Geography of Plants and Animals

NATIONAL ATLAS OF SWEDEN

Vittangi
Njalla
Jokkmokk
LAPPLAND
NORR-
BOTTEN
Kalix
Torne älv
Torneå
Sarek
Siberian Jay
Luleå
Lycksmyren
Hawk Owl
Skellefteå
Andro-
meda
Norwegian
Lemming
Beaver
Umeå
Razorbill
Bonden
JÄMTLAND
ANGERMANLAND
MEDELPAD
Sundsvall
HÄRJEDALEN
Eagle Owl
HÄLSING-
LAND
Skuleberget
Hudiks-
vall
Camberwell
Beauty
Städjan
Black-throated
diver
GÄSTRIK-
LAND
Mora
Älvkarleby
Moor-king
Falun
VÄRMLAND
DALARNA
Cuckoo and White
Wagtail
UPPLAND
Uppsala
Karlstad
Globe Flower
SÖDER-
NÄRKE MANLAND
Södertälje
Åmål
DALS-
LAND
ÖSTER-
GÖTLAND
BOHUSLÄN
Vänern
Marie-
stad
Vänersborg
Norrköping
Nyköping
Färö
Lidra
VÄSTER-
GÖTLAND
Swallowtail
Jön-
köping
Visby
Borås
SMÅLAND
Göteborg
GOTLAND
HALLAND
Twinflower
Bream
ÖLAND
Kullen
Växjö
Kalmar
Stenbrohult
BLEKINGE
Ottenby
Hoburgen
SKÅNE
Red deer
Seam Holly
Lund
Malmö
Avocet
G. BRUSEWITZ

Four of Linnaeus' five provincial journeys started and ended at Uppsala. The journey to Dalarna in 1734, however, started and ended at Falun. The illustrations are of events or phenomena mentioned in Linneaus' journals.

Geography of Plants and Animals

SPECIAL EDITORS

Lena Gustafsson and Ingemar Ahlén

THEME MANAGER

Swedish University of Agricultural Sciences

National Atlas of Sweden

SNA Publishing will publish between 1990 and 1996 a government-financed National Atlas of Sweden. The first national atlas, *Atlas över Sverige*, was published in 1953–71 by *Svenska Sällskapet för Antropologi och Geografi, SSAG* (the Swedish Society for Anthropology and Geography). The new national atlas describes Sweden in seventeen volumes, each of which deals with a separate theme. The organisations responsible for this new national atlas are *Lantmäteriverket, LMV* (the National Land Survey of Sweden), *SSAG* and *Statistiska centralbyrån, SCB* (Statistics Sweden). The whole project is under the supervision of a board consisting of the chairman, Sture Norberg and Thomas Mann (LMV), Staffan Helmfrid and Åke Sundborg (SSAG), Frithiof Billström and Gösta Guteland (SCB) and Leif Wastenson (SNA). To assist the board and the editors there is a scientific advisory group of three permanent members: Professor Staffan Helmfrid (Chairman), Professor Erik Bylund and Professor Anders Rapp. For this theme Ph D Ulf Gärdenfors, Professor Bengt Jonsell and Reader Sören Svensson has been coopted to the advisory group as a specialist. A theme manager is responsible for compiling the manuscript for each individual volume. The National Atlas of Sweden is to be published in book form both in Swedish and in English, and in a computer-based version for use in personal computers.

The English edition of the National Atlas of Sweden is published under the auspices of the *Royal Swedish Academy of Sciences* by the National Committee of Geography with financial support from *Knut och Alice Wallenbergs Stiftelse* and *Marcus och Amalia Wallenbergs Stiftelse*.

The whole work comprises the following volumes (in order of publication):

CHIEF EDITOR	Leif Wastenson
EDITORS	Staffan Helmfrid, Scientific Editor
	Ulla Arnberg, Editor of *Geography of Plants and Animals*
	Margareta Elg, Editor
	Märta Syrén, Editor
PRODUCTION	LM Maps, Kiruna
SPECIAL EDITORS	Lena Gustafsson and Ingemar Ahlén
TRANSLATOR	Michael Knight
GRAPHIC DESIGN	Håkan Lindström
LAYOUT	Typoform/Gunnel Eriksson, Stockholm
REPRODUCTION	LM Repro, Luleå
COMPOSITION	Bokstaven Text & Bild AB, Göteborg
DISTRIBUTION	Almqvist & Wiksell International, Stockholm
COVER ILLUSTRATION	Axel Ljungquist/N

First edition
© SNA
Printed in Italy 1996

ISBN 91–87760–04–5 (All volumes)

ISBN 91–87760–36–3 (Geography of Plants and Animals)

Contents

Sweden's Natural History

"Carta Marina" was published by Olaus Magnus in Venice in 1539. It consists of nine connected woodcuts with a total area of 170×125 cm and was in its time the largest printed map in the world. It contains a wealth of figures and scenes and is intended to give the Scandinavian countries a place of honour in the world. It has given rise to a large number of interpretations and studies by ethnologists, historians and zoologists.

People's understanding of plants and animals in Sweden in the earliest times was coloured by folklore and strictly concerned with their usefulness. There was no need for knowledge over and above that needed to survive on the bounties of nature. The inhabitants of the Scandinavian countries did not develop any deep understanding of natural history until the arrival of Christianity and the monks. The latter created herb gardens in their monasteries, prepared healing decoctions and cured the sick with medicinal plants.

Thus the natural sciences were from the very beginning connected with medicine. There was very little interest in nature itself and any such interest was fiercely opposed by scholastic theologians, for whom Aristotle had once and for all created a picture of the world that was acceptable to the Church.

The Reformation of the 16th century led to an impoverishment of Sweden's spiritual life. The monasteries were dissolved and their precious libraries of books scattered or vandalised—"Sacrilege!". The herb gardens ran to weed and many scholars fled the country in despair.

THE GREAT ACHIEVEMENTS OF OLAUS MAGNUS

In the transitional period between the Middle Ages and modern times the Catholic Archbishop of Sweden, *Olaus Magnus* (1490–1557) lived in exile in Italy, working on his magnum opus, "The History of the Nordic People" — 22 volumes and 476 chapters illustrated with 481 woodcuts. But not even here was much personal experience of nature to be found. Although Olaus Magnus, purveying papal indulgences, was one of the first scholars to visit Norrland, one has to search deep and long in his fanciful texts to find any first-hand descriptions of the Nordic countryside. Unfortunately his texts are to a large extent nothing more than a compilation of classical or medieval sources. Nevertheless, his impressive work must be considered to be the first comprehensive description of the Nordic countryside.

Other important names from this period are *Sigfridus Aronus Forsius* (1550–1624), who was one of the first to describe plants without concentrating on their usefulness; and *Johannes Franckenius* (1590–1661), who became the first to hold the title of Professor Botanices et Anatomices at Uppsala. He has been called "the father of Swedish botany". King Johan III's physician, the Italian *Apollonius Menabenus* (c. 1540–1603) was the first to give a detailed description of the moose, which by that time had been exterminated in Western Europe.

THREE GENERATIONS OF RUDBECKIUS AT UPPSALA

A scholar who, like so many of his contemporaries, received his education in Germany, was *Johannes Rudbeckius* (1581–1646). He became a professor at Uppsala University in 1604, but his contribution to research in the natural sciences was made outside the university, which was dominated by scholasticism. For several years he ran a private "preparatory" school in Uppsala at which botany studies were encouraged by letting the pupils "on Sundays after Evensong" take part in "herbationes" on the outskirts of the town. Rudbeckius had brought this idea back with him from his student years at Wittenberg, and these excursions were later to be revived by Linnaeus.

LIBER XX.

De mixtis Pifcibus cum Hirundinibus.

Olaus Magnus' history books are a mixture of fables, personal observation and various compilations taken from classical writers. That he followed Aristotle faithfully is evident in many places. For example, he perpetuated the ancient belief that swallows hibernate during the winter. The picture shows Nordic fishermen pulling swallows up in their seine.

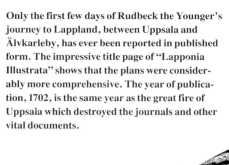

Only the first few days of Rudbeck the Younger's journey to Lappland, between Uppsala and Älvkarleby, has ever been reported in published form. The impressive title page of "Lapponia Illustrata" shows that the plans were considerably more comprehensive. The year of publication, 1702, is the same year as the great fire of Uppsala which destroyed the journals and other vital documents.

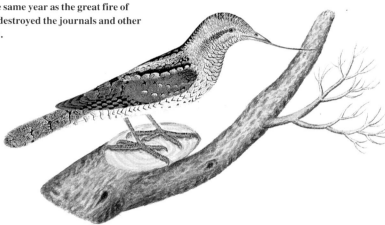

On 22 May 1695 at Älvkarleby Rudbeck the Younger shot and sketched a wryneck *Jynx torquilla*, making it the first scientifically described bird in the history of Swedish ornithology. A woodcut in "Lapponia Illustrata" based on this water-colour was also the first published picture of a scientifically described Swedish bird.

O. Rudbeck the Elder

O. Rudbeck the Younger

Despite these individual efforts interest in the natural sciences in Sweden was poor in the late 16th and early 17th century. Many of the doctoral theses connected with zoology or botany that were presented at this time seem to have served mainly as academic acrobatics or philological fancies.

Any independent investigations which were more than just respectful confirmations of Aristotles' words were looked upon with deep suspicion by the church, which systematically sabotaged any attempt at academic liberation. But by the late 17th century the theologians had begun to retreat from their positions under pressure from the new times. Aristotles' dominance over the sciences was finally about to be broken.

6 000 PLANTS CARVED IN WOOD

Olof Rudbeck the Elder (1630–1702) stands like a giant of learning at the threshold of the new age. He was the son of Johannes Rudbeckius and soon became the dominant force at Uppsala University, where his most important work was within the field of medicine, with the discovery of the lymphatic vessels as his crowning achievement. He himself probably considered his mighty "Atlantica" with its fantastic visions of Sweden's glorious history and his huge but never-completed "Campus Elysii" to be his masterpieces. The latter work was planned to reproduce—in natural size—some 7,000 plant forms carved in woodcuts and coloured by hand. About 7,000 blocks had been carved and printing of Campus had just begun in 1701 when the devastating fire of Uppsala took place the following autumn, totally obliterating the whole of Rudbeck's magnificent work.

Alongside Campus Rudbeck was working on a separate set of illustrations in twelve folio volumes, presenting more than 6,000 species. Miraculously these were saved from the flames and later came to Leufsta, the home of Charles de Geer.

A more permanent monument to Rudbeck as a botanist, however, was the large botanical garden which he created at Svartbäcken for the training of medical students. Rudbeck's garden differed from other similar gardens abroad in that it did not merely present beautifully decorative plants and exotic rarities but also gave plenty of room to native plants of more modest appearance.

RUDBECK THE YOUNGER AND LAPPLAND

Two professors of medicine, *Lars Roberg* (1664–1742) and *Olof Rudbeck the Younger* (1660–1740), dominated the golden scientific age of the Enlightenment. They were their opposites in both appearance and character. Roberg was a bohemian, notoriously miserly, a bachelor who dressed badly and cared nothing for outward appearances; Rudbeck was a more socially competent professor and amiable aesthete. When Roberg saw Rudbeck's magnificent illustrations of birds, his comment was "anatomically poor". He would probably have preferred to see the roller dissected than in its splendid plumage! This says a good deal about the difference between the two men, but as learned scholars they were each other's equal and both were excellent artists.

In 1695 Rudbeck embarked on an expedition to Lappland. The journey, which started in May, went from Uppsala to Torneå, where the midnight sun awaited them in the middle of June. From there he proceeded to Torne träsk and then on to Kvikkjokk and Lule Lappland, after which he returned to Österbotten. He and his assistants filled a large sketch book with drawings of many animals and plants that were unknown to science at that time, some of which were used in the famous "Fogelboken".

LINNAEUS—A WORLD-FAMOUS NAME

One of Olof Rudbeck the Younger's favourite pupils was *Carl Linnaeus* (1707–1778), who was so inspired by his teacher's drawings and descriptions of the unknown Lappland that he set off on a one-man expedition to the north only a few years later in 1732. This resulted in two notable works: "Flora Lapponica" (1737) and his travel book "Iter Lapponicum", first printed in an English translation in London in 1811.

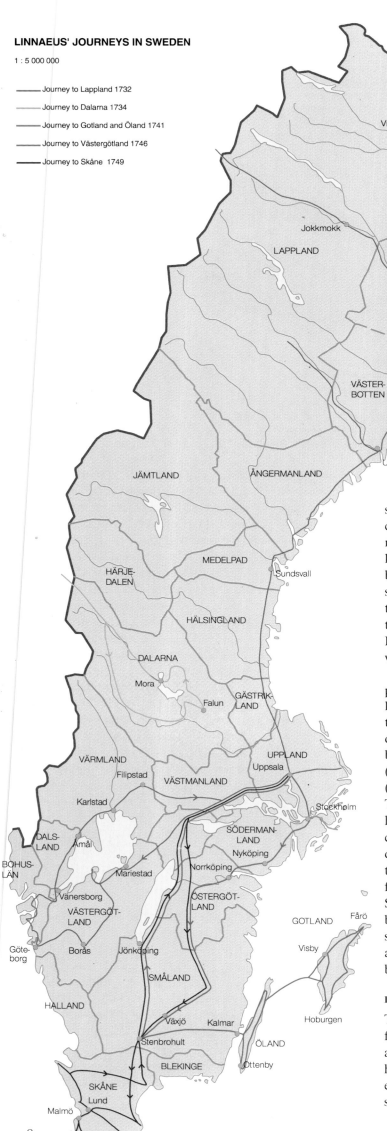

———— Journey to Lappland 1732
———— Journey to Dalarna 1734
———— Journey to Gotland and Öland 1741
———— Journey to Västergötland 1746
———— Journey to Skåne 1749

Vittangi

Jokkmokk

LAPPLAND

NORR-
BOTTEN

Torneå

Luleå

Skellefteå

VÄSTER-
BOTTEN

JÄMTLAND

ÄNGERMANLAND

Umeå

MEDELPAD

HÄRJE-
DALEN

Sundsvall

HÄLSINGLAND

DALARNA

Mora

GÄSTRIK-
LAND

Falun

UPPLAND

VÄRMLAND

Filipstad

Uppsala

VÄSTMANLAND

Karlstad

Stockholm

DALS-
LAND

Åmål

SÖDERMAN-
LAND

Nyköping

BOHUS-
LÄN

Mariestad

Norrköping

Vänersborg

ÖSTERGÖT-
LAND

VÄSTERGÖT-
LAND

GOTLAND

Fårö

Göte-
borg

Borås

Jönköping

Visby

SMÅLAND

HALLAND

Hoburgen

Växjö

Kalmar

Stenbrohult

ÖLAND

Ottenby

BLEKINGE

SKÅNE

Lund

Malmö

Carl Linnaeus. Oil painting by J H Scheffel, 1739 Linnés Hammarby.

The map shows the approximate routes that Linnaeus followed on his provincial journeys. He himself quotes an inscription at Jukkasjärvi Church in Lappland, but in fact he never went there! He turned south at Vittangi because of the cold weather at the end of August. (S1)

Linnaeus went on his great research expedition to Dalarna in 1734, commissioned by the County Governor at Falun, Reuterholm. The following year we find him with the banker Clifford in Holland, where he stayed for two years, establishing contacts with the most influential scientists of his time. At the age of 28 Linnaeus was already a famous and widely respected man of science.

During the 1730s Linnaeus displayed amazing productivity. He published one epoch-making work after the other and by the end of this decade he had published his great botanical reform, "Systema Naturae" (1735), "Fundamenta Botanica" (1736) and "Flora Lapponica" (1737). The world lay at the feet of this brilliant and diligent young man, but he chose to return to Sweden and settled down in Stockholm as a general practitioner. Linnaeus was one of the founders of the Royal Academy of Sciences in 1739; he succeeded Rudbeck as professor of botany at Uppsala in 1742 and the year before began a series of journeys to the provinces by visiting Öland and Gotland.

LINNAEUS INSPIRED THE POETS

These journeys to the provinces, financed by the Estates of the Realm and reported in Swedish, not Latin, have become part of the Swedish literary heritage. Suddenly the landscape of 18th-century Sweden emerges from the mists of history in the clear light of dawn in all the glory of its leafy groves, verdant pastures, luxuriant hayfields, park-like meadows, dark forests and smoking burn-beaten clearings. Everything is recorded with sharp-eyed curiosity—not only the smallest plant or insect but also the ways of building farm fences, the dress of haymakers, the design of farming equipment and much more. The important aspect of utility was however the real purpose of the journeys.

Linnaeus left his mark on most of his century, not merely in the field of botanical research. He opened wide the window on nature, inspiring poets like Gyllenborg, Oxenstierna, Creutz and Bellman. Headed by the king and queen, he gathered around him naturalists, nature lovers, aristocrats, merchants and clergymen while, like a spider in the web, he stayed in Uppsala, collecting objects and information that his disciples sent him from all corners of the country and the world.

He encouraged clergymen and private persons out in the provinces to send in reports and finds, and this was just the beginning of a steady stream of parish histories, local floras, botanical inventories, reports on migrant birds and flower calendars. The latter were particularly valuable from a utilitarian point of view since they gave farmers useful advice about the right times to sow and harvest crops.

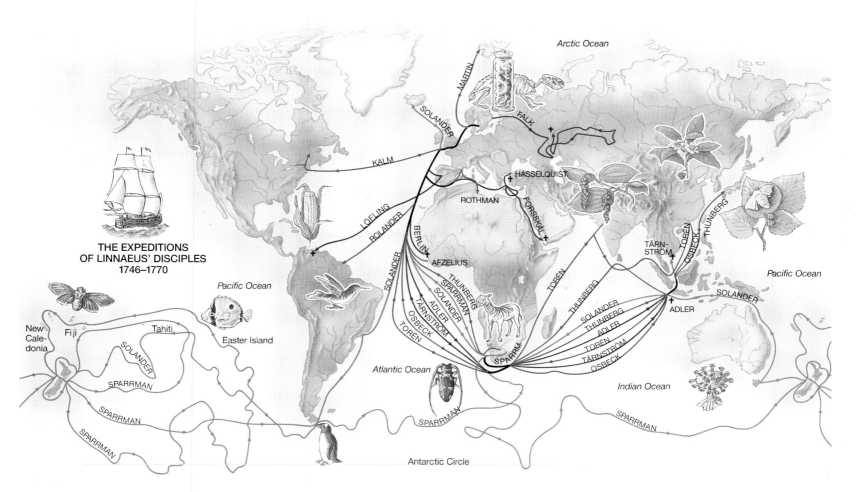

THE EXPEDITIONS
OF LINNAEUS' DISCIPLES
1746–1770

	Solander's and Sparr-man's expeditions
	Did not survive the journey
	Other disciples' expeditions

LINNAEUS' DISCIPLES

After Linnaeus had established his sexual system and scientific methods for classification, botanical expeditions became more rewarding, and many of his disciples—"apostles" as he called them—crossed the world to gather extensive collections for their master. They all made major contributions to science through their extensive collections, travel journals and research work. The greatest of them was *Daniel Solander*, who accompanied James Cook on his voyage round the world on the Endeavour in 1768 together with an admirer of Linnaeus', Sir Joseph Banks. This voyage inspired the British navy always to have on board a naturalist to collect specimens and make observations, among them Darwin and Huxley. (S2)

Gustaf von Paykull
1757–1826

Samuel Ödmann
1750–1830

Soon a number of versatile gentlemen followed in Linnaeus' tracks; *A. A. Hülphers* travelled to the Norrland counties, *Johan Fischerström* described in both lyrical and factual language Lake Mälaren in 1785, *J. C. Linnerhielm* began a series of cultural visits to southern and central Sweden in the 1780s, *A. F. Sköldebrand* painted and sketched his way through Norrland to the North Cape at the turn of the century, *Per Tham* described his erratic journey through central Sweden in the 1790s and the colourful art philosopher *C. A. Ehrensvärd* depicted his travel adventures with Linnean versatility and satirical acuity.

THE REVIVAL OF ORNITHOLOGY

The science of taxidermy was now beginning to develop, and wealthy collectors like *A U Grill* at Söderfors, *Charles De Geer* at Leufsta, *Gustaf von Carlson* at Mälby, *Gustaf von Paykull* at Wallox-Säby and other scholarly amateurs created impressive private museums for their treasures. De Geer was an entomologist of international repute. The study of insects had become a fashionable science not least thanks to *Carl Clerck* who published two magnificent volumes on butterflies and spiders. Zoology, however, had stagnated since the days of the great Rudbeck up until the 1780s, when the science of ornithology was revived.

A number of skilled field workers opened the way for a modern science, initially with the discreet request that Linnaeus' obsolete "Fauna Suecica" be republished in a heavily revised edition.

Admittedly, a prominent disciple of Linnaeus, *Anders Johan Retzius* (1742–1821) had compiled a survey of zoology ten years before—"Introduction to Zoology" (1772)—based on Linnaeus' theories, but a more comprehensive and critical examination of species and genuses was not carried out until a clergyman *Samuel Ödmann* (1750–1830) and later a physician, *Peter Gustaf Tengmalm* (1754–1803) published many excellent papers in the Royal Academy of Science's journals.

Ödmann has rightly been called

C. P. Thunberg, a disciple of Linnaeus, published the modest fauna "Description of Swedish Animals" in 1798. The Latin scholar Adolf Törneros wrote: "Thunberg's head is like Noah's Ark. In it there is a male and a female of all living things."

J. W. Palmstruch
1770–1811

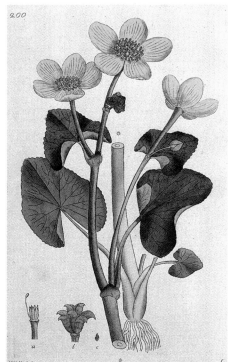

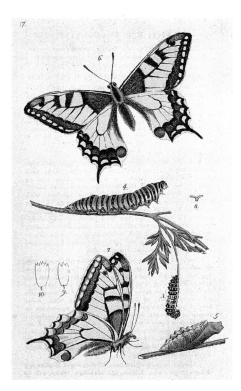

The brilliant artist J. W. Palmstruch illustrated not only the famous work "Swedish Botany" in eleven volumes (1801–1840) but also "Swedish Zoology" (1806–1809) in two volumes. The marsh marigold *Caltha palustris* and the stately swallowtail butterfly *Papilio machaon*.

"Sweden's first ornithologist". During the last twenty years of the 18th century he carried out research which led to a series of splendid monographs on island birds.

Tengmalm was one of the first to make a survey of local birds in Sweden, at Almare-Stäket in Uppland, published in 1783. Tengmalm became more internationally famous for his classic investigation of the species of the owl family (1793), which had baffled taxonomists ever since the publication of Linnaeus' "Systema Naturae". Tengmalm was honoured by having *Strix Tengmalmi* named after him. Nowadays, however, the scientific name of this little owl has been changed, but in England it is still called Tengmalm's Owl.

MAGNIFICENT BOOKS

Some of Sweden's magnificent nature books of international class were published at this time. The great illustrated work presenting Gustaf von Carlson's bird collection, "Museum Carlsonianum" (1786–1789), was compiled by *Anders Sparrman* (1748–1820), a disciple of Linnaeus', who also published "Swedish Ornithologie", comprising a large number of hand-coloured etchings.

The great work "Swedish Botany" published in eleven volumes (1801–1840) by *J W Palmstruch*, an army officer, draughtsman and engraver, was also of the same high artistic merit.

Anders Sparrman
1748–1820

By the end of the 18th century research in the natural sciences had moved towards increasing specialisation. In the wake of the golden age of Linnaeus, many scientists emerged who are usually rather generally termed Linnaeans without having had any close contact with their master. They were Linnaeans in spirit and followed his methods closely, at the same time as they occasionally allowed themselves a critical and stubborn attitude.

THE BERGIUS BROTHERS AND BOTANY

Let us go back in time a little, to the two brothers *Peter Jonas* (1730–1790) and *Bengt Bergius* (1723–1784), who helped Linnaeus to publish the important tenth edition of "Systema Naturae". Later, when these two wealthy bachelors had settled down at Bergielund on the northern outskirts of Stockholm and established something like a botanical institue there, their relationship to Linnaeus became chillier. A great deal of the botanical material sent back to Sweden by travellers abroad soon began to bypass Linnaeus and go to Bergielund; the centre of botanical research began to shift from Uppsala to Stockholm.

The greatest contribution made by Peter Jonas was to donate in his will Bergielund and its library and herbarium of more than 9,000 species, including many typical examples, to the Royal Academy of Sciences. His donation also comprised a professor's chair for research and the training of horticulturists. Following the wishes of the donator, the first Professor Bergianus was *Olof Swartz* (1760–1818), who carried out important morphological studies of the orchid family and helped to establish the system of the cryptograms.

Erik Acharius (1757–1819), a physician and lichen specialist, was one of Swartz's closest friends and also an important contributor to the system of cryptograms. Like Swartz he was a skilled draughtsman.

A group of scientists who prided themselves on being "Linnaeans in spirit" were ready to take over. One of the most dogmatic of them was *Göran Wahlenberg* (1780–1851), a frequent visitor to Lappland, whose studies of plant geography were to be of great value for future research in this field. Other post-Linneans were, for example, *Elias Fries* (1794–1878) "the father of Swedish fungi botany" and Lund scientists like *C. A. Agardh, J E Wikström, C. J. Hartman* and *J. W. Zetterstedt*.

The brothers Bengt and Peter Jonas Bergius had large collections and an extensive library at their country house Bergielund. It was a centre for botanists and natural scientists in the late 18th century.

Sven Nilsson
1787–1883

Wikström (1789–1856) succeeded Olof Swartz as Professor Bergianus in 1818. He published an important work entitled "Stockholm's Flora" (1840), which also contains the first local survey of all the occurrences of animal groups in and round the city.

The eccentric professor of botany J. W. Zetterstedt (1785–1874) also divided his favours between flora and fauna. He even became internationally famous as an entomologist, mainly thanks to his basic work in fourteen volumes on Swedish flies, "Diptera Scandinaviae" (1842–1860), which is still used today by fly specialists.

Zetterstedt was about the same age as his Lund colleague *Sven Nilsson* (1787–1883), zoologist, geologist, archeologist and more, who left his mark on zoological research in Sweden throughout most of the 19th century. As the dynamic head of the Royal Academy of Sciences he played an important part in moving its offices to new premises and in planning the new National Museum of Natural History. He published a classic work "Scandinavian Fauna" and made valuable contributions in the field of zoological geography during a journey through Sweden and Norway in 1816.

When this journey was repeated in 1826, he was accompanied by four assistants, the youngest of whom, 17-year-old *Sven Lovén*, was to become a famous pioneer in the field of marine biology.

As the 19th century approached, natural science publications became more and more difficult to grasp. Universal geniuses like Rudbeck, Linnaeus, Nilsson and Retzius no longer had a place in scientific research; more and more specialisation was what was expected.

Among the first naturalists to use

Wilhelm von Wright
1810–1887

"Fish of Scandinavia" (1836–1857) with hand-coloured plates by Wilhelm von Wright was one of the most beautiful zoological works of the 19th century. He used newly caught fish as his models and noted that even the scales in each row of scales agreed with the model. Female of the blue wrasse *Labrus bimaculatus*.

the new technology of the printing industry were the Finnish brothers *Magnus* and *Wilhelm von Wright*, who produced "Swedish Birds" (1828–1838), lithographs printed in an edition of less than 100, all coloured by hand.

ENGLISH NATURALISTS DISCOVER SWEDEN

Even in the briefest description of naturalists in Sweden, we should not forget all the many inquisitive, adventurous foreign scientists who travelled to the north of Sweden in search of the mysteries of Ultima Thule.

Llewyn Lloyd, "the English bear hunter" who came to Sweden in the early 19th century, acquired over the years an impressive field experience of Swedish animal life which he described in several valuable books. A contemporary of Lloyd's was *H. H. Wheelwright*, hunter and collector, who based himself in Värmland. He wrote two books which were never translated into Swedish but which helped to make foreigners curious about Swedish natural history, "A Spring and Summer in Lapland" (1864) and "Ten Years in Sweden" (1865). In the 1850s the wealthy English egg collector *John Wolley* contributed to our knowledge of the relatively unknown bird life of the Arctic regions of Scandinavia.

CLERGYMEN AND PHYSICIANS

Until long into the 19th century there were above all two professions that dominated natural history research: clergymen and physicians. The world of Swedish plants and animals was to a great extent explored by amateurs, some of whom tried their consciences when dividing their time between God the Father and the Goddess

Flora. Doctors, at any rate, could claim that it was part of their profession to study herbal plant life, and they contributed greatly to research.

Swartz, Tengmalm, Hartman and Acharius, all physicians, have already been mentioned; among the naturalist clergymen Samuel Ödmann, a true scholar, *C. U. Ekström,* an expert on birds and fish and *Clas Bjerkander,* an active collector should also be remembered. One more physician who should be mentioned is *J. P. Westring* (1753–1833) from Norrköping, whose beautiful work "History of Lichen Dyeing" (1805) belongs to an old tradition of utilitarian books on botany.

ELIAS FRIES — A WORLD-FAMOUS FUNGUS EXPERT

A central figure of the mid–19th century onwards was the gentle botanist Elias Fries. He was the only really outstanding botanical researcher in Uppsala for many years. As an expert on wild fungi Fries gained a world-wide reputation, although he hardly succeeded in persuading Swedes to eat mushrooms—his great mycological flora was written in Latin.

A contemporary of Fries was the eccentric Göran Wahlenberg—"more Linnean than Linnaeus", though he never met the master in person. He wrote "The Flora of the Uppsala District" and carried out significant research in the field of plant geography. Wahlenberg was one of those in the Royal Academy of Sciences who indignantly rejected any attempt to revise and modernise Linnaeus' Flora and Fauna. The zoologist Samuel Ödmann and the botanist C. J. Hartman, however, realised that the time was ripe for a revision. The former's proposed revisions were rejected by the Academy without much discussion,

Hawk's nest by Bruno Liljefors, 1886. Liljefors is one of the foremost nature painters of all time, who created a style followed by many of today's artists. He portrayed animals, often in motion, in a Darwinian spirit, as well as hunting scenes and romantic landscapes. In the late 1880s he collaborated with Gustaf Kolthoff, painting the landscape backgrounds for a natural-historical diorama at Uppsala, which led to the establishment of the Biological Museum in Stockholm in 1893.

Gustaf Kolthoff was a keen amateur photographer, but this is the only known photograph of the famous taxidermist at work.

Elias Fries 1794–1878

but Hartman's flora was reprinted several times. It deviated in many respects from Linnaeus' system, was written in Swedish (!) and as a result was violently criticised by Wahlenberg.

SPECIALISED AND POPULARISED RESEARCH

The increasing precision of instruments and research methods both broadened and deepened scientists' knowledge of natural history. New discoveries in Quaternary geology upset many old prejudices about the evolution of our planet.

The Swedes' feeling for Nature is seen as a national characteristic, reflecting a great many efforts in the 19th century to popularise and stimulate people's interest. Modernised collections at the National Museum of Natural History, the "dioramas" at the Biological Museum, the foundation of the Swedish Touring Club, the establishment of the first nature reserve (Stora Karlsö, 1880) and the long series of popular handbooks devoted to the natural sciences which were published during the 19th century bear witness to the general public's increasing thirst for information.

A. W. Malm (1821–1882), curator of the Göteborg Natural History Museum, is a characteristic representative of the social-minded researchers of his time. He wrote a two-volume book on the vertebrate animals of Göteborgs and Bohuslän and became

famous for his exhibition of a stranded young blue whale. Erroneously identifying it as an unknown species, he affectionately named it after his wife *Balaenoptera Carolinae*. To make it a real public attraction the whale was "converted" into a small café with blue wallpaper studded with gold stars!

"ROYAL CARLSON"

Several important and lavish works of popular natural history were published in the second half of the 19th century. *Wilhelm Lilljeborg* (1816–1903) published a fauna of Norway and Sweden in five thick volumes in 1870, and *Carl Gustaf Thompson*, an entomologist, published 1859–1868 his great work in ten volumes on beetles, "Scandinavia's Coleoptera". *Gustaf Kolthoff* and *L. A. Jägerskiöld* published "Nordic Birds" in 1898, heralding the future golden age of bird books.

A naturalist who should not be forgotten in this context is *August Emmanuel Carlson*, known as "Royal Carlson" because Karl X was one of his ancestors! Carlson was the author of the much used handbook "Swedish Birds" 1894, which can be seen as a predecessor of our many modern field handbooks. But the first handbook of all was *I. Ad. af Ström's* "Swedish Birds", which was printed as early as 1839 in a handy pocket format with illustrations by Wilhelm von Wright.

MAGNIFICENT ILLUSTRATIONS

A splendid work in which modern printing technology was used to the full was *Dr Paul Rosenius'* (1865–1957) mighty "Sweden's Birds and Nests" in 255 booklets published 1913–1954. These contained magnificent photographs of nesting sites and habitats as well as excellent colour illustrations by *Gustaf Swenander*. With its six huge volumes comprising 2,430 pages it is our most exhaustive ornithological work of all time.

Of great importance for Sweden's rapidly growing interest in Nature was *Bengt Berg's* (1885–1967) epoch-making documentation in pictures of birds and habitats. His books "Lake Tåkern", "Stora Karlsö" and "The Last White-tailed Eagles", for example, were also important contributions to the debate on nature conservation. The concept of nature conservation was in the air. If it is true to say that the interest of Swedes in natural history had been dominated by hunters, their role was now to be taken over by conservationists, idealists who were armed with cameras and binoculars, not guns.

Of course botanists, too, benefited from improved printing technology. Floras which were both expensive and practical to use were published: from *C. A. M. Lindman's* "Pictures of Nordic Flora" (1901–1905) with original but improved engravings taken from Palmstruch's famous "Swedish Botany" to the classic school flora "Krok-Almquist", which has been reprinted 27 times since 1883! An impressive standard work is "Wild Plants of the Nordic Countries" by *Torsten Lagerberg, G. E. Du Rietz* and *J A Nannfeldt*, the first edition of which appeared in the 1930s; it was the first flora to contain colour photographs of plants in their natural habitats.

Since the middle of the 20th centurys there has been an extensive publication of expensive handbooks, especially for birds and flowers. Two typical examples are Bo Mossberg's brilliant illustrations in "Nordic Flora" and Lars Jonsson's internationally famous "Birds in Nature".

GROWING INTEREST IN PLANT AND ANIMAL GEOGRAPHY

When the chair of plant biology was established at Uppsala University in 1897, botany was divided up into various areas of research – plant geography, plant sociology and ecology. Under the leadership of the legendary *Rutger Sernander* (1866–1944) botany became a popular subject even for those outside the experts' circle. He had Linnaeus' ability to gather round him a faithful band of disciples who could popularise his subject.

Plant geography became an increasingly extensive field of research

Carl Fries 1895–1982

The illustrations in Carl A. M. Lindman's very popular "Flora of the Nordic Countries" (1901–1905) were in part reworkings of J. W. Palmstruch's engravings in "Swedish Botany" (1802–1809). The water avens *Geum rivale*.

in which Sernander's disciples G E Du Rietz, *Th C Fries* and *Erik Almquist* played important roles. *Eric Hultén's* great "Atlas of Plant Distribution in Scandinavia" (1950) and *Hugo Sjörs'* "Nordic Plant Geography" (1956) were of great significance for this research work.

Animal geography was well represented in "The History of Animal Distribution on the Scandinavian Peninsula " (1922), by Professor *Sven Ekman* (1876–1964).

THE SWEDISH MUSEUM OF NATURAL HISTORY

Under the dynamic leadership of *Einar Lönnberg* the National Museum of Natural History in Stockholm and its researchers played an important role in spreading information about natural history. Darwin's theory of evolution was accepted early on, and among many well-known scientists who worked here, mention should be made of explorer and botanist *N. J. Andersson*, polar explorer *A. E. Nordenskiöld*, zoologist and taxidermist *Wilhelm Meeves* and the gruff but efficient fish expert *F. A. Smitt*.

The scientific journal "Fauna & Flora" launched by Lönnberg in 1906 was of great importance.

HUMANIST AND SCIENTIST

"The Living Landscape of Sweden" by *Sten Selander* (1891–1957) has become something of a bible for the biologists and nature-lovers of our time. The combination of humanist and scientist also characterised *Carl Fries* (1895–1982), who in a number of books threw light on mankind's role

in the development of the Swedish landscape.

Mårten Sjöbeck was the pioneer in the field of the farmer's role in the cultivated landscape. He worked at the State Railway Board and was commissioned in the 1930s to depict the Swedish landscape as seen from the railway network in a series of what might be called cultural-historical guide books.

POPULAR INTEREST IN NATURAL HISTORY

In the 1940s the Swedish Society for the Conservation of Nature had about 5,000 members; 50 years later the figure was more like 200,000. Local societies devoted to nature study are flourishing throughout the length and breadth of the country; ornithological societies have thousands of members. Sweden's first bird station was inaugurated in 1946 on the southern tip of Öland and has been followed by many others. Bird-watching towers—often combined with nature conservation measures—have been erected at almost every lake worth mentioning. The Swedish section of The World Wide Fund for Nature, founded in 1974, has become an important factor in the nature conservation movement, collecting some 80 million kronor annually.

Perhaps we in our insecure and stressed age are becoming more aware of the value of having a clean and well-preserved natural environment around us. Perhaps we realise that we Scandinavians are privileged to live in a landscape which, by European standards, is enviably untouched.

From the Ice Age to the Present Day

Seen over a long period of time the composition of plants and animals in Sweden has been in a continual state of change, mainly because of changes in the climate. Since the last Ice Age mankind's influence on the environment has also played a significant role.

The climate of the Quaternary was characterised by alternating glacials and interglacials. During the extensive ice ages the zones of vegetation in Europe moved southwards; trees and species that needed warmth were forced to "hibernate" in southern Europe. But after every ice age they spread northwards again.

More or less the same plant and animal species occurred during the various interglacials, but in different combinations and quantities. Our knowledge of plant and animal history is based mainly on the analysis of lake sediments and peat deposits. Pollen analysis is the most important method used when researching the history of vegetation, but analyses of seeds and other plant remains also provide useful information. Animal bones tell us about the history of fauna; they often used to be found when digging for peat, but nowadays most bone records are made in connection with archeological excavations.

Immigration of Plants and Animals

Plants and animals colonised Scandinavia from several directions. Most species came from the south via the land-bridges which used to connect the Continent and the Scandinavian peninsula across what today is Denmark. Many species also came from the east to Finland and northern Sweden. South-westerly immigration was important for Norway; parts of the North Sea between the British Isles, southern Norway and Jutland were dry land in the late Ice Age and functioned as "springboards".

14,000–12,000 YEARS B.P.

During the Oldest Dryas, Bölling and Younger Dryas the landscape which had only just emerged from the melting inland ice was first covered by an arctic desert, which later developed into sub-arctic tundra and steppe. The vegetation was characterised by the first wave of immigrant plants— a mixture of northern mountain plants and southern, continental steppe vegetation. This could be called a steppe-tundra. The mountain avens *Dryas octopetala*, the rock rose *Helianthemum nummularium*, various species of mugworts *Artemesia* spp., the mountain sorrel *Oxyria digyna* and the cornflower *Centaurea cyanus* occurred in the same areas—a combination which is entirely impossible today.

The mammoth was the first large mammal which immigrated when the inland ice retreated over 14,000 years B.P. to reveal the first narrow strip of south-west Skåne. Until about 12,000 years B.P. there are very few traces of higher land animals; apart from the mammoth they are limited to one record of a moose and one of a whooper swan.

12,000–11,000 YEARS B.P.

During the Alleröd the climate improved and the first forest plants came in a second wave of immigration. These created a "park-tundra"

Diagram with time scales, climate curve and general vegetation graph for the period following the melting of the inland ice. Absolute age is given in ¹⁴C years. The ¹⁴C time scale may be translated into calendar years for the last 10,000 years. The actual age for the late glacial period is 1,000–2,000 older than the ¹⁴C age. The dates in the text refer to ¹⁴C years.

The mammoth *Mammuthus primigenius*, weighing up to five tonnes, was a common herbivore on the tundra steppes of Europe and an important prey. Over 20 records have been made in Sweden, the latest from about 13,000 years B.P.

The mountain avens *Dryas octopetala* was one of the most characteristic flowers of the tundra steppe.

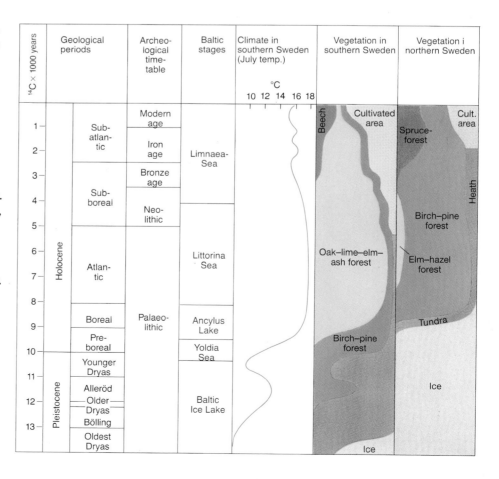

1:20 000 000

- ☐ Ice-sheet
- ☐ Ocean
- ■ Lake
- ■ Land

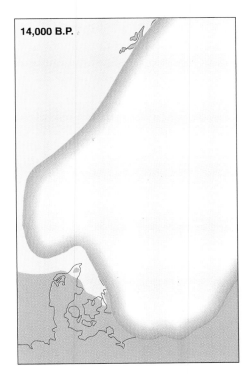

14,000 B.P.

11,000 B.P.

birch   pine

The paleogeographic maps on pages 15–17 show the melting of the inland ice, land contours in relation to the present shoreline and immigration routes for the most important kinds of trees. The time periods are chosen with regard to changes in the connections between the Baltic Sea and the North Sea. (S3–S9)

Birch, aspen and rowan were among the first trees that entered Sweden afte the Ice Age.

The giant deer
Megaloceros giganteus

of isolated trees and copses of birch, pine, aspen, rowan and wild-cherry.

The immigration of higher land animals was initially inhibited by a large river which drained the Baltic Ice Lake through the Sound. But about 11,200 years B.P. the land had risen so much that a land bridge was formed across the Danish islands. In spite of water obstacles immigrating reindeer arrived about 11,700 years B.P., followed a little later by the giant deer, moose and wild horse.

The next arrivals were probably the wolf, brown bear and wolverine, but so far there have been no records in Sweden to support this theory. Isolated records also prove the occurrence of fox, forest hare, vole and willow grouse. Remains of perch, pike-perch, burbot and pike have also been made in lake sediments. These fish must have reached Sweden via the waters of the Baltic Ice Lake, but not a single record of fish is known from its deposits.

11,000–10,500 YEARS B.P.

The first part of the Younger Dryas was characterised by a cold climate with sparse vegetation, permafrost and land movement. The land bridge across Denmark was broken about 10,800 years B.P. when the Sound once more became the outlet of the Baltic basin.

Deterioration in the climate is immediately reflected in animal records; from the period 10,900–10,600 years B.P. there are hardly any mammal

A pollen diagram from Blekinge illustrating the history of trees and changes in the open landscape in late and post-glacial times. The dates are in ¹⁴C years.

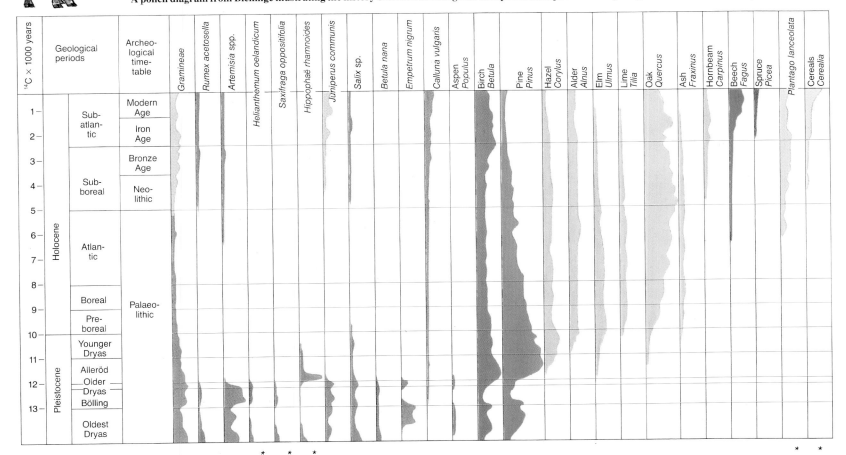

* Enlarged 10x

10,300 B.P.

birch

birch

10,000 B.P.

pine

pine

The aurochs
Bos primigenius

records. Many of the plants that had immigrated previously also disappeared, but it is possible that the birch survived in sheltered places.

The marine fauna was typical of a harsh arctic or sub-arctic climate during this period, but there were also occurrences of cosmopolitan species. There are also records of polar bear, great seal, ringed seal, Greenland seal, Greenland whale and white whale. Sea fish are known from records of polar cod, capelin and salmon species.

10,500–9,200 YEARS B.P.

Approximately 10,500 years B.P. there was a fairly rapid improvement in the climate. A few hundred years later the land bridge via Denmark arose again and continued until about 9,200 years B.P., when the Great Belt opened up. During this period the Baltic Sea drained through a broad sound in central Sweden, which inhibited immigration to the north.

The land bridge in the south was the entry point during this period for many of our plants and mammals.

A third wave of immigration led to the establishment of birch and pine forests with many forest plants as well as lake and shore plants. Reindeer, brown bear, wolf and perhaps lynx returned, but the reindeer disappeared again about 500 years later when hazel established itself and began to form woods together with pine on fertile soils in southern Sweden. The humus content of mineral soils continued to increase, which paved the way for many new plant species. At the same time many bryophytes and lichens decreased greatly, primarily to the detriment of reindeer.

The land bridge was crossed by most of our land mammals, for example the aurochs, bison, moose, red deer, roe deer, wild boar, wolf, fox, pine marten, weasel, badger, wild cat, lynx, squirrel and hedgehog. Probably the pond tortoise followed the same route. The earliest record of the aurochs is from 10,100 years B.P., but the largest number of records dates from the period 9,200–7,800 years B.P. Records of the European bison are concentrated to the period 9,500–8,700 years B.P. Many of the other species have not been found earlier than 9,000–8,500 years B.P., but they probably arrived before then.

9 200–8 000 YEARS B.P.

Approximately 9,200 years B.P. the Great Belt opened up and the land bridge to the Continent was broken. Zealand and several other Danish is-

The history of the tree line in the Swedish mountains reflects changes in the climate; 8,000–7,000 years ago it was almost 200 m higher than today, and pine and alder were more common in the mountain forests.

Even today we find pine stumps from these ancient forests on the mountain heaths. Seven thousand years ago the tree line, and in particular the upper limit for pine, started to be pushed downwards at the same time as the mountain birch forest was forming a forest zone close to the mountains. The cause was probably a change from a warm, dry climate to a cool, damp one.

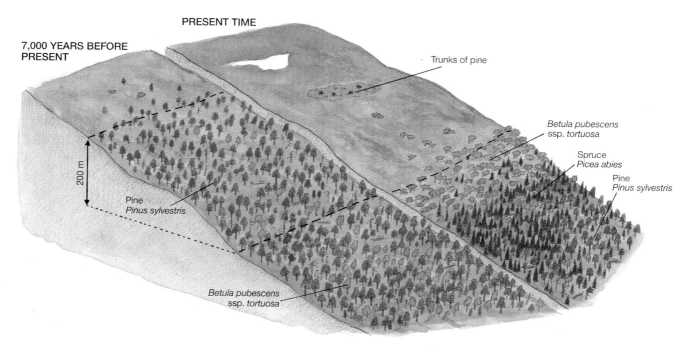

PRESENT TIME

7,000 YEARS BEFORE PRESENT

200 m

Trunks of pine

Betula pubescens ssp. *tortuosa*

Spruce *Picea abies*

Pine *Pinus sylvestris*

Pine *Pinus sylvestris*

Betula pubescens ssp. *tortuosa*

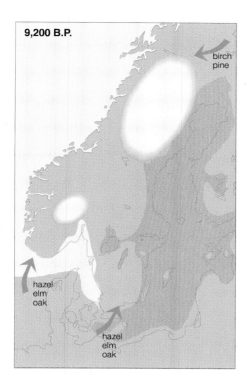

9,200 B.P.

birch pine

hazel elm oak

hazel elm oak

7,000 B.P.

grey alder

lime ash

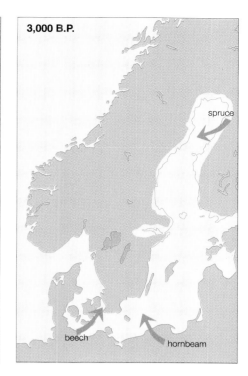

3,000 B.P.

spruce

beech

hornbeam

Ice-sheet
Ocean
Lake
Land

Wild boar *Sus scrofa*

Pond tortoise
Emys orbicularis

lands were connected to Sweden until about 8,000 years B.P., when the Sound reopened.

The Boreal was probably the warmest period following the last glaciation. This was the beginning of a warm period (9,000–5,000 years B.P.), when rich forest vegetation was established in southern Sweden. First came hazel, elm and oak, then lime and ash.

Red deer, roe deer and wild boar spread slowly and were not common until the oak forests began to expand. The aurochs seems to have disappeared at a fairly early date.

The Boreal was also the great period of colonisation in northern Sweden. After the great ice sheet had rapidly melted away, tundra plants arrived, followed by forest and bog plants. Birch and pine colonised the dry ground and willow and grey alder the damp ground.

The ice sheets that remained prevented animal immigration from the east, perhaps for as long as up to about 8,000 years B.P. That is why the first animals came to Norrland from the south. Moose, for example, could spread to northern Sweden via the central Swedish depression as soon as it dried up about 9,000 years B.P. By this time the reindeer was already extinct in southern Sweden, so it probably came to northern Sweden via Finland some time about 8,000 years B.P.

Fish and bird life became increasingly rich, which may be ascribed to changes in coastal environments when those parts of the North Sea which up

to then had been land were covered by water. When the English Channel opened up about 8,500 years ago, more warmth-dependent marine fauna could move into the North Sea and thus reach the coast of Sweden.

8,000–5,000 YEARS B.P.

During the Atlantic nemoral forests predominated in southern Sweden — on fertile soils mainly lime, elm and ash, on poorer and stonier soils oak. Pine forests survived on light, thin deposits. Nemoral trees spread as far north as the coast of southern Norrland, and hazel and elm right up to Jämtland. The rest of northern Sweden was dominated by vast forests of birch and pine.

5,000 YEARS B.P. – THE PRESENT

The Sub-Boreal and Sub-Atlantic periods were characterised by progressively cooler and damper climates, but also by the influence of mankind. About 5,000 years B.P. agriculture and cattle rearing were introduced; sheep, goats, pigs and cattle became common in southern Sweden. They required grazing grounds and sources of fodder, at the same time as fields were being created to cultivate a variety of crops. This meant that the landscape became more and more dominated by man.

Forests were cleared, often by fire, and temporary, later more permanent fields and pastures were created. Elm, lime and ash declined, as did oak. Ever since the Bronze Age haymaking has resulted in meadows; in southern Sweden meadows of tall

herbs were formed on what used to be alder bogs as early as 3,000 years ago. During the Bronze Age animals were let out to graze in the forests closest to the villages, a practice which grew increasingly common. This resulted in a varied landscape of heath, meadow and forest vegetation. This increasingly open cultivated landscape encouraged the immigration of new species, mainly weeds and cultivated plants.

The way in which mankind altered the landscape also affected the fauna to a great extent. The animals of the cultivated landscape, the hedgehog and the badger, for example, were encouraged, whereas forest animals like wild cat, lynx and bear suffered. Surprisingly enough the large predators, despite increased hunting, managed to survive in southern Sweden almost up to the present day.

As late as 4,000–3,000 years B.P. two new species of tree arrived from the south: beech and hornbeam. They succeeded in penetrating as far north as Mälardalen, but hornbeam was never more than a rather uncommon species of southern Sweden.

In northern Sweden the nemoral forest species became increasingly rare during the Sub-Boreal period. Birch and pine had to compete with spruce, which began to be fairly common along the coast of Norrland about 3,000 years B.P. Only during the past 2,000 years, however, has spruce become a dominant species. It reached its southernmost limit in Skåne-Blekinge as late as during the last 300 years.

The Younger Dryas —10,500 years B. P.

1:10 000 000

	Ice–sheet
	Tundra
	Present land, covered by water
●	Landscapes described

(S10)

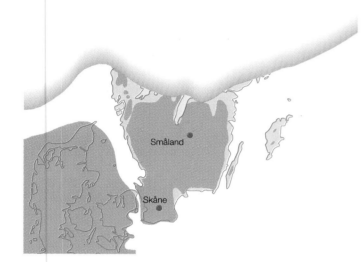

The Småland highlands were a bleak, arctic landscape whose proximity to the inland ice was very evident. Cirque glaciers occurred on some mountain slopes. Snow-patch vegetation consisting of dwarf birch, willow and bryophytes was common. The ground was covered with vegetation only in the most favourable places. On drier, lighter soils there were grass meadows with mugworts and a few dry-meadow herbs. Heath vegetation requiring humus had not yet developed here.

SKÅNE

After the cold temperate climate of the Alleröd, lasting some 1,000 years, there was a serious deterioration of the climate during the first part of the Late Dryas. The inland ice ceased to melt and began to edge southwards again from central Sweden. The level of the oceans was almost 100 m lower than today, but as large areas of land were still compressed by the ice, the coastline at that time was considerably above today's level throughout almost the whole of Sweden. There was a bleak archipelago along the west coast and the climate was arctic with summer temperatures of 8–10 °C. The ground was permanently frozen and unstable on account of land movement. The winds blew fiercely across large areas bare of vegetation. Snow-drifts built up on the leeside and often developed into cirque glaciers.

The landscape in Skåne was exposed to the sun and winds and there were great variations in temperature and humidity. Countless pools of water gathered in hollows in the ground since the ground underneath was usually frozen even in summer.

On south-facing slopes steppe-like vegetation consisting of mugworts, rock rose and other dry-meadow plants competed with mountain plants such as mountain avens. Dwarf willow, bryophytes and ferns grew in the hollows. On north-facing slopes or flat areas there was a layer of humus which allowed heath plants such as crowberry *Empetrum* spp., dwarf birch *Betula nana* and heathers to establish themselves. Willow bushes and marsh-meadow plants found a foothold in damp hollows. At least in southern Skåne isolated clusters of mountain birch and juniper could be found. At times there would be both reindeer and wild horses on the tundra, accompanied by quite a number of birds and rodents.

The Early Boreal
—9,000 years B. P.

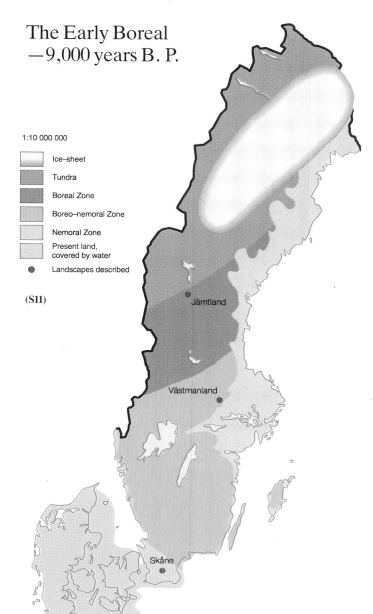

1:10 000 000

- Ice-sheet
- Tundra
- Boreal Zone
- Boreo–nemoral Zone
- Nemoral Zone
- Present land, covered by water
- Landscapes described

(S11)

Jämtland

Västmanland

Skåne

A large expanse of inland ice still spread across northern Sweden. The broad sound in central Sweden was now dry, which made it easier for plants and animals to spread to the north. The warm, dry climate also encouraged this colonisation on virgin land. Only a narrow belt of tundra remained along the edge of the ice sheet. Animals and plants came to this tundra from the south, west and north and the mountain vegetation began to resemble that of our own time more closely. The Boreal pine-birch zone had its southern limit immediately north of the present biological Norrland boundary. To the south lay an area of mixed forest: pine and birch with isolated nemoral trees. The predominance of hazel in Skåne means that we can place this area in the continental nemoral forest zone.

JÄMTLAND

South Jämtland lay close to the tree limit. The forest consisted of birch and pine which became a belt of bush vegetation at the edge of the ice sheet: sea buckthorn *Hippophaë rhamnoides* on dry ground and willow species *Salix* spp. on damp ground. There was also mountain vegetation like our own. There are no animal records, but moose had probably come as far north as this, perhaps together with wolf, bear and wolverine.

VÄSTMANLAND

Pine and birch forest predominated, but there was a good deal of hazel here as well. Nemoral trees were considerably less common here than in southern Sweden. The central Swedish landscape was characterised by the expanding coastal landscape. No finds of bones from higher animals are recorded, but it may be presumed that moose, bear and wolf were present.

SKÅNE

Pine-hazel forests were a type of vegetation which does not exist in present-day Sweden. There were also many species that require warm conditions like ivy *Hedera helix*, mistletoe *Viscum album*, great fen-sedge *Cladium mariscus* and royal fern *Osmunda regalis*. The higher fauna are recorded in many bone finds of moose, aurochs, European bison, red deer, roe deer, wild boar, bear, wolf and badger.

The Late Atlantic
—5,000 years B. P.

1:10 000 000

- Tundra
- Boreal Zone
- Boreo–nemoral Zone
- Nemoral Zone
- Present land, covered by water
- ● Landscapes described

(S12)

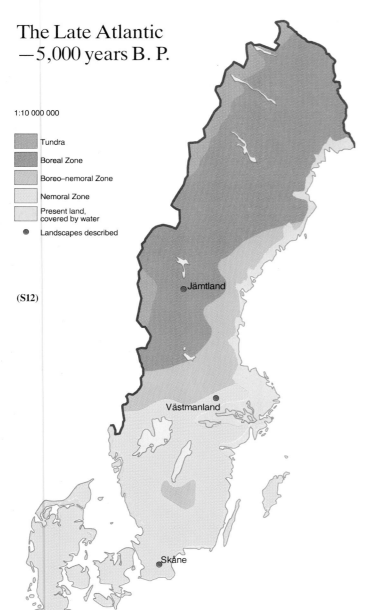

The inland ice had totally disappeared 8,000 years B.P. Probably even the small cirque glaciers in the mountains disappeared during the Atlantic. The tree limit was 150–200 m higher than today. The Boreal pine-birch forest region lay further north and the mixed forest region consisting of pine-birch and elm-oak-lime now comprised the coast of Norrland up to South Västerbotten and the lower reaches of the Norrland river valleys. Nemoral forests dominated the whole of southern Sweden. The northern limit of several warm-period species like the large-leaved lime *Tilia platyphyllos*, mistletoe, ivy, royal fern, water chestnut *Trapa natans* and pond tortoise was further north during this period. Red deer, roe deer and wild boar were common in southern Sweden, whereas moose was the dominant large animal in northern Sweden. In general the fauna of southern Sweden was rich: wild cat, beaver, otter, badger, bear and many other species were to be found.

JÄMTLAND

The landscape was largely covered with forest. Low pines grew on the mountains at the tree limit. In the central, low-lying forests birch and pine were predominant, with grey alder and willow in moist places. Elm and hazel flourished on south-facing slopes. Dwelling sites indicate that moose, bear, wolverine, beaver and otter were hunted, as well as birds like merganser, capercaillie and divers.

VÄSTMANLAND

A rich mixed forest grew here, with pine and birch on poor soils and nemoral forest on good soils round lakes and sea lochs. A rich fauna of moose, red deer, wild boar, wolverine, bear and wild cat could be found, as well as many sea species, not least grey seal.

SKÅNE

Nemoral forest, with oak and lime on dry ground and elm and ash on moister ground, completely dominated the landscape. A rich fauna meant many dwelling sites. Bone records show that red deer and wild boar, among other animals, were hunted intensively. Wild cat and pond tortoise were to be found, but moose had disappeared entirely, at least from southern Skåne. Evidence has been found of a large number of bird and fish species, mainly at dwelling sites. About this time small-scale farming was introduced as a complement to hunting, fishing and gathering.

The Sub-Atlantic
—1,000 years B.P.

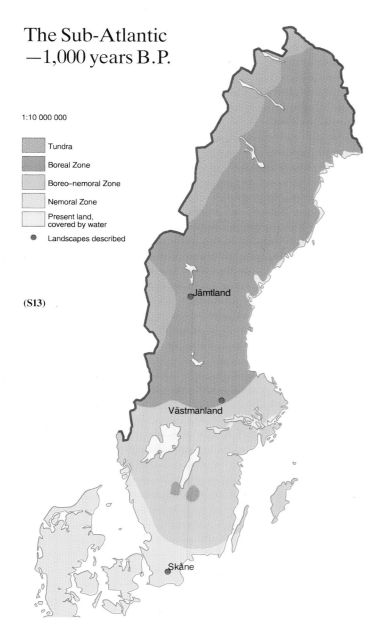

1:10 000 000

- Tundra
- Boreal Zone
- Boreo–nemoral Zone
- Nemoral Zone
- Present land, covered by water
- ● Landscapes described

(S13)

The temperature was lower and humidity higher in the sub-Atlantic. Cirque glaciers formed again in the mountains and the tree limit moved down. Bogs became larger throughout the country.

The boreal coniferous forest now consisted of both pine and spruce. Its southern limit had moved to the present biological Norrland boundary. In the mixed forest region to the south pine, spruce and birch grew on poor soils. Nemoral forest grew on better soils, especially close to cultivated land. In the southernmost coastal landscape beech and hornbeam also grew now in the nemoral forest.

The open cultivated landscape, characterised by meadows and pastures, dates from this period, the late Iron Age. The open landscape, together with intensive hunting, led to a considerable reduction in the higher wild fauna in southern Sweden.

JÄMTLAND

The tree limit now ran along more or less the same line as today, and the forest closest to the limit, then as now, consisted of dwarf birch. The rest of the forest was dominated by pine, spruce and birch. Farms breeding cattle grew up in favourable locations. Man had begun to domesticate reindeer, but wild reindeer also existed. The animal most commonly hunted was still moose.

VÄSTMANLAND

The landscape was dominated by coniferous forest of pine and spruce, but in favourable places there were also nemoral trees and an open, cultivated landscape of fields, meadows and pasture land. The previously rich fauna had been decimated, partly because the area now lay further from the coast and partly because of changes in the vegetation and hunting by man. Moose and bear were the predominant species.

SKÅNE

In Skåne there was now an open cultivated landscape of fields and meadows round the villages and vast grazing lands in the outfields between the villages. Semi-open woods of beech, oak and saplings were to be found mainly on the granite Skåne horsts. Much of the wild fauna had been driven away from the inhabited areas, but wolves still made winter raids on the villages and bear and lynx could also be seen in the surviving forest land, especially in northern Skåne.

21

Helianthemum
oelandicum

Artemisia
oelandica

Ranunculus
illyricus

Gypsophila
fastigiata

Bartsia
alpina

The present alvar vegetation on Öland and Gotland is a mixture of mountain and steppe plants.

Holly, water chestnut, mistletoe and royal fern are examples of plants that had a wider distribution in the warm period.

Water chestnut
Trapa natans

Holly *Ilex aquifolium*

Royal fern
Osmunda regalis

Mistletoe
Viscum album

Relict Plants in the Present

Most tundra plants died out at the end of the late glacial period, but a few species have managed to survive right up to the present. Both steppe and mountain plants grow in the limestone areas of Gotland and Öland and in Västergötland. Examples of relict steppe plants from the late glacial steppe tundra are Öland rock rose *Helianthemum oelandicum, Gypsophilia fastigiata*, great burnet *Sanguisorba officinalis, Ranuculus illyricus*, alvar mugwort *Artemesia oelandica* and *A. rupestris*. Alpine sawwort *Saussurea alpina*, alpine butterwort *Pinguicula alpina* and alpine bartsia *Bartsia alpina* are examples of relict alpine plants.

During the warm period there were a number of plants requiring warm conditions which have now become extinct or whose distribution has moved southwards or westwards. Holly *Ilex aquifolium* is a tree found in the west which was more common in southern Norway, Denmark and Halland-Bohuslän during the Atlantic. Only one specimen of wild holly now grows in Sweden. Water chestnut *Trapa natans* was common in Götaland, but it suffered a serious decline during the Sub-Boreal-Sub-Atlantic. Its last known occurrence was in Lake Immeln, Skåne, in 1913. Mistletoe *Viscum album* was also widespread in southern Sweden but today has a relict-like distribution mainly round Lake Mälaren. Royal fern *Osmunda regalis* used to be common along streams and in fens in Götaland but is now considerably rarer.

Southern Forests —2,000 Years of Change

The appearance and composition of forests are in a continuous state of flux. The forests we see today are the product of climate and human activity and should not be seen as a final stage.

Mankind can affect forests directly by silviculture or agriculture or indirectly, for example by grazing cattle in forests, which affects the kind of tree species that can develop. Other forms of indirect influence are culling wild species or changes in soil nutrients caused by pollution.

The climate is the driving force behind changes in the distribution of species. A warmer climate means that most species of trees can spread northwards, but will have to retire to the south if it gets colder or wetter. In many cases it is changes in the winter climate or its relation to the summer climate that determine whether a species is favoured or not rather than the mean annual climate.

The maps on next page show the possible composition of the forests in southern Sweden 2,000 and 1,000 years B.P. They are based on pollen counts from some 40 locations. The results have been converted to show the relative quantities of trees of each species. This method gives some idea of the mixture of tree species in forests in older times but tells us nothing about the total amount of forest land. The maps showing the situation today are based on figures from the National Forest Survey.

MORE DECIDUOUS TREES BEFORE

Two thousand years ago there were many more deciduous trees in southern Sweden that there are today. Spruce had not yet come to this part of the country. The deciduous forests mainly consisted of nemoral species like oak, lime, ash, elm and maple. These species have become fewer and fewer throughout the whole of the period and are in a very weak position today.

Beech had its widest distribution about one thousand years ago, but was less common 2,000 years B.P. Today it is the most common nemoral tree in Skåne. The "Little Ice Age" brought cold winters and during the past thousand years beech has been losing ground to spruce, which has immigrated from both north and east. This is the result of both a changing climate and human activity.

FORESTRY HAS FAVOURED PINE AND SPRUCE

During the past 100–200 years forestry has favoured spruce at the expense of beech and other deciduous trees, which had already been losing ground to beech. In addition a great deal of open land has been planted with spruce.

The proportion of pine increased between 2,000 and 1,000 years B.P. This may have been the result of a change in climate which began about 500 B.C. We can see a larger proportion of pine in the eastern parts of Sweden and because there is a drier climate here forest fires have played a more significant role than in

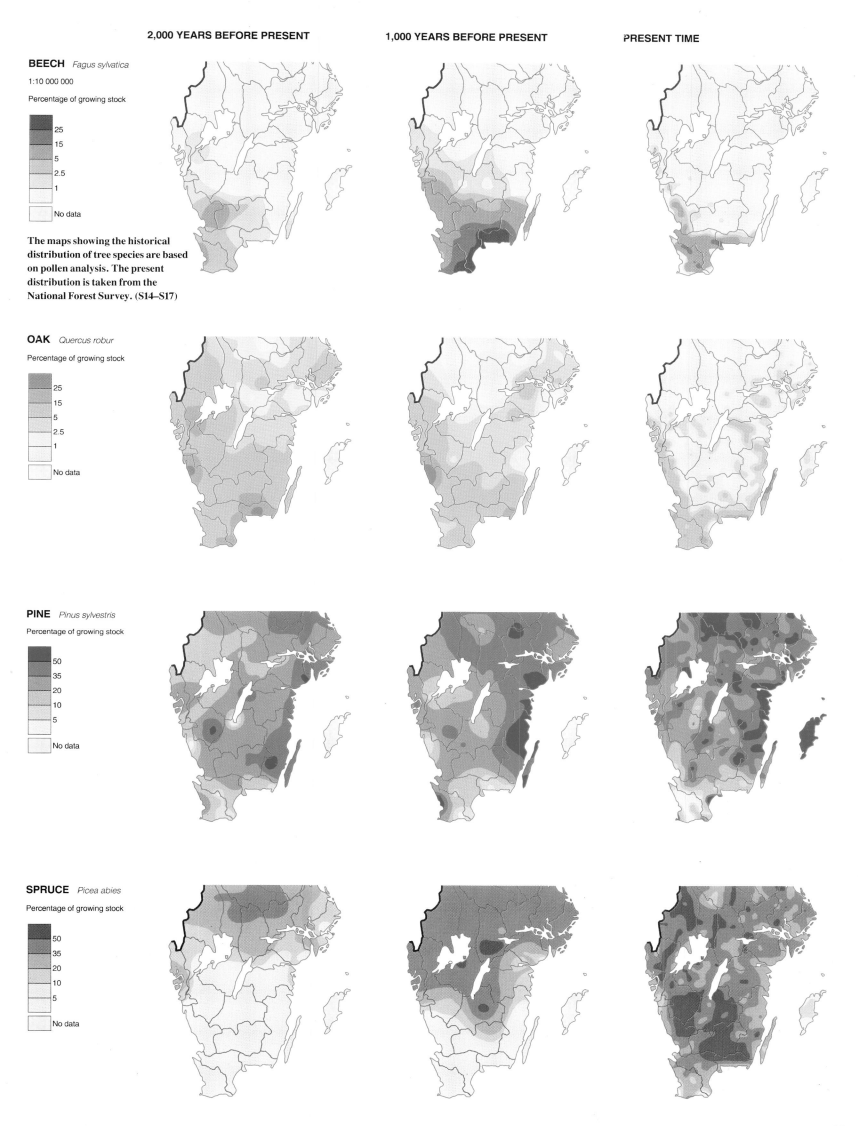

2,000 YEARS BEFORE PRESENT   1,000 YEARS BEFORE PRESENT   PRESENT TIME

BEECH *Fagus sylvatica*

1:10 000 000

Percentage of growing stock

25
15
5
2.5
1

No data

The maps showing the historical
distribution of tree species are based
on pollen analysis. The present
distribution is taken from the
National Forest Survey. (S14–S17)

OAK *Quercus robur*

Percentage of growing stock

25
15
5
2.5
1

No data

PINE *Pinus sylvestris*

Percentage of growing stock

50
35
20
10
5

No data

SPRUCE *Picea abies*

Percentage of growing stock

50
35
20
10
5

No data

23

TYPE OF FOREST

1:10 000 000

- Birch
- Oak–birch
- Oak–alder–lime–hazel
- Beech
- Pine–beech/lime–juniper
- Pine–birch
- Spruce–pine–birch
- Pine
- Spruce
- No data

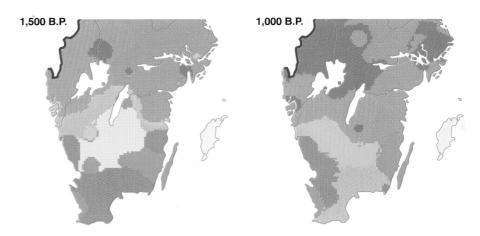

2,000 B.P.   **1,500 B.P.**   **1,000 B.P.**

The composition of the forests has changed noticeably in the past 2,000 years, mainly as a result of human activities. Spruce has expanded very rapidly and the nemoral forests are in decline today. (S18)

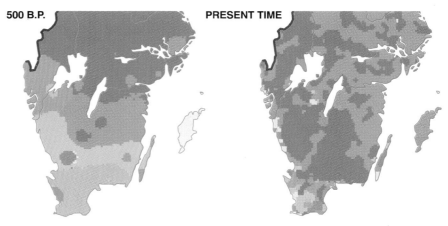

500 B.P.   **PRESENT TIME**

Mixed forests of pine, hazel and nemoral trees are hardly to be found in Sweden today, but were widespread a few thousand years ago. The picture is from Latvia.

---

the west. Pine is ecologically well adapted to surviving forest fires. In the southernmost parts of Sweden the proportion of pine has increased somewhat during the past 500 years. Today's farming methods allow pine to grow on good soil where it would, under natural conditions, disappear as a result of competition from tree species that demand more nutritious soil.

NEMORAL TREES UNCOMMON TODAY

The more intensively the land was exploited by man, the more the nemoral forests decreased. Intensive forest grazing in the 18th and 19th centuries primarily affected the trees that cattle preferred. Nemoral trees are relatively uncommon in today's forest landscape.

FOREST TYPES HAVE CHANGED DRAMATICALLY

The maps showing different types of forests give an idea of the way in which the whole landscape has changed. The forests in which spruce predominate have expanded greatly during the period and are today almost pure spruce forests. Other types have been driven out; the rich mixed forests of pine, birch and nemoral trees, for example, which were widespread 2,000 years ago, have disappeared completely. There are few traces of the open mixed coniferous forests with beech or other nemoral trees which were common 500 years ago.

The past 500 years have been the worst period for beech forests and their decline is very evident. Beech forests never consisted of beech trees alone; there were always considerable

numbers of oak, lime and other nemoral trees. The rich, nemoral forests which covered large parts of Skåne have almost disappeared. A strong contributory factor has certainly been the extensive draining of the plains.

It is difficult to imagine the natural vegetation at a particular spot since changes take place continuously. When studying the role played by mankind in changes in the vegetation, it is important to choose a time scale within which the climate has not changed too much.

Our knowledge of the composition and appearance of forests in the past can be used to make forestry more environmentally friendly today. If the natural forest at a particular place can be imitated, it will give the natural flora and fauna a chance to survive, or even return if it has already disappeared.

Geographical Classifications of Plants and Animals

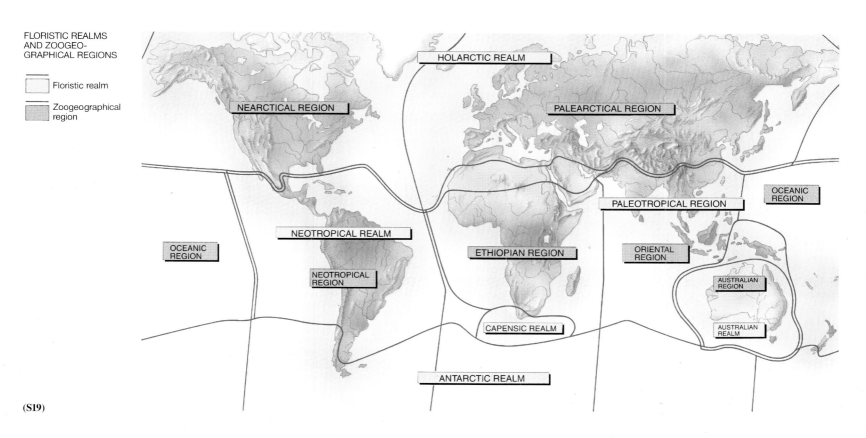

FLORISTIC REALMS
AND ZOOGEO-
GRAPHICAL REGIONS

☐ Floristic realm

▨ Zoogeographical
region

(S19)

ZOOGEOGRAPHICAL PROVINCES

1:10 000 000

■ Arctic Province

Boreal Province

■ North–east Scandinavian area

■ North–east Baltic coast area

☐ Middle Scandinavian area

South Scandinavian Province

☐ Middle Swedish Lowlands

☐ South Swedish Uplands

☐ Öland and Gotland

■ Nemoral area

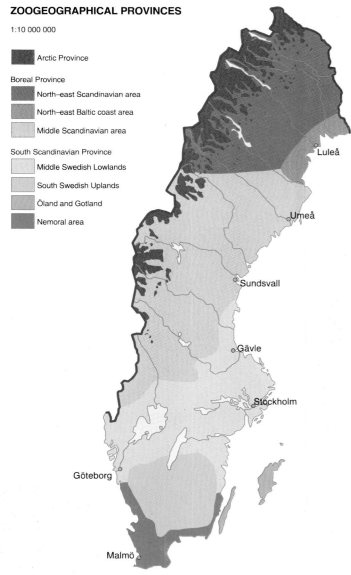

Different parts of the earth have similar plant and animal life, which is above all the result of historical factors. In fact some 250 million years ago the land mass consisted of one single large continent—*Pangea*—which later split up into smaller units. Since then plants and animals have developed; the family relationships in the fauna and flora reflect earlier contact between now separated land masses.

ZOOGEOGRAPHICAL PROVINCES

Sweden is usually divided into three zoogeographical provinces, which may in turn be divided into different areas. This division was made as early as the 1920s. Swedish zoogeography has been a neglected subject in recent years and there is a lack of modern analyses and revisions.

Species typical of the *Arctic Province* or mountain zone are arctic fox, lemming, shore lark, snow bunting and char. Species found in the *Boreal Province* or northern Scandinavian forest region are grey red-backed vole, bean goose, willow grouse and grayling. Hedgehog, mole, coot, marsh harrier and sand lizard are species that belong to the *South Scandinavian Province*. (S20)

The earth is usually divided into regions with similar flora or fauna and various systems, all more or less alike, are used to categorize the plants and animals.

The animal regions are the *Australian, Ethiopian, Nearctic, Neotropical, Oceanic, Oriental* and *Palaearctic*. The Palearctic and Nearctic regions form together the *Holarctic* region.

In plant geography the Nearctic and Palaearctic regions together form the *Holarctic* realm. The Ethiopian, Oriental and Oceanic regions are combined to form the *Palaetropical* realm. And the southernmost part of the globe is distinguished as the *Antarctic* realm. The *Cape* realm comprises the southern tip of Africa, which has a very special flora with many endemic species, that is, species limited to a certain geographical area. There is no equivalent in the zoogeographical world.

VEGETATION ZONES

- ☐ Ice
- ☐ Tundra, alpine vegetation
- ☐ Coniferous forest
- ☐ Coniferous forest with large proportions of broad–leaved deciduous trees
- ☐ Broad–leaved, deciduous forest
- ☐ Broad–leaved evergreen forest
- ☐ Grassland and steppe
- ☐ Semidesert and desert
- ☐ Savanna, savanna shrubland, dry forest
- ☐ Tropical—subtropical rainforest, mountain rain forest

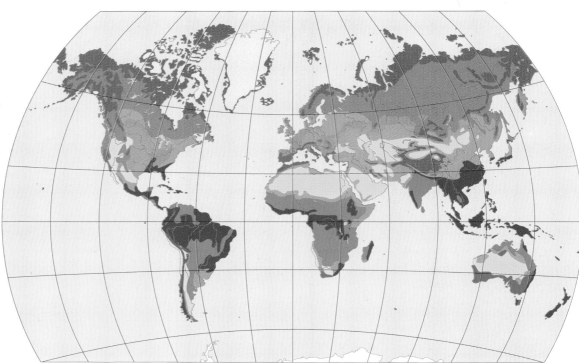

(S21)

The alpine zone comprises bare mountains and consists of low vegetation, with many bryophytes and lichens. Kaskasavagge, Kebnekaise.

Below left. Boreal coniferous forest is found north of the biological Norrland boundary. Spruce and pine are the totally dominant tree species. The southern limit of the boreal zone coincides with the northern limit of the oak. Åsbo, Hälsingland.

Below right. The boreonemoral zone lies south of the biological Norrland boundary and is dominated by coniferous forests, but nemoral trees also occur.

26

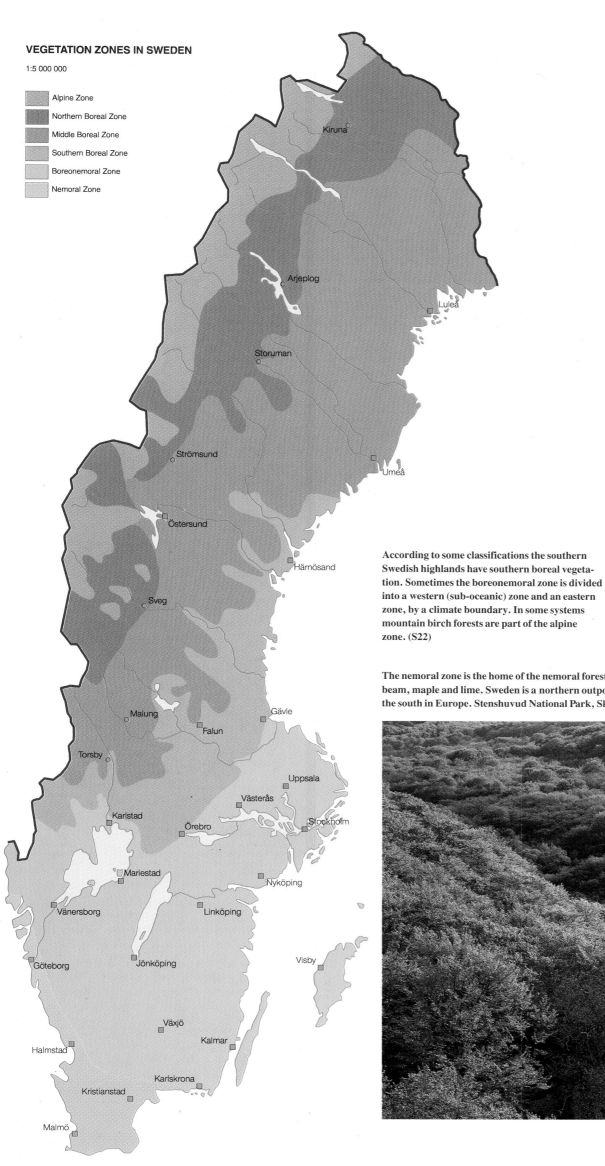

VEGETATION ZONES IN SWEDEN

1:5 000 000

- Alpine Zone
- Northern Boreal Zone
- Middle Boreal Zone
- Southern Boreal Zone
- Boreonemoral Zone
- Nemoral Zone

Kiruna

Arjeplog

Luleå

Storuman

Strömsund

Umeå

Östersund

Härnösand

Sveg

Malung

Gävle

Falun

Torsby

Uppsala

Västerås

Karlstad

Örebro

Stockholm

Mariestad

Nyköping

Vänersborg

Linköping

Göteborg

Jönköping

Visby

Växjö

Kalmar

Halmstad

Kristianstad

Karlskrona

Malmö

According to some classifications the southern Swedish highlands have southern boreal vegetation. Sometimes the boreonemoral zone is divided into a western (sub-oceanic) zone and an eastern zone, by a climate boundary. In some systems mountain birch forests are part of the alpine zone. (S22)

VEGETATION ZONES

The classification is based above all on the predominant tree species; it is in a continuous state of refinement and change, but its main features are constant.

Alpine Zone: Bare mountain.
High Alpine: Boulders and patterned ground with sparse plant coverage.
Middle Alpine: Grass and scrub heathland.
Low Alpine: Scrub heathland.

Boreal Zone: Coniferous forests. Nemoral trees very rare. Aspen and birch common. Few cultivated areas. Large mire area.
Northern Boreal: Sparse coniferous forests containing many birch trees. Mountain birch forests.
Middle Boreal: The coniferous zone proper.
Southern Boreal: Nemoral trees occur.

Boreonemoral (Hemiboreal) Zone: Northern limit coincides with the northern limit of oak. Mixed forests of pine, spruce, deciduous trees (mainly aspen and birch but also some nemoral species) are common. Large cultivated areas on the plains. Large mire areas in the west.

Nemoral Zone: Northern limit coincides with the natural southern limit of spruce. The forests consist largely of nemoral trees (mainly beech, oak, elm, ash, maple, lime). Beech is the characteristic tree species. Large cultivated areas; small mire area.

The nemoral zone is the home of the nemoral forests, mostly of beech and oak but also elm, ash, hornbeam, maple and lime. Sweden is a northern outpost of this vegetation zone, which is more common to the south in Europe. Stenshuvud National Park, Skåne.

27

Various Types of Distribution

DISTRIBUTION TYPES: VASCULAR PLANTS IN THE NORDIC COUNTRIES (EXCEPT ICELAND)

NORTHERN

NORTH–EASTERN

SOUTHERN

SOUTH–CENTRAL

WESTERN

CONTINENTAL

ALPINE SPECIES

This classification is based on a numerical analysis of distribution maps for some 730 taxa from various map collections. Species spread by human beings and taxa and taxonomic groups of uncertain status are not included. Only information from Sweden, Norway, Denmark and Finland has been used. (S23)

Species have different distribution areas, which vary according to environmental requirements, immigrant history and the influence of man. Biologists have tried to group species with similar distributions into distribution types. The division depends on the scale: distribution types may be discerned, for example, for a part of Sweden, all of Sweden, Scandinavia, Europe and the world.

Vascular Plants

As with other groups of organisms the distribution of vascular plants is governed by Sweden's north–south orientation. There is also an east–west gradient, but this is much weaker. Traditionally the Nordic Countries without Iceland have often been used as an area for the division of the distribution types of vascular plants.

Some species occur throughout Scandinavia, such as common chickweed *Stellaria media,* field horsetail *Equisetum arvense,* bottle sedge *Carex rostrata,* juniper *Juniperus communis* and wavy hairgrass *Deschampsia flexuosa.*

SOUTH–EASTERN DISTRIBUTION

SEASHORE SPECIES

Northern species occur in northern Norway, Sweden and Finland. Many of them are found in mountain areas but also in the lowlands. Among them are northern moonwort *Botrychium boreale* and mountain butterbur *Petasites frigidus.*

North-eastern species are mainly found in the most northern and north-eastern parts of Sweden and northern Finland, for example, *Carex disperma.*

Southern species are most common in Denmark, but some also occur in the south of Sweden and southernmost Finland and in south and south-west Norway. Among them are hornbeam *Carpinus betulus,* common cudweed *Filago vulgaris* and square-stalked St John's wort *Hypericum tetrapterum.*

Southern-central species are a group found south of limes norrlandicus (the biological Norrland boundary) in Sweden. Among them are leafless hawksbeard *Crepis praemorsa,* agrimony *Agromonia eupatoria* and coralroot *Cardamine bulbifera.*

Western species are a fairly small group found primarily in Norway but also in Denmark, south-west Sweden and Jämtland. Examples of western species that occur in Sweden are bog asphodel *Narthecium ossifragum* and lemon-scented fern *Oreopteris limbosperma.*

Continental species are found mainly in eastern Scandinavia, in areas with little precipitation and cold winters. *Calypso bulbosa,* yellow wintergreen *Pyrola chlorantha* and *Salix starkeana* are among them.

Alpine species form a large group found in the mountain areas of Scandinavia. They include russet *Carex saxatilis,* Scandinavian primrose *Primula scandinavica, Cassiope hypnoides* and snow pearlwort *Sagina nivalis.*

Looking at Sweden alone, it is possible to distinguish a few distribution types:

South-eastern species occur primarily on Öland and Gotland but also in south-east Skåne and Blekinge. These species are found mostly in open, warm, lime-rich places such as sandy heaths or alvars. Such habitats are outposts for species which are more common in steppe-like landscapes in South-east Europe. Yellow pheasant's eye *Adonis vernalis* and *Ranuculus illyricus* are two examples.

Seashore species occur only along the coast. Sea rocket *Cakile maritima, Puccinellia retroflexa* and sea milkwort *Glaux maritima* belong to this group.

OCEANIC DISTRIBUTION

Scapania gracilis

1:20 000 000

(S24)

CONTINENTAL DISTRIBUTION

Mannia fragrans

(S25)

Oceanic species of bryophytes flourish in the mist and spray of waterfalls. Djupadal, Västergötland.

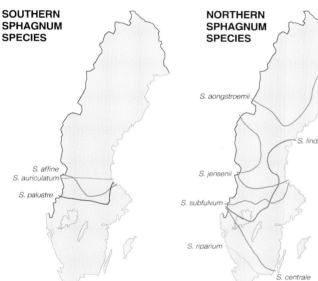

SOUTHERN SPHAGNUM SPECIES

S. affine
S. auriculatum
S. palustre

The lines indicate the northern limits of the main distribution areas of the species. (S26)

Sphagna dominate the bottom layers of most mires.

NORTHERN SPHAGNUM SPECIES

S. aongstroemii
S. lindbergii
S. jensenii
S. subfulvum
S. riparium
S. centrale

The lines indicate the southern limits of the main distribution areas of the species. (S27)

Continental species of bryophytes find a home on the rocky outcrops of Öland and Gotland.

SPHAGNA FOUND THROUGHOUT SWEDEN

Sphagnum angustifolium
S. capillifolium
S. compactum
S. fallax
S. fimbriatum
S. fuscum
S. girgensonii
S. magellanicum
S. papillosum
S. russowii
S. squarrosum
S. subsecundum
S. teres
S. warnstorfii

Bryophytes

Bryophytes are found mainly in damp places such as marshy woods, mires, shady ravines and cliffs. Their distribution pattern differs from that of lichens and fungi, for example; precipitation and humidity are of far greater importance for bryophytes.

Oceanic bryophyte species require continual high humidity and are therefore found in places which have many days of rain. The most characteristic oceanic bryophytes are found on the west coast but also occur in a belt running from south-west Skåne to south-west Värmland, round Storlien and in certain very wet parts of the western mountains, for example round Tärna and Lycksele. Oceanic bryophytes also need mild winters, which the sea and the warm Gulf Stream help to provide. To a certain extent proximity to the sea also characterises bryophytes in the rest of southern and central Sweden, since these parts enjoy mild south-westerly winds throughout the year. Some oceanic species may even occur inland if the lower precipitation there is compensated by less evaporation, in mountain districts, for example. The snow there also provides shelter from low winter temperatures. Finally, oceanic species may occur close to a waterfall in its spray or mist zone.

Continental bryophyte species, that is, species which require dry, warm summers and cold winters, are almost non-existent in Sweden. One of the few exceptions is *Mannia fragrans*, which occurs in the east and appears to be better adapted to a steppe-like climate with long periods of drought.

Sphagna. Most of Sweden's 40 or so Sphagna are exclusively wetland mosses. Several of them are well adapted to living in acid mires (mires with low pH). Sphagna predominate in the bottom layers of most mires, thereby accounting for a large proportion of Sweden's peat production.

A few species are generalists that can exist in many environments, but most species have specialised in specific environments. Differences in the distribution patterns of Sphagna are probably largely due to the climate.

The rare lichen *Usnea longissima* is found only in old coniferous forests.

The beautiful lichen *Solorina crocea* grows on the ground, mostly in the mountains.

The lichen *Verrucaria maura* is found along the coasts of Sweden, where it grows on rocks, forming a clear zone.

The lichen *Lobaria amplissima* is a large, rare foliose lichen that grows on nemoral trees, above all in south-west Sweden.

Lichens

Lichens are an important part of vegetation; in some areas they are the totally dominant form of ground-cover. Boulders and rocks are often completely covered with corticolous lichens which in fact give the rocks their colour. If the lichen disappears, for example on rocks round a strong source of pollution, the bare rock will often have a contrasting lighter colour.

In general the lichen share of the vegetation increases the further north you go. Lichens are also found higher up in the mountains than vascular plants—they can even survive on the highest peaks.

With regard to distribution, lichens can be divided into geographical or climatic groups. The chemical composition of the bedrock is another important factor in the distribution of lichens. Limestone bedrock, for example, is very unevenly distributed in Sweden.

DISTRIBUTION TYPES: LICHENS

1:20 000 000

Southern species usually have a wider distribution in the rest of Europe—Sweden is the northernmost outpost. (S28)

Northern species are found in the northernmost part of Sweden and in the mountains. There are also species that are limited to the upper parts of the mountains. (S29)

SOUTHERN
Physconia grisea

NORTHERN
Solorina crocea

EASTERN
Ramalina dilacerata

CONIFEROUS SPECIES
Usnea longissima

COASTAL
Verrucaria maura

OCEANIC
Lobaria amplissima

LIME–DEPENDENT
Caloplaca flavescens
Limestone bedrock/calcareous deposits

Corticolous lichens can grow on rocks, often creating beautifully coloured patterns.

Eastern species (above left) are not so common in Sweden, but have their main distribution in the eastern part of the boreal zone—the taiga. (S30)

Coniferous forest species are more or less widespread in the boreal zone. (S31)

Coastal species are dependent on salt or brackish water, often forming clear zones like the *Verrucaria maura* zone. (S32)

Oceanic species are found in areas with a mild, moist climate, as in south-west Sweden. (S33)

Lime-dependent species are found in a few relatively limited areas in Sweden. These species seldom occur in all calcareous areas but other factors such as climate appear to be important. (S34)

The spores of fungi are very small and can be transported over long distances by the wind, which helps them to spread.

Fungi

The ease with which fungi dispers means that it is often easier for them to find suitable habitats than for flowering plants. Thus their distribution within a relatively small area like Sweden probably reflects the current climate, the soil and the like; they do not to such an extent as flowering plants display historical migrational patterns.

One example of this is *Laurilia sulcata*, a fungus bound to spruce in mountainous, virgin-like forests. It has a clear bicentric distribution, like several alpine flowering plants. For flowering plants this is presumed to reflect different migrational routes, but for this fungus, which is favoured by a continental climate, it is presumed to be due to the more oceanic climate of the lower mountains in Jämtland and Tröndelag.

The distribution of many species of fungi in Sweden reflects their hosts.

Thus *Piptoporus betulinus* is common on birch throughout Sweden, but not all bracket fungi on birch follow this pattern. *Daedaleopsis septentrionalis* is common on birch only in northern Sweden, so its distribution is probably due to climatic conditions. Climatic conditions are also certainly the reason for the distribution of *Haploporus odorus*, which has a clear northern distribution, although it is bound to sallow, a substrate found throughout Sweden.

The form of *Puccinia persistens* which has as its host both liverleaf *Hepatica nobilis* and various species of grass such as common couch *Elymus repens* and bearded couch *E. caninus* has a very restricted distribution in coastal districts of eastern central Sweden.

Several rare species of fungi which form mycorrhiza with nemoral trees such as oaks or limes are distributed in parts of central Sweden and on Öland and Gotland, but they are not found in Skåne or on the west coast, nor in Denmark. A fungus of this kind is *Cortinarius praestans*.

Many fungi have a nemoral distribution; they accompany the beech in Sweden even though they are not always bound to beech trees. One of them is *Mycena crocata*, which is common in beech woods but is also found in elm groves, though only within the distribution area of the beech.

Amanta citrina is one of the boreonemoral fungi, that is, the fungi that are not found north of the northern limit of the oak. It is common in southern Sweden in both oak and beech woods, but also in pine forests. Pine is found throughout Sweden, but this fungus is wholly restricted to the boreonemoral zone, apart from one record in the Sundsvall district.

SOME DISTRIBUTION TYPES: FUNGI

1:20 000 000

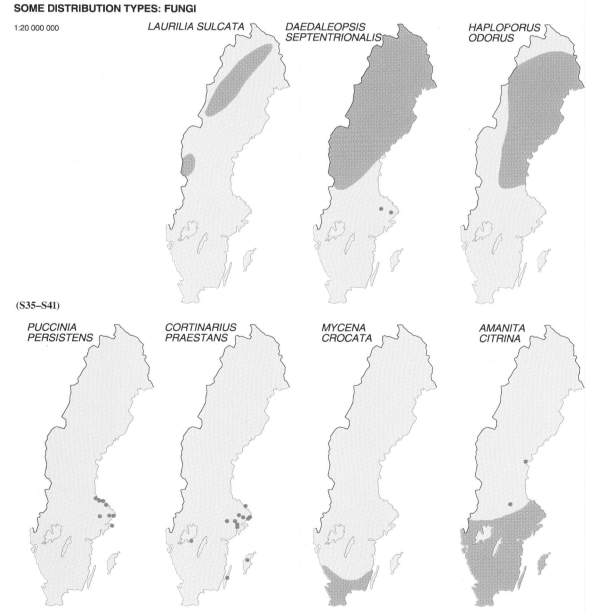

LAURILIA SULCATA — DAEDALEOPSIS SEPTENTRIONALIS — HAPLOFORUS ODORUS

(S35–S41)

PUCCINIA PERSISTENS — CORTINARIUS PRAESTANS — MYCENA CROCATA — AMANITA CITRINA

The fungus *Mycena crocata* is a southern species found only within the distribution area of the beech.

31

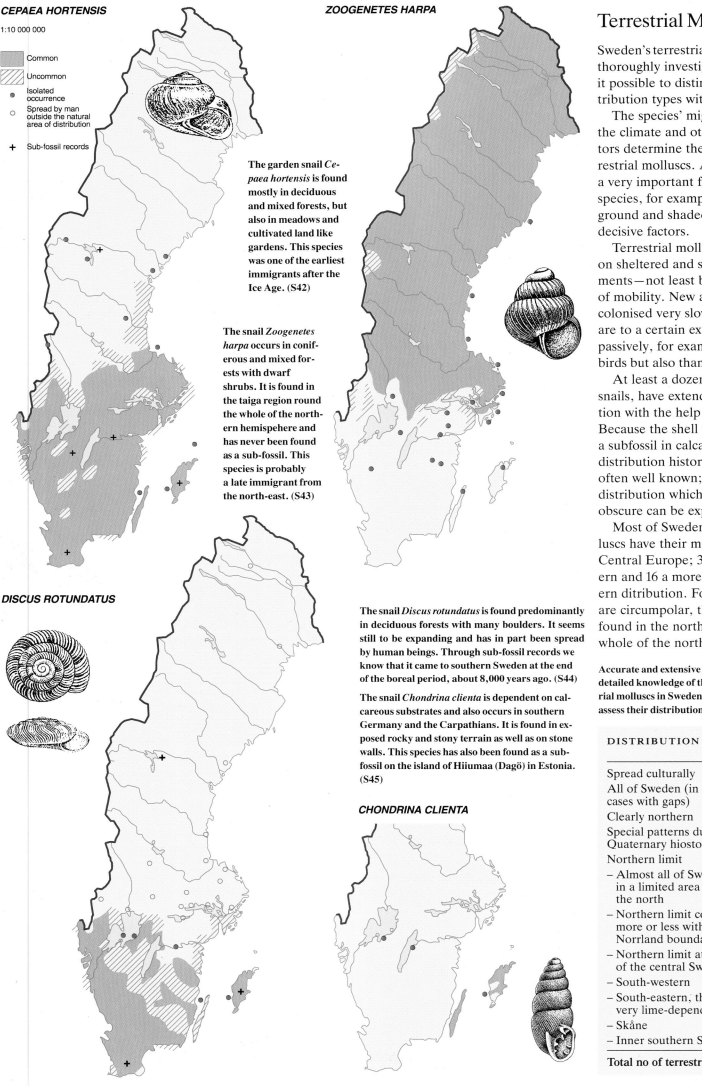

CEPAEA HORTENSIS

1:10 000 000

- ▨ Common
- ▨ Uncommon
- ● Isolated occurrence
- ○ Spread by man outside the natural area of distribution
- + Sub-fossil records

The garden snail *Cepaea hortensis* is found mostly in deciduous and mixed forests, but also in meadows and cultivated land like gardens. This species was one of the earliest immigrants after the Ice Age. (S42)

The snail *Zoogenetes harpa* occurs in coniferous and mixed forests with dwarf shrubs. It is found in the taiga region round the whole of the northern hemispehere and has never been found as a sub-fossil. This species is probably a late immigrant from the north-east. (S43)

ZOOGENETES HARPA

DISCUS ROTUNDATUS

The snail *Discus rotundatus* is found predominantly in deciduous forests with many boulders. It seems still to be expanding and has in part been spread by human beings. Through sub-fossil records we know that it came to southern Sweden at the end of the boreal period, about 8,000 years ago. (S44)

The snail *Chondrina clienta* is dependent on calcareous substrates and also occurs in southern Germany and the Carpathians. It is found in exposed rocky and stony terrain as well as on stone walls. This species has also been found as a sub-fossil on the island of Hiiumaa (Dagö) in Estonia. (S45)

CHONDRINA CLIENTA

Terrestrial Molluscs

Sweden's terrestrial molluscs have been thoroughly investigated, which makes it possible to distinguish various distribution types with great certainty.

The species' migrational history, the climate and other ecological factors determine the distribution of terrestrial molluscs. Access to lime is a very important factor for some 30 species, for example. Likewise damp ground and shaded habitats are often decisive factors.

Terrestrial molluscs are dependent on sheltered and stable environments—not least because of their lack of mobility. New areas are usually colonised very slowly. But molluscs are to a certain extent able to spread passively, for example by means of birds but also thanks to human beings.

At least a dozen species, mainly snails, have extended their distribution with the help of human beings. Because the shell is preserved as a subfossil in calcareous soil, the distribution history of the species is often well known; features of their distribution which would otherwise be obscure can be explained.

Most of Sweden's terrestrial molluscs have their main distribution in Central Europe; 35 have a more western and 16 a more continental—eastern ditribution. Four of the species are circumpolar, that is, they are found in the northern parts of the whole of the northern hemisphere.

Accurate and extensive surveys have given us very detailed knowledge of the distribution of terrestrial molluscs in Sweden. This makes it possible to assess their distribution types in detail.

DISTRIBUTION TYPES	Number
Spread culturally	20
All of Sweden (in some cases with gaps)	17
Clearly northern	5
Special patterns due to Quaternary hiostory	4
Northern limit	70
– Almost all of Sweden except in a limited area in the north	13
– Northern limit corresponding more or less with the biological Norrland boundary	18
– Northern limit at or just north of the central Swedish lakes	11
– South-western	6
– South-eastern, the majority very lime-dependent	13
– Skåne	5
– Inner southern Sweden	4
Total no of terrestriral molluscs	**116**

Endemism

Endemism means that a *taxon*, a systematic unit like a family, genus or species, is only found within a limited area such as a mountain peak, a river system, a country or a continent. An endemic species can either have arisen inside the area or have previously had a wider distribution but has now become extinct in all the other areas.

The number of endemic species and how clearly they differ from their related species is to a large extent dependent on the length of time the flora and fauna have developed within that area. Since Scandinavia was completely covered with ice until only about 13,000 years ago, our fauna and flora have been here for a relatively short time. The number of endemic species which have arisen since the Ice Age is therefore small.

Examples of areas with a large number of endemic species are the Galapagos and Hawaii.

Primula scandinavica

Saxifraga osloënsis

Papaver laestadianum

Papaver laestadianum has a very restricted distribution and differs only slightly from closely-related species.

Primula scandinavica, the Scandinavian primrose, is a hybrid that has stabilised as a species by an increased number of chromosomes. It is clearly different from the parent species.

Saxifraga osloënsis has a similar history and exemplifies endemics with a distribution in central Sweden. The parent species still live north and south of as well as within the distribution area of *S. osloënsis.*

Helianthemum oelandicum, the Öland rock-rose, and the grass *Deschampsia bottnica* belong to species groups which have probably had a continuous distribution area throughout much of Europe ever since the ice age. This distribution pattern has split up and the isolated populations have become separate species. (S46)

Deschampsia bottnica

Helianthemum oelandicum

VERY FEW ENDEMIC VASCULAR PLANTS

Of Sweden's phanerogams (flowering plants) fewer than ten species (c. 0.5%) are endemic to Sweden. The corresponding proportion for the Canary Islands, for example, is about 50% and for some other islands even higher. At the sub-species and variety level there are considerably more endemics, but there is great uncertainty about their taxonomic classification.

Our Swedish endemics, both at the species and the lower level, are mostly concentrated in the mountain regions and the Baltic Sea area, in particular on Öland and Gotland. There are also a few which probably originated in the central Swedish basin, that is, the area round the great lakes. A number are also considered to have arisen by adapting to the environments that agriculture created. Since agriculture has only existed in Sweden for about 6,000 years, such species must have evolved rapidly.

ENDEMIC VERTEBRATES

There are no endemic vertebrates at the species level in Sweden, but one at the subspecies level, the Gotland subspecies of the grass snake *Natrix natrix gotlandica,* which is only known on Gotland. If the area is enlarged to include Fennoscandia, there is one Swedish species that is endemic, the mountain lemming *Lemmus lemmus,* and at the subspecies level there are several: the Baltic Sea races of the ringed seal *Phoca hispida botnica,* the lesser black-backed gull *Larus fuscus fuscus* and the black guillemot *Uria grylle grylle,* the nominate race of the ptarmigan *Lagopus mutus mutus* and the Swedish subspecies of the pipit *Anthus petrosus littoralis.* Finally, mention should be made of the nominate race of the red deer *Cervus elaphus elaphus,* which has now become mixed through hybridisation everywhere except in Sweden.

Fish in Scandinavia have been greatly influenced by the recurrent ice ages. An interesting case of such species is our common vendace (which gives us that delicious roe). It was probably during the latest ice age that a spring-spawning population developed from the normal autumn-spawning species of vendace. It is likely that these populations coexisted later in ice-dammed lakes which formed south of the edge of the ice during the

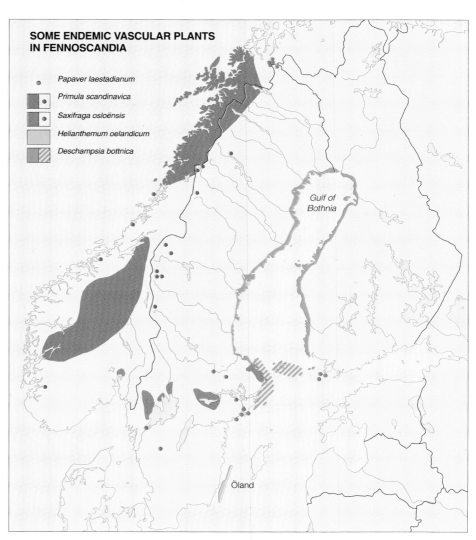

SOME ENDEMIC VASCULAR PLANTS IN FENNOSCANDIA

- Papaver laestadianum
- Primula scandinavica
- Saxifraga osloënsis
- Helianthemum oelandicum
- Deschampsia bottnica

Gulf of Bothnia

Öland

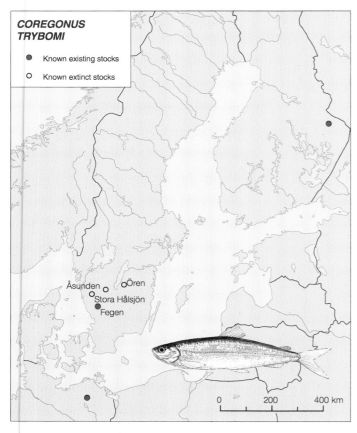

COREGONUS TRYBOMI

● Known existing stocks
○ Known extinct stocks

Åsunden ○ ○ Ören
○ Stora Hålsjön
● Fegen

0   200   400 km

The spring-spawning cisco *Coregonus trybomi* occurred at the turn of the century in four Swedish lakes. It has probably disappeared from Åsunden, Hålsjön and Ören. Today, as far as we know, it lives only in Fegen. Apart from this occurrence it has also been found in recent times in one lake in Finland and one in northern Germany. (S47)

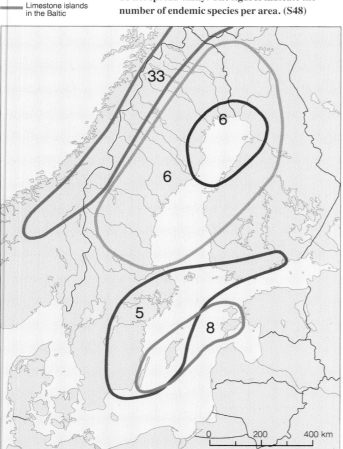

— Alpine area
— Bothnian Bay
— "Generally" northern distribution
— "Generally" southern distribution
— Limestone islands in the Baltic

DISTRIBUTION TYPES OF ENDEMIC MOTHS IN FENNOSCANDIA

Of all butterflies and moths presumed to be endemic, almost all are microlepidopterans that do not spread easily. The figures indicate the number of endemic species per area. (S48)

33
6
6
5
8

0   200   400 km

latest ice age. When the ice retreated towards the north, both species probably colonised a large number of lakes. In Sweden the spring-spawning species, which was given the scientific name *Coregonus trybomii* probably spread south from a refuge in the ice-locked Lake Vättern when the ice advanced southwards for a short period down the Vättern valley.

Coexistence is possible since the spring-spawning species lives in deeper water than the autumn-spawning species. So the two species seem to have been able to coexist only in lakes deeper than 30 m which have not been affected by eutrophication. As far as we know, spring-spawning vendace are to be found in three lakes in Sweden, Finland and northern Germany. Thus it is endemic to the Baltic Sea area.

ARE THERE ENDEMIC INSECTS IN SWEDEN?

Some 25,000 species of insects have been found in Sweden. Approximately 300 of these have not been found anywhere else in the world. So are they endemic to Sweden?

If we look more closely at these species we discover that, among well-studied insect groups, there are hardly any species which are known only in Sweden. Among our 1,000 or so large butterflies there is only one; among the 1,700 microlepidopteras there are six, two of which may, in fact, belong to two widespread species (uncertain species separations) and the remaining four may very well also exist in other parts of the world.

Of the 725 or so species of aculeates (bees, ants, wasps) in Sweden, there are only two leaf-cutting bees, described as late as 1983, which, as far as we know, only exist in Sweden. Among the other 8,000 species of aculeates there are probably about two hundred species that so far have only been found in Sweden, but this group is largely unknown.

Of the 6,000 or so species of dipterans (mosquitoes and flies) that are known in Sweden, at least 130 have only been found here. Dipterans are, however, a relatively unknown group, both in Sweden and abroad; judging by the pattern in well-known insect groups several ought also to be found elsewhere in the world.

Thus we cannot with any certainty claim that there are any endemic species of insects in Sweden. If we extend the geographical scale to look at Scandinavia as a unit, we find isolated species which are probably endemic to that area. But at the sub-species level there are probably real endemics even in Sweden.

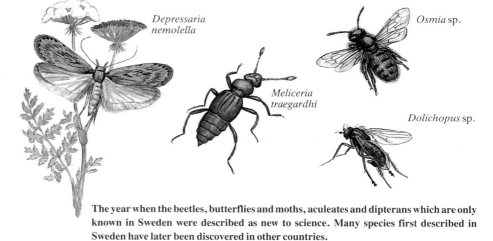

Depressaria nemolella

Meliceria traegardhi

Osmia sp.

Dolichopus sp.

The year when the beetles, butterflies and moths, aculeates and dipterans which are only known in Sweden were described as new to science. Many species first described in Sweden have later been discovered in other countries.

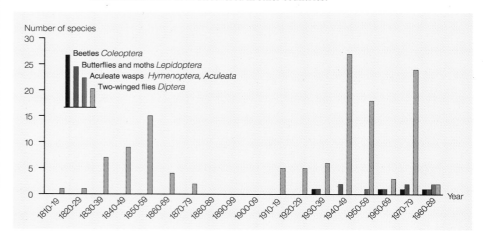

Number of species

■ Beetles *Coleoptera*
■ Butterflies and moths *Lepidoptera*
■ Aculeate wasps *Hymenoptera, Aculeata*
■ Two-winged flies *Diptera*

Year: 1810-19, 1820-29, 1830-39, 1840-49, 1850-59, 1860-69, 1870-79, 1880-89, 1890-99, 1900-09, 1910-19, 1920-29, 1930-39, 1940-49, 1950-59, 1960-69, 1970-79, 1980-89

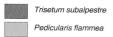

■ *Trisetum subalpestre*

■ *Pedicularis flammea*

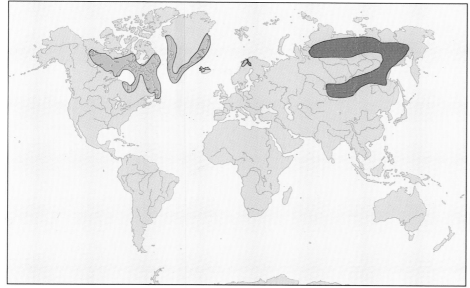

Trisetum subalpestre, a type of oat, grows in a few valleys in the northernmost part of Scandinavia and in a large area east of the Russian river Yenisey. One theory is that the species immigrated from the east but then died out in European Russia.

Some 30 species, including *Pedicularis flammea*, occurs in the Scandinavian mountains, on Greenland and in arctic North America. Some scientists consider this to be proof that the species survived in Scandinavia during the last Ice Age, others believe in long-distance dispersal. (S49)

● *Aradus frigidus*

● *Pinosomus tricopterus*

■ *P. trichopterus frigidus*

▨ *P. trichopterus latens*

Disjunctions

Disjunction means that a species occurs in two or more different distribution areas. It is also possible to speak of disjunction within a limited area such as Sweden, even though the distribution of the species outside this area may be continuous. Disjunctions may be caused, for example, by different waves of immigration, long-distance dispersal or by the species dying out in intermediate areas. Examples of relict occurrences are found among the species of the Öland alvar, for example. There live a large number of species that only occur here in northern Europe. But they also occur in eastern and south-eastern European steppe areas, in north-east Siberia and in some of Europe's southern mountain areas.

PINGUICULA ALPINA

1:20 000 000

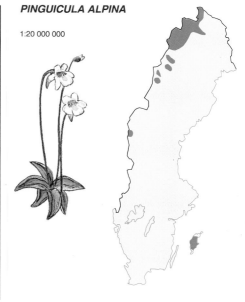

The fact that alpine butterwort *Pinguicula alpina* and *Euphrasia salisburgensis* grow in such very different places as in mountain districts and on Gotland would suggest separate immigration routes. (S52, S53)

EUPHRASIA SALISBURGENSIS

● *Salda henschii*

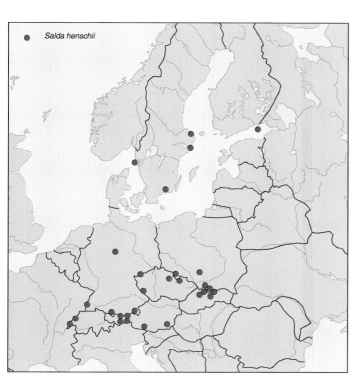

The beetles *Aradus frigidus* and *Pinosomus trichopterus* are thought to have survived on Öland ever since the island was covered with tundra steppe after the Ice Age. (S50)

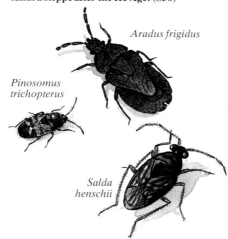

Aradus frigidus

Pinosomus trichopterus

Salda henschii

The beetle *Salda henschii* is an example of another relict disjunction type, namely those species that are found in areas which have recently become accessible through land uplift but which otherwise are mainly found in the mountain regions of Northern and Central Europe. (S51)

Limes Norrlandicus—Where the Taiga Begins

The northern coniferous forest region —or taiga—is the largest continuous forest type in the world. In Eurasia it stretches from Iceland and Scotland to the Bering Straits, almost half way round the world. In Sweden the taiga's transition to more southerly types of landscape is particularly abrupt; here northern and southern species meet in a fascinating way. This boundary—or rather transitional zone—is called *limes norrlandicus*, the biological Norrland boundary.

A PHYSICAL GEOGRAPHICAL BOUNDARY...

The biological Norrland boundary coincides with the southern limit of the Norrland terrain. It is here that the central Swedish plains change into hilly upland and the mountains increase in height from 100–200 m to 300–500 m. The countryside below limes norrlandicus is to a large extent an old coastal plain dating back to the time of the Cambrian Sea.

The area immediately south of limes norrlandicus is below the highest level the sea rose to after the inland ice disappeared, the *highest shoreline*. Below the highest shoreline clays and other nutrient-rich deposits are predominant; above it, however, there is usually nutrient-poor till.

Several climate limits coincide closely with limes norrlandicus, particularly in the west. These include the mean temperature for most months, the duration of snow cover and the dates when spring and winter begin.

...AND A HUMAN GEOGRAPHICAL BOUNDARY

Limes norrlandicus also reflects differences in human living conditions. The density of population decreases rapidly in the north. North of the border forestry is the dominant industry, while to the south it is agriculture. The border coincides with the northern limit of medieval towns and the southern limit of the summer shealing system.

The shealing system was at one time an extensive form of cattle farming in northern Sweden. In the winter the cattle were kept at the main farm, but were moved up to the shealings in the summer. Where there was a shortage of pasture land it was necessary to move several times each season.

A PLANT AND ANIMAL BOUNDARY

Nemoral forests stop at limes norrlandicus and common alder is replaced by grey alder. A large number of vascular plants have a continuous distribution south of this border, but only occur sporadically north of it. There are considerably fewer species that are found to the north. Differences in climate mean that mires of the fen type predominate north of the border and bogs south of it.

Typical examples of birds found south of limes norrlandicus are the tawny owl, the green woodpecker and many lake birds of the plains, whereas the brambling, the great grey shrike and the willow grouse are birds that are found north of it.

There is also a connection between the distribution of plants and animals. The presence of wood mice, for example, is clearly related to limes norrlandicus. This is because the number of plant species with large seeds which can be hoarded is larger to the south. Seed-eaters like wood mice are thereby limited in their distribution to the north.

The line of limes norrlandicus seems to be particularly unclear in the

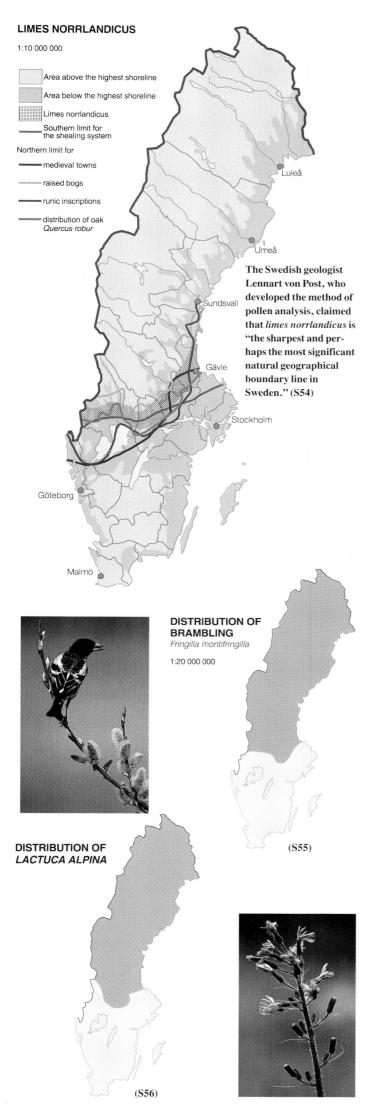

LIMES NORRLANDICUS

1:10 000 000

- Area above the highest shoreline
- Area below the highest shoreline
- Limes norrlandicus
- Southern limit for the shealing system

Northern limit for

- medieval towns
- raised bogs
- runic inscriptions
- distribution of oak *Quercus robur*

Luleå

Umeå

The Swedish geologist Lennart von Post, who developed the method of pollen analysis, claimed that *limes norrlandicus* is "the sharpest and perhaps the most significant natural geographical boundary line in Sweden." (S54)

Sundsvall

Gävle

Stockholm

Göteborg

Malmö

DISTRIBUTION OF BRAMBLING
Fringilla montifringilla

1:20 000 000

(S55)

DISTRIBUTION OF *LACTUCA ALPINA*

(S56)

The northern boundary of woods dominated by oak *Quercus robur* corresponds fairly closely with limes norrlandicus. Photograph from the southern Dalälven.

east. If the northern limit of the oak is taken as a benchmark, it runs approximately to Gävle on the east coast. Sten Selander in "The Living Landscape of Sweden" mentions some 50 vascular plants that do not occur north of limes norrlandicus. According to modern distribution data about 20 of these occur a little further up the coast of Norrland, including hazel, which is sometimes considered to be a particularly important distinguishing species.

Hardly any zoologists or botanists have researched limes norrlandicus since the 1950s. The question therefore arises as to whether this shift up the coast is the result of the species moving northward or because of improved knowledge.

BOUNDARY FOR POPULATION VARIATIONS

Regular and large population fluctuations of lemmings and voles, for example, are a typical feature of many species in the Scandinavian taiga. Population variations among small rodents also affect other species—if there is plenty of food for predators they will have many offspring and vice versa.

Populations of mountain hares and black grouse also vary cyclically in the north, but not in southern Sweden. The explanation is that when voles in-

crease in number, the predators that live on small rodents enjoy an abundance of food. Alternative prey like forest birds and mountain hares are then left more or less in peace.

The mosaic-like southern Swedish landscape of forests and cultivated land makes it easier for predators to find their prey there. Generally speaking predators consume the whole population of small rodents, so the population density remains the same from year to year. In northern Sweden, however, small rodents are protected by the snow during this vulnerable period, so predators are not so effective and the population of small rodents can build up.

Bank vole
Clethrionomys glareolus

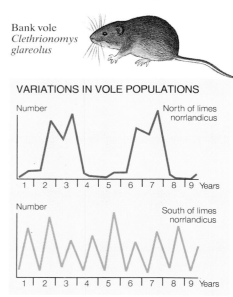

VARIATIONS IN VOLE POPULATIONS

Number — North of limes norrlandicus

1 2 3 4 5 6 7 8 9 Years

Number — South of limes norrlandicus

1 2 3 4 5 6 7 8 9 Years

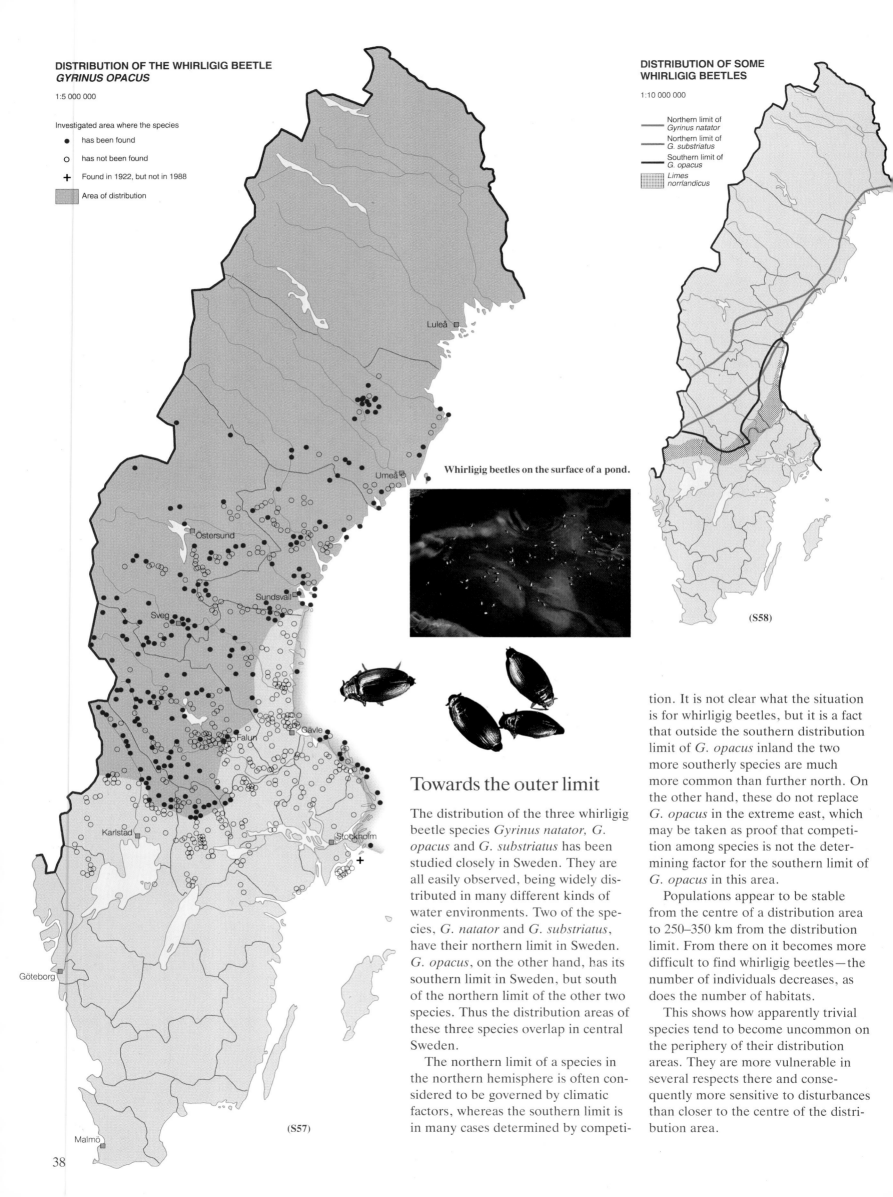

Investigated area where the species

● has been found

○ has not been found

✛ Found in 1922, but not in 1988

▨ Area of distribution

Luleå

Umeå

Östersund

Sundsvall

Sveg

Falun

Gävle

Karlstad

Stockholm

Göteborg

Malmö

(S57)

Whirligig beetles on the surface of a pond.

— Northern limit of
Gyrinus natator

— Northern limit of
G. substriatus

— Southern limit of
G. opacus

▨ *Limes
norrlandicus*

(S58)

Towards the outer limit

The distribution of the three whirligig beetle species *Gyrinus natator*, *G. opacus* and *G. substriatus* has been studied closely in Sweden. They are all easily observed, being widely distributed in many different kinds of water environments. Two of the species, *G. natator* and *G. substriatus*, have their northern limit in Sweden. *G. opacus*, on the other hand, has its southern limit in Sweden, but south of the northern limit of the other two species. Thus the distribution areas of these three species overlap in central Sweden.

The northern limit of a species in the northern hemisphere is often considered to be governed by climatic factors, whereas the southern limit is in many cases determined by competi-

tion. It is not clear what the situation is for whirligig beetles, but it is a fact that outside the southern distribution limit of *G. opacus* inland the two more southerly species are much more common than further north. On the other hand, these do not replace *G. opacus* in the extreme east, which may be taken as proof that competition among species is not the determining factor for the southern limit of *G. opacus* in this area.

Populations appear to be stable from the centre of a distribution area to 250–350 km from the distribution limit. From there on it becomes more difficult to find whirligig beetles—the number of individuals decreases, as does the number of habitats.

This shows how apparently trivial species tend to become uncommon on the periphery of their distribution areas. They are more vulnerable in several respects there and consequently more sensitive to disturbances than closer to the centre of the distribution area.

Ecosystems

Sweden covers an area of about 45 million hectares, some 41 million of which are land and the rest lakes and watercourses. It has a variety of landscapes, ranging from mountains and coniferous forests in the north to deciduous forests and cultivated fields in the south.

The term *nature type* is used to broadly distinguish various types of environments such as *mountains*, *forests*, *mires*, *cultivated fields* and *lakes* and *the sea*.

An *ecosystem* is a functional unit of nature comprising a *biotic* part, its organisms and their interaction, and an *abiotic* part, comprising the chemical and physical conditions such as the soil, the air and the water. An ecosystem may be described with respect to the species living there but also in the form of processes such as food webs and energy flows. An ecosystem is often more clearly delineated than a nature type; thus mountains or forests can be divided into different kinds of ecosystems. Ecosystems are also used for very small parts of nature, for example "the ecosystem of a tree stump" or "the rock pool as an ecosystem".

A *biotope* is a limited piece of nature, for example a precipice or a river ravine; it really refers to an environment characterised by certain plant and animal communities. Thus

The Swedish landscape is dominated by forests, which cover more than half of its area. Wetlands are also common, comprising one fifth of its area. (S59)

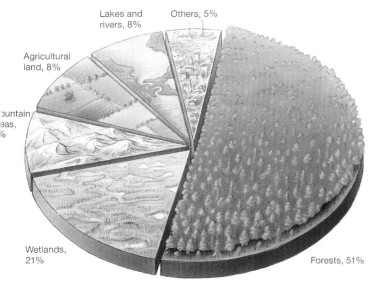

Lakes and rivers, 8%

Others, 5%

Agricultural land, 8%

Mountain areas, %

Wetlands, 21%

Forests, 51%

MAJOR HABITATS

1:5 000 000

Forest

Open landscape

Wetland

Mountain area above tree–line

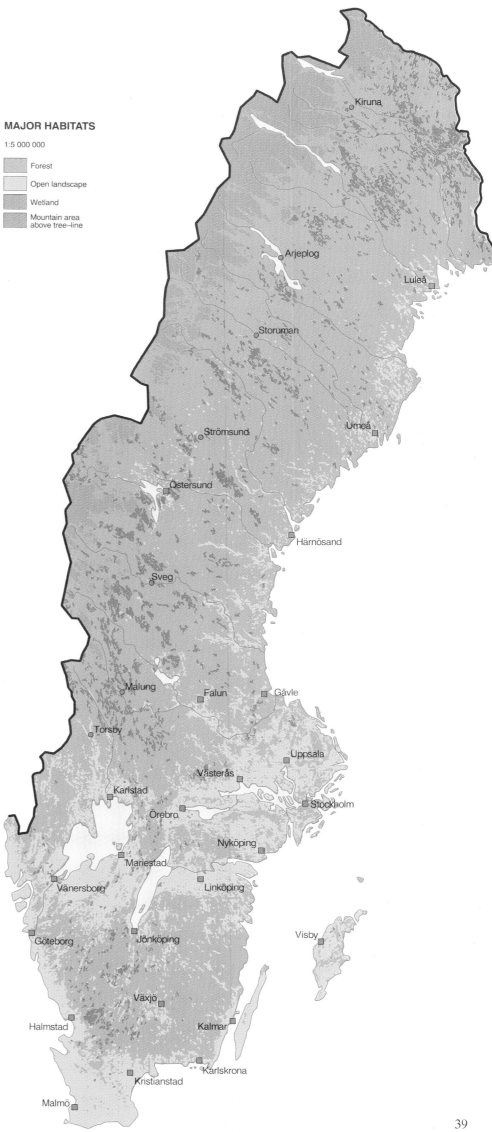

Vegetation Types of the Nordic Countries, 1994

ALPINE VEGETATION

Snow-free exposed mountain heath
- Exposed mountain heath on poor soil
- Exposed mountain heath on intermediate soil
- Exposed mountain heath on rich/calcareous soil

Snow-covered vegetation
- Heath vegetation on poor soil
- Heath vegetation on rich/calcareous soil
- Short-herb meadow on poor soil
- Short-herb meadow on rich/calcareous soil
- Bracken vegetation
- Tall-herb meadow
- Willow vegetation

Snowfield vegetation (on loose ground)
- Snowfield vegetation on poor soil
- Snowfield vegetation on rich/calcareous soil
- High-arctic-alpine vegetation on rich soil

WOODLANDS

Coniferous woodland
- Pine woodland
  - Lichen/dwarf-shrub/herb/swamp-types
- Spruce/fir woodland
  - Dwarf-shrub/fern/low herb/tall herb/swamp-types
- Other coniferous woodlands

Deciduous woodland
- Birch and aspen woodland
  - Mountain birch forests of lichen/dwarf-shrub/grass/herb-types
  - Birch forests of dwarf-shrub/herb/swamp-types
  - Aspen forest
- Beech and hornbeam woodland
  - Beech forest of dwarf shrub-grass/herb-types
  - Hornbeam forest
- Oak, elm, ash and lime woodland
- Alder woodland
- Other deciduous woodland

Mixed deciduous coniferous woodland
- Mature woodland of lichen/dwarf-shrub/grass/herb/swamp-types
- Immature deciduous-coniferous woodland

MIRES

Bog vegetation
- Woodland bog vegetation
- Dwarf-shrub hummock vegetation
- Firm carpet bog vegetation
- Water-logged carpet bog vegetation

Poor fen vegetation
- Woodland or scrub fen carr
- Dwarf-shrub hummock poor fen vegetation
- Firm carpet poor fen vegetation
- Water-logged carpet poor fen vegetation

Intermediate fen vegetation
- Woodland or scrub intermediate fen carr
- Firm carpet intermediate fen vegetation
- Water-logged carpet intermediate fen vegetation
- Intermediate swamp vegetation

Rich fen vegetation
- Woodland or scrub rich fen carr
- Firm carpet rich fen vegetation
- Water-logged carpet rich fen vegetation
- Rich swamp vegetation

Spring fen vegetation
- Intermediate spring fen vegetation
- Rich spring fen vegetation

SEASHORES

Epilittoral vegetation
- Sea-cliff and shingle vegetation
- Embryonic sand dunes
- Sand dunes
- Fixed sand dunes

Geolittoral vegetation
- Drift vegetation
- Upper geolittoral vegetation
- Lower geolittoral vegetation
- Lower geolittoral brackish vegetation
- Pan vegetation
- Sea-cliff vegetation

Hydrolittoral vegetation
- Helophyte vegetation
- Short-stem vegetatiom (Isoetid vegetation)

Sublittoral vegetation
- Long-stem vegetation

OPEN CULTIVATED HEATH AND GRASSLAND

Heathland
- Dwarf shrub heathland
- Wet dwarf-shrub heathland
- Grass heathland
- Sandy grass heathland
- Limestone pavement heath (alvar)

Meadowland
- Dry meadow
- Mesic meadow
- Wet meadow

FRESHWATER VEGETATION

Reed and herb (freshwater) vegetation (Helophytes)
- Sparse reed vegetation
- Dwarf reeds
- Tall reeds

Fixed floating vegetation (Nymphaeids)
- Large-leaved water lilies
- Small-leaved water lilies
- Narrow-leaved water lilies

Long-stem vegetation (Elodeids)
- Long-stem vegetation in oligotrophic lakes
- Long-stem vegetation in eutrophic lakes
- Long-stem vegetation with charophyte algaes

Short-stem vegetation (Isoetids)
- Short-stem vegetation in oligotrophic lakes
- Short-stem vegetation in calcareous lakes

Free-floating vegetation (Pleustophytes)
- Duckweeds
- Bryophytes

Running water
- Floods and springs
- Stream and river vegetation

VEGETATION ADAPTED TO SPECIAL SOIL PROPERTIES

Cliff and scree vegetation
- Poor rock vegetation
- Rich rock vegetation
- Serpentine rock vegetation
- Scree vegetation

Alluvial vegetation
- Coarse-grained deposit vegetation
- Fine-grained deposit vegetation

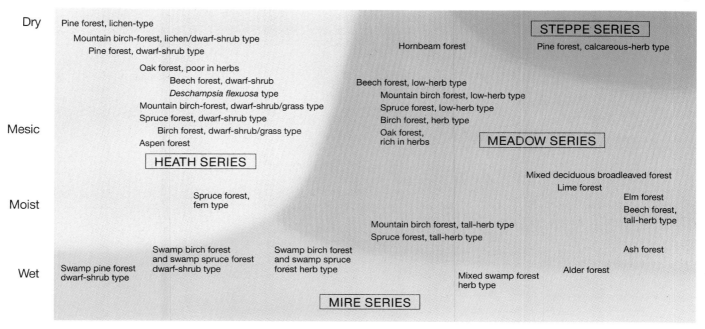

Poor soils — Rich soils

Dry
- Pine forest, lichen-type
- Mountain birch-forest, lichen/dwarf-shrub type
- Pine forest, dwarf-shrub type
- Oak forest, poor in herbs
- Beech forest, dwarf-shrub
- *Deschampsia flexuosa* type
- Mountain birch-forest, dwarf-shrub/grass type
- Spruce forest, dwarf-shrub type
- Birch forest, dwarf-shrub/grass type
- Aspen forest
- Hornbeam forest
- **STEPPE SERIES**
- Pine forest, calcareous-herb type
- Beech forest, low-herb type
- Mountain birch forest, low-herb type
- Spruce forest, low-herb type
- Birch forest, herb type
- Oak forest, rich in herbs

Mesic
- **HEATH SERIES**
- **MEADOW SERIES**
- Mixed deciduous broadleaved forest
- Lime forest
- Elm forest
- Beech forest, tall-herb type

Moist
- Spruce forest, fern type
- Mountain birch forest, tall-herb type
- Spruce forest, tall-herb type
- Ash forest

Wet
- Swamp pine forest dwarf-shrub type
- Swamp birch forest and swamp spruce forest dwarf-shrub type
- Swamp birch forest and swamp spruce forest herb type
- Mixed swamp forest herb type
- Alder forest
- **MIRE SERIES**

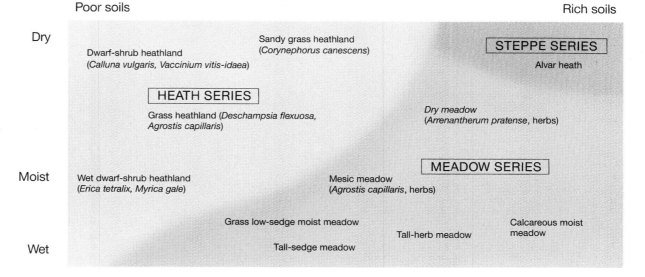

Poor soils — Rich soils

Dry
- Dwarf-shrub heathland (*Calluna vulgaris, Vaccinium vitis-idaea*)
- Sandy grass heathland (*Corynephorus canescens*)
- **STEPPE SERIES**
- Alvar heath

- **HEATH SERIES**
- Grass heathland (*Deschampsia flexuosa, Agrostis capillaris*)
- Dry meadow (*Arrenantherum pratense*, herbs)

- **MEADOW SERIES**

Moist
- Wet dwarf-shrub heathland (*Erica tetralix, Myrica gale*)
- Mesic meadow (*Agrostis capillaris*, herbs)

- Grass low-sedge moist meadow
- Tall-herb meadow
- Calcareous moist meadow

Wet
- Tall-sedge meadow

The vegetation types of forests and cultivated land may be placed along gradients reflecting soil nutrient and moisture conditions; they then form various groups called meadow, heath, steppe and mire series.

Vegetationstyper i Norden

The report of the Nordic Council of Ministers "Vegetation Types of the Nordic Countries" comprises some 450 units.

the term biotope is often used when animals and plants are in focus.

A habitat is an environment in which a certain species lives. For mobile animals this means that a habitat may embrace several biotopes. In practice the term biotope is used in Sweden for both habitat and biotope, whereas in English it is often the reverse, that is, habitat is used for both concepts.

In comparison with the rest of Europe Sweden has a great many forests and wetlands. The large number of lakes and watercourses and its long coastline also give Sweden its special character. The proportion of cultivated land, on the other hand, is small and actually decreasing; it has decreased by about 30% since the 1940s.

A nature type is never stable but is in a constant state of change. Developments since the Ice Age from tundra via the nemoral forests of the warm period to today's forests and cultivated landscape shaped by the hand of man give some idea of the dynamic forces involved. The natural landscape is shrinking, giving way to ecosystems created by human beings; today we use more than one million hectares of land for roads, buildings, car parks, gardens and industrial sites.

Ecosystem types may be divided into smaller units such as *vegetation types* which have a characteristic composition of plant species. Vegetation types are often used to describe environmental conditions.

Vegetation Types of the Nordic Countries

The Nordic Council of Ministers has created a classification of vegetation types common to the Nordic Countries in which characteristic plant species, geographical distribution and ecological requirements are given for each type. The primary aim was to create units for land use planning, but the same units can be used to provide information about the landscape, when producing vegetation maps, for example.

The division and descriptions of the Scandinavian vegetation types are based on scientific literature, and on information from scientists and biologists active in nature conservation and other types of physical planning.

Apart from being used to develop vegetation maps in Sweden, the Nordic vegetation types have also been integrated in a broader scheme throughout Europe. They have, for example, formed the basis for northern sections of the 1:3 million vegetation map which the Council of Europe published in 1987. Work is in progress for the production of a vegetation map for the whole of Europe at the scale of 1:2.5 million.

The Scandinavian vegetation types are also recorded in the EU classification system CORINE/BIOTOPES for nature resource planning at the European level.

VEGETATION MAP OF AN ALPINE AREA

Akkatjåkko 1974 m.a.s.l.

Alajaure
914 m.a.s.l.

Alkajaure
756 m.a.s.l.

Virihaure
579 m.a.s.l. Staloluokta

Amphibolite

Schist, often calcareous,
and marble

Amphibolite
and mica schist

Granite and quartzite

Blocky areas
Grass heath
Heath
Meadow
Birch forest

The bedrock determines the landscape and vegetation in the mountains—in the west there is easily weathered calcareous slate, hard and high amphibolite massifs form Sarek and the eastern part is dominated by precambrian bedrock. The flower-rich mountains are mainly found in the schist districts in the west. The thin red line marks the position of the profile on height and bedrock above the vegetation map.

Among the alpine louseworts *Pedicularis oederi* represents the southern region, where it grows on the limestone mountains of Jämtland, while *Pedicularis hirsuta* is found in the northern high mountain areas. *Pedicularis flammea* is one of the characteristic flowers of the "Virihaure flora". (S60)

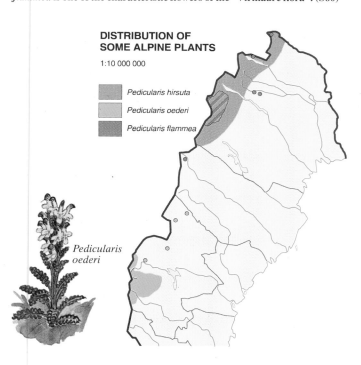

DISTRIBUTION OF SOME ALPINE PLANTS

1:10 000 000

Pedicularis hirsuta
Pedicularis oederi
Pedicularis flammea

Pedicularis oederi

The Mountains

A large part of the mountain chain, especially on the west side, has a local maritime, moist climate due to its proximity to the Atlantic and the west winds which bring precipitation to the mountain slopes. To the east these west winds are blocked by high mountains, so the climate is of a more continental type with warm summers, cold winters and less precipitation. Such areas may also occur locally in valleys where cold air "runs down" the mountain sides and collects at the bottom.

The varying bedrock composition causes large regional differences in vegetation. Owing to the thin overburden the bedrock in the mountains, in contrast to the rest of Sweden, is of far greater significance for plant life than the type of deposition. Also precipitation, temperature, insolation and topography determine to a large extent the vegetation of the mountain chain. The distribution of the individual species may, however, be more difficult to explain.

Birdspecies with more than 50% of their populations in mountain areas. The diagram shows the estimated number of breeding pairs.

* = red-listed species.

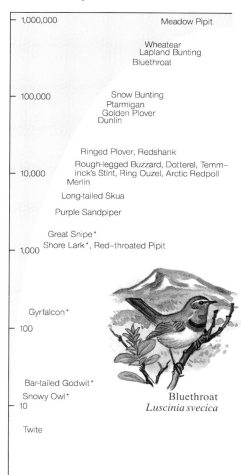

1,000,000 — Meadow Pipit

Wheatear
Lapland Bunting
Bluethroat

100,000 —
Snow Bunting
Ptarmigan
Golden Plover
Dunlin

Ringed Plover, Redshank
Rough-legged Buzzard, Dotterel, Temminck's Stint, Ring Ouzel, Arctic Redpoll
10,000 — Merlin

Long-tailed Skua

Purple Sandpiper

Great Snipe*
1,000 — Shore Lark*, Red-throated Pipit

Gyrfalcon*

100 —

Bar-tailed Godwit*
Snowy Owl*
10 —

Twite

Bluethroat
Luscinia svecica

0 —

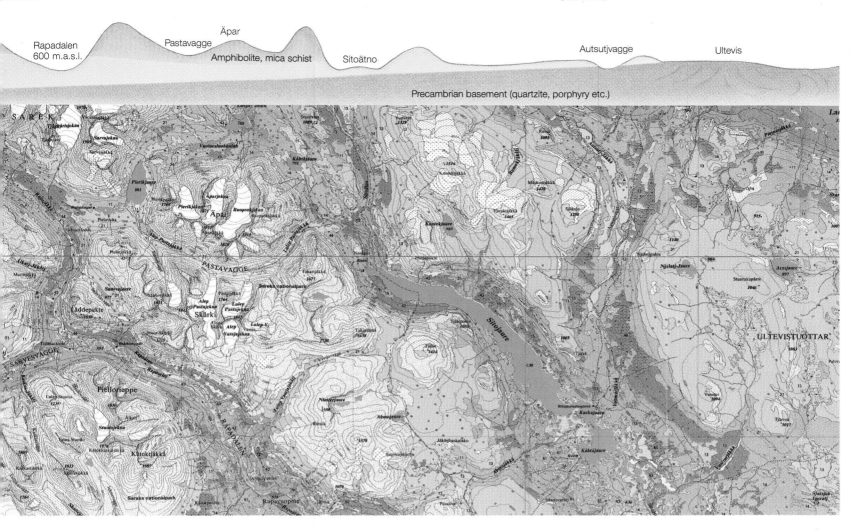

Rapadalen 600 m.a.s.l. — Pastavagge — Äpar — Amphibolite, mica schist — Sitoätno — Autsutjvagge — Ultevis

Precambrian basement (quartzite, porphyry etc.)

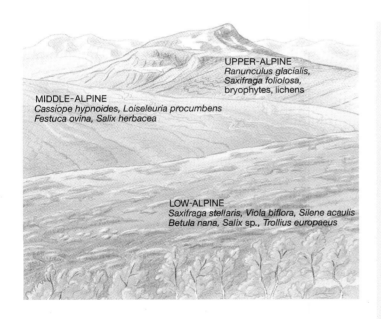

UPPER-ALPINE
Ranunculus glacialis,
Saxifraga foliolosa,
bryophytes, lichens

MIDDLE-ALPINE
Cassiope hypnoides, Loiseleuria procumbens
Festuca ovina, Salix herbacea

LOW-ALPINE
Saxifraga stellaris, Viola biflora, Silene acaulis
Betula nana, Salix sp., Trollius europaeus

VEGETATION ZONES

The *low-alpine zone* is dominated by meadows and heaths. The meadows of grass and herbs are found in the upper part of the zone or at the bottom of hollows where the snow remains for a long time. Towards the *middle-alpine zone* the meadowland changes into grassy heaths where the vegetation becomes more sparse. In the *upper-alpine zone*, where freezing and weathering forces affect the ground, the individual species do not manage to create a continuous plant cover.

FROM PADJELANTA IN THE WEST TO ULTEVIS IN THE EAST

The mountain chain is very old, so most of it has already been worn down. What remain are the hard, resistant amphibolites. To the west the mountains are lower and rounded where the soft schists have been eroded. To the east, on the Ultevis plateau, as at the base of Sarek's mountain valleys, the hard bedrock crops out.

Padjelanta means "The Highland" and is a landscape of soft shapes. Thanks to its calcareous bedrock these mountains are rich in flowers. Mountain avens *Dryas octopetala* and a number of species that grow on limestone heaths set their mark on the landscape. Large parts of Padjelanta have a very special flora and are among the most interesting parts of the Swedish mountain world; here we find species like *Arnica angustifolia* and *Carex nardina*. In contrast, the heaths on the Ultevis bedrock east of Sarek are extremely poor in species, with Northern crowberry *Empetrum hermaphroditum* as the dominant species.

The sun often shines on the large lakes to the west when the clouds hang heavy over Sarek, with its peaks more than 2,000 metres above sea level. Here the moist air masses are forced another few hundred metres higher, re-sulting in high precipitation and snow that lies for many months. In the deeply cut valleys facing south on the mountain the sun warms the ground twenty-four hours a day during the summer, and in this greenhouse climate herbs and ferns flourish, forming two-metre-high thickets of blue alpine lettuce *Lactuca alpina*, *Aconitum lycoctonum*, globe flower *Trollius europaeus*, garden angelica *Angelica archangelica* and ostrich fern *Matteuccia struthiopteris*. The meadows of low herbs cover great stretches of the slopes, but at higher altitudes soon give way to boulders and glaciers.

East of the high mountains the Precambrian bedrock takes over at Ultevis, a rolling plateau about 1,000 m above sea level. Here the precipitation is lower and the climate more continental. The vegetation is more like that of the tundra and is extremely poor in species. In the bogs of the high plateaus we have our southernmost large areas of permanently frozen bogland where the winter cold penetrates deep into the ground, not thawing during the short summer. Grassy heaths of three-leaved rush *Juncus trifidus* and stiff sedge *Carex bigelowii* and shrub heaths of northern crowberry are very common.

More than half of Sweden's species occur in a forest environment. Invertebrates are the group with by far the largest number of species, followed by the macrofungi.

Forests

Sweden is a country of forests; of its 23 million or more hectares of productive forest land, 90% consists of coniferous forest and the remainder of deciduous forests, of which nemoral woodlands account for only about 1%.

Nemoral woodlands are only found in the southern parts of Sweden. Pine forests are most common in the north, while spruce forests are most common in the south. Most of the pine and spruce forests are young; approximately 85% are not yet ready for final felling. A large percentage of the nemoral forests, however, are old.

More than 99% of productive forest land below the mountain coniferous forests is used for silviculture, often of an intensive nature. Silviculture has radically changed the forests; there is not much natural forest left. In the coniferous forest belt of northern Sweden, the *taiga*, however, there are still fragments of natural forest which give us some idea of what the forests once looked like. In the taiga fires used to be a very significant factor which greatly influenced the forests' structure and the species occuring there.

The southern Swedish forest landscape has been influenced by agriculture and forest grazing by cattle for several thousand years. There is no longer any trace of the virgin forests. Forests close to villages and farms have also been affected by hay and foliage harvesting. The forests of the old agricultural landscape had very high biological values: they were open, varied and contained many species of trees. The influence of agriculture has now decreased dramatically or come completely to an end. Instead the forests have been taken over for silviculture. We now have a southern Swedish forest landscape in a highly overgrown state, dominated more and more by spruce.

AREA, MILL. HA

Deciduous forest, 1.3 (6%)
Mixed forest, 1.5 (7%)
Nemoral forest, 0.15 (1%)
Coniferous forest, 19.5 (87%)

GROWING STOCK, MILL. FOREST m³

Beech, 19 (<1%)
Oak, 27 (1%)
Birch, 285 (10%)
Other deciduous trees, 96 (3%)
Pine, 1,078 (39%)
Spruce, 1,244 (45%)

Birdspecies with more than 50% of their populations in forest areas. The diagram shows the estimated number of breeding pairs.
* = red-listed species.

10 milj — Chaffinch, Willow Warbler

Robin

Song Thrush, Garden Warbler, Goldcrest
Dunnock, Great Tit
Blackbird, Redwing, Brambling
Fieldfare, Pied Flycatcher, Willow Tit, Spotted Flycatcher

1,0 milj — Tree Pipit, Coal Tit, Blue Tit, Redpoll, Siskin
Tree Creeper
Blackcap
Wren, Crested Tit, Jay, Crossbill, Bullfinch
Willow Grouse, Black Grouse, Lesser Whitethroat, Chiffchaff
Redstart
Hazel Hen, Great Spotted Woodpecker, Wood Warbler, Marsh Tit, Nuthatch, Mistle Thrush, Siberian Jay
Capercaillie*, Woodcook, Cuckoo, Icterine Warbler, Siberian Tit

100 000

Green Woodpecker, Waxwing, Thrush Nightingale, Long-tailed Tit, Parrot Crossbill, Green Sandpiper, Tengmalm's Owl

Black Woodpecker*

Sparrow Hawk, Pygmy Owl, Three-toed Woodpecker*, Raven, Nutcracker*, Hawfinch*, Pine Grosbeak
Goshawk*

10 000

Honey Buzzard*
Hawk Owl, Nightjar, Lesser Spotted Woodpecker*, Collared Flycatcher, Ural Owl*

Wood Lark

Read-breasted Flycatcher*, Redpoll (ssp. *cabaret*)

1 000

Great Greay Owl*
Golden Eagle*

Eagle Owl*
Grey-headed Woodpecker*

Golden Oriole*
100 — Chaffinch
Fringilla coelebs

White-backed Woodpecker*, Two-barred Crossbill

Greenish Warbler*, Arctic Warbler*, Serin*
10

Black Kite

Hazel-hen
Bonasia bonasia
Black Stork*, Middle Spotted Woodpecker*
0

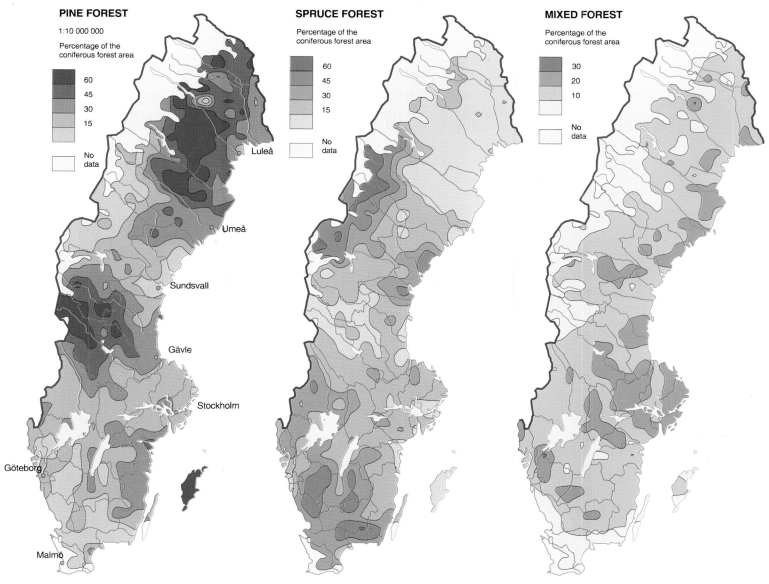

PINE FOREST

1:10 000 000

Percentage of the coniferous forest area

- 60
- 45
- 30
- 15
- No data

Luleå
Umeå
Sundsvall
Gävle
Stockholm
Göteborg
Malmö

SPRUCE FOREST

Percentage of the coniferous forest area

- 60
- 45
- 30
- 15
- No data

MIXED FOREST

Percentage of the coniferous forest area

- 30
- 20
- 10
- No data

Pine forests are predominant in north-eastern Norrland and north-western Svealand and on Gotland. (S61)

Spruce forests are common in southern Sweden but also on the coast and in the interior of central Norrland. (S62)

Mixed forests are not as common as pure pine or spruce forests, but they are fairly evenly distributed throughout the country. (S63)

CONIFEROUS FORESTS

Coniferous trees are found in all the vegetation zones except the alpine, but spruce is not considered a natural species in the nemoral zone. Pine forests are the most common kind, covering an area of some 9 million ha, followed by spruce forests with approximately 7 million ha and mixed coniferous forests with about 4 million ha.

The composition of the fauna and flora in a mixed coniferous forest varies greatly according to soil conditions, climate and historical factors. The northern coniferous forest, the taiga, is poorer in species than the more southerly. In the south the existence of a large number of species is usually connected with the occurrence of nemoral trees such as oak, beech, elm, ash, maple and lime.

Coniferous forests on calcareous soils are usually those richest in species, often containing a large number of rare species. This is because soil conditions allow a large number of species and because there are plenty of deciduous trees in such forests. Forests on calcareous ground are not widespread in Sweden and are found in Dalsland, Östergötland, Uppland, round Lake Siljan and in Jämtland, for example. One sign that Sweden's forests are poor in nutrients is that only about 5% of the forest land has mull-like soil, that is, the type in the most nutrient-rich forests.

NUMBER OF SPECIES IN CONIFEROUS FORESTS

	1	2	3	4	5
Vascular plants	56	64	79	69	76
Bryophytes	79	97	91	82	65
Lichens	172	208	158	104	92
Fungi	683	861	993	839	727
Mammals	21	24	23	22	23
Birds	75	75	65	58	62
Amphibians and reptiles	3	3	3	3	3
Total	1,089	1,332	1,412	1,177	1,048

The area of coniferous forest in the different zones varies from one million ha in the south (zones 4 and 5) to about seven million ha in the north (zones 1 and 2), which partly explains the difference in the number of species. (S64)

1
2
3
4
5

45

Coniferous forests may be categorised in various ways. They can be divided into heath and meadow series according to nutrients and soil water conditions. A blueberrry-spruce forest will then belong to the heath series and a spruce forest containing tall herbs to the meadow series. In silviculture vegetation—together with other conditions such as soil and type of hydrology—is also used to assess how much biomass an area of forest land can produce. Its potential productivity is expressed as its site quality class. The vegetation is categorised as, for example, lichen type, tall-herb type, narrow-leaved grass type or cowberry type. Approximately 65% of coniferous forests are of the dry-mesic type and approximately 35% of the moist-wet type. Almost 75% has vegetation dominated by shrubs, about 15% crowberry/lichen and the remainder, 10%, is of the tall-herb or grass type.

TYPES OF GROUND VEGETATION
following Hägglund-Lundmark's system.

— *Bottom layer* = bryophytes and lichens that grow on the ground
— *Field layer* = herbs, grasses, sedges, dwarf shrubs, ferns, horsetails and club mosses.

Lichen class: Lichens comprise at least 25% of the bottom layer. Divided into *lichen-rich type* (lichens comprise 25–50% of the bottom layer) and *lichen type* (lichens comprise >50% of the bottom layer).

Bryophyte class: Bryophytes comprise at least 50% of the bottom layer. Also includes types which almost completely lack a bottom layer. The description follows the order given below. When the composition meets the requirement for a type the description is complete.
— *Herb types*: A certain number of typical nutrient-demanding species must be present. Divided into *tall-herb type* and *low-herb type*.
— *Ground lacking a field layer*: the ground layer covers <6% of the ground and there are few or no herbs.
— *Grass types*: grasses, bracken *Pteridium aquilinum* and herbs cover >25% of the field layer. Divided into *broad-* and *narrow-leaved grasses*.
— *Sedge-horsetail type*: sedges, wood horsetail *Equisetum sylvaticum*, cloudberry *Rubus chamaemorus* and bog-bean *Menyanthes trifoliata* together cover more than 25%.
— *Dwarf shrub types*: Account is taken of the amount of blueberry, cowberry, crowberry and heather respectively. Cover of herbs, grasses, ferns and club mosses which do not meet the requirements listed above is included. Four different dwarf shrub types are distinguished which are determined and added to reach at least 50%: *blueberry type*, *cowberry type*, *crowberry-heather type* and *poor dwarf shrub type*.

LICHEN TYPES

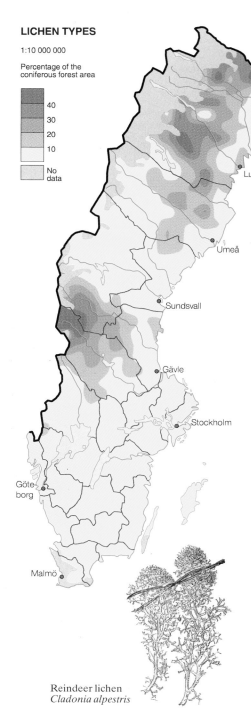

1:10 000 000

Percentage of the coniferous forest area

40
30
20
10
No data

Reindeer lichen
Cladonia alpestris

The lichen types are found in dry pine forests and are most common in Norrbotten, northern Kopparberg and southern Jämtland. (S68)

Wood crane's bill
Geranium sylvaticum

Liverleaf
Hepatica nobilis

Dwarf cornel
Cornus suecica

SAMPLE PLOTS WITH *GERANIUM SYLVATICUM*

1:20 000 000

Percentage

15
7.5
4.0
Missing
No data

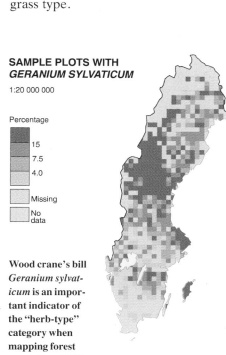

Wood crane's bill *Geranium sylvaticum* is an important indicator of the "herb-type" category when mapping forest vegetation. (S65)

SAMPLE PLOTS WITH *HEPATICA NOBILIS*

Percentage

15
7.5
4.0
Missing
No data

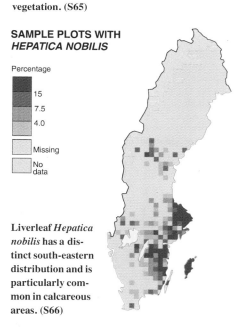

Liverleaf *Hepatica nobilis* has a distinct south-eastern distribution and is particularly common in calcareous areas. (S66)

SAMPLE PLOTS WITH *CORNUS SUECICA*

Percentage

15
7.5
4.0
Missing
No data

Dwarf cornel *Cornus suecica* has two different distribution areas: coastal and mountain areas in Norrland and south-west Sweden. (S67)

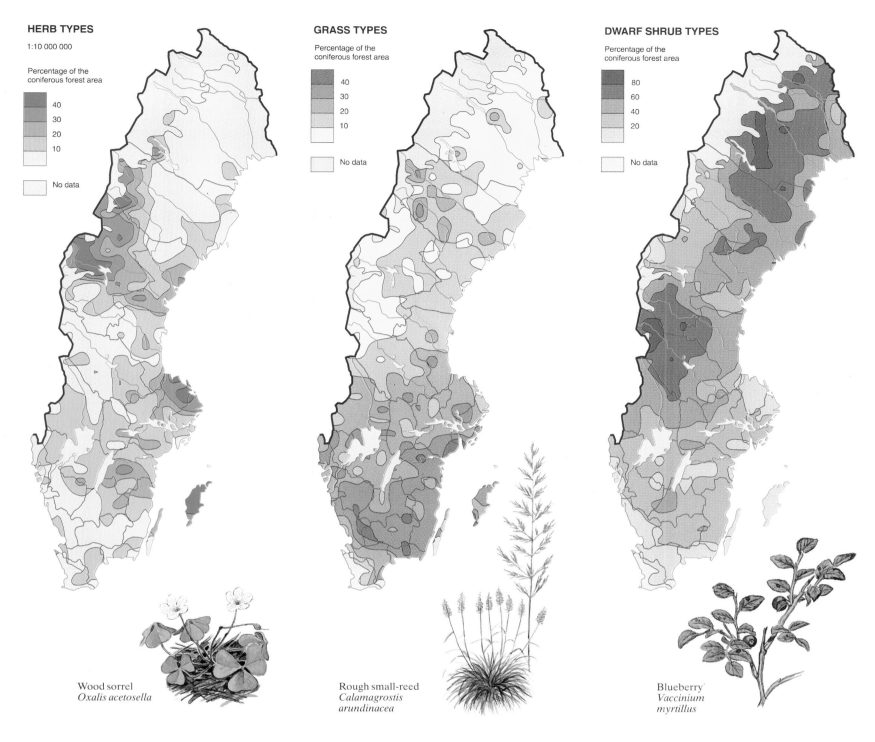

HERB TYPES

1:10 000 000

Percentage of the
coniferous forest area

- 40
- 30
- 20
- 10

No data

Wood sorrel
Oxalis acetosella

GRASS TYPES

Percentage of the
coniferous forest area

- 40
- 30
- 20
- 10

No data

Rough small-reed
*Calamagrostis
arundinacea*

DWARF SHRUB TYPES

Percentage of the
coniferous forest area

- 80
- 60
- 40
- 20

No data

Blueberry
*Vaccinium
myrtillus*

The nutrient-rich herb type is found above all in calcareous areas in, for example, Jämtland, Uppland, Gotland and Skåne. (S69)

The grass type is considerably more common in southern than in northern Sweden. (S70)

The dwarf shrub type is by far the most common of the ground vegetation types and is particularly dominant in northern Sweden. (S71)

Mountain coniferous forest is the forest area that lies immediately east of the mountain chain. It consists of productive forest land, that is, land with a wood-producing potential exceeding 1 forest m³ total volume per hectare and year, but which is difficult to regenerate. At present mountain coniferous forest covers about 1.5 million hectares, a third of which is protected in nature reserves. Between the mountain areas above the tree line and the mountain coniferous forests there are zones of non-productive coniferous forest and mountain birch forests, amounting altogether to just over 1.3 million hectares. A characteristic feature of mountain coniferous forests is that large parts of them are old; 38% are more than 140 years old. The corresponding figure for the coastal municipalities in Norrbotten and Västerbotten is hardly 4%.

Mountain coniferous forest is not a homogeneous forest landscape. In Dalarna and Härjedalen pine forests are predominant, in Jämtland and southern Lappland spruce forests. In the most north-eastern part of Lappland there are flat areas with a very sparse mixture of pine and mountain birch. The reason why there is such a relatively large percentage of old forest is that the mountain coniferous forests have not been accessible for silviculture. The stands also have a much more variable age structure compared with the cultivated forests. There is a rich variety of old trees and standing and fallen dead trees in various stages of decomposition.

Plenty of precipitation combined with low temperatures and a short vegetation period results in large areas of wetland and wet forest types. The moist climate has also meant that forest fires have occurred less frequently than in other northern coniferous forests.

Diagrammatic profile of various forest classifications of areas close to the mountains.

MOUNTAIN CONIFEROUS FORESTS, 1990

1:5 000 000

- Percentage of Sweden's total area of mountain coniferous forest, per county
- Percentage of protected area of the mountain coniferous forest in the county
- Mountain coniferous forest limit
- Forest
- Open landscape
- Mountain area above tree-line

Kiruna
683,000 ha
45%

49%

Norrbotten County

342,000 ha
23%

Luleå

29%

Västerbotten County

435,000 ha
29%

5%

Umeå

Jämtland County

Östersund

Härnösand

46,000 ha
3%

57%

Kopparberg County

Gävle

Falun

There are all told 1.5 million ha of mountain coniferous forest, half of which is in the county of Norrbotten. In comparison with the forests in lowland areas a large proportion of the mountain coniferous forests are old. (S72)

BOUNDARIES IN ALPINE AND ADJACENT AREAS

m
1,500

1,000

Area above tree-line

Tree limit

Salix region

Limit of coniferous forest

Limit of productive forest

Limit of mountain coniferous forest

500

Mountain birch forest

Mountain coniferous forest

Limit of forest difficult to regenerate

0

Forest difficult to regenerate

"Normal" forest

Umeå

Gulf of Bothnia

300

200

100

0 km

Maple leaves in autumn

NEMORAL WOODLAND

Elm, ash, oak, lime and maple have long been classified as nemoral trees. Since 1984 hornbeam, beech and wild cherry are also counted as nemoral trees in the legislation that guarantees the survival of nemoral forests. In contrast to nemoral the term common is used of deciduous trees such as alder, aspen and birch. A deciduous tree which has been introduced into Sweden and is biologically—though not legally—a nemoral tree is sycamore *Acer pseudoplatanus*. This species is spreading in the deciduous forests of southern Sweden.

Most nemoral species came to Sweden as early as about 9,000 years ago, but hornbeam and beech came about 4,000 years later. The nemoral forests had their widest distribution during the post-glacial warm period about 8,000–5,000 years ago.

Nemoral trees occur in today's Swedish landscape in very many different habitats: as cultivated or spontaneously growing trees in both plantations and natural forests; as isolated trees; in groves or avenues in agricultural landscapes; in natural pastures; and in parks and gardens. Some of these species—especially beech—form stands in today's forests.

Today's forests have very varied origins and appearances. There are very small relics of the more virgin nemoral forests, but considerable areas have survived in more or less unchanged form as forest meadows. A considerable part of the original nemoral forests' flora and fauna are considered to have been able to survive in these tree and bush-covered areas with unbroken continuity since the warm period. If this land is allowed to become overgrown, the forest that grows up is called "primary natural forest". Thus land where trees and bushes have grown throughout time has a different and richer flora than forestland that was previously completely open, in the form of fields, for example.

Nemoral forests are found on many different kinds of soil, from the very poorest and driest (oak) to the richest (elm) or on very moist land (ash). Most of the arable land in southern Sweden would have been nemoral or mixed forest if it had not been for human intervention.

Natural forests with nemoral trees comprise many different species of trees and bushes, except on the very

Beech *Fagus sylvatica* prefers rich, calcareous soil, but not heavy clay. It is sensitive to spring frosts. (S73)

Oaks can grow on most kinds of soils. They are sensitive to frost, but very resistant to storms. The pedunculate oak *Quercus robur* is more common than the sessile oak *Q. petraea*. (S74)

Norway maple *Acer platanoides* is hardy, but needs rich and calcareous soil to develop well. (S75)

Lime *Tilia cordata* flourishes on clayey soil. It has a good suckering ability but does not seem to regenerate with seeds except in very good years. (S76)

Ash *Fraxinus excelsior* is light-prefering and needs calcareous, rich soil with plenty of moving surface water. It is particularly sensitive to spring frosts. (S77)

There are three native species of elm: wych elm *Ulmus glabra*, small-leaved elm *U. minor* and *U. laevis*. Dutch elm disease is a serious threat to elms in Sweden. (S78)

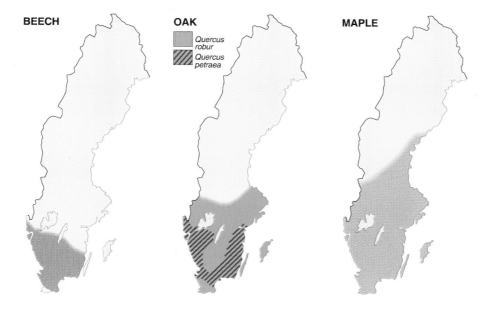

BEECH

OAK

Quercus robur
Quercus petraea

MAPLE

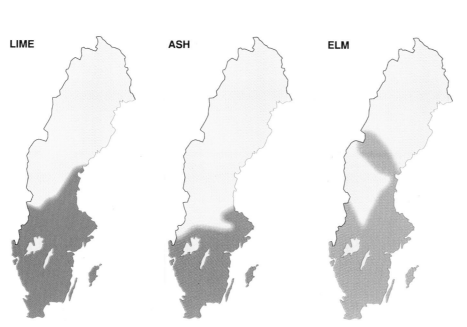

LIME

ASH

ELM

AGE STRUCTURE OF THE NEMORAL FOREST

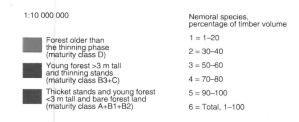

1:10 000 000

Forest older than
the thinning phase
(maturity class D)

Young forest >3 m tall
and thinning stands
(maturity class B3+C)

Thicket stands and young forest
<3 m tall and bare forest land
(maturity class A+B1+B2)

Nemoral species,
percentage of timber volume

1 = 1–20

2 = 30–40

3 = 50–60

4 = 70–80

5 = 90–100

6 = Total, 1–100

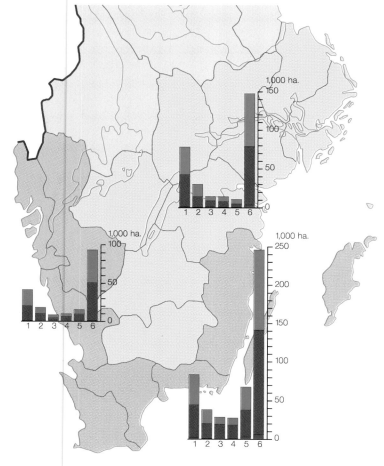

Many of the nemoral forests are very old compared with most coniferous forests. A large proportion of nemoral forests are therefore mature for felling, according to the forestry classification. (S79)

The proportion of nemoral trees has to be at least 70% if a forest is to be counted as nemoral. Beech is the most common tree, followed by oak. (S80, S81, S82)

In the spring before the leaves come out and when there is plenty of light on the ground there is often a tremendous show of flowers in nemoral forests. Spring pea *Lathyrus vernus* in flower.

poorest soil. There are often several layers of trees representing different ages and species and one or two layers of bushes. Together with old, dying or dead deciduous trees and good soil these forests provide suitable conditions for a rich variety of species that is unique in Swedish forests. Several of the nemoral trees, mainly oak and beech, are hosts for a very large number of species of bryophytes, lichens, fungi and invertebrates. They are accordingly a kind of key organism for biological diversity.

Several nemoral trees—especially maple, lime, elm and ash—have a favourable effect on soil conditions because their leaf litter has a high pH. Ash, elm, maple and old oak and beech trees are rich-bark trees, that is, their bark is good for bryophytes and lichens because of its high pH. Many of these epiphytes have else-

where been seriously affected by acidification and have difficulty in finding suitable habitats in southern and central Sweden.

From a European point of view Sweden's nemoral forests seem very rich in species and relatively untouched. The relatively low level of air pollution load in Sweden has, in spite of everything, given us perhaps the best long-term prospects in Europe for preserving the rich diversity of the nemoral forests.

Thanks to good light conditions before the trees come into leaf, which for many species of trees occurs late, many woodland areas develop thick and colourful carpets of anemones, gageas, buttercups and the like. The spring song of birds and this floral richness in nemoral forests is one of the most delightful of nature experiences.

NEMORAL FOREST OLDER THAN THE THINNING PHASE

Percentage of forest area

35
25
15
5
1
0.1

No data

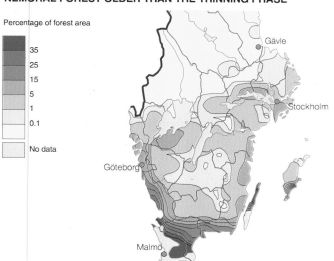

NEMORAL FOREST, EXCLUDING BEECH

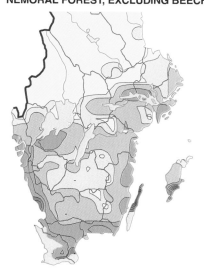

BEECH FOREST

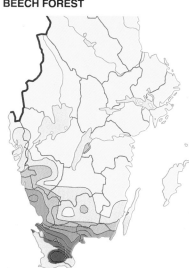

WETLAND TYPES

1:5 000 000

Dominating type of wetland

- Bog
- Fen
- Mixed mire
- Wet meadow/heath
- Inundated wetlands
- Wet forest; swamp
- No data

Kiruna

Arjeplog

Luleå

Storuman

Strömsund

Umeå

Östersund

Härnösand

Sveg

Malung

Gävle

Falun

Torsby

Uppsala

Västerås

Karlstad

Örebro

Stockholm

Mariestad

Nyköping

Linköping

Vänersborg

Visby

Göteborg

Jönköping

Växjö

Kalmar

Halmstad

Karlskrona

Kristianstad

Malmö

All wetland types except mixed mires occur in most of the country. The map does not show the distribution but where a certain wetland type is dominant. (S83)

Alpine wetlands, 0.2 mill. ha (2%)

Bog 1.3 mill. ha (14.5%)

Wet forest; swamp 2.6 mill. ha (28%)

Fen, 3.7 mill. ha (40%)

Inundated wetlands, 0.4 mill. ha (4%)

Wet meadow or heath, 0.1 mill. ha (1%)

Mixed mire 1 mill. ha (10.5%)

Note that mires can be covered with forest and are in certain cases designated as "swamp forests". Data, April 1994, based on the National Wetland Survey and the National Forest Survey.

The predominant type of wetland as far as area is concerned within a 5 x 5 km square is marked with a dot of a certain colour. Most types occur in most of Sweden. The maps on this page and the next page are not, in other words, distribution maps of the various types but show where a certain type of wetland dominates the total area of wetland in the district.

These maps are based on the National Wetland Survey, whose smallest items vary from county to county. This inconsistency probably affects the maps somewhat. There would probably be an even greater difference if the small wetlands had also been included; swamp forests, for example, would have a far more dominant position in certain areas.

Wetlands

Wetland is a collective term for several types of moist and wet vegetation. They occur in all the main groups of vegetation such as alpine, forest, shore, cultivated land, fresh water and mire. Only the last-mentioned is completely included in the term wetland. There are also different opinions about the definition of wetland. Here we use the definition most commonly used in Sweden in, for example, the National Wetland Survey of the National Environmental Protection Agency which includes mires, wet meadows, moist heaths, marshy meadows, swamp forests, reed beds and clayey bottoms which sometimes dry up, but not open water in lakes and the sea.

It is practical to have a collective name for all these wet environments. They are often of great zoological value, regardless of type. They are also threatened environments in that they are vulnerable to hydrological disturbances as a result of draining or water regulation, for example.

Inundated wetland is a collective term for the wetlands that get their water from lakes or watercourses. Marshy meadows (close to a shore), shore meadows, flooded land and reed beds are examples of types included in this group.

Wet forests are wetlands covered by forest. The term is used with varying meanings in various contexts. Here

Birdspecies with more than 50% of their populations in mire areas. The diagram shows the estimated number of breeding pairs.
* = red-listed species.

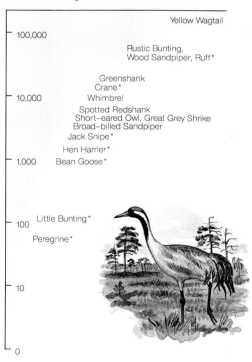

Yellow Wagtail

100,000

Rustic Bunting, Wood Sandpiper, Ruff*

Greenshank
Crane*

10,000

Whimbrel
Spotted Redshank
Short–eared Owl, Great Grey Shrike
Broad–billed Sandpiper
Jack Snipe*
Hen Harrier*

1,000

Bean Goose*

Little Bunting*

100

Peregrine*

10

0

51

Mires belong to Sweden's most unspoilt habitats; many of them have had an undisturbed development for thousands of years. Ko-mosse in Västergötland.

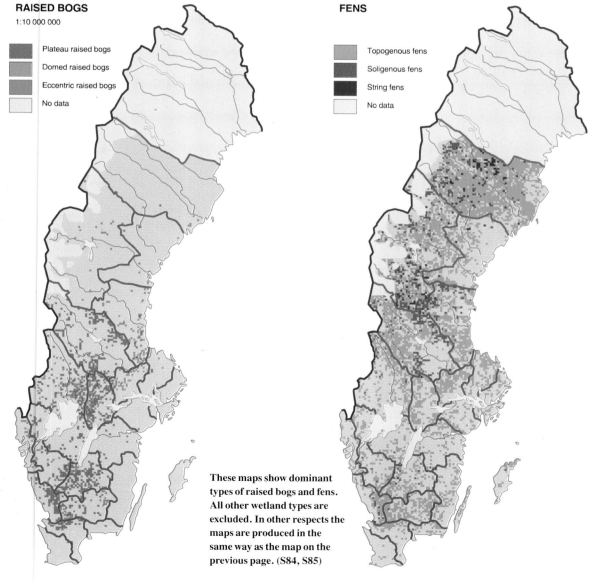

RAISED BOGS

1:10 000 000

- Plateau raised bogs
- Domed raised bogs
- Eccentric raised bogs
- No data

FENS

- Topogenous fens
- Soligenous fens
- String fens
- No data

These maps show dominant types of raised bogs and fens. All other wetland types are excluded. In other respects the maps are produced in the same way as the map on the previous page. (S84, S85)

we refer to wetlands—except bogs—where the tree crowns cover at least 60–70% of the ground.

Bogs, fens and *mixed mires* are different types of *mires*, that is, peat-forming wetlands with the exception of those close to shores.

Wet meadows and *wet heaths* are non-peat-forming wetlands which are often part of vegetation affected by cultivation.

Alpine wetland is used here as a collective term for many different types of wetland that occur in the mountains, including large, shallow mires, moist heaths, moist meadows and inundated wetlands. These have not been surveyed by the Environmental Protection Agency and are relatively unknown but are characterised by alpine species.

TYPES OF MIRES

The word mire is a collective term for bogs, fens and mixed mires.

Bogs get their water from direct precipitation only; this water has not passed across land. This means that there is a very limited supply of nutrients and minerals and the range of species is relatively small. On raised bogs the peat has accumulated so that the surface is noticeably higher than the surrounding land. *Domed raised bogs* have a domed surface with a concentric patterns of strings and hollows. *Plateau raised bogs* are domed mostly at the edges and are flat on top. *Eccentric raised bogs* are a sloping form of raised bogs. Other lower, flat or sloping types of bogs occur but are not shown on the map.

Fens, unlike bogs, also get their water from the surrounding land and are usually divided into "poor", "intermediate" and "rich", mainly according to the availability of minerals. Some fens have a typical pattern of strings (raised strips of peat) and hollows (wet hollows containing fen vegetation). These fens are called *string fens*. Other fens are called *topogenous fens* or *soligenous fens*.

As the name suggests, *mixed mires* consist of a mixture of small areas of bogs and fens.

TYPES OF VEGETATION

The maps on the following two pages show the main distribution of a small sample of types of wetland vegetation. Isolated occurrences may be found far outside the distribution recorded here. The maps are based on the National Wetland Survey.

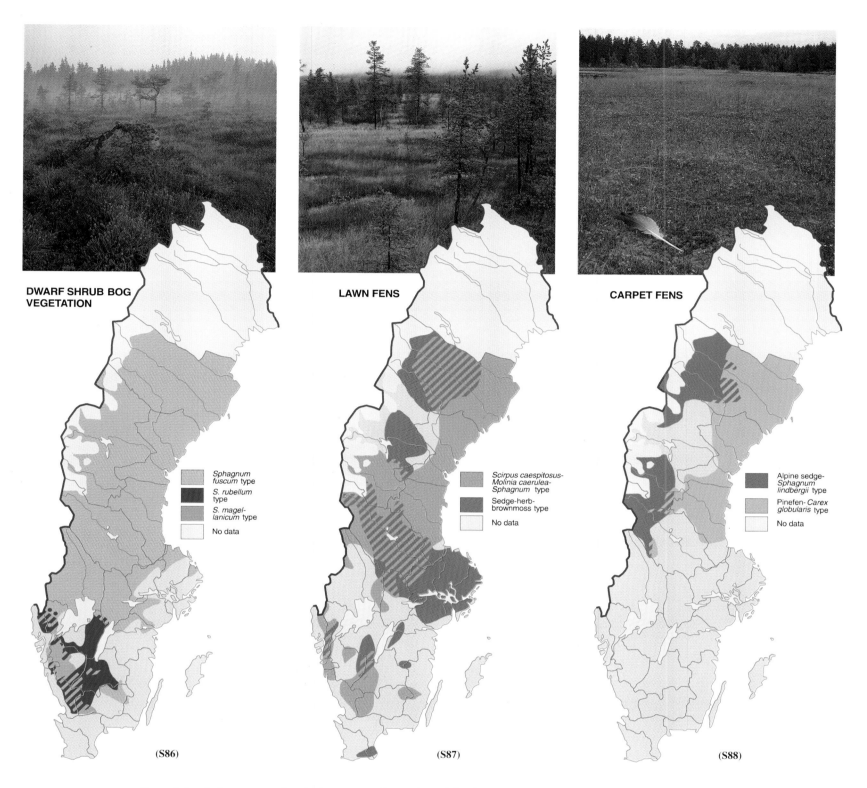

DWARF SHRUB BOG VEGETATION

- Sphagnum fuscum type
- S. rubellum type
- S. magellanicum type
- No data

(S86)

LAWN FENS

- Scirpus caespitosus-Molinia caerulea-Sphagnum type
- Sedge-herb-brownmoss type
- No data

(S87)

CARPET FENS

- Alpine sedge-Sphagnum lindbergii type
- Pinefen-Carex globularis type
- No data

(S88)

Dwarf shrub bog vegetation is dominated in the field layer by species of heather *Calluna vulgaris*, crowberry *Empetrum* spp., bog rosemary *Andromeda polifolia*, dwarf birch *Betula nana*, bog bilberry *Vaccinium uliginosum*, cross-leaved heather *Erica tetralix*, cloudberry *Rubus chamaemorus* and hare's-tail cottongrass *Eriophorum vaginatum*. The bottom layer is dominated by Sphagna, sometimes accompanied by other mosses and reindeer lichens. The map records three types distinguished by the dominant moss species: *Sphagnum magellanicum* type, *S. rubellum* type and *S. fuscum* type. Sometimes intermediate types are more common than the "pure" types.

Lawn fens. The book "Vegetation Types of the Nordic Countries" lists twelve different types, two of which are presented on the map.

The *Scirpus caespitosus—Molinia caerulea—Sphagnum* type contains certain sub-oceanic species like bog asphodel *Narthecium ossifragum* in south-west Sweden. In the north it occurs together with a similar type in string fens.

The sedge-herb-brown moss type is very varied and rich in species. All types occur, ranging from intermediate fens containing, for example, *Sphagnum warnstorfii*, to rich fens containing brown mosses and *Schoenus ferrugineus*. This type often has many orchids.

Carpet fens, as the name suggests, are softer; you sink down into them when you walk. The map shows one of 15 varieties described in "Vegetation Types of the Nordic Countries".

The alpine sedge-Sphagnum type is one variant which is dominated by *Sphagnum lindbergii*.

Pine fens of the sedge type often have scattered pines and are dominated by dwarf shrubs and *Carex globularis* in the field layer. The bottom is often dominated by Sphagna mixed with forest mosses. This type occurs almost exclusively on mires with a peat depth of 0.5 m or less.

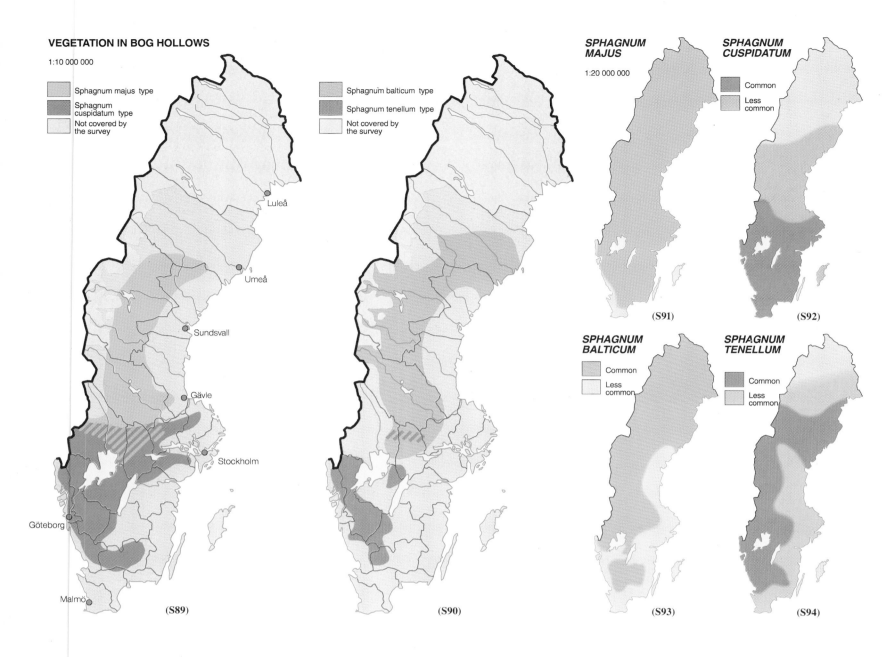

VEGETATION IN BOG HOLLOWS

1:10 000 000

- Sphagnum majus type
- Sphagnum cuspidatum type
- Not covered by the survey

- Sphagnum balticum type
- Sphagnum tenellum type
- Not covered by the survey

Luleå
Umeå
Sundsvall
Gävle
Stockholm
Göteborg
Malmö

(S89)

(S90)

SPHAGNUM MAJUS

1:20 000 000

SPHAGNUM CUSPIDATUM
- Common
- Less common

(S91)

(S92)

SPHAGNUM BALTICUM
- Common
- Less common

SPHAGNUM TENELLUM
- Common
- Less common

(S93)

(S94)

BOG HOLLOW VEGETATION

Hollows in bogs often have a bottom of mud and wet peat that either lacks almost all vegetation or is dominated by Sphagna—a carpet community. Carpet communities are usually divided into four types mainly according to the dominant Sphagna in the bottom layer: the *Sphagnum cuspidatum* type, the *S. majus* type, the *S. tenellum* type and the *S. balticum* type.

In the field layer one often finds rannoch-rush *Scheuchzeria palustris* and white beak-sedge *Rhynchospora alba*. Other vascular plants which may occur are, for example, hare's-tail cottongrass *Eriophorum vaginatum* and cranberry *Vaccinium oxycoccus*.

Sphagnum cuspidatum type. The bottom layer is dominated by *S. cuspidatum*, but other bog hollow Sphagna may occur, most commonly perhaps *S. tenellum*. This is one of the wettest bog hollow types with so much water that the floating Sphagnum species

justifies its name by "floating" in the hollows.

Sphagnum majus type. This type is rather similar to the preceding one, being mainly distinguished by *S. majus*, which occurs practically all over Sweden and has taken over the role of the more southerly *S. cuspidatum*. Rannoch-rush is often the only dominant species in the field layer. A similar type of vegetation occurs in extremely poor fens in large parts of Norrland.

Sphagnum tenellum type. *Sphagnum tenellum* dominates the bottom layer, but there is often *S. cuspidatum* as well. White beak-sedge dominates the field layer. This type occurs in somewhat less wet hollows than the two previous types and is the most south-westerly of the hollow types. *Sphagnum tenellum*, however, occurs in most of Sweden and apart from in the hollows it is found, for example, in

extremely poor fens, quite often as a pioneer species on bare peat.

Sphagnum balticum type. The field layer here is dominated by rannoch-rush and hare's-tail cottongrass, the bottom layer by *Sphagnum balticum*. Other species of Sphagnum that often occur are *S. magellanicum* or *S. majus*. The balticum type is the most northerly and is limited to the north by the northern boundary of the bog hollows proper. Like *Sphagnum tenellum* it is relatively dry. In Norrland it merges without a clear boundary into the carpet fen type. *Sphagnum balticum* occurs throughout Sweden but seems to avoid the south-west coast. Strangely enough it has two rather different habitats, one in wet carpets, and the other as isolated individuals in dwarf shrub-tussock vegetation in for example the bogs of the southern Swedish highlands.

The occurrence of species in wetlands is based on the National Wetland Survey. A total distribution picture would look rather different for the species that also occur in other types of environments. The maps show the main distribution of the species. For common alder, *Tricophorum caespitosum*, *Myrica gale* and *Ledum palustre*, the map shows where the species is predominant in a vegetation type. For *Sphagnum angermannicum*, *S. strictum* and *S. molle* all known habitats are shown, even those outside the National Wetland Survey. (S95—S104)

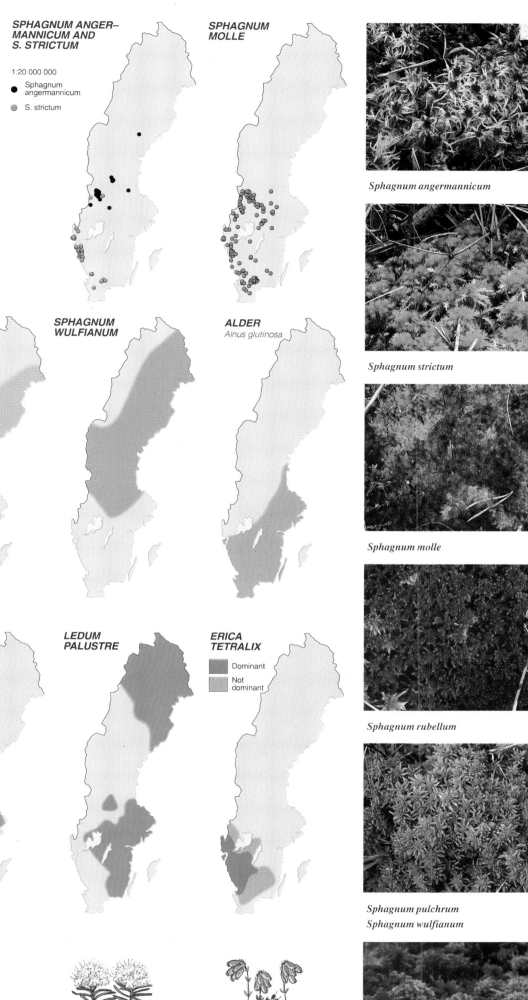

SPHAGNUM ANGER–MANNICUM AND S. STRICTUM

1:20 000 000
- Sphagnum angermannicum
- S. strictum

SPHAGNUM MOLLE

Sphagnum angermannicum

Sphagnum strictum

Sphagnum molle

Sphagnum rubellum

Sphagnum pulchrum
Sphagnum wulfianum

SPHAGNUM RUBELLUM

SPHAGNUM PULCHRUM

SPHAGNUM WULFIANUM

ALDER
Alnus glutinosa

TRICOPHORUM CAESPI–TOSUM

MYRICA GALE

LEDUM PALUSTRE

ERICA TETRALIX

- Dominant
- Not dominant

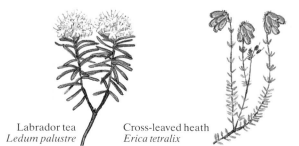

Labrador tea
Ledum palustre

Cross-leaved heath
Erica tetralix

1:5 000 000

- Ancient open pasture
- Ancient pasture with birch
- Ancient pasture with oak
- Heathland with heather
- Ancient shore pasture
- Ancient pasture with mixed deciduous trees
- Alvar
- Ancient pasture rich in shrubs or open
- Old type of grazed forest
- Other
- No data

Area, hectares

- 40,000
- 20,000
- 10,000
- 5,000
- 1,000

Area of various pasture types in Sweden.

Breckland thyme
Thymus serpyllum

All in all there is about 280,000 ha of valuable pastureland (grazing grounds), unevenly distributed throughout the country; the main concentrations are in Älvsborgs County, Kalmar County and Gotland. (S105)

The Cultivated Landscape

The smiling open cultivated landscape that we almost take for granted nowadays has developed over thousands of years with the assistance of the scythe, the plough and grazing cattle. Approximately 6,000 years ago we changed from a nomadic fishing and hunting life to cultivating the land. To begin with the fields were temporary slash-and-burn areas, which became permanent during the Iron Age (400 B.C.–1050 A.D.).

Cattle required large areas to meet their grazing needs and wandered freely in forests and other outlying land. Close to farms, in the infields, there were enclosures to keep the cattle out of the cultivated fields. Grasses, sedges and herbs were collected from every kind of land to make winter fodder for the cattle. The mild climate in south-west Sweden allowed the cattle there to be kept outdoors in the winter, and large heaths were created by regularly burning the vegetation.

During the late 18th century the cultivated landscape began to change its character as a result of land reform, new cultivation methods and later the draining of lakes and wetlands. This transformation has continued at an increasingly rapid pace in our own times.

PASTURELAND

Most of the forests of Götaland, Svealand and in the coastal districts of Norrland used to be grazed, which created open, light forests. Today there is about 600,000 ha of pastureland (= grazing grounds), most of which is ploughed, sown and manured fields. Forest grazing has practically ceased and the forests have closed in, but a keen eye can still detect traces in the form of old juniper bushes, decayed fence posts and collapsed stone walls.

The National Survey of Meadow and Pastureland reports about 200,000 ha (some 6% of all agricultural land) as being valuable for nature conservation. Of this area 98% is pastureland; most of it is open and treeless, while tree-covered grazing grounds of conservation value comprise only about 40,000 ha. The pure birch and oak meadows, which have become a kind of symbol of summer Sweden, cover less than 15,000 ha and may well become rare in the future unless they get conservation-oriented management.

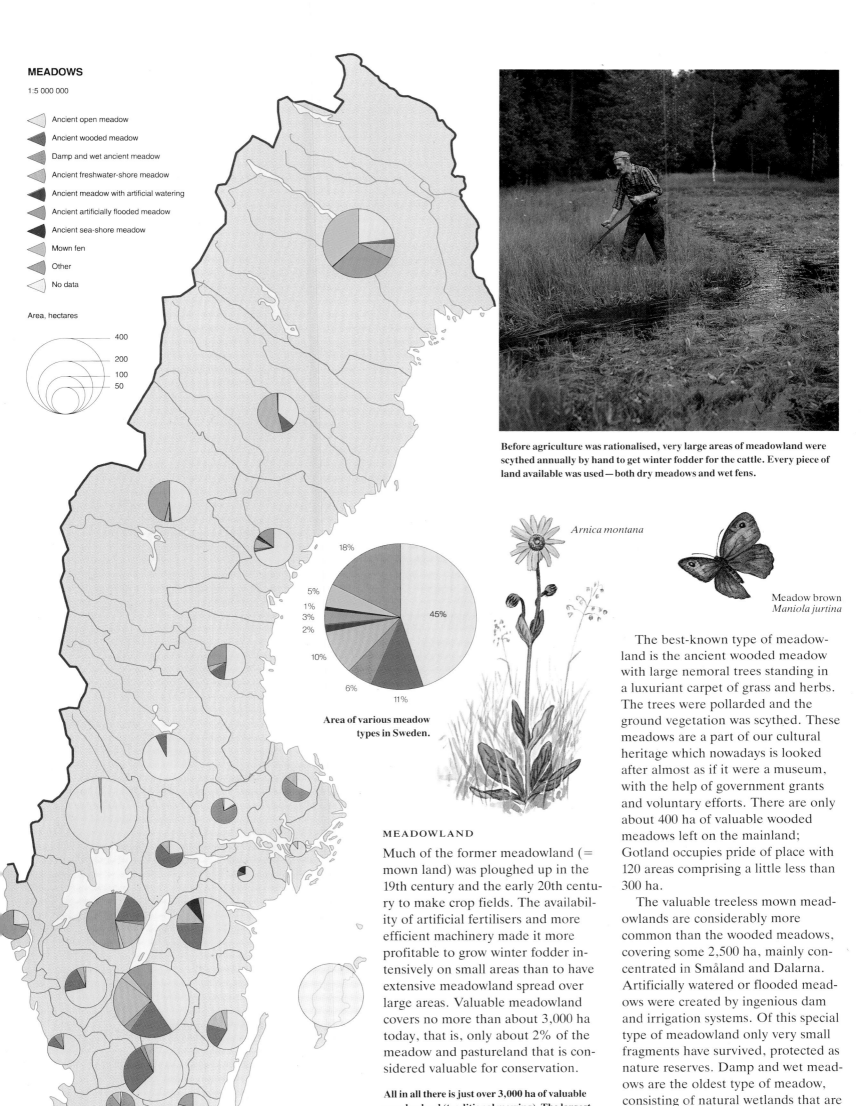

MEADOWS

1:5 000 000

Ancient open meadow

Ancient wooded meadow

Damp and wet ancient meadow

Ancient freshwater-shore meadow

Ancient meadow with artificial watering

Ancient artificially flooded meadow

Ancient sea-shore meadow

Mown fen

Other

No data

Area, hectares

400

200

100

50

Area of various meadow types in Sweden.

Arnica montana

Meadow brown
Maniola jurtina

Before agriculture was rationalised, very large areas of meadowland were scythed annually by hand to get winter fodder for the cattle. Every piece of land available was used — both dry meadows and wet fens.

MEADOWLAND

Much of the former meadowland (= mown land) was ploughed up in the 19th century and the early 20th century to make crop fields. The availability of artificial fertilisers and more efficient machinery made it more profitable to grow winter fodder intensively on small areas than to have extensive meadowland spread over large areas. Valuable meadowland covers no more than about 3,000 ha today, that is, only about 2% of the meadow and pastureland that is considered valuable for conservation.

All in all there is just over 3,000 ha of valuable meadowland (traditional mowing). The largest areas are in the counties of Jönköping, Norrbotten and Värmland. (S106)

The best-known type of meadowland is the ancient wooded meadow with large nemoral trees standing in a luxuriant carpet of grass and herbs. The trees were pollarded and the ground vegetation was scythed. These meadows are a part of our cultural heritage which nowadays is looked after almost as if it were a museum, with the help of government grants and voluntary efforts. There are only about 400 ha of valuable wooded meadows left on the mainland; Gotland occupies pride of place with 120 areas comprising a little less than 300 ha.

The valuable treeless mown meadowlands are considerably more common than the wooded meadows, covering some 2,500 ha, mainly concentrated in Småland and Dalarna. Artificially watered or flooded meadows were created by ingenious dam and irrigation systems. Of this special type of meadowland only very small fragments have survived, protected as nature reserves. Damp and wet meadows are the oldest type of meadow, consisting of natural wetlands that are regularly flooded, along rivers, for example.

Pastureland forms a diminshing remnant of the old cultivated landscape. Most animals nowadays are let out to graze on cultivated fields. Unfertilised natural grazing grounds are among our richest biotopes.

Above right. Many types of weeds which used to be common in the fields are now uncommon as a result of fertilizers, herbicides and effective weeding of the sowings. The common poppy *Papaver rhoeas* in a cornfield.

There used to be plenty of pollarded trees in the old enclosed land. Their foliage was used as fodder and pollarding meant that the trees could become very old. A rich flora and fauna of bryophytes, lichens, fungi and insects were often connected to these trees.

In the past 100 years natural meadowland and pastureland has greatly decreased, while ploughed grazing land has increased noticeably.

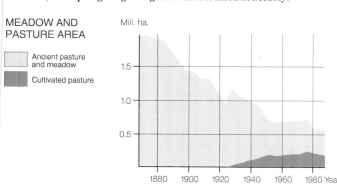

MEADOW AND PASTURE AREA

☐ Ancient pasture and meadow
■ Cultivated pasture

Mill. ha.

RICH FLORA AND FAUNA

The ancient cultivated landscape favoured a rich variety of species and most of our rarest species are found only in the remnants of our ancient system of cultivation. In infields and mown meadows there used to be plenty of large nemoral trees. There were probably more than 100 million pollarded trees in Sweden at the beginning of the 19th century.

The ancient unfertilised pastures are among the richest in species of vascular plants and they also contain many special ground fungi. Many of these species have become uncommon today, driven out by rapid-growing herbs and grass that are favoured by nitrogen.

In the old days, much to the farmers' dismay, the fields were rich in weeds. Today these species are protected as rarities and in some places special weed fields have been created. Another contributory factor to the rich biodiversity in the old cultivated landscape was the multiplicity of small biotopes like the edges of fields, islands of uncultivated land in fields and road and ditch banks.

TODAY'S AND TOMORROW'S CULTIVATED LANDSCAPE

There is today great uncertainty about the future of Sweden's cultivated landscape. The surrounding world in the form of the EU and the world market will be decisive in determining whether and how the land will be used. Grants may reward conservational measures, but spruce plantations on former fields may become very profitable. We see today the development of extensive farming, concentrating on ecologically cultivated products. From a biological point of view there is no doubt that a varied and open landscape is preferable to a closed one dominated by coniferous forests.

Birdspecies with more than 50% of their populations in the cultivated landscape. The diagram shows the estimated number of breeding pairs.
* = red-listed species.

Number	Species
1,000,000	Yellowhammer, Starling, Woodpigeon, Sky Lark, White Wagtail, Tree Sparrow, House Sparrow, Magpie, Whinchat, Hooded Crow, Jackdaw, Greenfinch, Swallow
	House Martin, Wood Warbler, Linnet
	Lapwing, Snipe
100,000	Pheasant, Red-backed Shrike
	Scarlet Rosefinch, Ortolan Bunting
	Stock Dove*, Marsh Warbler, Rook, Buzzard, Curlew, Tawny Owl*, Wryneck
	Partridge*
10,000	Long-eared Owl, Yellow Wagtail* (ssp. *flava*), Grasshopper Warbler
	Goldfinch
	Kestrel*
	Hobby, Corncrake*, Barred Warbler
1,000	
	Kite*, Dunlin* (ssp. *schinzii*), Black-tailed Godwit*
100	Montagu´s Harrier*
	Peregrine*, Quail*, River Warbler
	Blyth´s Reed Warbler
	Hoopoe*
10	
	Corn Bunting*
0	

Yellowhammer
Emberiza citrinella

Corncrake
Crex crex

MEADOW AND PASTURE CLASS I – III

1:5 000 000

Percentage area of agricultural land in the municipality

- 30
- 15
- 10
- 5
- 3
- 1
- 0
- No data

Kiruna

Arjeplog

Luleå

Storuman

Umeå

Strömsund

Östersund

Härnösand

Sveg

Malung

Falun

Gävle

Torsby

Uppsala

Västerås

Karlstad

Örebro

Stockholm

Mariestad

Nyköping

Vänersborg

Linköping

Göteborg

Visby

Jönköping

Växjö

Kalmar

Halmstad

Karlskrona

Kristianstad

Malmö

(S107)

SURVEYS OF MEADOW AND PASTURELAND

Between 1987 and 1990 the National Environmental Protection Agency carried out a National Survey of Meadow and Pastureland. Assessments of conservation values were based on biological and to some extent cultural criteria. Sites were divided into three classes.

Large areas of the most valuable land are now covered by agreements with the owners who receive compensation for managing them. From 1996 there will be grants from the EU programme for the environment.

Jönköping County has reported 2,373 sites containing valuable meadow and pastureland. The pasque flower *Pulsatilla vulgaris* grows mainly in dry meadows with deep, sandy and gravelly soil. All in all 689 such dry meadows were recorded in the survey; pasque flowers were recorded in 187 of them. The distribution of the pasque flower follows important deposits of sand and gravel in the county; it is less common in dry meadows with thin cover, close to rock outcrops, for example. Despite the frequency of dry meadows with a rich flora in the rocky landscape east of Lake Vättern, the pasque flower is uncommon there.

VALUABLE MEADOW AND PASTURE IN JÖNKÖPING COUNTY

1:1 500 000

(S108)

Pasque flower
Pulsatilla vulgaris

DRY MEADOWS AND OCCURENCE OF PASQUE FLOWER

- ○ Dry meadows
- • Pasque flower *Pulsatilla vulgaris*
- Glaciofluvial sediments

(S109)

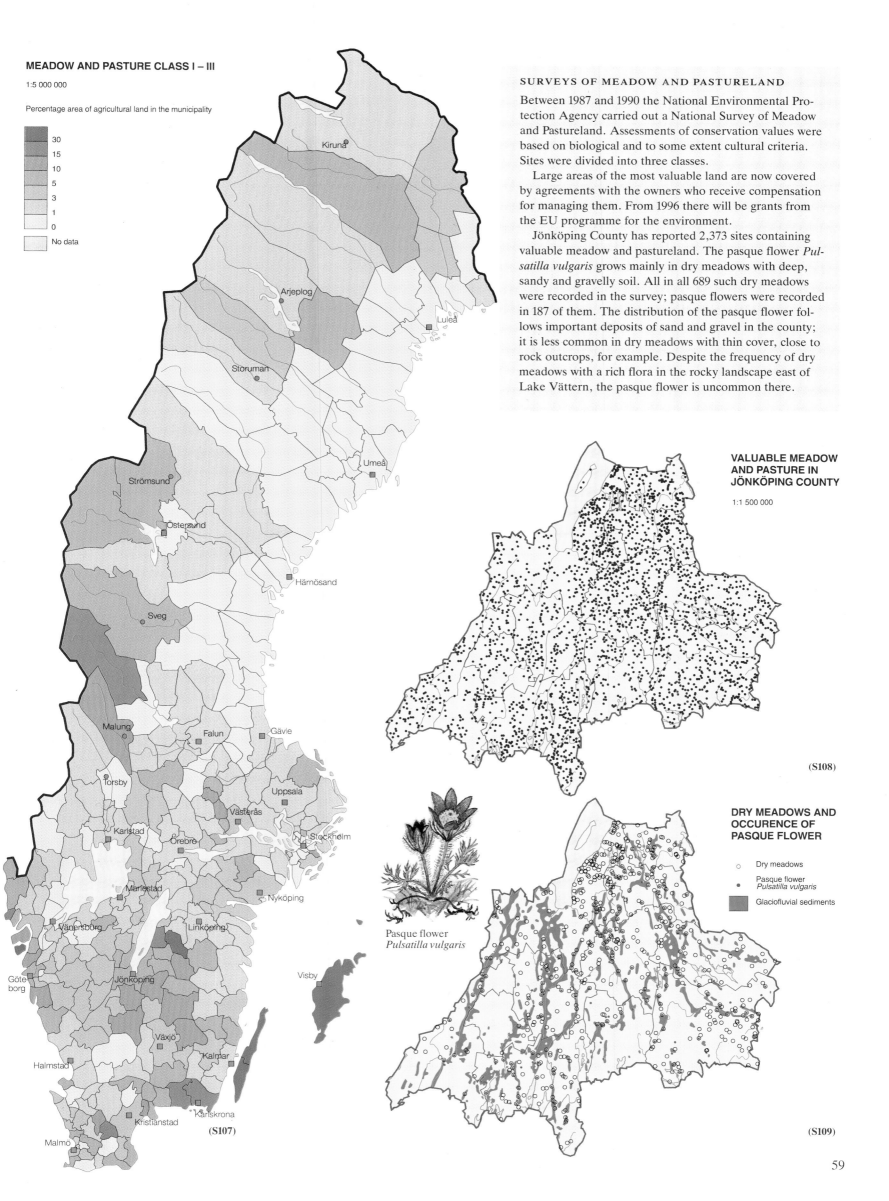

59

Dawn on the Great Alvar. The impressive scenery of this open, flat alvar landscape with its diversity of plant habitats and stone walls is emphasised by the shifting light.

The golden plover *Pluvialis apricaria* is a typical bird on the alvar.

The Öland rock rose *Helianthemum oelandicum*, which is found only on Öland, is a characteristic species on the shallow cover of the alvar. In June it flowers beautifully against the reddish-brown calcareous soil.

ALVAR

In the southern parts of the limestone areas there are vast flat areas of a very special type called *alvar*. The combination of thin overburden, limestone bedrock and relatively low precipitation on alvar ground has resulted in a special, rich flora and fauna.

Apart from the usual Scandinavian plants there are a multitude of species that are mainly distributed in other, often more distant climes. There are those that have immigrated during warm eras and remained although the climate became colder; these are called *warm-period relicts*. Another group of species came when the inland ice had melted and the land was covered with bleak mountain heaths. Since alvar ground has a similar winter climate to alpine areas—with wind, snow and ice—these *glacial relicts* have remained. There are also a few *endemics*, that is, species that are found only here and which have developed characteristics in their isolation that distinguish them from related species.

Among animals there are also many examples of unusual species such as the grasshopper *Bryodema tuberculata*, which is found on the steppes of south-east Europe and in Asia, but which also occurs in places in western Europe, including Öland. The grasshopper *Omocestus haemorrhoidalis* is mainly found from Central Europe to East Asia, but also in Sweden on both Öland and Gotland as well as in Skåne and on the hill called Kinnekulle. Several other insects have a similar distribution. A species of very small moth by the name of *Bucculatrix laciniatella* is found only on Öland, however.

Alvar ground has been exploited by human beings ever since Prehistoric times for hunting, and later for grazing and even for small-scale cultivation. On Stora Alvaret, for example, there are no fewer than 48 remains of Iron Age settlements. Trees and juniper bushes were used widely for fuel, creating, together with grazing, an open landscape. Linnaeus records in his travel journal of 1741 that the alvar stretched from Öland's southernmost tip up to Borgholm. This open and at times over-exploited area has today at its northern tip a young forest (Mittlandsskogen). This forest was able to develop after about one third of the island's population had emigrated to North America between 1880 and 1910.

As grazing and wood-cutting decrease the littoral banks meadows are colonised by juniper bushes and pine trees, while birch and shrubby cinquefoil *Potentilla fruticosa* spring up in the hollows. What can grow is governed by the summer drought, which makes it impossible to survive except in filled crevices in the rock. This is grassland that has been kept open by nature for thousands of years. The great problem today on most alvar ground with thick cover is the spread of scrub. By creating nature conservation areas and paying grants for clearance and fencing for cattle, attempts are now being made to control the growth of scrub on Stora Alvaret.

ALVAR GROUND IN SCANDINAVIA AND THE BALTIC STATES

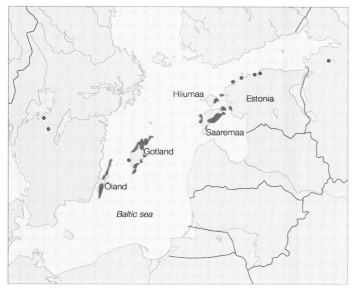

Alvars are found on limestone bedrock. In Västergötland (Kinnekulle and Falbygden), on Öland and in western Estonia the bedrock consists of Ordovician limestone, whereas other alvars are on Silurian bedrock. (S110)

DISTRIBUTION OF *LOXOSTEGE MANUALIS* IN EUROPE

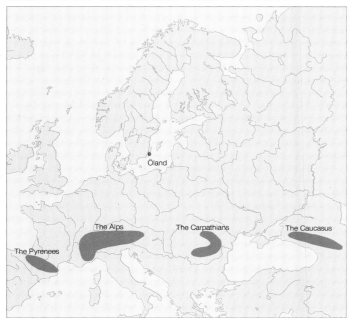

ALVAR GROUND ON ÖLAND AND GOTLAND

1:1 250 000

Alvar ground

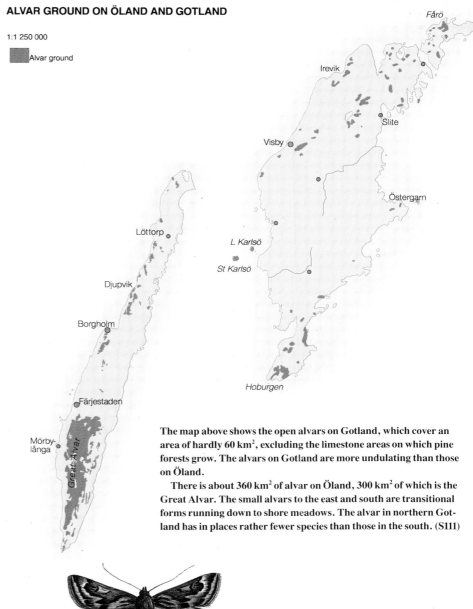

The map above shows the open alvars on Gotland, which cover an area of hardly 60 km², excluding the limestone areas on which pine forests grow. The alvars on Gotland are more undulating than those on Öland.

There is about 360 km² of alvar on Öland, 300 km² of which is the Great Alvar. The small alvars to the east and south are transitional forms running down to shore meadows. The alvar in northern Gotland has in places rather fewer species than those in the south. (S111)

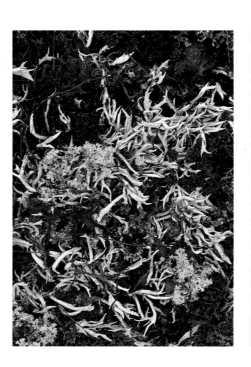

The microlepidoptera *Loxostege manualis* is an example of a southern species which is also found on Öland (a relict of the warm period). (S112)

DISTRIBUTION OF *THAMNOLIA VERMICULARIS* IN EUROPE

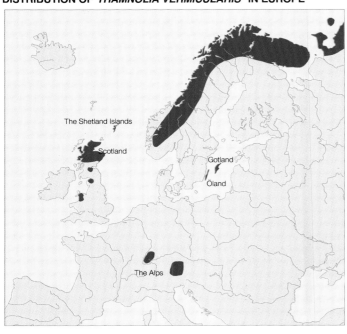

The lichen *Thamnolia vermicularis* is a species that occurs in Sweden's mountain districts. It is also found on Öland's and Gotland's alvar grounds as a relic of the time after deglaciation when there was an arctic climate here (glacial relict). The species is most frequent on thin calcareous soils with little frost movement. It is sensitive to being trodden on, as this easily crushes the hollow branches. *Thamnolia vermicularis* is widespread outside Europe and is also found in mountain tracts in the southern hemisphere.

The Plant Environment of the Alvar

More than 400 sample plots on the Öland alvars have been investigated with regard to plant species, soil type, depth of deposit, moisture and the like. The photographs show some main types of plant habitats and how they are realted to soil, moisture and soil depth. The thick deposits are dominated by littoral sand and gravel (silicate soil); the thin layers are calcareous.

DRY AND MODERATELY MOIST ENVIRONMENTS

Fissure-restricted alvar vegetation provides a home for many unusual species. The province flower of Öland, the Öland rock rose *Helianthemum oelandicum*, dominates the fissures in the photograph.

Alvar fescue communities consist of a sparse, tussocky covering relatively poor in species which often dries up in the height of summer. During the late winter they are subject to violent frost action.

Alvar dry meadows occur on the thick shore deposits. This environment is very rich in relatively small plant species. Within 10 x 10 cm sample areas up to 27 species of vascular plants have been recorded!

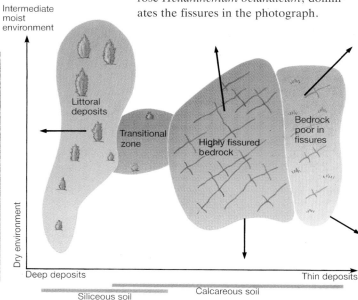

Karst alvar is an extreme environment of deep, open fissures and bare limestone bedrock. The favourable microclimate of the fissures encourages several plants of the nemoral woodland, which would not otherwise survive on the dry alvar ground. Small snails eat the lichens round the fissures baring the limestone.

Temporary pools are the periodically water-filled hollows which are found here and there on the alvar. The plant covering is usually completely dried up in the summer. Brown mosses and a few vascular plants, including dwarf plantain *Plantago tenuiflora*, grow in the dry, often thin, calcareous mud.

MOIST AND WET ENVIRONMENTS

Alvar moist meadows are found in hollows containing fine-grained deposits and good water-retaining properties. The dominant grass there is blue moor-grass *Sesleria caerulea* along with sedges and a small number of herbs. The low, yellow-flowering shrubby cinquefoil *Potentilla fruticosa* is common in this environment.

Alvar lakes form in large hollows where there is water throughout the year. The reed *Phragmites australis*, the tufted-sedge *Carex elata* and rushes *Scirpus* spp often grow in the middle of the lakes, surrounded by open water is rich in water plants.

If a sea-shore meadow is to develop, the coast must be shallow and the land has to be kept open, by grazing, for example. Beautifully formed sea-shore meadows are to be found at the southern tip of Öland.

Sea-shore Meadows

Sea-shore meadows may develop along shallow, low coasts. As a result of land elevation new sea-shore meadows are slowly but continuously created along large parts of the Swedish coastline. Other significant factors for the development of sea-shore meadows are that the area has been affected by grazing or hay-making over a long period of time, that it is regularly flooded and that the soil contains relatively large amounts of fine particles. Grazing prevents sea-shore meadows from becoming overgrown with trees, bushes and high grass, in particular reed. Large areas have become overgrown since the 1950s, particularly along the coast of Norrland.

Since many sea-shore meadows are regularly flooded by salt water, the plants growing there must be able to stand some salt. The vegetation in

sea-shore meadows forms more or less evident belts. This is because the plant species can stand being submerged in salt water to varying degrees.

The shore is usually water-soaked below the mean water line, and here sea club-rush *Scirpus maritimus*, grey club-rush *Scirpus tabernaemontani* and reed dominate large stretches of our coastline. On the shores of the Bothnian Bay grey club-rush is common, but reed and sea club-rush are usually absent. Instead there are smaller species such as needle spike-rush *Eleocharis acicularis*. Above the mean water line up to the highest water line creeping bent *Agrostis stolonifera*, saltmarsh *Juncus gerardi* and red fescue *Festuca rubra* are dominant.

Many species of birds have their densest populations on grazed sea-shore meadows. This is particularly true of waders, including rare species such as Kentish plover, the southern subspecies of dunlin and avocet. The black-tailed godwit nests mainly on sea-shore meadows on Öland and Gotland. The curlew, ruff and yellow wagtail are examples of species that can also occur inland but which are mainly found on sea-shore meadows in southern and central Sweden. Other more common birds that nest on sea-shore meadows are oystercatcher, lapwing, redshank and ringed plover. The sea-shore meadows along our coasts are also of great importance as resting places for many species of birds. In particular migrating waders, geese and ducks are dependent on coastal areas with shallow beaches and low shore vegetation.

The occurrence of species within other groups of organisms than vascular plants and birds on sea-shore meadows is less well known. Among the batrachians the green toad *Bufo viridis* and natterjack *Bufo calamita* are found in southern Swedish shore environments. Of Sweden's lepidoptera some 20 Noctuidae, 17 species of Tortricidae, Pyralidae and Tineidae and two species of Geometridae occur on sea-shore meadows.

Sea-shore meadows occur along flat shores on certain parts of our coasts. (S114)

Salinity is an important environmental factor for some plant species. They form zones from the west coast to the Bothnian Sea. (S115)

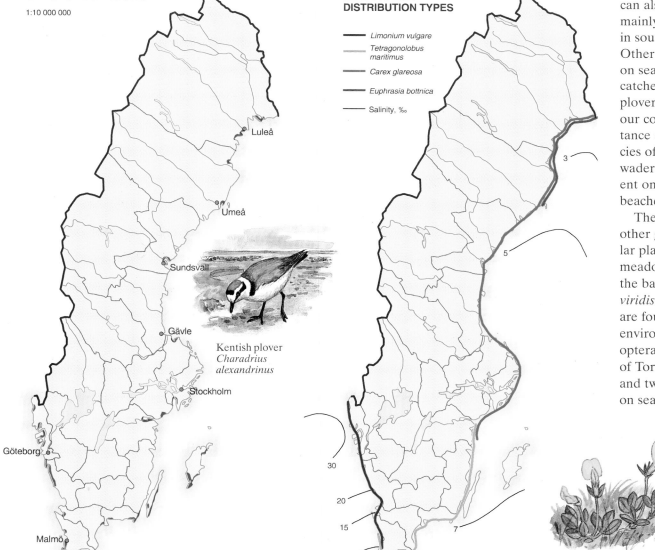

SEA-SHORE MEADOWS

1:10 000 000

Luleå

Umeå

Sundsvall

Gävle

Stockholm

Göteborg

Malmö

Kentish plover
Charadrius alexandrinus

SALINITY AND DISTRIBUTION TYPES

— *Limonium vulgare*
— *Tetragonolobus maritimus*
— *Carex glareosa*
— *Euphrasia bottnica*
— Salinity, ‰

3

5

30

20

15

7

10

Dragon's teeth
Tetragonolobus maritimus

63

There are often several different environments in towns which can give a very rich variety of vascular plants. At Långholmen in Stockholm, for example, there are unusually many water plants, where the fresh water of Lake Mälaren meets the brackish water of the Baltic.

Urban Flora and Fauna

Towns are built and dominated by human beings. A surprisingly large number of organisms have made towns their home, but most of them live unnoticed by us.

An urban environment offers quite a few advantages compared with natural environments, but also disadvantages. Among the advantages are a more favourable local climate, as shown by more snow-free days, and a longer vegetation period. Some of the disadvantages are, for example, a lack of water on hot summer days, air pollution and—for animals— a grave risk of being killed by the heavy traffic. Supplies of food for birds are usually good during the critical winter months thanks to feeding by people. This encourages breeding to begin early.

URBAN VEGETATION

There is great similarity between the flora in Swedish towns, and the differences are mainly due to the size of the towns and their latitude; the further south, the larger the number of species. After Stockholm the town with the largest number of species is Göteborg. The most common plants in Swedish towns are without doubt annual meadow grass *Poa annua*, common chickweed *Stellaria media* and knotgrass *Polygonum aviculare*— all weeds that are found throughout the world.

There are some 1,300 wild vascular plants, including those that have escaped from cultivation, in Stockholm.

Madwort *Asperugo procumbens* is a poor competitor and grows in flower beds, on waste tips and often on bare ground under bridges where it is favoured by nitrogen emissions from the traffic. This species has diminished as towns have been cleaned up. (S116)

No other flower is so closely connected with palaces and country houses as the wild tulip *Tulipa sylvestris*. It spreads by forming new bulbs but because it flowers infrequently it has not been cultivated much since the 19th century.

MADWORT AND WILD TULIP IN STOCKHOLM

- ● Madwort
  Asperugo procumbens

Wild tulip *Tulipa sylvestris* growing in
- △ castle parks
- ◉ old town gardens
- ▣ other old properties

Wild tulip

Madwort

The great tit *Parus major* is one of the commonest birds in towns thanks to winter feeding and all the parks with their hollow trees and bird boxes. But this tit has chosen to build its nest in a cellar ventilator!

It is primarily availability of vegetation that determines how rich animal life is in towns. So in town centres there are very few species, whereas out in the residential areas with their many gardens there is an amazing variety of animal life. (S117)

ANIMALS IN CENTRAL LUND

The old town centre

Rock Dove *Columba livia*
House Sparrow *Passer domesticus*

Old parks

Hedgehog *Erinaceus europaeus*
Pipistrelle Bat *Pipistrellus pipistrellus*
Red Squirrel *Sciurus vulgaris*
Tree Sparrow *Passer montanus*
Great Tit *Parus major*
Blue Tit *Parus caeruleus*
Blackbird *Turdus merula*
Greenfinch *Carduelis chloris*
Chaffinch *Fringilla coelebs*

New parks

Hedgehog *Erinaceus europaeus*
Blackbird *Turdus merula*
Linnet *Carduelis cannabina*

Residential areas

Hedgehog *Erinaceus europaeus*
Northern Bat *Eptesicus nilssonii*
House Mouse *Mus musculus*
Great Tit *Parus major*
Blue Tit *Parus caeruleus*
Pied Flycatcher *Ficedula hypoleuca*
Redstart *Phoenicurus phoenicurus*
Starling *Sturnus vulgaris*
Blackbird *Turdus merula*
Garden Warbler *Sylvia borin*
Lesser Whitethroat *Sylvia curruca*
Thrush Nightingale *Luscinia luscinia*

University and industrial areas

Rabbit *Oryctolagus cuniculus*
Common Rat *Rattus norvegicus*
Jackdaw *Corvus monedula*
Rook *Corvus frugilegus*
Magpie *Pica pica*

This large number is due to the wide variety of environments: backyards, parks, woodland, harbours, railways, mills, fields, nurseries and waste tips.

Many cultivated flowers have survived or run wild on demolition sites and abandoned allotments. More recently it is those that have run wild and become naturalised that have enriched the urban flora, whereas at the turn of the century it was mainly trade and communications with foreign countries that brought in new species. There is also countryside less affected by human activities, like coniferous and deciduous forests, fens and bogs, in or close to towns. The most central bog in Stockholm is at Hammarbyhöjden, only about 4 km from the city centre, but most of the other wetlands have been drained.

The least affected flora and fauna in Stockholm's most densely populated district are found on rocks that are too steep to be built on, as in Fredshällparken and Eriksdalslunden.

Stockholm lies at the meeting point of fresh and brackish water in Lake Mälaren and the Baltic, so it has both lake and skerry vegetation, giving it unusually many species of water plants. Fresh and brackish water plants meet in the open water round Långholmen and Reimersholme, and this area probably has most phanerogamous underwater plants in Sweden—24 species, 12 of which are species of *Potamogeton*.

Common rat
Rattus norvegicus

URBAN FAUNA

The richness of higher animal life in a town is mainly determined by its plant life, since animals are dependent on vegetation for their food and protection. The supply of vegetation is worst in the old town centre, the "concrete jungle", and best in the residential areas.

The parkland of suburbia usually consists of a rather poor environment of large areas of grass and monotonous bush and tree vegetation where few birds can flourish. But its proximity to the open countryside makes it possible for mammals to move in, especially small mammals like water voles, bank voles and field mice. If the parks are sufficiently large, foxes and badgers can also live there.

The vegetation of residential areas is more varied, especially their shrubs and plants. This encourages a wide range of insects which attract hedgehogs and bats. Typical garden birds are blackbird, willow warbler, great tit, blue tit, pied flycatcher and robin.

The range of urban bird fauna is in a constant state of change as new species become urbanised. The fieldfare, for example, used to be a forest bird but today it nests in most towns. The collared dove has come to Sweden from the south and spread northwards to coastal towns in Götaland and Svealand. Other species that are showing a tendency to become town dwellers are hawfinch and dunnock.

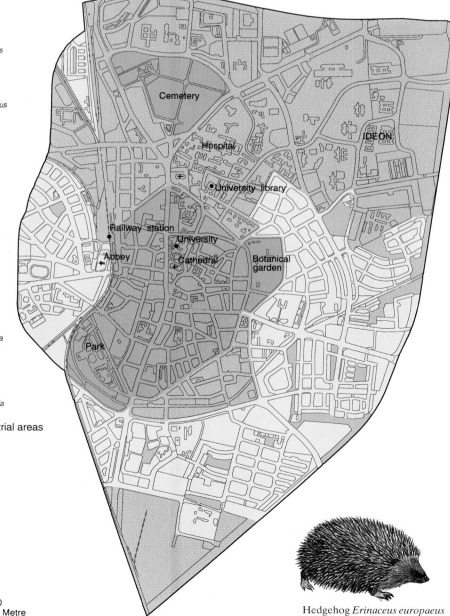

Hedgehog *Erinaceus europaeus*

0   100   200   300
|___|___|___|___| Metre

Species Diversity

"Living mire". Lithograph by Agneta Gussander.

The title of this volume indicates that there are two great kingdoms of organisms: *plants* and *animals*. But life is probably not so simple. Research in the past few years, above all in the field of DNA studies, has considerably increased our insight into relationships in the lower levels of the tree of evolution, though there is still great uncertainty about such relationships.

A five-kingdom system was proposed in the 1970s: *bacteria, protista, fungi, plants* and *animals*. This system has now proved to be inadequate and is only a small step forward compared with dividing all eukaryotic organisms (species with a cell core) into the two groups of plants and animals. There is as yet no accepted complete classification system.

NUMBER OF SPECIES IN SWEDEN AND IN THE WORLD

Probably only between a tenth and a fifth of the total number of species in the world are known and have been described. The organisms that are thought to be best known are birds, mammals, reptiles and amphibians. Those that are least well known are one-celled organisms (bacteria and Protista) and roundworms (Nematoda).

The group with most species is insects, which, as far as we know, comprise about 55% of all the world's species. There are many gaps in our knowledge of this group, and it is here that in all probability most future discoveries will be made. The fungus group, forming today 5% of all described species on earth, is also considered to comprise a large number of species not yet described. Our lack of information about the number of species is greatest in the tropical forests, but much is also unknown in the temperate zone.

Our knowledge of species and their distribution in Sweden is better than in most other countries thanks to our long floristic and faunistic tradition

dating back to Linnaeus' time. Many professional botanists and zoologists have contributed to the description and classification of species, but skilful amateurs have also contributed detailed information over the past two centuries.

There is, however, great variation in our knowledge of where in Sweden the species are to be found. When the information from different provinces is compiled, there is a risk that inaccurate assessments will be made, that, for example, the same importance is attached to isolated records as to numerous records. In general the south of Sweden is better surveyed than the north. The interior of Norrland is one of the least-well surveyed areas, with regard to all groups of species.

Despite our relatively good knowledge of the distribution of species, it is rather unusual for this information to have been collected in national maps. The reason is that plant and animal geography, which was an important branch of research in the early part of the 19th century, has not been given much attention during the past few decades.

NUMBER OF KNOWN SPECIES

Various attempts have been made to estimate the actual number of species on earth, resulting in anything between two and 150 million. However, a reasonable estimate is around ten million. The table on the next page shows *the number of species known today*. The figures for Sweden include species that were originally introduced. For fish and birds the first figure indicates the number of reproducing species, while the figure in brackets represents the total number of species observed.

The reliability of these figures varies greatly. For many species groups we have very good information, while for others there are no modern lists or systematic revisions—here the figure given is "a best estimate". The most unreliable figures are generally speaking for "primitive" fungi and one-celled organisms.

An example is the one-celled parasites called microsporidians, of which 1,300 species are known today. There is a great deal to suggest that most animals host at least one microsporidian which is specific to the species. If this is so, estimates of the total number of species are doubled!

Group of organisms in English		No. of known species globally	in Sweden

PROCARYOTAE	procaryotes		
BACTERIA	eubacteria	5,000	2,500
ARCHAEA	archaebacteria	300	40

EUCARYOTAE	eucaryotes		
PROTISTA	unicellular eukaryotic organisms	50,000	5,000
Sarcomastigophora	flagellates, amoebas	20,000	1,000
Labyrinthomorpha	gregarines, coccidians	40	5
Apicomplexa	microsporidians	5,000	100
Microspora	myxosporidians	1,300	70
Myxozoa		1,200	20
Ascetospora		30	1
Ciliophora	ciliates	8,000	1,000
Chrysophyta		12,000	1,100
Chrysophyceae	golden algae	1,000	500
Xanthophyceae	yellow-green algae	600	80
Bacillariophyceae	diatoms	10,000	550
Haptophyta		500	25
Pyrrophyta	dinoflagellates	2,500	250
Cryptophyta	cryptomonades	200	80
Euglenophyta	euglenids	1,000	280
Acrasida	cellular slime molds	20	3
Myxogastrea	plasmodial slime molds	600	175
Plasmodiophorida		50	4

FUNGI	fungi	80,000	10,000
Mastigomycota		1,200	300
Eumycota		80,000	10,000
Zygomycotina	zygomycetes	700	300
Ascomycotina	sac fungi	35,000	4,500
	(lichens)	18,000	2,000
	(others)	15,000	2,500
Deuteromycotina	fungi imperfecti	20,000	2,500
Basidiomycotina	basidiomycetes	25,000	3,000
Teliomycetes	rust and smut fungi	13,500	700
Phragmobasidio-mycetes		475 / 80	
Hymenomycetes	mushrooms and their allies	11,000	2,100
Gasteromycetes	puffballs, stinkhorns etc.	700	100

PLANTAE	plants	290,000	5,000
Rhodophyta	red algae	4,000	190
Phaeophyta	brown algae	1,500	150
Chlorophyta	green algae	15,000	1,600
Charophyta	stoneworts	440	34
Bryophyta	bryophytes	14,000	1,050
Anthoceropsida	hornworts	300	2
Marchantopsida	liverworts	6,000	260
Bryopsida	mosses	8,000	780
Lycophyta	club mosses	1,300	10
Sphenophyta	horsetails	22	9
Pteridophyta	ferns	9,000	47
Coniferophyta	conifers	610	6
Magnoliophyta	flowering plants	250,000	1,900
Magnoliopsida	dicotyledons	190,000	1,400
Liliopsida	monocotyledons	60,000	500

ANIMALIA	animals	1,250,000	34,000
Porifera	sponges	5,000	170
Mesozoa		50	4
Cnidaria	cnidarians	9,000	210
Scyphozoa	jellyfish	200	8
Hydrozoa	hydrozoans	2,000	150
Anthozoa	sea anemone and corals	6,000	50
Ctenophora	comb-jellies	50	4
Platyhelminthes	flatworms	13,000	960
Turbellaria	free-living flatworms	13,000	960
Digenea	flukes	5,000	200
Monogenea	monogenes	1,100	40
Cestoda	tapeworms	4,000	370
Xenoturbellida		1	1
Nemertea	ribbonworms	900	90
Gnathostomulida		80	4
Rotatoria	rotifers	1,500	700
Acanthocephala	spiny-h.worms	1,150	30
Gastrotricha	gastrotrichs	460	65
Priapulida	priapulids	9	3
Loricifera		10	1
Kinorhyncha		100	15
Nematoda	roundworms	12,000	1,000
Nematomorpha	hair-worms	230	5
Tardigrada	water bears	400	61
Sipunculida	peanut worms	320	10
Pogonophora	pogonophorans	80	1
Echiurida	spoonworms	140	3

EUCARYOTAE	eucaryotes		
Annelida	annelids or bristle-worms	12,000	690
Polychaeta	marine annelids	8,000	490
Oligochaeta	earthworms	3,000	167
Hirudinea	leeches	500	25
Entoprocta	entoprocts	150	28
Cycliophora		1	1
Bryozoa	sea-mats	4,000	170
Phoronida	phoronids	10	5
Brachiopoda	lampshells	335	5
Arthropoda	arthropods	1,000,000	28,200
Myriapoda	centipeds, millipeds etc.	13,000	90
Hexapoda	insects	950,000	24,700
Protura	proturans	500	4
Collembola	springtails	6,000	170
Diplura	two-tailed bristletails	800	5
Archaeognatha	bristletails	350	3
Zygentoma	silverfish	370	2
Ephemeroptera	mayflies	2,100	48
Odonata	dragonflies	5,000	56
Blattodea	cockroaches	4,000	5
Orthoptera	grasshoppers, crickets	20,000	39
Dermaptera	earwigs	1,800	4
Plecoptera	stoneflies	2,000	38
Psocoptera	book-lice	3,000	63
Phthiraptera	biting/sucking lice	3,500	150
Thysanoptera	thrips	4,500	99
Hemiptera	bugs	72,000	1,740
Megaloptera	alder-flies	300	5
Raphidioptera	snake-flies	180	4
Neuroptera	lacewings and ant-lions	5,000	65
Coleoptera	beetles	370,000	4,400
Strepsiptera	stylops	550	7
Mecoptera	scorpion flies	500	5
Siphonaptera	fleas	2,400	54
Diptera	two-winged flies	120,000	5,930
Trichoptera	caddies-flies	7,000	220
Lepidoptera	butterflies and moths	150,000	2,700
Hymenoptera	wasps and their allies	150,000	8,900
Crustacea	crustaceans	40,000	1,500
Chelicerata	chelicerates	75,000	1,900
Araneae	spiders	35,000	715
Opiliones	harvestmen	5,000	20
Pseudoscorpiones	false scorpions	2,000	21
Acari	mites and ticks	30,000	1,100
Pycnogonida	sea-spiders	1,000	16
Mollusca	Molluscs	50,000	640
Caudofoveata		70	6
Solenogastres	solenogasters	180	3
Polyplacophora	chitons	1,000	11
Gastropoda	snails, whelks etc.	38,000	430
Prosobranchia		20,000	170
Ophisthobranchia		2,000	120
Pulmonata		16,000	142
Bivalvia	bivalve molluscs	8,000	170
Scaphopoda	tusk shells	350	5
Cephalopoda	squids, octopods etc.	600	15
Hemichordata	hemicordates	85	5
Enteropneusta	acorn worms	70	4
Pterobranchia	pterobranchs	15	1
Chaetognatha	arrow worms	70	7
Echinodermata	echinoderms	5,500	75
Crinoidea	sea-lillies and feather stars	80	2
Asteroidea	starfish	1,500	22
Ophiuroidea	brittle-stars	2,000	18
Echinoidea	sea urchins	950	14
Holothuroidea	sea cucumbers	900	19
Chordata	chordates	48,000	525 (820)
Tunicata	tunicates	2,000	50
Appendicularia	appendicularians	70	3
Thaliacea	salps	50	1
Ascidacea	sea squirts	1,900	42
Cephalochordata	lancelets	25	1
Craniata	vertebrates	46,100	475 (773)
Pteraspidomorphi	hagfishes	32	1
Cephalaspidomorphi	lampreys	31	3
Chrondrichthyes	cartilaginous fishes	800	7 (28)
Osteichthyes	bony fishes	21,000	127 (204)
Amphibia	amphibians	4,100	13
Reptilia	reptiles	6,500	6
Aves	birds	9,200	245 (450)
Mammalia	mammals	4,500	69

TOTAL		1,675,000	55,000

Genes

Species

Nature types

BIODIVERSITY

There are many definitions of biodiversity. Some are very detailed and exact, others are brief—"life on earth", for example. Most of them usually state that biodiversity is found at three levels: *genes*, *species* and *ecosystem* levels.

Biodiversity can be calculated in various ways. The most usual one is based on the number of species per geographical area. Usually the abundance and the spatial distribution of the organisms are also taken into account. In its 1993 Bill the government defines biodiversity as "variation within and among species and in the ecological systems".

To be counted as belonging to one of the six regions a species has to have at least 5% of its total occurrence in that region. Thus isolated records are not included. (S118)

TERRESTRIAL VERTEBRATES

1:10 000 000

Number of species / region

- Reptiles and amphibians
- Birds
- Mammals

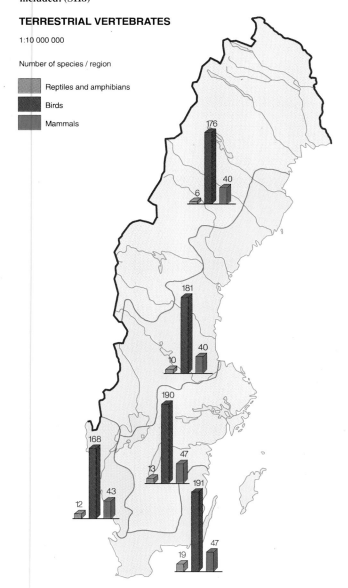

Decrease of Species towards the North

The number of species of flora and fauna varies geographically and according to the ecosystem. As a result of continuous change, local extinction and new establishment the number also varies with time. In general the flora and fauna are richest in species in the tropics and poorest towards the poles. This is also true within Sweden, Scandinavia and Europe.

Mammals

The number of species of mammals in Sweden is geographically relatively equally distributed. Of Sweden's 66 species almost half are spread throughout the country, 22 are limited to the south part and 14 to the north part.

Only the bat group, with 14 species in Sweden, has an evident increase in number of species in the south. The number of species increases linearly, reaching about 25 species in Central Europe. Within the Arctic Circle only one species, *Eptesicus nilssoni*, has adapted to the long winters and a short but insect-rich summer. Some of the species living in southern Sweden are dependent on a long season of flying insects and are unable to survive such a long hibernation.

Small rodents are another numerous group of mammals. Several of our

17 species are tied to the boreal ecosystem; seven are found all over the country, while only four are found solely in southern Sweden. Several species on the continent could very well live in southern Sweden, but they did not get there before the land bridge between Denmark and Skåne was definitely broken about 8,000 years ago.

Birds

Birds differ considerably from most other groups of animals in their greater mobility. Almost 80% of the species leave Sweden during the autumn and spend the winter in areas with more congenial conditions.

Thanks to their ability to migrate periodically, only a few species of Swedish birds have a distribution that is directly limited by the climate. One example is the mute swan, whose long breeding and fledgling period restricts their ability to settle in the interior of Norrland. A very large number of bird species, on the other hand, are dependent on a certain vegetation and their distribution is thus only indirectly affected by the climate. The fact that the climate is not so important is well illustrated by the occurrence of species like the garganey, shoveler and Caspian tern which nest very locally, and are usually rare, in suitable habitats over almost the whole of the country.

Many species are strictly tied to one particular habitat—mountain heaths (dotterel etc), Norrland mires (greenshank etc), or rich plain lakes (bittern etc), for example. These special habitat requirements mean that the number of bird species is always

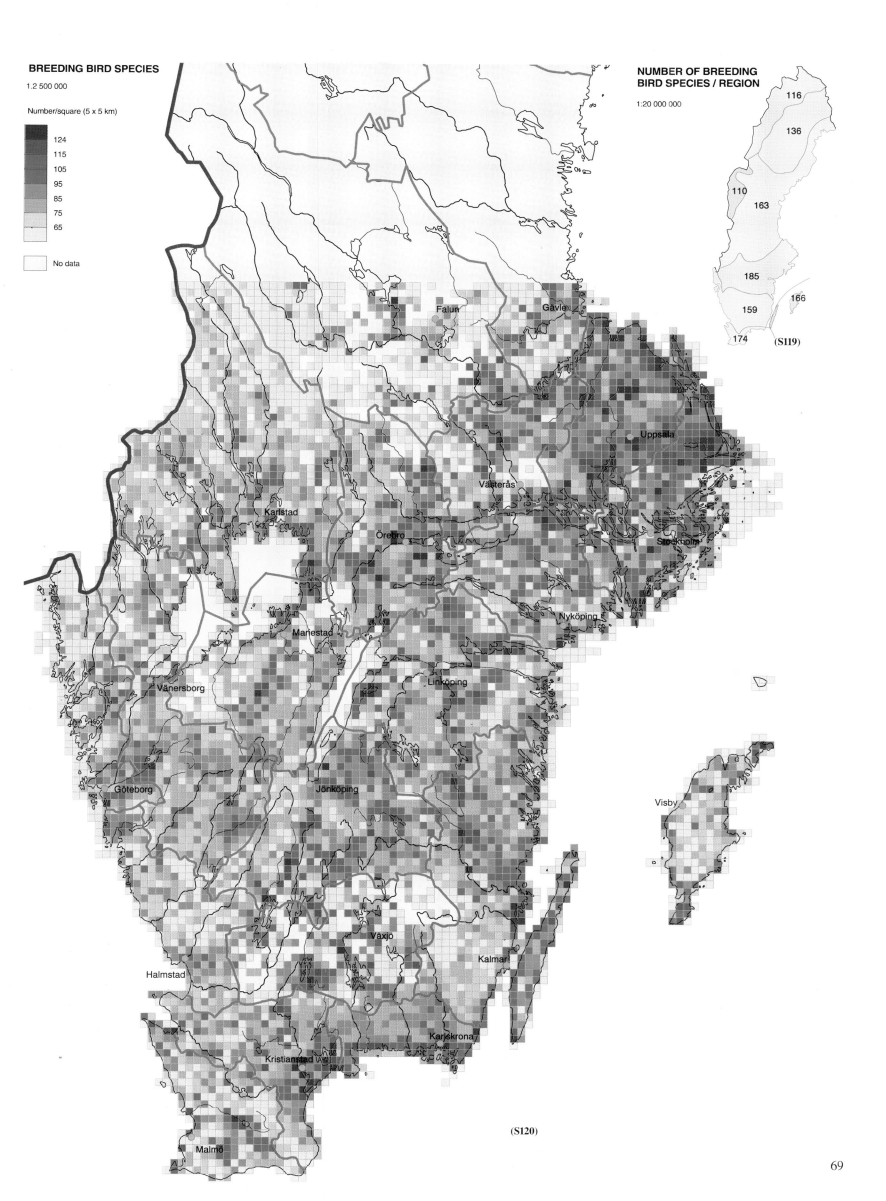

BREEDING BIRD SPECIES

1.2 500 000

Number/square (5 x 5 km)

124
115
105
95
85
75
65

No data

NUMBER OF BREEDING
BIRD SPECIES / REGION

1:20 000 000

116
136
110
163
185
166
159
174
(S119)

Falun
Gävle
Uppsala
Västerås
Karlstad
Örebro
Stockholm
Nyköping
Mariestad
Linköping
Vänersborg
Visby
Göteborg
Jönköping
Växjö
Kalmar
Halmstad
Karlskrona
Kristianstad
Malmö

(S120)

69

The dotterel *Charadrius morinellus* lives in a special environment, mountain heaths.

The adder *Vipera berus* is found all over Sweden except in the far north.

NUMBER OF FISH SPECIES PER REGION

1:10 000 000

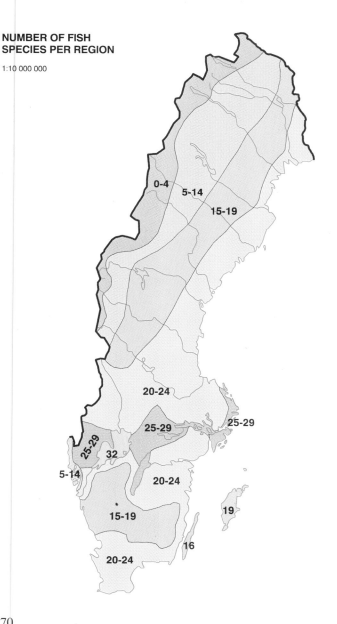

larger in heterogeneous environments than in more homogeneous ones—something that applies as much in mountain districts as in the southern Swedish broad-leaved forests.

Dependence on climate combined with great mobility means that the number of bird species, in contrast to most other groups of organisms, decreases relatively little in Sweden along a north-south gradient. It is in fact only in mountain districts and in the interior of northern Norrland that the number of species is noticeably much lower than in the rest of Sweden. The total number of breeding species is almost identical south and north of the biological Norrland boundary *limes norrlandicus* (203 species all told south of the boundary and 202 north of it).

Amphibians and Reptiles

There are only six species of reptiles in Sweden. Four of these occur throughout the country, or most of it. Only two, the sand lizard and the smooth snake, live in southern Sweden. Reptiles love warmth, so this group does not have many species north of the Mediterranean area.

Among Sweden's 13 amphibians the increase in the number of species towards the south is very noticeable. The reason is that the development of amphibian larvae usually requires a long season. Small frogs also prob-

ably need time to prepare themselves for hibernation.

Fish

The number of species of fish in lakes and watercourses is determined by the species' immigration history, human activities and climatic developments since the Ice Age up to the present day. There is a total of some 150 species of fish in Sweden in seas, lakes and watercourses.

Sweden's fresh water was first colonised by char and thereafter by a number of other species adapted to cold water, mainly salmon type, which spread northward as the ice receded. Later when it was warmer, families like the perches and the roaches immigrated from the south and south-east.

As the temperature rose, most of the salmon-type fish were driven out of the lakes in southern and central Sweden. Populations of char, whitefish and vendace there are relics of colder periods. Similarly, perch and roach are relics of warmer periods in southern mountain regions and sheatfish a relict in Södermanland and Småland.

Human beings have introduced mainly whitefish, pike and perch-pike in new waters—for food and for recreational fishing—which has resulted in the disappearance of less competitive species. Hydro-electric power plants have also reduced the spread of species dependent on running water during some phase of their life, for example salmon, grayling, asp and dace.

Invertebrates

The geographical distribution of the 4,000 or more invertebrates that live in Swedish seas generally speaking corresponds to the salinity of the water. Thus the greatest number of species occur off the coast of Bohuslän, whereas there is a very small number furthest north in the Bothnian Bay.

In general it is true to say that, of Sweden's 30,000 or so terrestrial and freshwater insect species, the number decreases from south to north. For many groups, however, we lack detailed knowledge of their distribution. But it is possible to see relatively reliable patterns for well-studied insect groups like butterflies and beetles, although the numbers in certain mountainous provinces are probably somewhat underestimated.

BEETLE AND BUTTERFLY SPECIES

1:5 000 000

Proportion of total number of Coleoptera
and Lepidoptera species in the country, %

- 70
- 60
- 50
- 40
- 30
- 20

— Province border

Number of species

- 6,000
- 4,000
- 2,000
- 1,000

◄ Butterflies

◄ Beetles

Torne
Lappmark

Lule
Lappmark

Pite
Lappmark

Norrbotten

Luleå

Lycksele
Lappmark

Åsele
Lappmark

Västerbotten

Jämtland

Ångerman-
land

Umeå

Härjedalen

Medelpad

Hälsingland

Dalarna

Gästrikland

Uppland

Värmland

Västman-
land

Dalsland

Närke

Stockholm

...huslän

Söderman-
land

Göteborg

Öster-
götland

Väster-
götland

Småland

Halland

Öland

Skåne

Blekinge

Malmö

Gotland

Three species of predace-
ous diving beetles: *Dytis-
cus dimidiatus* (above),
Colymbetes striatus (left)
and *Ilybius fuliginosus*
(right).

(S122)

PREDACIOUS DIVING BEETLES

1:10 000 000

Number of species
per square (50 x 50 km)

- 100
- 90
- 80
- 70
- 60
- 50
- 40
- 30
- 20
- 10

☐ Peak
value

22

32

43

53

63

74

HOW SHOULD SURVEY RESULTS BE INTERPRETED?

The map shows the number of species
of diving beetles (Coleoptera: Dytisci-
dae and Noteridae) per 50×50 km
square. This material is based on private and museum collections and the
values range from zero to 104. If these
values are adjusted mathematically,
a gradient appears showing a decrease
in the number of species towards the
north and north-west. It is, however,
uncertain whether this is a true trend
or whether it rather shows where the
most intensive collections were made.
Isolated peak values may, however, be
presumed to indicate that there was intensive collecting, so they are relatively
comparable. The number of species
then does seem to decrease towards
the north, i.e. 104 in Skåne, 96 round
Stockholm, 84 along the river Vindel-
älven and 86 at Abisko. But only the
future can prove whether these areas
are especially rich in species or only
well surveyed. (S123, S124)

71

There are some 2,000 species of vascular plants in Sweden (herbs, grasses, sedges, ferns, trees, shrubs). They often produce an impressive show of flowers, as in this meadow at the height of summer.

Vascular plants

There is a total of some 2,000 vascular plants in Sweden. The number of species increases more towards the south within the vascular plant group compared with several other groups such as birds, bryophytes and lichens.

"Atlas of Sweden", 1966, presents the first and so far the only detailed map of the number of vascular plant species quoting about 1,000 in the far south and about 200 in the far north: Of the 360 or so vascular plants which occur in forests about 300 are found in the far south but in the mountain regions only just over 90.

It has long been known that the number of vascular plants is closely related to calcareous soil. Areas with limestone bedrock or lime-rich soils— above all Öland, Gotland, parts of Skåne, Västergötland, Östergötland and Uppland and the areas round Lakes Siljan and Storsjön—have a richer range of vascular plants than regions poor in lime.

Bryophytes, Lichens and Macrofungi

The survey of bryophytes in western Sweden shows that half of Sweden's bryophyte species can be found in an area of about 50 km^2, provided the area is relatively varied and contains a "normal" number of habitats. There is much that indicates that the same is true of lichens and fungi.

Within most groups of species there is firstly a large group of rare species and secondly a smaller group of common and widespread species. Of Sweden's lichens, for example, more than half are known to exist in less than 100 sites in the country. The rare species are often geographically limited, demanding very special environments. The occurrence of such rare species differs therefore if one compares a 50 km^2 area in Gästrikland, for example, with an equally large area in Halland. The second large group, of widespread and common species, is found in virtually every square kilometre of Sweden.

One of Sweden's most common plants is probably the green alga *Trebouxia* sp. This is found in the lichen *Hypogymnia physodes*, which grows on almost every branch of trees in various types of forests throughout the country.

NUMBER OF VASCULAR PLANT SPECIES

1:10 000 000

- 1,000
- 900
- 750
- 500
- 400
- 300
- 200

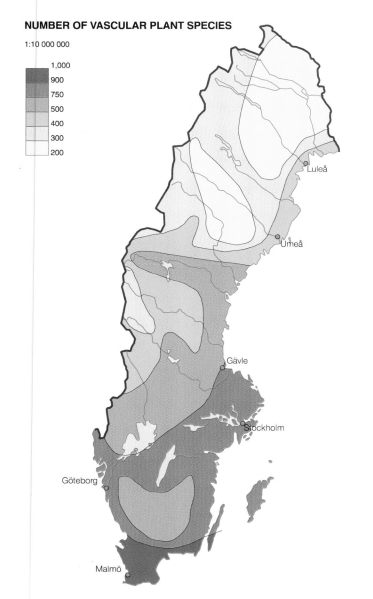

NUMBER OF VASCULAR PLANT SPECIES IN FORESTS

1:20 000 000

- 300
- 275
- 175
- 90

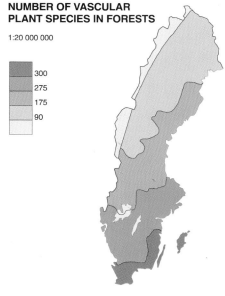

The vascular plants of the forest, like the total number of vascular plants, are considerably more numerous in the south than in the north of Sweden. (S125, S126)

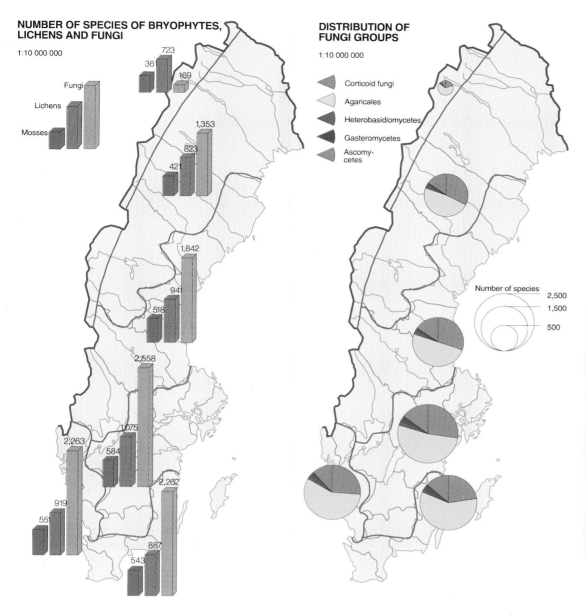

NUMBER OF SPECIES OF BRYOPHYTES, LICHENS AND FUNGI

1:10 000 000

Fungi
Lichens
Mosses

723
361
169
1,353
823
42
1,842
941
518
2,558
1,075
2,263
584
2,262
919
551
887
543

DISTRIBUTION OF FUNGI GROUPS

1:10 000 000

Corticoid fungi
Agaricales
Heterobasidiomycetes
Gasteromycetes
Ascomy-
cetes

Number of species

2,500
1,500
500

The reason why there are relatively many bryophytes in south-west Sweden may be that they flourish in an oceanic climate. Fungi and lichen cope more easily with an inland climate and flourish on calcareous soil, as on Öland and Gotland, for example.

The largest number of species of fungi are in eastern central Sweden. The reason why there are so few fungi in the mountains is that many of them live on or together with trees, so they do not exist above the tree line. (S127, S128)

Mycorrhiza is a form of interaction between fungi and trees. The small roots of trees are surrounded by fungus mycelium which provides these roots with minerals and water, while the fungus gets sugar in exchange. The 800 or so species of mycorrhiza-forming fungi consist mainly of large ground fungi, including the most important edible fungi.

Spruce, pine, beech, oak and birch are important mycorrhiza hosts for macrofungi. Elm, ash and maple lack mycorrhiza. More than half of the mycorrhiza species can live together with several kinds of tree, sometimes both coniferous and deciduous trees.

A very large number of bryophytes, lichens and fungi are adapted to living on trees, both dead and living. Sometimes bryophytes and lichens form a mosaic-like carpet.

SUBSTRATES AND NUMBER OF SPECIES

During the past few years scientists have begun to investigate how many species of bryophytes, lichens and macrofungi are tied to different substrates, that is, the surface—wood or ground—on which the plant or fungus lives. This makes it possible to present figures for the number of species that are tied to different kinds of trees.

Trees. Most bryophytes, lichens and macrofungi are tied to trees. There are species that have specialised in certain kinds of trees, certain parts of trees and certain ages of trees.

Some 700 bryophytes and lichens prefer deciduous trees, while about 550 prefer to grow on coniferous trees. One possible explanation of this difference is that Sweden has about 20 different kinds of deciduous trees but only a few species of coniferous trees. Oak, aspen and ash are the deciduous trees that have the greatest number of species of lichens and bryophytes. Spruce has almost twice as many species as pine.

The relationship between the number of species and area is a very steep curve from zero up to about 10 km², where the number begins to level out.

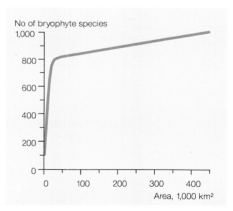

The majority of Sweden's 3,000 or so macrofungi live on trees in symbiosis with them in the form of mycorrhiza. Spruce has most species. Other host trees with many species are pine, beech, oak and birch. Among the fungi there is a group of species—pathogens—that damage and often in the end kill the host tree. This group comprises only a small proportion of all the macrofungi in the forests but are of far greater economic significance for the forest owners.

73

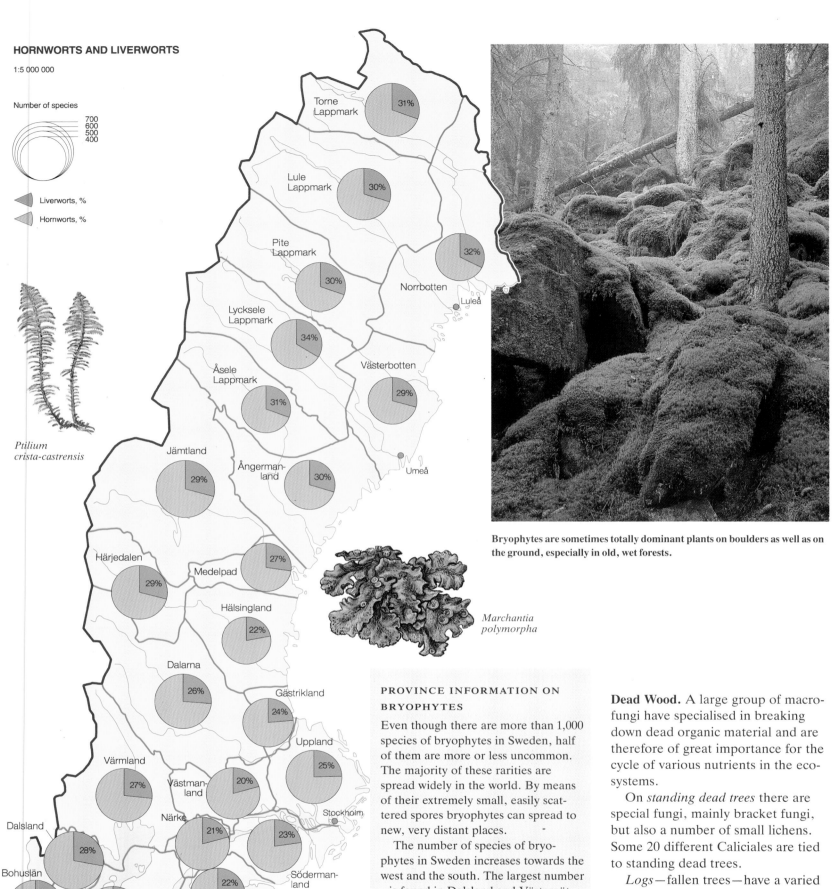

HORNWORTS AND LIVERWORTS

1:5 000 000

Number of species

700
600
500
400

Liverworts, %

Hornworts, %

Ptilium crista-castrensis

Torne Lappmark 31%

Lule Lappmark 30%

Pite Lappmark 30%

Norrbotten 32%

Luleå

Lycksele Lappmark 34%

Åsele Lappmark 31%

Västerbotten 29%

Umeå

Jämtland 29%

Ångermanland 30%

Härjedalen 29%

Medelpad 27%

Hälsingland 22%

Marchantia polymorpha

Dalarna 26%

Gästrikland 24%

Uppland 25%

Värmland 27%

Västmanland 20%

Närke 21%

Södermanland 23%

Stockholm

Dalsland

Bohuslän 28%

24%

25%

Östergötland 22%

Gotland 20%

Göteborg

Västergötland

Småland 24%

Halland 25%

Öland 18%

Skåne 24%

Blekinge 21%

Malmö

Bryophytes are sometimes totally dominant plants on boulders as well as on the ground, especially in old, wet forests.

PROVINCE INFORMATION ON BRYOPHYTES

Even though there are more than 1,000 species of bryophytes in Sweden, half of them are more or less uncommon. The majority of these rarities are spread widely in the world. By means of their extremely small, easily scattered spores bryophytes can spread to new, very distant places.

The number of species of bryophytes in Sweden increases towards the west and the south. The largest number is found in Dalsland and Västergötland, but different groups differ somewhat. *Liverworts*, which altogether make up about a quarter of all Sweden's bryophytes, are particularly common in western Sweden.

The largest group of bryophytes, *mosses*, comprises some 760 species. This group is richest in southern Sweden, especially in Västergötland and Dalsland. The smallest number of species of mosses seems to be in the coastal districts of Norrbotten and Västerbotten, but this may be due to a lack of surveys. (S129)

Dead Wood. A large group of macrofungi have specialised in breaking down dead organic material and are therefore of great importance for the cycle of various nutrients in the ecosystems.

On *standing dead trees* there are special fungi, mainly bracket fungi, but also a number of small lichens. Some 20 different Caliciales are tied to standing dead trees.

Logs—fallen trees—have a varied growth of bryophytes, lichens and fungi that varies according to the size, of the tree, how long it has lain on the ground, whether the wood is very rotted and if it is lying in a dry or a wet spot. Bryophyte growth is often very evident on fallen spruce. Lichens are fewer in number of species and prefer pine. But it is fungi that form the largest number of species on old windthrows; they are found on the underside or inside them. Spruce and pine windthrows have the largest number of species.

Northern Sweden

Southern Sweden

The diagrams show how many species of bryophytes, lichens and fungi grow on various types of tree species in northern and southern Sweden. They also show the distribution of species among living trees, snags and logs.

B = bryophytes, L = lichens, F = fungi. The figures show the number of species of each group in northern/southern Sweden.

SCOTS PINE
Pinus sylvestris

B	0/0
L	51/46
F	5/7

B	0/0
L	23/20
F	29/33

B	6/6
L	12/10
F	132/140

NORWAY SPRUCE
Picea abies

B	0/0
L	106/71
F	5/6

B	0/0
L	20/19
F	35/40

B	15/13
L	13/10
F	187/190

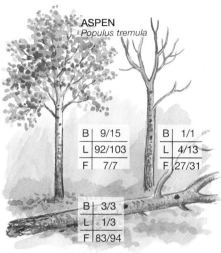

ASPEN
Populus tremula

B	9/15
L	92/103
F	7/7

B	1/1
L	4/13
F	27/31

B	3/3
L	1/3
F	83/94

BIRCH
Betula pendula/
B. pubescens

B	1/1
L	92/71
F	14/15

B	1/1
L	10/19
F	54/60

B	1/1
L	8/5
F	107/121

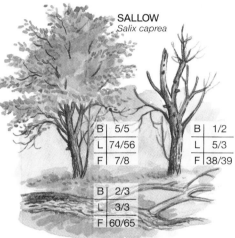

SALLOW
Salix caprea

B	5/5
L	74/56
F	7/8

B	1/2
L	5/3
F	38/39

B	2/3
L	3/3
F	60/65

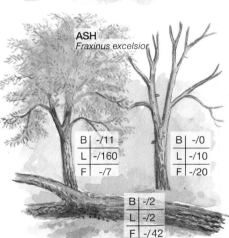

ASH
Fraxinus excelsior

B	-/11
L	-/160
F	-/7

B	-/0
L	-/10
F	-/20

B	-/2
L	-/2
F	-/42

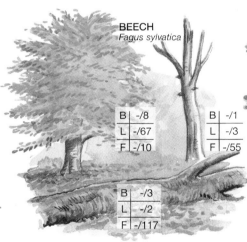

BEECH
Fagus sylvatica

B	-/8
L	-/67
F	-/10

B	-/1
L	-/3
F	-/55

B	-/3
L	-/2
F	-/117

OAK
Quercus robur

B	-/6
L	-/133
F	-/14

B	-/1
L	-/9
F	-/56

B	-/2
L	-/3
F	-/76

	Bryophytes	Lichens
Limestones	200	330
Intermediate bedrock	180	200
Silicates	220	740

Cliffs and Boulders. Since stone is a permanent surface, slow-growing organisms have a chance of developing there in peace and quiet. Bryophytes are predominant on shaded and moist cliffs and boulders, while lichens usually grow on exposed rocks and on boulders lying out in the open. A decisive factor for the appearance of lichens and bryophytes is the chemical composition of the rock, its structure and its hardness. Rocks containing calcareous minerals will have a very different flora.

Ground. A very large number of bryophytes, lichens and fungi grow directly on the ground. On dry, poor soils where seeding plants find it difficult to survive, reindeer lichens manage very well. Mosses predominate in shaded and moist environments. On mountain heaths both lichens and mosses play a very important role as pioneer plants on bare ground and in places which are exposed to wind. At least 100 bryophytes are to be regarded as pioneers on bare ground and will be found where roads meet, on paths and in clearings, but also at places which have been disturbed naturally such as under uprooted stumps in forests and on the banks of lakes and watercourses.

Patterns in Genetic Variation

In the past few decades new molecular-genetic methods, DNA analyses, have been developed and are beginning to be used in both botany and zoology. These very powerful methods make it possible to answer questions concerning the relationship, origin, age and distribution of species in a way that we could only dream about before. It is probable that many previous theories and ideas about our flora and fauna will be revised thanks to these new developments.

DNA ANALYSIS REVEALS VOLES' HANKY-PANKY

The bank vole *Clethrionomys glareolus* is the most common mammal, found all over Sweden from Skåne to Lappland. There was great astonishment when geneticists discovered that there were very great differences between the mitochondria DNA (mt-DNA) of the northern and southern populations—so great that they really should be treated as separate species. The astonishment was no less when it turned out that mt-DNA from the northern voles was almost identical with that of another species, the red vole (northern red-backed vole) *Clethrionomys rutilus*. How could this be? The probable explanation is to be found in events during and just after the last time the inland ice melted.

The red vole, which is only found in the far north of Sweden and to the east, probably came from the north-east directly after the ice had melted in this part of Sweden, about 9,000 years ago. At the same time and from the same direction came bank voles from Finland and the southern Baltic region. It is well known that animals from different species can mate when there is a shortage of partners of one species. It is likely that male bank voles mated with female red vole, resulting in fertile daughters which inherited mt-DNA from their red vole mothers. Bank voles came to Sweden at an early date from the south and followed the melting ice northward. We know that the southern and northern voles eventually met somewhere in the area of Sollefteå, because there is a clear 40–50 km wide transitional zone here; north of it there are only bank voles with red-vole mt DNA and south of it they only have bank-vole mt DNA.

CLOSEST RELATIVES OF HÄRJEDAL BEARS IN FRANCE?

The brown bear *Ursus arctos* is spread through Europe with small, isolated populations in Spain, France and Italy, for example, and larger, continuous occurrences in south-east Europe, Russia, Finland and Sweden. A first genetic analysis of mt-DNA shows that there are two distinct groups, a northern-eastern group and a western-southern group, and that the latter can in turn be divided into two sub-groups. The interpretation is that the two main groups separated a long time ago and that they did not remix because of the inland ice sheets. The group found in the Balkan region, for example, is considered to have been prevented from expanding by the ice that covered the Alps.

The Swedish bear population is clearly divided; the bears in the south in Dalarna–Hälsingland–Härjedalen are most closely related to those in France and Spain, while the more northerly ones are more like those in Finland and Russia. This has been interpreted to mean that bears immigrated to Sweden after the Ice Age from two directions, the south and the north-east. Since female bears are very stationary, this original difference has survived up to the present. Future analyses will show whether these introductory DNA studies have revealed the immigration history of bears.

There is a clear transition zone between the southern and the northern bank vole *Clethrionomys glareolus* near Sollefteå. The northern bank vole has received its mt-DNA from the northern red-backed vole *C. rutilus*, which suggests that hybridisation occurred between the two species, probably during immigration from the north-east after the inland ice had melted. (S130)

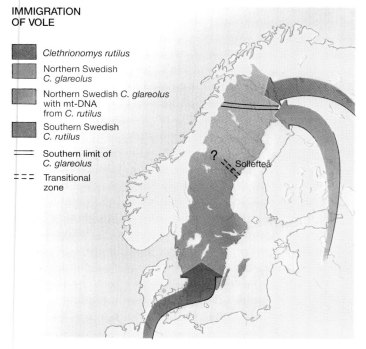

IMMIGRATION OF VOLE

- *Clethrionomys rutilus*
- Northern Swedish *C. glareolus*
- Northern Swedish *C. glareolus* with mt-DNA from *C. rutilus*
- Southern Swedish *C. rutilus*
- Southern limit of *C. glareolus*
- Transitional zone

Bank vole (above) and red vole (below)

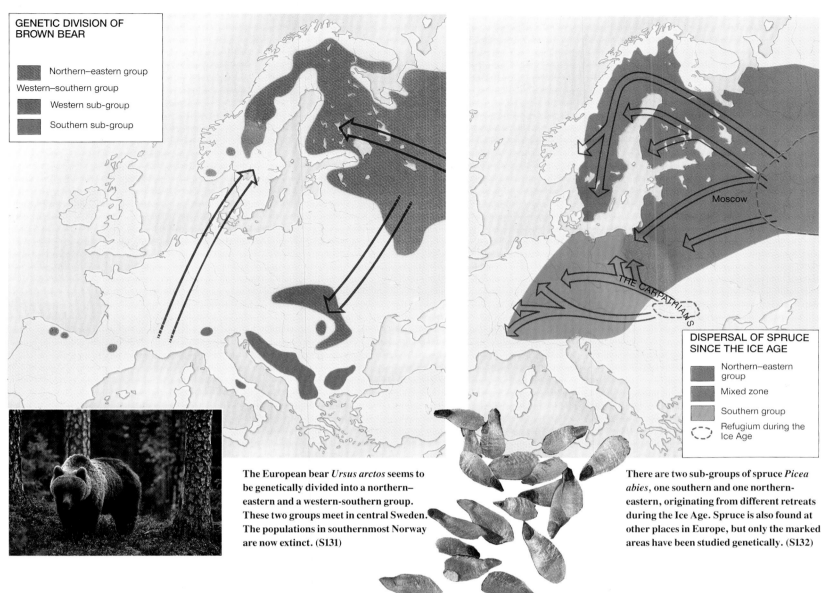

GENETIC DIVISION OF BROWN BEAR

- Northern–eastern group
- Western–southern group
  - Western sub-group
  - Southern sub-group

DISPERSAL OF SPRUCE SINCE THE ICE AGE

- Northern–eastern group
- Mixed zone
- Southern group
- Refugium during the Ice Age

The European bear *Ursus arctos* seems to be genetically divided into a northern–eastern and a western-southern group. These two groups meet in central Sweden. The populations in southernmost Norway are now extinct. (S131)

There are two sub-groups of spruce *Picea abies*, one southern and one northern-eastern, originating from different retreats during the Ice Age. Spruce is also found at other places in Europe, but only the marked areas have been studied genetically. (S132)

Since the scorpion senna *Hippocrepis emerus* requires warm, calcareous habitats, it is considered to have come to Sweden a long time ago, when the climate was more favourable.

EUROPEAN SPRUCES HAVE DIFFERENT ORIGINS

Pollen analysis indicates that spruce in Europe was pushed back during the last Ice Age to two areas in particular: a small area in the Carpathians and a larger area near Moscow. Isozyme analyses of spruce from various parts of Europe show that the genetic variation is fairly high in most of the area. But it is considerably lower in Central Europe, probably because the spruce spread there from the genetically impoverished mountain area to the south. Three genetically related sub-groups may be distinguished: a north-eastern one comprising Russia, Finland and Sweden, a southern one comprising Southern and Central Europe and an intermediate zone in

East Poland. Swedish spruce belong to the north-eastern type, having spread to Sweden from the north-east.

SCORPION SENNA — A RELICT PLANT AND LATE IMMIGRANT

The rare pea plant scorpion senna *Hippocrepis emerus* is found naturally in Sweden only at a few places on Öland and Gotland and at one place in southernmost Norway. These populations are isolated from each other and are also a long way from the main area of distribution in southern Europe.

A genetic analysis of DNA and isozymes revealed that the Öland and Gotland populations are most closely related. The explanation has been sought in their immigration history: perhaps the species came from different places and at different times to Sweden and Norway. One occurrence on a roadside bank in Uppsala proved to have a much higher degree of genetic variation. It probably came with a seed mixture which originated in southern Europe and which was used to sow the bank recently.

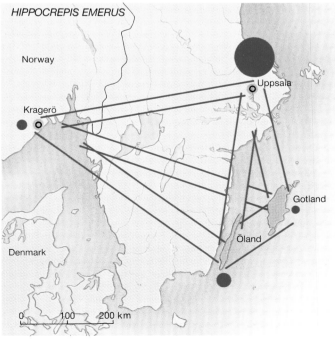

HIPPOCREPIS EMERUS

Norway

Kragerö

Uppsala

Gotland

Öland

Denmark

0   100   200 km

Populations of the scorpion senna *Hippocrepis emerus* on Öland and Gotland show close relationship with each other. The Uppsala population has considerably greater genetic variation. It has been introduced and probably originates from southern Europe.

The lines indicate the degree of similarity between populations. The circles show the amount of genetic variation. (S133)

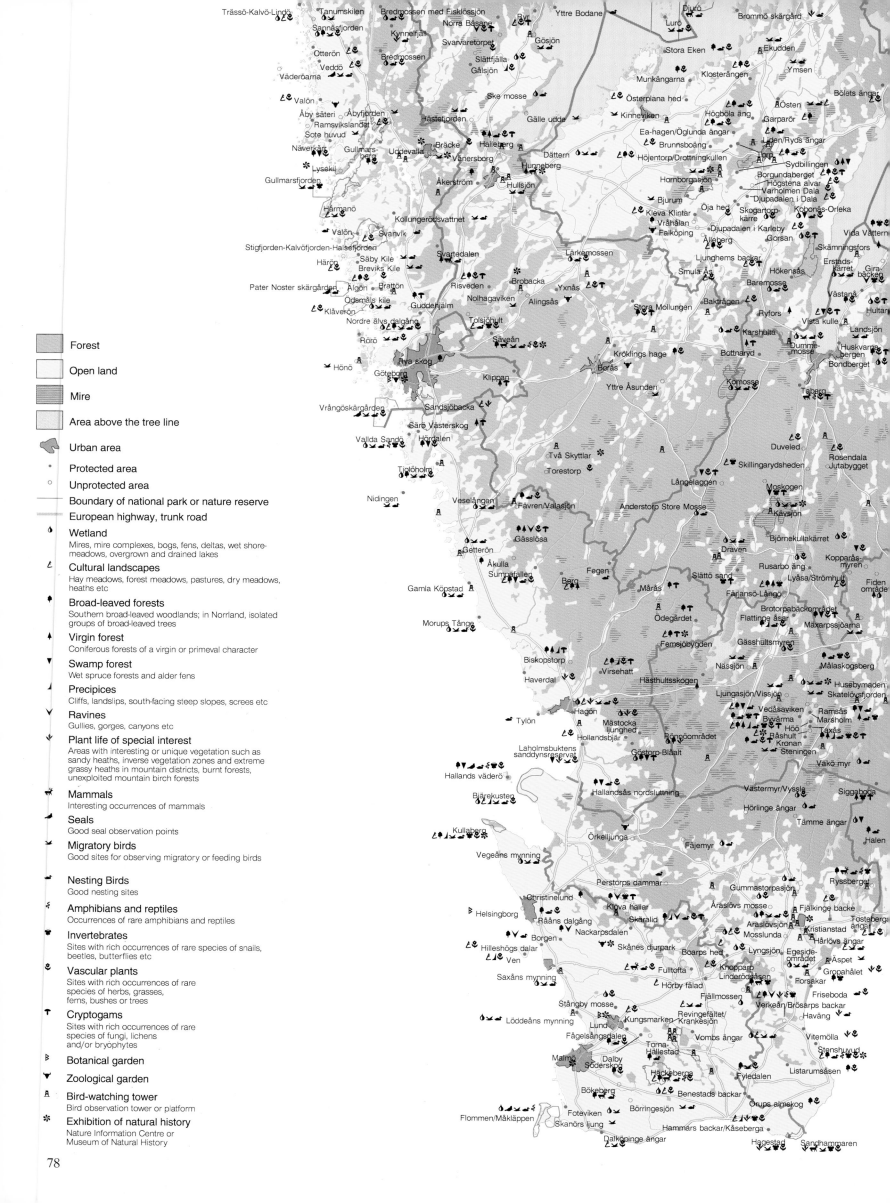

Forest

Open land

Mire

Area above the tree line

Urban area

Protected area

Unprotected area

Boundary of national park or nature reserve

European highway, trunk road

Wetland
Mires, mire complexes, bogs, fens, deltas, wet shore-meadows, overgrown and drained lakes

Cultural landscapes
Hay meadows, forest meadows, pastures, dry meadows, heaths etc

Broad-leaved forests
Southern broad-leaved woodlands; in Norrland, isolated groups of broad-leaved trees

Virgin forest
Coniferous forests of a virgin or primeval character

Swamp forest
Wet spruce forests and alder fens

Precipices
Cliffs, landslips, south-facing steep slopes, screes etc

Ravines
Gullies, gorges, canyons etc

Plant life of special interest
Areas with interesting or unique vegetation such as sandy heaths, inverse vegetation zones and extreme grassy heaths in mountain districts, burnt forests, unexploited mountain birch forests

Mammals
Interesting occurrences of mammals

Seals
Good seal observation points

Migratory birds
Good sites for observing migratory or feeding birds

Nesting Birds
Good nesting sites

Amphibians and reptiles
Occurrences of rare amphibians and reptiles

Invertebrates
Sites with rich occurrences of rare species of snails, beetles, butterflies etc

Vascular plants
Sites with rich occurrences of rare species of herbs, grasses, ferns, bushes or trees

Cryptogams
Sites with rich occurrences of rare species of fungi, lichens and/or bryophytes

Botanical garden

Zoological garden

Bird-watching tower
Bird observation tower or platform

Exhibition of natural history
Nature Information Centre or Museum of Natural History

Places of
Biological Interest

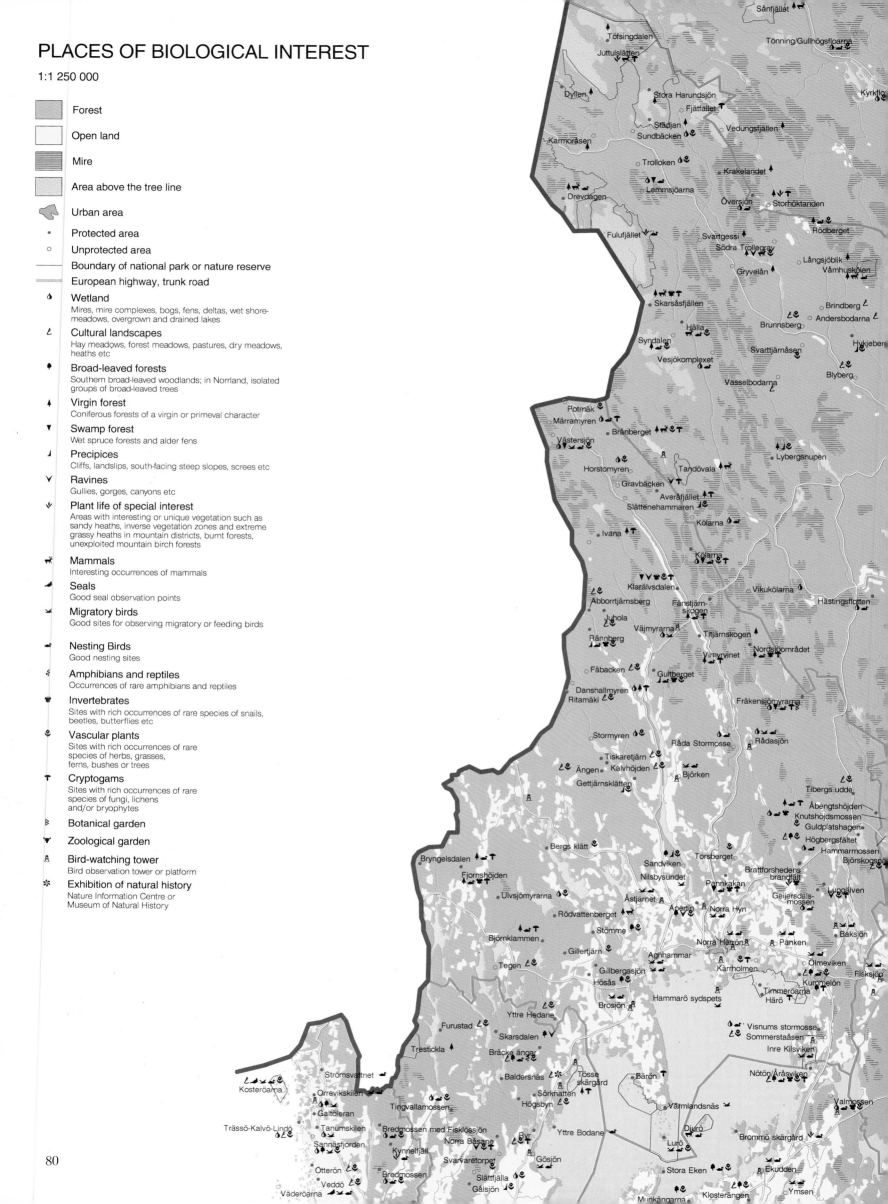

PLACES OF BIOLOGICAL INTEREST

1:1 250 000

Forest	
Open land	
Mire	
Area above the tree line	

Urban area

· **Protected area**

○ **Unprotected area**

— **Boundary of national park or nature reserve**

═ **European highway, trunk road**

◊ **Wetland**
Mires, mire complexes, bogs, fens, deltas, wet shore-meadows, overgrown and drained lakes

∠ **Cultural landscapes**
Hay meadows, forest meadows, pastures, dry meadows, heaths etc

♠ **Broad-leaved forests**
Southern broad-leaved woodlands; in Norrland, isolated groups of broad-leaved trees

▲ **Virgin forest**
Coniferous forests of a virgin or primeval character

▼ **Swamp forest**
Wet spruce forests and alder fens

⊿ **Precipices**
Cliffs, landslips, south-facing steep slopes, screes etc

Y **Ravines**
Gullies, gorges, canyons etc

↯ **Plant life of special interest**
Areas with interesting or unique vegetation such as sandy heaths, inverse vegetation zones and extreme grassy heaths in mountain districts, burnt forests, unexploited mountain birch forests

🦌 **Mammals**
Interesting occurrences of mammals

◢ **Seals**
Good seal observation points

🦅 **Migratory birds**
Good sites for observing migratory or feeding birds

🦆 **Nesting Birds**
Good nesting sites

§ **Amphibians and reptiles**
Occurrences of rare amphibians and reptiles

🦋 **Invertebrates**
Sites with rich occurrences of rare species of snails, beetles, butterflies etc

🌿 **Vascular plants**
Sites with rich occurrences of rare species of herbs, grasses, ferns, bushes or trees

⊤ **Cryptogams**
Sites with rich occurrences of rare species of fungi, lichens and/or bryophytes

⅄ **Botanical garden**

⅄ **Zoological garden**

🄰 **Bird-watching tower**
Bird observation tower or platform

❋ **Exhibition of natural history**
Nature Information Centre or Museum of Natural History

PLACES OF BIOLOGICAL INTEREST

1:1 250 000

Forest

Open land

Mire

Area above the tree line

Urban area

· Protected area

○ Unprotected area

— Boundary of national park or nature reserve

═ European highway, trunk road

Wetland
Mires, mire complexes, bogs, fens, deltas, wet shore-meadows, overgrown and drained lakes

Cultural landscapes
Hay meadows, forest meadows, pastures, dry meadows, heaths etc

Broad-leaved forests
Southern broad-leaved woodlands; in Norrland, isolated groups of broad-leaved trees

Virgin forest
Coniferous forests of a virgin or primeval character

Swamp forest
Wet spruce forests and alder fens

Precipices
Cliffs, landslips, south-facing steep slopes, screes etc

Ravines
Gullies, gorges, canyons etc

Plant life of special interest
Areas with interesting or unique vegetation such as sandy heaths, inverse vegetation zones and extreme grassy heaths in mountain districts, burnt forests, unexploited mountain birch forests

Mammals
Interesting occurrences of mammals

Seals
Good seal observation points

Migratory birds
Good sites for observing migratory or feeding birds

Nesting Birds
Good nesting sites

Amphibians and reptiles
Occurrences of rare amphibians and reptiles

Invertebrates
Sites with rich occurrences of rare species of snails, beetles, butterflies etc

Vascular plants
Sites with rich occurrences of rare species of herbs, grasses, ferns, bushes or trees

Cryptogams
Sites with rich occurrences of rare species of fungi, lichens and/or bryophytes

Botanical garden

Zoological garden

Bird-watching tower
Bird observation tower or platform

Exhibition of natural history
Nature Information Centre or Museum of Natural History

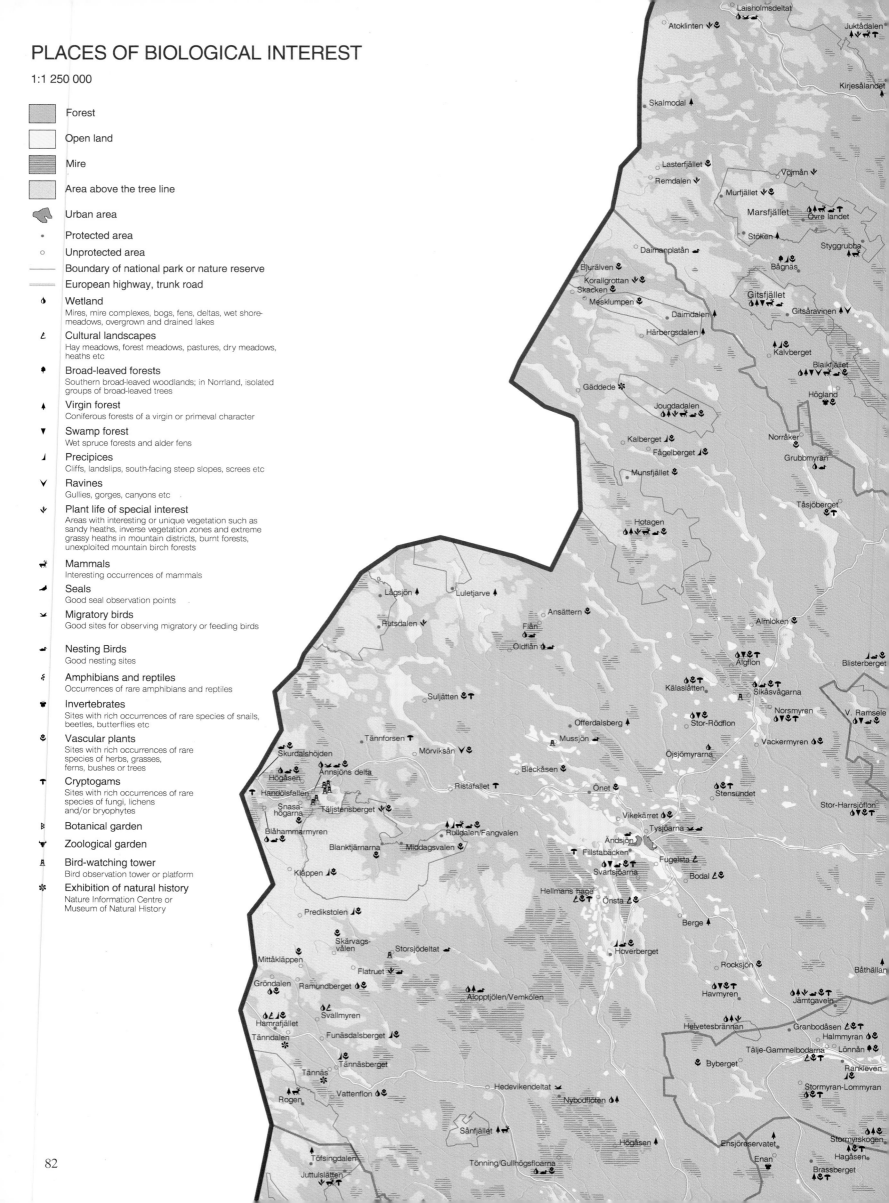

Matsorliden
Nalovardo
Nakteberget
Gammelstadsviken
Lamburträsk
Porsnäsfjärden
Skvalpen
Brännliden
Kartudalen
Blaiken
Degerforsheden
Kyrkberget
Fågelmyrkölen
Skikkisjöberget
Vithattsmyrarna
Brännberget
Kvarnklodden
Svansele
Ostträsket
Lycksamyran
Kryddgrovan
Storåliden
Kalkstenstjärn
Buberget
Innerviksfjärdarna
Altarliden
Nästansjömyrarna
Vitbergen
Fetsjön
Sikmyran
Jättungsmyran
Alsberget
Lycksele
Bjuröklubb
Arasjö
Storbacken
Tuggensele
Gäddsjömyran
Gärdefjärden
Botsmarksträsket
Hertsånger
Vallsjöskogen
Degerö-Stormyr
Åströmforsen
Eldsjö-Flakamyran
Orrböle
Rataskär
Stenbithöjden
Balberget
Björnlandet
Brånsjön
Stockholmsgata
Umeå
Skeppsviksskärgården
Lillsjöslåttern
Ängsbacka
Stora Tuvan
Vändåtberget
Herrbergsliden
Holmöarna
Bågaliden
Långrumpskogen
Junsele
Kålhuvudet
Torsmyran
Tågsjöbrännan
Snöanskärgården
Storsandskäret
Järnäs-udden
Bonden
Kronoören
Gideåbergsmyrarna
Öfjärden
Idbyfjärden
Prästflon
Helgumsjöns delta
Balesudden
Gränkälen
Trysunda
Billtjärn
Svartnäsudden
Hästråberget
Skuleskogen
Döraberget
Skuleberget
Villmyran
Omneberget
Gnäggen
Vällingsjö
Halsviksravinen
Rigåsen
Ringkallen
Barstaön
Sursundet/Norasundet
Rotsidan
Valletjärnarna
Bråtan
Svedjan
Vättaberget
Västanåfallet
Kärringberget
Fåren
Sundsjöåsen
Indalsälvens delta
Långharsholmen
Smedsgården
Stornäset
Selångerssjön
Sundsvall
Måckelmyran
Klövberget
Skrängstasjön
Mingen
Korpåsen
Brämön
Malungsfluggen
Björkökusten

83

PLACES OF BIOLOGICAL INTEREST

1:1 250 000

Forest

Open land

Mire

Area above the tree line

 Urban area

• Protected area

○ Unprotected area

——— Boundary of national park or nature reserve

═══ European highway, trunk road

◊ **Wetland**
Mires, mire complexes, bogs, fens, deltas, wet shore-meadows, overgrown and drained lakes

ᴌ **Cultural landscapes**
Hay meadows, forest meadows, pastures, dry meadows, heaths etc

♠ **Broad-leaved forests**
Southern broad-leaved woodlands; in Norrland, isolated groups of broad-leaved trees

▲ **Virgin forest**
Coniferous forests of a virgin or primeval character

▼ **Swamp forest**
Wet spruce forests and alder fens

⌐ **Precipices**
Cliffs, landslips, south-facing steep slopes, screes etc

∨ **Ravines**
Gullies, gorges, canyons etc

↓ **Plant life of special interest**
Areas with interesting or unique vegetation such as sandy heaths, inverse vegetation zones and extreme grassy heaths in mountain districts, burnt forests, unexploited mountain birch forests

🦌 **Mammals**
Interesting occurrences of mammals

◢ **Seals**
Good seal observation points

↙ **Migratory birds**
Good sites for observing migratory or feeding birds

↩ **Nesting Birds**
Good nesting sites

ξ **Amphibians and reptiles**
Occurrences of rare amphibians and reptiles

✷ **Invertebrates**
Sites with rich occurrences of rare species of snails, beetles, butterflies etc

❧ **Vascular plants**
Sites with rich occurrences of rare species of herbs, grasses, ferns, bushes or trees

⊤ **Cryptogams**
Sites with rich occurrences of rare species of fungi, lichens and/or bryophytes

ß **Botanical garden**

⏛ **Zoological garden**

Ä **Bird-watching tower**
Bird observation tower or platform

❅ **Exhibition of natural history**
Nature Information Centre or Museum of Natural History

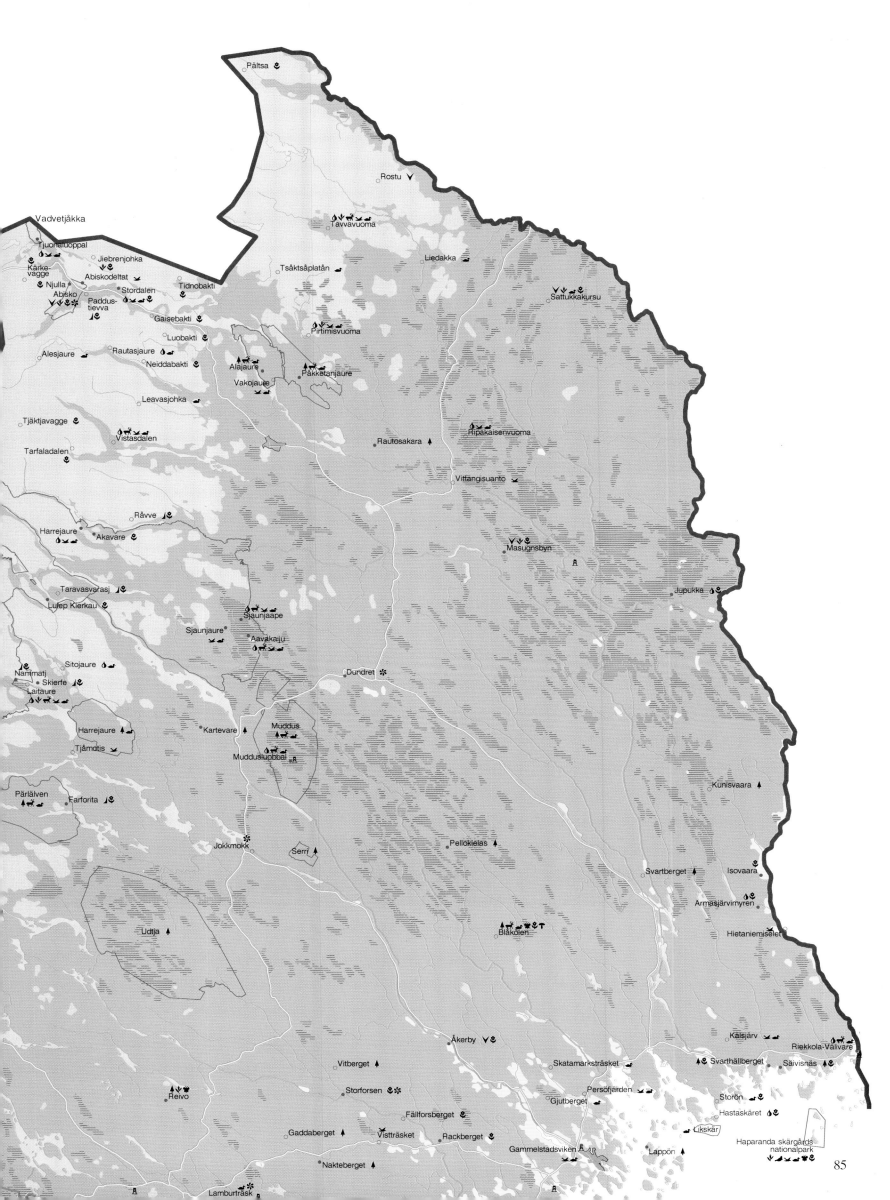

Pältsa

Rostu

Tavvavuoma

Liedakka

Tsåktsåplatån

Sattukkakursu

Vadvetjåkka

Tjuonatjoppal

Jiebrenjohka

Kärke-
vagge

Abiskodeltat

Njulla

Tidnobakti

Abisko

Stordalen

Paddus-
tievva

Gaisebakti

Pirtimisvuoma

Luobakti

Alesjaure

Rautasjaure

Neiddabakti

Alajaure

Påkketanjaure

Vakojaure

Leavasjohka

Tjäktjavagge

Rautosakara

Ripakaisenvuoma

Vistasdalen

Tarfaladalen

Vittangisuanto

Råvve

Harrejaure

Akavare

Masugnsbyn

Taravasvarasj

Jupukka

Lulep Kierkau

Sjaunjaape

Sjaunjaure

Aavakaiju

Sitojaure

Nammatj

Dundret

Skierfe

Laitaure

Harrejaure

Kartevare

Muddus

Tjåmotis

Muddusluobbal

Kunisvaara

Pärlälven

Farforita

Jokkmokk

Pellokielas

Serri

Svartberget

Isovaara

Armasjärvimyren

Udtja

Hietaniemiselet

Blåkölen

Åkerby

Käisjärv

Riekkola-Välivare

Vitberget

Skatamarksträsket

Svarthällberget

Säivisnäs

Persöfjärden

Storön

Reivo

Storforsen

Gjutberget

Hastaskäret

Fällforsberget

Likskär

Gaddaberget

Vistträsket

Rackberget

Haparanda skärgårds
nationalpark

Gammelstadsviken

Lappön

Nakteberget

85

Lamburträsk

Changes in Flora and Fauna

Nature is dynamic. In prehistoric times most changes took place slowly, in step with changes in the climate—apart from dramatic events like volcanic eruptions and earthquakes. Today it is without any doubt we humans that cause the greatest changes, and at a speed never before imagined.

The transformation of virgin natural forests into a cultivated landscape began slowly with the first farmers during the Stone Age, and culminated in the intensive cultivation of the 19th century. Since then technology has given us yet more power to transform nature.

Forestry, agriculture, air pollution and *urbanisation* are the four most important factors that have affected animal and plant life in modern Sweden. These activities nearly always lead to a uniform landscape in which the mix of species is altered and its diversity is reduced. But we can perhaps see some light in the darkness; a new way of thinking is developing in which environmental considerations are expected, as a matter of course, to influence all types of land use. Natural values should not simply be isolated in reserves but be seen everywhere. Species and biotopes should be taken into consideration whenever tree felling, crop cultivation, road building and town planning are being discussed. Perhaps large-scale and brutal methods will gradually be replaced by multiple use and variation?

Flora and fauna are affected by land use. Biodiversity is most impoverished by large-scale, standardised methods in silviculture and agriculture—and of course by air pollution and increasing urbanisation.

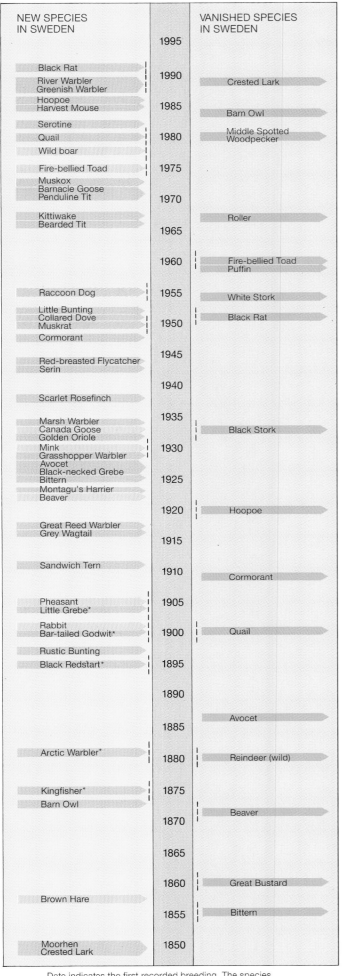

NEW SPECIES IN SWEDEN / Year / VANISHED SPECIES IN SWEDEN

New species in Sweden	Year	Vanished species in Sweden
	1995	
Black Rat	1990	Crested Lark
River Warbler / Greenish Warbler	1990	
Hoopoe / Harvest Mouse	1985	Barn Owl
Serotine		Middle Spotted Woodpecker
Quail	1980	
Wild boar		
Fire-bellied Toad	1975	
Muskox / Barnacle Goose / Penduline Tit	1970	
Kittiwake / Bearded Tit	1965	Roller
	1960	Fire-bellied Toad / Puffin
Raccoon Dog	1955	White Stork
Little Bunting / Collared Dove / Muskrat	1950	Black Rat
Cormorant		
Red-breasted Flycatcher / Serin	1945	
	1940	
Scarlet Rosefinch	1935	Black Stork
Marsh Warbler / Canada Goose / Golden Oriole		
Mink / Grasshopper Warbler	1930	
Avocet / Black-necked Grebe / Bittern	1925	
Montagu's Harrier / Beaver	1920	Hoopoe
Great Reed Warbler / Grey Wagtail	1915	
Sandwich Tern	1910	Cormorant
Pheasant / Little Grebe*	1905	
Rabbit / Bar-tailed Godwit*	1900	Quail
Rustic Bunting	1895	
Black Redstart*		
	1890	
	1885	Avocet
Arctic Warbler*	1880	Reindeer (wild)
Kingfisher*	1875	
Barn Owl	1870	Beaver
	1865	
	1860	Great Bustard
Brown Hare	1855	Bittern
Moorhen / Crested Lark	1850	

* Date indicates the first recorded breeding. The species probably existed in Sweden earlier

Date uncertain

Spontaneous immigration

Introduced

Introduced to a neighbouring country, later an immigrant

SPECIES VANISH — OTHERS IMMIGRATE

Many species in Sweden increase or decrease in number, at least during certain periods, which also leads to new distribution areas. Now and again new species immigrate while others vanish. Those that vanish usually require specialised living conditions and cannot maintain their populations when their biotopes shrink. Such developments are usually identical in other parts of Europe.

The new species are, in many cases, those that have extended their distribution areas as new biotopes are created or altered. In the last hundred it is above all years the growth of weeds and scrub—both on land and in water—that has made it possible for new species to establish themselves in Sweden. Thanks to their mobility birds can find these new or altered environments more quickly than other organisms. This is clearly illustrated by the list of species that have immigrated spontaneously. Greater protection from hunting and shooting, both in Sweden and along the birds' migration routes, has resulted in many species increasing greatly in population and geographical expansion. Human beings have also actively introduced several species, further adding to the fauna.

SPREAD OF THE HAZEL HEN

1:20 000 000

1900
1990

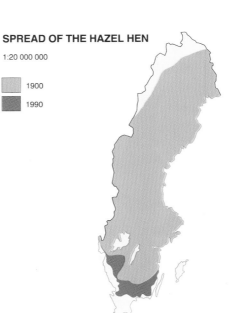

Changes in Bird Life

The number of Swedish bird species has remained amazingly stable ever since most species immigrated at the end of the last Ice Age about 10,000 years ago. Almost all the species that existed in Sweden then are still present. Not until the last few thousand years has mankind caused large changes, the most extensive of which are in forestry and agriculture.

We are unable to study in detail changes in the fauna before written documents began to occur in the 18th century, although sub-fossil records (non-fossilised remains, mainly bones) give some information about prehistoric distribution.

FORESTRY

The southern and central Swedish forests were greatly affected by human activities as early as 200–300 years ago; nevertheless, the differences compared with forests today are very great. The forests were also used for grazing, which, in combination with unsystematic felling, created a light, open and varied forest containing trees of different ages. Similarly fire used to have a considerable effect on forests, as a result of both spontaneous forest fires and slash-and-burn cultivation. Close to towns and in particular near mines and ironworks there was often a severe shortage of wood. Large areas in the interior of Norrland, however, were virtually unaffected by human activities until the rivers were exploited for floating and large-scale felling began in the mid-19th century.

Modern forestry methods have led

The musk ox *Ovibos moschatus* **was part of the European fauna during the Ice Age. There are no Swedish records dating from the postglacial period. Almost 50 years ago musk oxen were introduced at Dovre in Norway and in 1971 a group of five of them emigrated to Härjedalen, where they established a small population.**

The expansion of the hazel-hen *Bonasa bonasia* **into southern Sweden is probably due to increasing numbers of spruce plantations, but less hunting may also be an explanation. (S135)**

to denser and more uniform forests. The proportion of old forest is small and really full-grown forest is often completely absent. Draining has reduced the area of swamp forest and bogs enormously.

But the changes in the forests have not been entirely negative; measured in number of birds per hectare the fauna is probably greater today than a hundred years ago. Species like willow warbler, robin and chaffinch seem to have increased considerably in number since the beginning of the 20th century. In contrast birds which require old, full-grown forest, swamp forest or old deciduous forest containing a large number of dead trees for example capercaillie, lesser woodpecker and white-backed woodpecker have suffered badly. A lack of trees strong enough to nest in is a serious problem for, for example, golden eagles and white-tailed eagles. There are many instances of eagles' nests collapsing when they were built in trees that were not sturdy enough. Even species that prefer open forests with clearings such as nightjar and woodlark have decreased. Some species have, however, been able to compensate for this to some extent by using clear-cut areas instead.

To sum up, changes in the forests have mainly benefited a number of small birds, while larger and less common species have as a rule suffered.

AGRICULTURE

Sweden's 18th-century cultivated landscape was above all a landscape of pastures, heaths, meadows providing hay and leaf fodder, grazed forests and mown wetlands. This landscape favoured several species of birds that are now extinct or very rare in Sweden, such as the great bustard, roller, hoopoe and middle spotted woodpecker.

Land reform and new farming methods made great changes in the agricultural landscape in the first half of the 19th century. Wetlands were drained and meadows became fields or pastures; the area of ploughed land increased greatly.

Not all bird species suffered as a result of these developments; on the contrary, some species benefited. The lapwing, for example, seems to have been a fairly rare species up until the early 19th century, and the rook, which used to be found only in Skåne and on Öland and Gotland, spread during the second half of the century to the plains of Halland, Västergötland, Östergötland and Uppland.

Since 1945 the cultural landscape has changed radically. Pastures and grazing grounds have largely disappeared and fields have become much larger. The edge zones, which are of great importance for rich animal and plant life — road verges with meadow-like vegetation, borders of fields, stone walls and the like — have de-

Dunnock

White-backed woodpecker

The wood lark *Lullula arborea*, which has decreased greatly, used to be found in poor fields and half-open, grazed forests. To some extent forest clearings provide an alternative biotope.

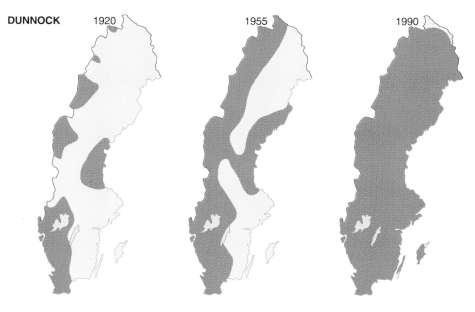

DUNNOCK   1920   1955   1990

The dunnock *Prunella modularis* began to expand about 1930 and 25 years later its distribution areas had merged. Dunnocks are typical "bush-creepers", often seen in young spruce plantations; they have benefited greatly from the expansion of shrubs in the landscape. (S136)

The white-backed woodpecker *Dendrocopos leucotos* needs forests with large numbers of old and dying deciduous trees. Its decrease is probably completely due to the obliteration of its habitat by modern forestry methods. (S137)

WHITE-BACKED WOODPECKER   1850   1950   1990

creased enormously. Wooded "islands" in fields have been removed and ponds drained or filled in. The intensive use of pesticicdes and herbicides has killed off many insects and weeds in the fields. From a biological point of view the result is an extremely poor landscape—a "cultivated desert"— and almost all species of birds in the agricultural landscape have decreased in the past few decades. Even hardy, common species like the wheatear and the house sparrow have become noticeably less common. The only bird species that have benefited from the changes are a few "undergrowth" species like the thrush nightingale, grasshopper warbler, marsh warbler and scarlet rosefinch, which at least temporarily flourish in bushes and/or high and dense herb vegetation on overgrown cultivated land.

The curlew *Numenius arquata* has become increasingly rare in southern and central Sweden's agricultural districts. Its decrease is at least partly due to less grazing of shore meadows and the conversion of old meadows and pastures for other agricultural use or for forestry.

The grasshopper warbler *Locustella naevia* was first observed in Sweden in 1913, and it probably bred for the first time in 1929. During the 1980's this species spread over much of southern Sweden. (S138)

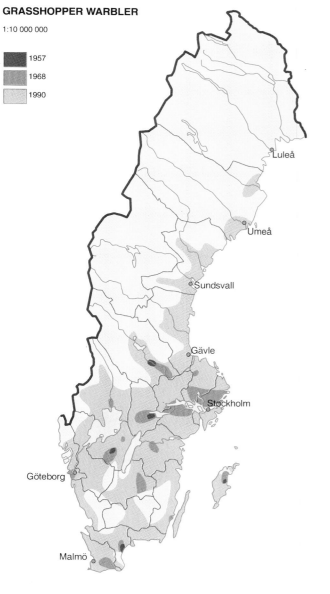

GRASSHOPPER WARBLER

1:10 000 000

- 1957
- 1968
- 1990

Grasshopper warbler

The roller has decreased greatly in parts of western and central Europe.

The distribution of the middle spotted woodpecker *Dendrocopos medius* used to be less well known than that of the roller *Coracias garrulus*, but the two species seem to have had similar distributions in Sweden during the 19th century. The middle spotted woodpecker, however, is restricted to oak groves, while the roller accepts other types of open terrain with scattered trees. The roller disappeared as a breeding bird on the mainland in 1943. It last bred on Fårö in 1967. The last middle-spotted woodpecker vanished from Östergötland in 1982. (S139, S140)

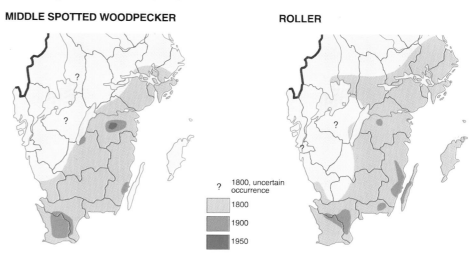

MIDDLE SPOTTED WOODPECKER   ROLLER

- ? 1800, uncertain occurrence
- 1800
- 1900
- 1950

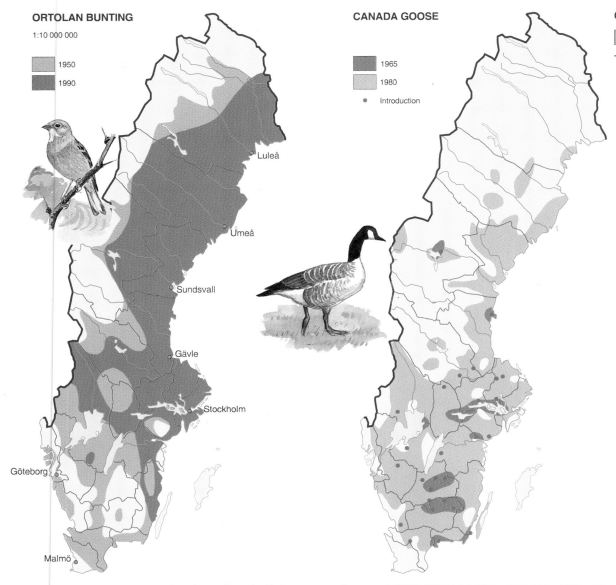

ORTOLAN BUNTING

1:10 000 000

- 1950
- 1990

Luleå

Umeå

Sundsvall

Gävle

Stockholm

Göteborg

Malmö

CANADA GOOSE

- 1965
- 1980
- Introduction

CORN BUNTING

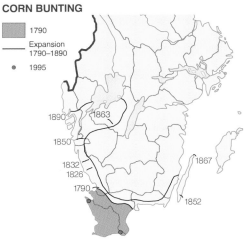

- 1790
- Expansion 1790–1890
- 1995

1890 · 1863
1850
1832
1826
1790
1867
1852

The corn bunting *Miliaria calandra* began to decrease already before the end of the 19th century and is now almost extinct in Sweden; only two very small relict populations remain in north-west and south-east Skåne. (S143)

TOXIC POLLUTANTS

During the 1950s and 1960s much of the bird life of southern and central Sweden's agricultural districts was obliterated by the organic mercury compounds that were used to treat seed. Species like the kestrel, rook, ortolan bunting, yellowhammer and corn bunting were almost completely exterminated. The effects of DDT were even more widespread. The peregrine falcon became almost extinct in Sweden and most of the white-tailed eagles along the east coast became sterile.

INTRODUCTION OF NEW SPECIES

Human beings have also affected bird life directly by introducing new species. The birds which have managed to establish themselves permanently in Sweden are, however, limited to three species: the Canada goose, the pheasant and the domestic pigeon. Of these it is really only the Canada goose that may be said to have established a breeding population that is independent of human beings.

The ortolan bunting *Emberiza hortulana* suffered badly from the use of pesticides in the 1960s. Since DDT and mercury-based pesticides have been forbidden it has recovered slightly, but it has never returned to the arable districts of southern Sweden, where the environment now is probably far too impoverished. (S141)

Above right. The Canda goose *Branta canadensis* was introduced into Sweden about 1930 at the south of Kalmarsund, but as late as 1965 it had a very limited distribution. During the 1970s it increased rapidly and by 1980 it had an almost continuous distribution area. (S142)

Right. Toxic substances like DDT and PCB reduced the hatchability of white-tailed eagles' eggs by 80%.

By the mid-19th century the white-tailed eagle *Haliaeetus albicilla* had already been decimated by hunting. This decline continued until about 1950, after which there was a slight recovery. But this was interrupted sharply when white-tailed eagles were dealt an almost fatal blow by toxic pesticides, in particular DDT. About 1970 the species was at its lowest ebb and most of those along the east coast had become sterile, but during the past decade they have begun to recover. Their distribution in Lappland is more or less unchanged, but the population in southern Sweden is expanding slowly and has begun to return to inland sites in eastern Götaland and Svealand.

WHITE-TAILED EAGLE

1:20 000 000

- + Sub-fossil records
- ? Uncertain occurrence
- Occasional new colonisation

1850   1970   1990

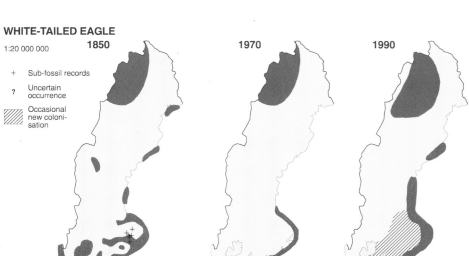

(S144)

In the territorial battles between the species it is usually the whooper swan that wins and it is possible that the mute swan (above) will gradually be forced away from parts of its distribution area.

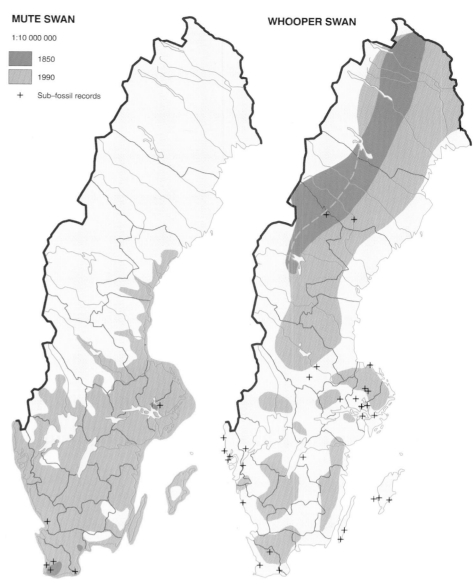

MUTE SWAN

1:10 000 000

▨ 1850

▨ 1990

+ Sub–fossil records

WHOOPER SWAN

Sub-fossil records show that the whooper swan *Cygnus cygnus* was fairly common, while the mute swan *Cygnus olor* was uncommon in prehistoric times. In the mid-19th century whooper swans had decreased greatly due to hunting. At present the two swans' distribution areas overlap in much of southern and central Sweden. (S145, S146)

HUNTING

Hunting has for a very long time affected Swedish animal life. Several mammals have been exterminated by over-hunting and many bird species have had their natural distribution and numbers greatly reduced for the same reason. Concerning birds, there are two groups in particular that have suffered: large birds that can be eaten, like geese and swans, and birds of prey, which have been considered competitors by hunters.

In the olden days whooper swans were probably found all over Sweden, as indicated by sub-fossil records and place names. By the mid-19th century ruthless hunting had reduced the species to a few pairs in the interior of Norrland; there was no recovery until after 1950, probably because the hunting laws were not very well observed in the Norrland breeding grounds.

The few sub-fossil records of mute swans indicate that this species was rather uncommon in prehistoric times. Around 1850 it began to expand, a process which accelerated after 1900 when it was in principle no longer hunted. By 1950 the mute swan

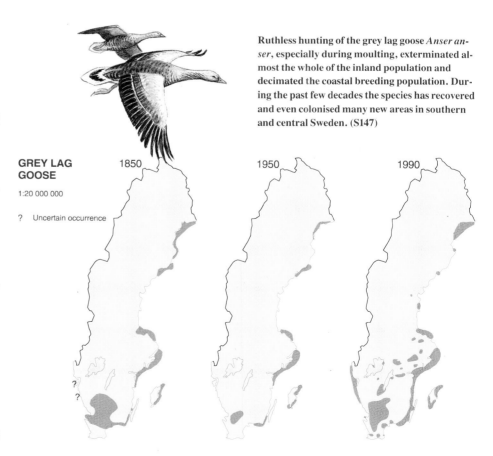

GREY LAG GOOSE

1:20 000 000

? Uncertain occurrence

1850 1950 1990

Ruthless hunting of the grey lag goose *Anser anser*, especially during moulting, exterminated almost the whole of the inland population and decimated the coastal breeding population. During the past few decades the species has recovered and even colonised many new areas in southern and central Sweden. (S147)

91

The number of cormorants *Phalacrocorax carbo* increased dramatically in the 1980's. There has certainly been some immigration from the other Baltic countries. Eutrophication of the Baltic may also have played a part, since it led to increased biological production in shallow water, resulting in more "coarse fish" and better feeding conditions for cormorants. (S148)

had colonised more or less the whole of Götaland and Svealand and parts of the coast of Norrland.

Among the birds of prey it is mainly the larger species like eagles, ospreys and harriers that have suffered. Although all birds of prey have suffered from persecution, the smaller species are less vulnerable since they are more difficult to locate and they breed more rapidly.

UNKNOWN CAUSE

In many cases the causes of changes in the fauna are unknown and we can only speculate as to the underlying factors. One example is the cormorant, which, judging by sub-fossil records, was widespread in southern and central Sweden in earlier times but was exterminated round the turn of the last century. It re-established itself at the end of the 1940s in Kalmarsund, increasing slowly at first, but in recent years the population has exploded. The reason for this explosion is not clear.

DISTRIBUTION OF THE CORMORANT

1:10 000 000

Number of nests

● 1,000–
● 100–1,000
· 1–100
◎ New colony

1980

1988

1994

Luleå

Umeå

Sundsvall

Gävle

Stockholm

1990

1992

Göteborg

Malmö

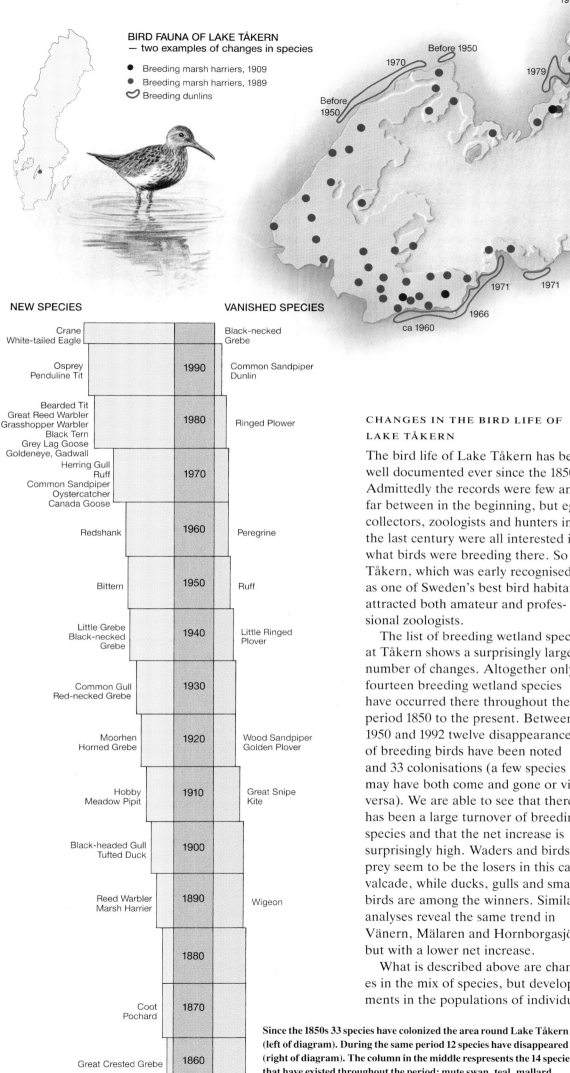

BIRD FAUNA OF LAKE TÅKERN
— two examples of changes in species

● Breeding marsh harriers, 1909
● Breeding marsh harriers, 1989
◡ Breeding dunlins

1979
1967
Before 1950
1970
1979
Before 1950
1985
1981
1965   0   1000 m
1971   1971
ca 1960   1966

NEW SPECIES		VANISHED SPECIES
Crane White-tailed Eagle		Black-necked Grebe
Osprey Penduline Tit	1990	Common Sandpiper Dunlin
Bearded Tit Great Reed Warbler Grasshopper Warbler Black Tern Grey Lag Goose Goldeneye, Gadwall	1980	Ringed Plover
Herring Gull Ruff Common Sandpiper Oystercatcher Canada Goose	1970	
Redshank	1960	Peregrine
Bittern	1950	Ruff
Little Grebe Black-necked Grebe	1940	Little Ringed Plover
Common Gull Red-necked Grebe	1930	
Moorhen Horned Grebe	1920	Wood Sandpiper Golden Plover
Hobby Meadow Pipit	1910	Great Snipe Kite
Black-headed Gull Tufted Duck	1900	
Reed Warbler Marsh Harrier	1890	Wigeon
	1880	
Coot Pochard	1870	
Great Crested Grebe	1860	
	1850	

Since the 1850s 33 species have colonized the area round Lake Tåkern (left of diagram). During the same period 12 species have disappeared (right of diagram). The column in the middle respresents the 14 species that have existed throughout the period: mute swan, teal, mallard, garganey, shoveler, water rail, spotted crake, lapwing, snipe, curlew, common tern, yellow wagtail, sedge warbler and reed bunting.

CHANGES IN THE BIRD LIFE OF LAKE TÅKERN

The bird life of Lake Tåkern has been well documented ever since the 1850s. Admittedly the records were few and far between in the beginning, but egg collectors, zoologists and hunters in the last century were all interested in what birds were breeding there. So Tåkern, which was early recognised as one of Sweden's best bird habitats, attracted both amateur and professional zoologists.

The list of breeding wetland species at Tåkern shows a surprisingly large number of changes. Altogether only fourteen breeding wetland species have occurred there throughout the period 1850 to the present. Between 1950 and 1992 twelve disappearances of breeding birds have been noted and 33 colonisations (a few species may have both come and gone or vice versa). We are able to see that there has been a large turnover of breeding species and that the net increase is surprisingly high. Waders and birds of prey seem to be the losers in this cavalcade, while ducks, gulls and small birds are among the winners. Similar analyses reveal the same trend in Vänern, Mälaren and Hornborgasjön, but with a lower net increase.

What is described above are changes in the mix of species, but developments in the populations of individual

The decline of the dunlin *Calidris alpina* is due to the disappearance of grazed shore meadows. The map shows the areas round Tåkern where dunlin bred at the beginning of the century and the years when they last bred at each place. They last bred here in 1981, and the species has declined in other parts of Sweden as well.

The marsh harrier *Circus aeruginosus* was very close to extinction in Sweden at the turn of the century. Tåkern was one of the few places where it bred at that time. Since it was declared a protected species in 1919 it has increased, at first slowly but later more rapidly, both at Tåkern and elsewhere. The population at Tåkern stabilised around 1975 at 40–50 pairs, probably the largest number that the 10 km² or so of reedbeds can stand.

species are very varied. Two species which have occurred all the time but diminished in number are the mallard and the common snipe. Some colonisers have become very numerous, the greylag goose and the bearded tit, for example, while only a few pairs of others like the osprey and the redshank remain.

The changes in the biotopes at Tåkern partly explain the changes in the lake's bird life. The area of reed grew after the level of the lake was lowered in 1844 and the drought years of the 1930s, which favoured reed-loving species in general. On the other hand the reed harvest, both in summer and winter, was extensive until the 1940s, which meant that there was relatively little old reed. When reed harvesting decreased after the Second World War, the birds that build their nests in the reed or find their food there benefited. The area of shore meadows decreased up until about ten years ago, and during this period a number of species that lived on such meadows disappeared.

PHEASANTS AT TROLLEHOLM

Pheasants need areas of 3–5 ha of high grass to be able to breed, trees to sleep in and low grass or several sorts of crops for food. Possible biotopes of this kind have been investigated by field studies and interpreting air photographs of the Trolleholm estate in central Skåne.

When the size of fields increases, the edge zones decrease in length and the small biotopes disappear, the number of possible territories is reduced. Hunting statistics show that the pheasants in the Trolleholm area have decreased by about 70% since 1947. During this same period edge zones, road verges, ditch banks and stone walls have decreased by about 30%, and pools and wooded "islands" in fields by about 50%. Pheasant biotopes for breeding, feeding and shelter have diminished drastically.

The number of fields decreased from 354 small ones in 1947 to 132 large ones in 1978. As the fields grow larger, the zones along their edges, which are vital for wild life, become smaller and smaller.

Road verges, stone walls and streams form an important ecological infrastructure. In 1947 it was dense, but by 1978 it had disappeared; 56% of the stone walls and 48% of the watercourses had disappeared between 1947 and 1978.

In 1947 the important Islands of rough land and small ponds lay close together, but by 1978 more than 50% of them had been cleared or drained.

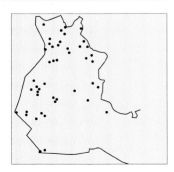

THE TROLLEHOLM ESTATE

Pheasant
*Phasianus
colchicus*

1947

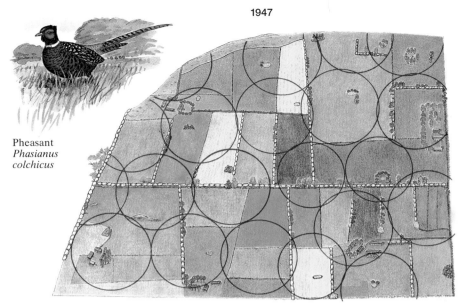

The Trolleholm estate in central Skåne, with trees, bushes, fields and stone walls drawn exactly from the old aerial photographs. There are at least 20 possible pheasant territories here (marked by circles).

1978

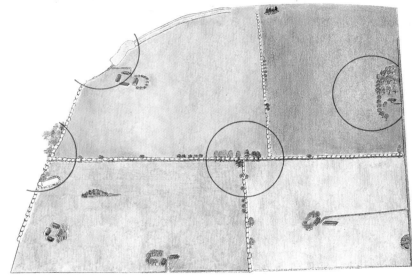

The small fields have been combined to make four large fields, empty of habitats. Only four of 15 stone walls are still standing and the small ponds have all gone. There are now only four possible pheasant territories.

2010?

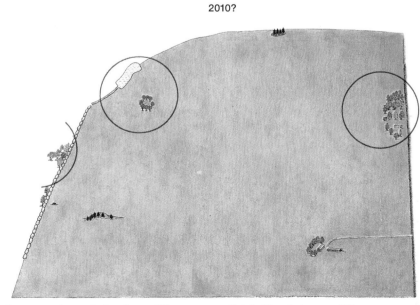

If such changes continue as before there will be no stone walls left. The whole area will be one great field of 150 ha—and there will be hardly any habitat for pheasants.

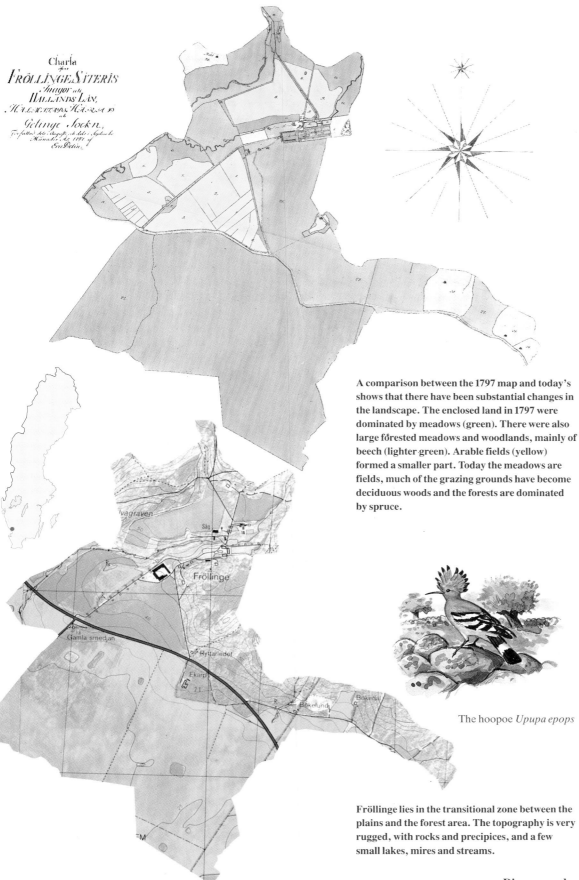

Between 1813 and 1814 Sven Nilsson, later a renowned professor of zoology at Lund, was a tutor at Fröllinge Manor near Halmstad. His detailed diary gives a fairly accurate picture of the bird life of that time. In 1976 Fröllinge's breeding bird life was surveyed as part of the national Swedish Bird Atlas project. A comparison of the breeding fauna in 1814 and 1976 provides interesting material which reflects the changes in the landscape.

The total number of species found was 100. Approximately two thirds were common to both years, while one third had either come or gone. The number of breeding species was fairly constant—at least 81 compared to 85; 15 species which existed in 1814 are reckoned to have disappeared by 1976, and 20 have arrived. In addition there have probably been large changes in the sizes of the populations, but of that we have no information. The species that have vanished are, for example, the white stork, roller and hoopoe, which were mainly connected with the old cultivated and forest landscapes. The species that have arrived are mainly birds that are favoured by the eutrophication of water and the establishment of spruce plantations or those that flourish in overgrown environments. Thus changes in the fauna are mostly the result of changes in human land use, both locally in and round Fröllinge and, in a larger perspective, throughout southern Sweden.

In 1814 the dominant forests were deciduous. The open land consisted of meadows and grazing ground and to a lesser extent of fields and heaths. The banks of the Slissån were cultivated as water meadows. Between 1814 and 1976 the forests underwent a radical change. To a large extent the deciduous forests have been replaced by spruce and pine. In comparison with other parts of Halland there is still a fair amount of beech forest. The open land round the estate is now mainly tilled. The Slissån has been straightened out and its banks are overgrown with bushes and alder.

The table shows how the bird fauna in the Fröllinge area changed between 1814 and 1976. The total number of species is 100. Question marks after names indicate uncertain records as a result of incomplete notes by Sven Nilsson, or because the species is judged to have lived in the Fröllinge area in 1814 although Nilsson did not mention it.

A comparison between the 1797 map and today's shows that there have been substantial changes in the landscape. The enclosed land in 1797 were dominated by meadows (green). There were also large forested meadows and woodlands, mainly of beech (lighter green). Arable fields (yellow) formed a smaller part. Today the meadows are fields, much of the grazing grounds have become deciduous woods and the forests are dominated by spruce.

The hoopoe *Upupa epops*

Fröllinge lies in the transitional zone between the plains and the forest area. The topography is very rugged, with rocks and precipices, and a few small lakes, mires and streams.

New species (n=20):		Common species (n=65):				Disappeared (n=15):
Goldeneye	Marsh warbler	Mallard	Green	Northern	Blue tit (?)	Black stork
Honey	Reed warbler	Goshawk	woodpecker	wheatear	Great tit	White stork
buzzard	Nutcracker	Sparrowhawk (?)	Black	Song thrush	Nuthatch	Red kite
Pheasant	Goldcrest (?)	Buzzard	woodpecker	Mistle thrush	Treecreeper	Capercaillie
Moorhen	Coal tit (?)	Grey partridge	Great spotted	Blackbird	Red-backed	Black grouse
Nightjar	Golden oriole	Lapwing	woodpecker	Icterine warbler	shrike	Golden plover
Long-eared	Bullfinch (?)	Snipe	Lesser spotted	Blackcap (?)	Jay	Dunlin
owl	Greenfinch (?)	Woodcock	woodpecker	Garden warbler	Magpie	Eagle owl
Fieldfare	Siskin (?)	Curlew	Sky lark	Whitethroat (?)	Jackdaw	Roller
Dunnock	Crossbill	Common	Swallow	Lesser white-	Hooded crow	Hoopoe
Thrush	Reed bunting	sandpiper	House martin	throat (?)	Raven	Middle spotted
Nightingale		Green	Tree pipit	Wood warbler	Starling	woodpecker
		sandpiper	Meadow pipit	Willow warbler	House sparrow	Woodlark
		Stock dove	Pied wagtail	Spotted flycatcher	Tree sparrow	Yellow wagtail
		Wood pigeon	Wren	Pied flycatcher	Chaffinch	Goldfinch
		Cuckoo	Robin	Long-tailed tit	Linnet	Ortolan
		Tawny owl	Redstart	Marsh tit	Hawfinch	bunting
		Swift	Whinchat (?)	Willow tit (?)	Yellowhammer	
		Wryneck		Crested tit		

ARION RUFUS

1:20 000 000

1892

1850'S

1906

There are 59 known occurrences of the red slug—the oldest records are dated. (S149)

Typical colouring of the red slug (above) and the Lusitanian slug.

Invertebrates

RED SLUGS

Two species of large red slugs have spread in Sweden with the help of human beings—the red slug *Arion rufus*, originally from Central Europe, and the Lusitanian slug *Arion lusitanicus*, originally from the Iberian peninsula. Although closely related and very similar in appearance, these two species have considerable differences in distribution and ecology. The red slug was first found in Sweden in the 1850s and has since then spread slowly. It still occurs only sporadically and causes no harm. In some cases the species was introduced intentionally; the well-known occurrences on Öland originate from those introduced by Queen Victoria when the summer palace Solliden was built in 1906.

The Lusitanian slug began to spread over much of West and Central Europe in the 1970s, mainly passively through the sale of plants and house plants. Thanks to its ability to self-fertilise and its large egg production it has spread rapidly. This slug often does great damage in cultivated fields and gardens, which has given it the name "the killer slug". The mild winters and rainy, moist summers of the late 1980s probably helped the species to establish itself in Sweden. It was first found here in 1975. Mass invasions and damage were reported for the first time from the Göteborg district in 1984.

The first record in eastern Sweden was made in Södermanland in 1983. Since 1988 it has spread like wildfire in the Stockholm region, and more slowly northward along the Baltic coast.

ARION LUSITANICUS

1985   **1988**   **1992**

1976

1975

1976

The first record of a Lusitanian slug was made in 1975. In 1988 it existed at 70 sites and in 1992 at 296! Note the concentration in the big-city regions. (S150)

CERATINA CYANEA

1:10 000 000

Number of records per 50 x 50 km square

7
5
3
1

1870 s   **1930 s**

1950 s   **1970 s**

(S151)

Little carpenter bee
Ceratina cyanea

LITTLE CARPENTER BEE

The first Swedish record of the little carpenter bee *Ceratina cyanea* was reported from Öland in 1871, the second 30 years later from Uppland. Up to the mid-1950s it was considered a relict and a great rarity. It was still uncommon in the 1960s, but in the 1970s records increased greatly in number.

It is impossible to explain simply why this bee has spread so rapidly. Probably it is the result of several interacting factors. Hollow raspberry canes and mugwort stalks, for example, are used for hibernation. Long, warm summers and an increase in suitable habitats like clear-cut areas with plenty of wild raspberries have encouraged it.

EUPHYDRYAS MATURNA

1:10 000 000

o Unspecified province record

? Uncertain occurence

−1899

1900–1949

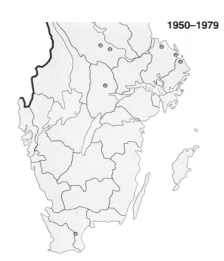
1950–1979

1980–1993

The scarce fritillary *Euphydryas maturna* belongs to the Nymphalidae family of butterflies. Its distribution area has decreased greatly both in Sweden and in other parts of Europe and it is one of the rarest butterflies in Western and Central Europe today. Since 1980 only one record has been reported in Uppland (two butterflies in 1987). Between 1992 and 1993 the population in Västmanland comprised about 1,000 individuals. (S152)

WHY HAS THE SCARCE FRITILLARY VANISHED?

The scarce fritillary *Euphydryas maturna* takes two to three years to develop from egg to fully fledged butterfly. The first-year caterpillars, which require a body temperature above +30°C to grow normally, live in groups in places sheltered from the wind with at least 4–5 hours of sunshine. The species has a few enemies, one of which is the parasite hymenopteran *Cotesia acuminata*. The degree of parasitation is determined during the last ten days before pupation. The hatching of the hymenopteran and its ability to fly during the spring are more dependent on high air temperatures than the black caterpillar, which can, in cold weather, find warm enough places in the sun for its development.

The scarce fritillary has decreased rapidly in Sweden in the past few decades. The most likely explanations are its vulnerability to the climate and changes in the environment. The species is favoured by continuous snow covering until April, although it requires high summer temperatures. Such conditions also lessen the risk of attack by hymenoptera. Another cause may be that the caterpillars are dependent on moisture and flourish best in very wet places by streams and fens. These environments have decreased as a result of draining and silviculture. Heavy grazing by moose may be yet another explanation of its decline, since the butterfly lays its eggs on ash or guelder rose leaves, which are one of the moose's favourite foods.

Changes in Forest Flora

Most forest plants, including trees, suffer from a shortage of nitrogen. As a result of airborne nitrogen pollutants large quantities of nitrogen have been deposited in forests during the past few decades, above all in the south-west of Sweden. Thanks to the National Forest Survey, which has operated since the 1920s, it is possible to follow changes in forest vegetation. Comparisons between vegetation data for middle-aged and old forests in southern Sweden between 1973–1977 and 1983–1987 reveal a noticeable increased distribution of narrow-leaved grass-type vegetation. One of the dominant species here is the wavy-hairgrass *Deschampsia flexuosa*. Hairgrass has proved to be greatly favoured by increased supplies of nitrogen, in contrast to blueberry and cowberry. The

Grasses, above all the wavy-hairgrass *Deschampsia flexuosa*, are spreading far and wide. Increasing nitrogen deposition—from traffic, for example—and intensive browsing of dwarf shrubs by wild herbivores are presumed to be the causes.

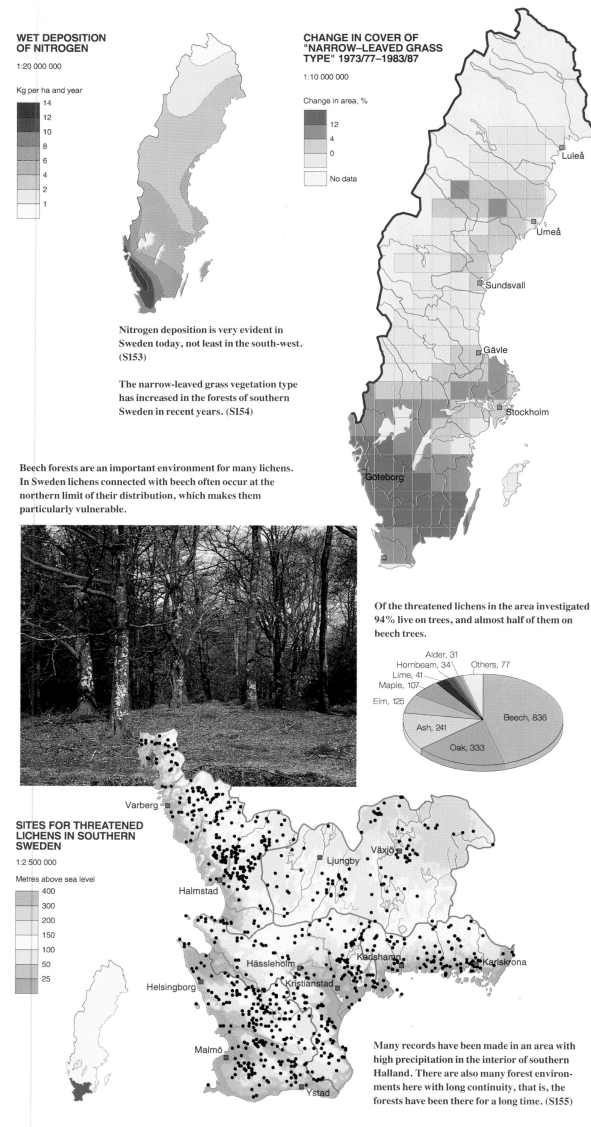

WET DEPOSITION OF NITROGEN

1:20 000 000

Kg per ha and year

- 14
- 12
- 10
- 8
- 6
- 4
- 2
- 1

Nitrogen deposition is very evident in Sweden today, not least in the south-west. (S153)

The narrow-leaved grass vegetation type has increased in the forests of southern Sweden in recent years. (S154)

Beech forests are an important environment for many lichens. In Sweden lichens connected with beech often occur at the northern limit of their distribution, which makes them particularly vulnerable.

CHANGE IN COVER OF "NARROW–LEAVED GRASS TYPE" 1973/77–1983/87

1:10 000 000

Change in area, %

- 12
- 4
- 0
- No data

Luleå
Umeå
Sundsvall
Gävle
Stockholm
Göteborg

Of the threatened lichens in the area investigated 94% live on trees, and almost half of them on beech trees.

Alder, 31
Hornbeam, 34
Lime, 41
Maple, 107
Elm, 125
Ash, 241
Oak, 333
Beech, 836
Others, 77

SITES FOR THREATENED LICHENS IN SOUTHERN SWEDEN

1:2 500 000

Metres above sea level

- 400
- 300
- 200
- 150
- 100
- 50
- 25

Varberg
Halmstad
Ljungby
Växjö
Hässleholm
Helsingborg
Kristianstad
Karlshamn
Karlskrona
Malmö
Ystad

Many records have been made in an area with high precipitation in the interior of southern Halland. There are also many forest environments here with long continuity, that is, the forests have been there for a long time. (S155)

increase in narrow-leaved grass types has therefore been explained as a reaction to the increase in nitrogen deposition in southern Sweden. It is also possible that more intensive grazing by roe deer is a reinforcing factor, since roe deer prefer blueberry foliage to wavy-hairgrass, which is left to flourish.

LICHENS IN SOUTHERNMOST SWEDEN

A lichen consists of an alga and a fungus that live in symbiosis. The alga provides the fungus with nutrients and the fungus gives the alga a stable and protected environment—a subtle but vulnerable form of mutual support. Many lichens are therefore very sensitive to changes in the environment and are strongly affected by air pollution and rapid changes in agricultural and forestry methods. This is particularly true in the most southerly parts of Sweden which are relatively densely populated and where air pollution and other human activities are especially evident. Great changes in the lichen flora during the past 150 years have been documented in this area by the "Threatened Lichens in Southern Sweden" project. A search has been made for 114 lichen species which were judged to be endangered, both in their previously known habitats and in other suitable places in the counties of Kronoberg, Blekinge, Kristianstad, Malmöhus and Halland. The project has also resurveyed all species of lichen in five smaller, early well-studied areas.

It is often difficult to determine why the distribution of lichens changes. Their occurrence is not only affected by human activities but is also due to historical factors, long-term changes in the climate and competition from other species.

The properties of the substrate, that is, the surface on which the lichen grows, are of great significance for its establishment. In southern Sweden many species today seem to occur on more basic substrates than before—probably to compensate for the increase in acid precipitation. At the same time more acid-tolerant species have become more common. Strong environmental influences have also made it less easy for many species to utilise several different kinds of substrate; they occur on fewer substrates than before.

Beech forests have proved to be a very important habitat for the threatened lichens in southernmost Sweden.

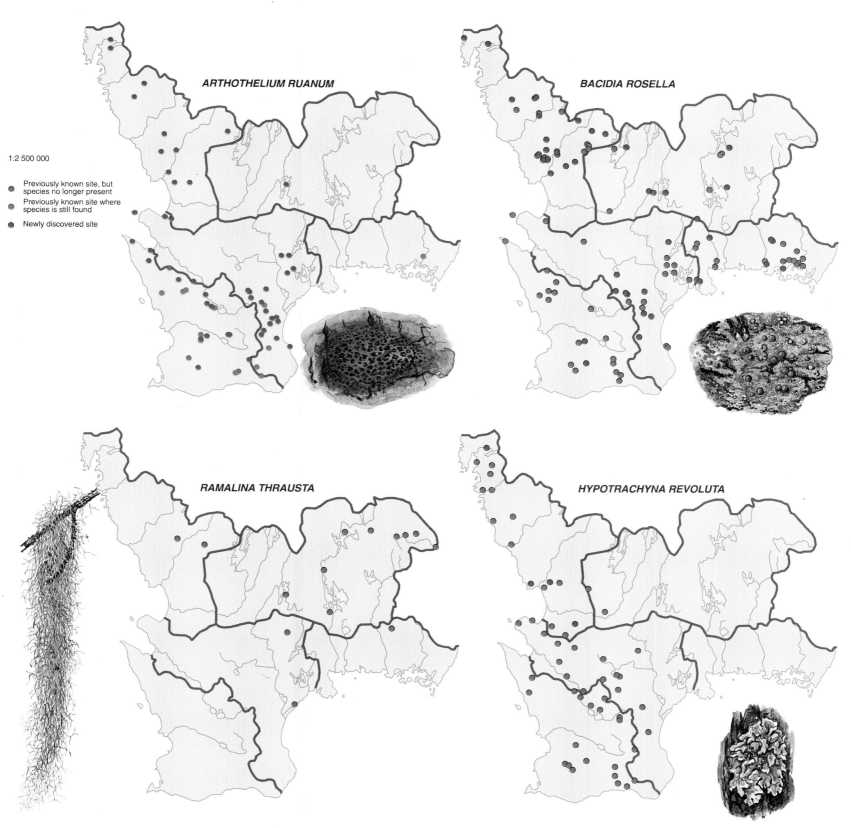

ARTHOTHELIUM RUANUM

BACIDIA ROSELLA

RAMALINA THRAUSTA

HYPOTRACHYNA REVOLUTA

1:2 500 000

- Previously known site, but species no longer present
- Previously known site where species is still found
- Newly discovered site

Arthothelium ruanum occurs in moist and shaded nemoral forests, often in stands of ash, and has been found in 12 of 15 old sites as well as in 42 new sites. The first Swedish record of this species was made in 1934 in Dalby Söderskog, and in 1948 it was known to exist at 15 sites within the area investigated. It seems clear that the species has spread in recent years. It has probably benefited from the fact that young, smooth-barked ash trees have become more common as a result of the agricultural landscape becoming overgrown. (S156)

Ramalina thrausta grows on spruce branches in mossy spruce forests on moist ground with a high level of nutrients and has not been found at any of the 14 old sites. The last known record in the area investigated was made in 1939. The old sites have been affected by felling since the original records were made. Felling makes the climate drier in surrounding stands, so this lichen has difficulty in surviving there, too. The species occurred very sparsely at many of the old sites as early as the 1930s, and collecting may have caused it to disappear there. (S158)

Bacidia rosella occurs in nemoral forests, avenues and church-yards and has been found in only 8 of 61 old sites, while 31 new sites have been found. All present records were made in or adjacent to long-established stands of trees, so the new sites probably represent old occurrences and indicate that the species has diminished greatly. This species is probably sensitive to air pollution, as it has disappeared to a large extent from sites which are in other respects unchanged, but it has probably also suffered from the effects of silviculture. Earlier investigations also suggest that the species used to form considerably larger colonies. (S157)

Hypotrachyna revoluta occurs mainly on common alder in alder fens. It shows a sharp reduction in occurrences, being found in only 3 of 51 old sites, while no more than 5 new sites have been located. The decline of this species is probably due to the fact that the common alder's normally low pH has been further decreased by air pollution. Most sites appear to be unchanged in other respects. This lichen probably also has poorer competitive powers than other similar lichens in the same environment. (S159)

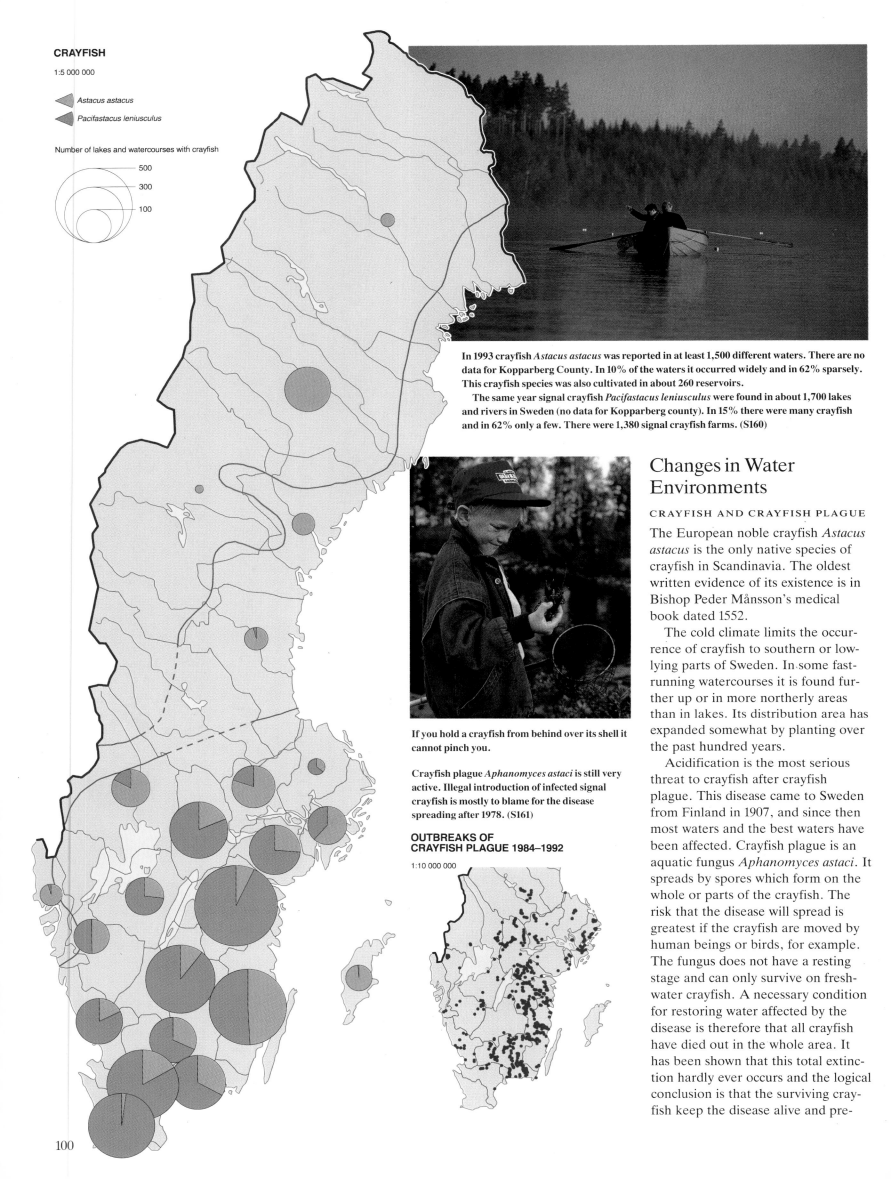

CRAYFISH

1:5 000 000

◄ *Astacus astacus*

◄ *Pacifastacus leniusculus*

Number of lakes and watercourses with crayfish

- 500
- 300
- 100

In 1993 crayfish *Astacus astacus* was reported in at least 1,500 different waters. There are no data for Kopparberg County. In 10% of the waters it occurred widely and in 62% sparsely. This crayfish species was also cultivated in about 260 reservoirs.

The same year signal crayfish *Pacifastacus leniusculus* were found in about 1,700 lakes and rivers in Sweden (no data for Kopparberg county). In 15% there were many crayfish and in 62% only a few. There were 1,380 signal crayfish farms. (S160)

If you hold a crayfish from behind over its shell it cannot pinch you.

Crayfish plague *Aphanomyces astaci* is still very active. Illegal introduction of infected signal crayfish is mostly to blame for the disease spreading after 1978. (S161)

OUTBREAKS OF CRAYFISH PLAGUE 1984–1992

1:10 000 000

Changes in Water Environments

CRAYFISH AND CRAYFISH PLAGUE

The European noble crayfish *Astacus astacus* is the only native species of crayfish in Scandinavia. The oldest written evidence of its existence is in Bishop Peder Månsson's medical book dated 1552.

The cold climate limits the occurrence of crayfish to southern or low-lying parts of Sweden. In some fast-running watercourses it is found further up or in more northerly areas than in lakes. Its distribution area has expanded somewhat by planting over the past hundred years.

Acidification is the most serious threat to crayfish after crayfish plague. This disease came to Sweden from Finland in 1907, and since then most waters and the best waters have been affected. Crayfish plague is an aquatic fungus *Aphanomyces astaci*. It spreads by spores which form on the whole or parts of the crayfish. The risk that the disease will spread is greatest if the crayfish are moved by human beings or birds, for example. The fungus does not have a resting stage and can only survive on fresh-water crayfish. A necessary condition for restoring water affected by the disease is therefore that all crayfish have died out in the whole area. It has been shown that this total extinction hardly ever occurs and the logical conclusion is that the surviving crayfish keep the disease alive and pre-

Sphagna on the lake bottom overgrown with blue-green algae

vent any restoration). The fact that some crayfish survive is not because they have developed resistance but because they have quite by chance not been infected. In most waters where the catch of crayfish is small the disease is still probably present.

The American signal crayfish *Pacifastacus leniusculus* was introduced into Sweden as an experiment in 1960. The background was that it had been possible to restore very few of all the infested waters in spite of extensive efforts. In addition the methods for preventing crayfish plague from spreading were both impractical and unreliable. There was good reason to assume that signal crayfish were comparatively more resistant to crayfish plague. This soon proved to be the case, but it was as a rule also a bearer of the disease.

DIATOMS AND ACIDIFICATION

Swedish lakes have a rich flora of microscopic algae which provide the nutritional base for the aquatic ecosystem. In a quite normal lake there will be several hundred kinds of diatoms. The composition of the diatom flora is determined first and foremost by the chemical composition of the lake.

Diatoms are 0.005–0.1 mm in size and have beautifully shaped shells. Lake water may contain several thousand individuals per litre without our noticing them. Diatoms also grow on water plants near the shore, on stones and on the lake bed. When these algae die, their silica shells are preserved in the bottom sediment. Every year new sediment is deposited and this process has been going on ever since the lake was formed. It is possible, from the composition of the species in these sediment layers, to draw conclusions as to changes in the lake's water quality. The pH value that a lake has had can be read quite accurately, making it possible to determine whether or not the lake has become acidified.

When the lakes were formed as the inland ice melted about 10,000 years ago, the pH value of the water was about 7. During the following thousands of years natural acidification took place, especially in lakes surrounded by thin, poor soils. Just over 2,000 years ago, during the Iron Age, mankind began to change the southern Swedish landscape more decisively. To create arable and grazing land forests were cleared and burnt. These activities culminated in the 19th century when, for example, Halland to a large part became virtually devoid of forest. Instead there were vast heaths which were burnt regularly.

This farming culture altered the state of the land, contributing to a rise in the pH in lakes. Thus many lakes had a higher pH than the strictly natural value when the industrial period proper began in the 20th century; then arable and grazing land was allowed to become overgrown and the acid deposition from fossil fuels began to have a serious impact.

Even though changes in land use may have contributed to acidification, there is no doubt that the main cause is acid deposition. Today the pH value in many lakes is much lower than ever before.

CHANGES IN DIATOM COMPOSITION IN A LAKE IN BOHUSLÄN

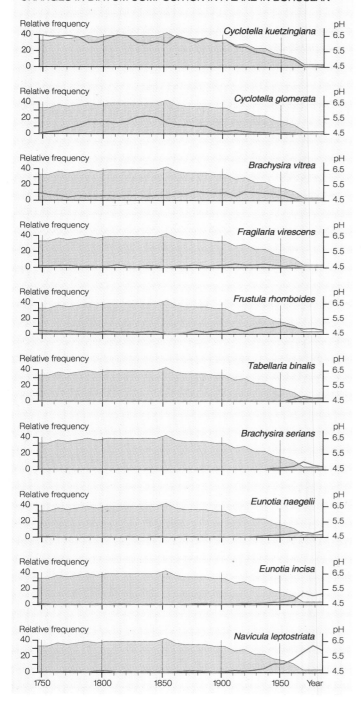

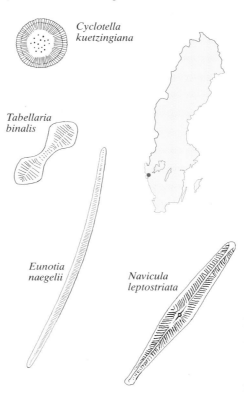

Cyclotella kuetzingiana

Tabellaria binalis

Eunotia naegelii

Navicula leptostriata

As a consequence of acidification in the 20th century the diatom flora of many lakes has changed dramatically. *Tabellaria binalis* was a rare species 40–50 years ago; today it is a characteristic species in hundreds of acidified lakes in southern Sweden.

The diagram shows how the flora has changed in a lake in Bohuslän during the past 250 years. Only a few of the most common species are given. The pH curve (right-hand y axis) has been calculated on the basis of the composition of the diatoms. The sediment has been dated using the lead isotope method (^{210}Pb). The percentage (left-hand y axis) shows what percentage of each species was found on the microscope slides.

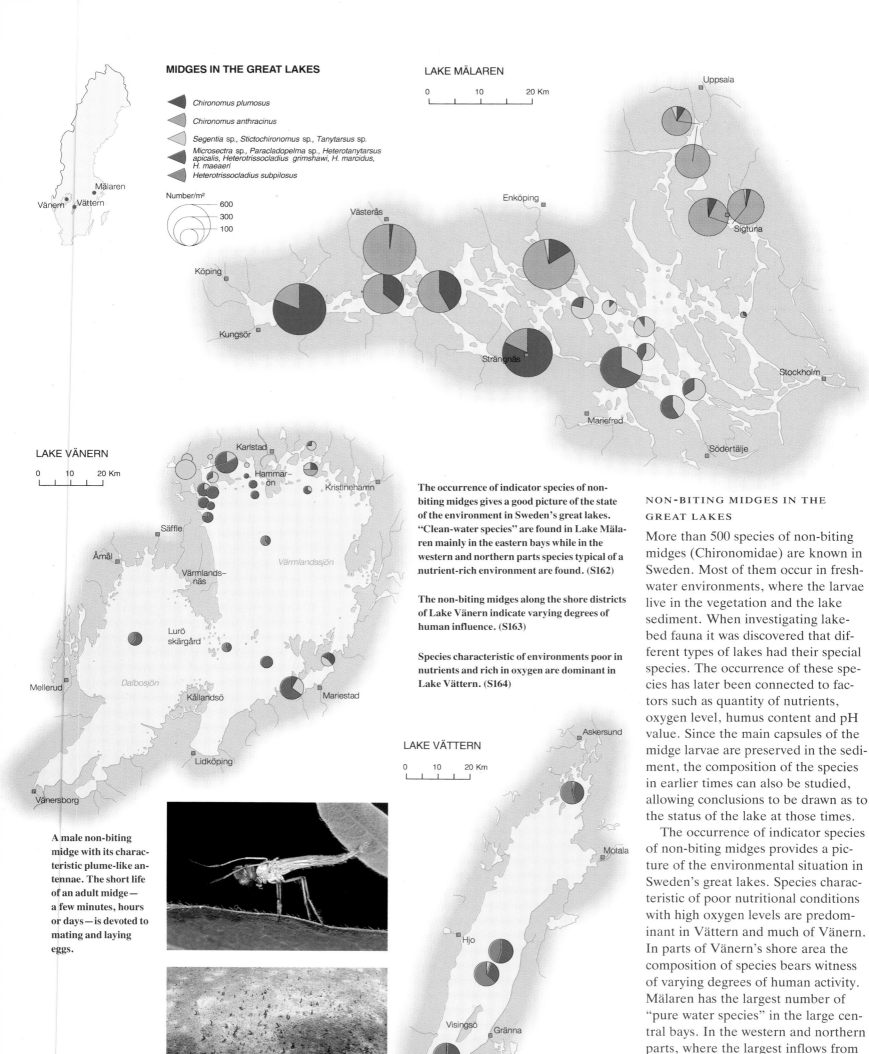

MIDGES IN THE GREAT LAKES

- *Chironomus plumosus*
- *Chironomus anthracinus*
- *Segentia* sp., *Stictochironomus* sp., *Tanytarsus* sp.
- *Microsectra* sp., *Paracladopelma* sp., *Heterotanytarsus apicalis, Heterotrissocladius grimshawi, H. marcidus, H. maeaeri*
- *Heterotrissocladius subpilosus*

Number/m²
600
300
100

LAKE MÄLAREN

0   10   20 Km

Uppsala
Enköping
Västerås
Köping
Kungsör
Strängnäs
Mariefred
Sigtuna
Stockholm
Södertälje

LAKE VÄNERN

0   10   20 Km

Karlstad
Hammarön
Kristinehamn
Säffle
Åmål
Värmlands-näs
Värmlandssjön
Lurö skärgård
Dalbosjön
Mellerud
Kållandsö
Mariestad
Lidköping
Vänersborg

The occurrence of indicator species of non-biting midges gives a good picture of the state of the environment in Sweden's great lakes. "Clean-water species" are found in Lake Mälaren mainly in the eastern bays while in the western and northern parts species typical of a nutrient-rich environment are found. (S162)

The non-biting midges along the shore districts of Lake Vänern indicate varying degrees of human influence. (S163)

Species characteristic of environments poor in nutrients and rich in oxygen are dominant in Lake Vättern. (S164)

A male non-biting midge with its characteristic plume-like antennae. The short life of an adult midge — a few minutes, hours or days — is devoted to mating and laying eggs.

Lake sediment with midge larvae living in tubes. The larval stage lasts from a couple of weeks up to several years.

LAKE VÄTTERN

0   10   20 Km

Askersund
Motala
Hjo
Visingsö
Gränna
Jönköping

NON-BITING MIDGES IN THE GREAT LAKES

More than 500 species of non-biting midges (Chironomidae) are known in Sweden. Most of them occur in fresh-water environments, where the larvae live in the vegetation and the lake sediment. When investigating lake-bed fauna it was discovered that different types of lakes had their special species. The occurrence of these species has later been connected to factors such as quantity of nutrients, oxygen level, humus content and pH value. Since the main capsules of the midge larvae are preserved in the sediment, the composition of the species in earlier times can also be studied, allowing conclusions to be drawn as to the status of the lake at those times.

The occurrence of indicator species of non-biting midges provides a picture of the environmental situation in Sweden's great lakes. Species characteristic of poor nutritional conditions with high oxygen levels are predominant in Vättern and much of Vänern. In parts of Vänern's shore area the composition of species bears witness of varying degrees of human activity. Mälaren has the largest number of "pure water species" in the large central bays. In the western and northern parts, where the largest inflows from surrounding land and the effluents from towns occur, the species which are typical of a nutritious environment, often poor in oxygen on the lake bed, are predominant.

Red-listed Species

The middle spotted woodpecker *Dendrocopos medius* is dependent on oak woods. Its former distribution extended up to Lake Mälaren, but the population has been extinct since the last successful breeding in Östergötland in 1980.

The World Conservation Union (IUCN), in cooperation with the *World Conservation Monitoring Centre*, compiles information about endangered animal and plant species in the world. These species are grouped into categories that express the probability of their survival or extinction. The results are published in *red lists*. Similar assessments of the threat to flora and fauna have also been made in geographically limited areas such as countries and regions.

The first Swedish red list of endangered and rare species, comprising vertebrates, was published in 1975. Since 1984 this work has been carried out by the *Swedish Threatened Species Unit* and its *expert committees*.

A large percentage of Sweden's animal and plant groups on land and in freshwater have now been assessed for risk of extinction. The red lists cover some 3,500 species today. Several revisions have been made for certain organisms, some for the better, but for the majority the situation has unfortunately deteriorated.

During the past few years we have also been able to get a clearer picture of the risks, that is, the factors that underlie the assessment that a species

0. Vanished. Species (taxa) vanished (or regarded as vanished) as reproducing populations. Only species vanished since 1850 included.

1. Endangered. Species (taxa) subject to great risk of vanishing as reproducing populations in the near future if the causal factors are not removed.

2. Vulnerable. Species (taxa) whose survival is not secured in the long term. Includes species seriously declining in numbers or geographical distribution and which may soon enter the endangered category.

3. Rare. Species (taxa) which at present are not immediately endangered or vulnerable, but are still at risk because their total populations are small or restricted to local areas or disseminating.

4. Care-demanding. Species (taxa) which do not belong to categories 1–3 but still require attention specific for each species.

Group of organisms / Threat category	0. Vanished	1. Endangered	2. Vulnerable	3. Rare	4. Care-demanding	Total	% of total no of species in Sweden
Mammals	2	3	9	4	5	23	33
Birds	8	5	14	13	51	91	37
Reptiles and amphibians	0	1	5	0	7	13	63
Fishes and lampreys	1	2	4	6	6	19	14
Invertebrates	111	206	521	263	776	1,877	
Beetles	49	150	315	107	445	1,066	24
Butterflies	9	28	74	39	183	333	12
Two-winged flies	21	6	28	37	14	106	>2
Wasps and their allies	26	4	39	24	28	121	>1
Molluscs	1	5	10	15	14	45	>7
Bugs	0	4	27	4	36	71	>4
Spiders, crustaceans and other invertebrates	5	9	28	37	56	135	>2
Vascular plants	32	92	118	104	99	445	c. 20
Stoneworts	3	9	8	4	3	27	c. 80
Macrofungi	8	80	138	117	185	528	c. 20
Lichens	22	73	82	18	43	238	c. 10
Bryophytes	18	26	37	126	34	241	c. 20
Total	**205**	**497**	**936**	**655**	**1,209**	**3,502**	

> indicates that a large number of species in the group of organisms have not been investigated.

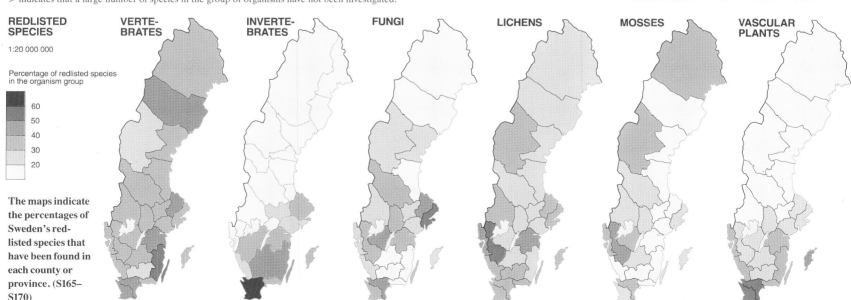

REDLISTED SPECIES

1:20 000 000

Percentage of redlisted species in the organism group

60
50
40
30
20

The maps indicate the percentages of Sweden's red-listed species that have been found in each county or province. (S165–S170)

VERTE-BRATES INVERTE-BRATES FUNGI LICHENS MOSSES VASCULAR PLANTS

Group of organisms / Type of habitat	Forest	Agricultural land	Cliffs and outcrops of bedrock*	Water and wetland	Sea and seashores	Alpine region	Total	Total number of red-listed species
Mammals	14	8	2	4	3	2	33	23
Birds	33	24	7	37	18	9	128	91
Amphibians and reptiles	6	9	0	9	2	0	26	13
Fishes	0	0	0	16	9	0	25	19
Invertebrates	969	868	17	400	110	3	2 367	1 876
Vascular plants	66	305	19	63	47	32	532	445
Stoneworts	0	0	0	21	8	0	29	27
Macrofungi	465	174	4	10	0	4	657	528
Lichens	159	84	76	10	0	4	333	238
Bryophytes	74	54	63	51	7	57	306	241
Total per habitat	**1 786**	**1 526**	**188**	**621**	**204**	**111**		

*outside the mountain area

Many species occur in several environments, e.g. the wolverine *Gulo gulo*, which lives both in forest and mountain areas. Thus the presence in habitats exceeds the total number of red-listed species.

RED-LISTED MAMMALS

0. Vanished
Black rat 1994
Reindeer c. 1880

1. Endangered
Bechstein's bat
Pond bat
Wolf

2. Vulnerable
Natterer's bat
Barbastelle
Arctic fox
Wolverine
Otter*
Lynx
Ringed seal
Grey seal*
Harbour porpoise

3. Rare
Nathusius' pipistrelle
Serotine
Harvest mouse
Northern
  birch-mouse

4. Care-demanding
Hedgehog
Noctule
Dormouse
Brown bear
Harbour seal

*species with regionally different threat status

The otter *Lutra lutra* used to live in practically every part of the country, but it has now decreased greatly and is no longer found in many parts of southern and central Sweden in particular. Photograph from an enclosure.

The lynx *Lynx lynx* which was under pressure from hunting and disease is now showing signs of a strong recovery. Photograph from an enclosure.

is in the danger zone. The serious effects of forestry and agriculture are very evident, but there are many other important factors such as nitrogen deposition, acidification, building work, disturbance and illegal collecting.

Information about each red-listed species is compiled in a fact sheet which is published for individual species or for whole animal and plant groups. The National Environmental Protection Agency works on producing programmes for a selected number of high-priority species and ensures that authorities, organisations and private individuals cooperate to carry these programmes out.

Mammals

Twenty-three of Sweden's 69 mammals are red-listed. However, an analysis of the development of the populations of the mammals shows that there are today more species with an increasing trend than a decreasing trend. Several species that used to be endangered or had even vanished from Sweden have now re-established strong positions or are expanding rapidly. This is true above all of moose, roe deer, beaver and wild boar. The black rat, which had disappeared from Sweden for several decades, is making a new attempt to establish itself in southern Sweden.

But the situation is serious for several mammals. The otter population has declined greatly and seals have long been at risk, even though there is now hope of recovery. No fewer than seven species of bats—half of them species that occur regularly—are red-listed. Bechstein's bat is now so rare that it is no longer observed even once a year. Some of the other species are also extremely uncommon and others have suffered from recent changes in forestry and agriculture.

THE LARGE CARNIVORES

In the late 1980s and early 1990s the populations of the large predators—with the exception of the wolverine—developed fairly favourably, but forecasts for the future vary.

Wolverines were declared protected animals in 1969. By then they had been hunted so fiercely that their situation was judged to be very serious. For a few years in the 1970s there were signs that the population was increasing, at least locally, but since then there has been no improvement. This species is the object of illegal hunting, especially round its dens. The total Swedish population is probably not more than about 100 individuals.

As late as 1986 there was still an open hunting season for lynxes in Sweden. But in that year the species was protected outside the reindeer-breeding areas and in 1991 this protection was enlarged to cover the whole of Sweden. The reason was alarming reports of declining populations. Hunting was probably the main reason, but disease (scab and feline distemper) may have played a part. As

DISTRIBUTION OF THE FOUR SPECIES OF LARGE CARNIVORES, 1990

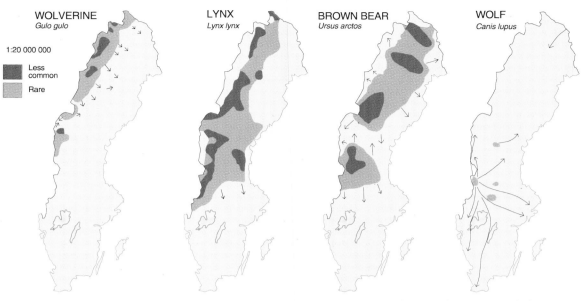

WOLVERINE
Gulo gulo

LYNX
Lynx lynx

BROWN BEAR
Ursus arctos

WOLF
Canis lupus

1:20 000 000

Less common

Rare

In the early 1990s there were about 25 wolves in Sweden. The population was at that time increasing slowly, but the species is still considered to be endangered. Photograph from an enclosure.

Compared with their original distributions the four large carnivores are geographically limited today. Three of them — wolf, bear and lynx — are now showing signs of trying to recolonize lost areas. (S171–174)

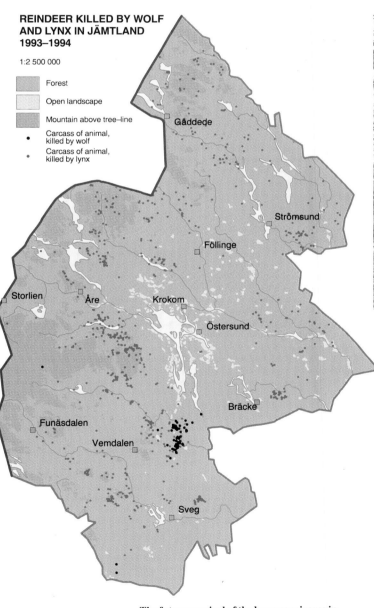

REINDEER KILLED BY WOLF AND LYNX IN JÄMTLAND 1993–1994

1:2 500 000

Forest

Open landscape

Mountain above tree–line

- Carcass of animal, killed by wolf

- Carcass of animal, killed by lynx

Gäddede

Strömsund

Föllinge

Storlien

Åre

Krokom

Östersund

Bräcke

Funäsdalen

Vemdalen

Sveg

The future survival of the large carnivores in northern Sweden is closely connected with the solution of the problems that they create for reindeer farming. During the period 1 July 1992–30/6 1993 108 cadavers were found in Jämtland that had been attacked by wolves and 776 that had been attacked by lynxes. (S175)

Roe-deer *Capreolus capreolus* killed by lynx *Lynx lynx* in Jämtland

a result of protection the population has evidently recovered; surveys in parts of central Sweden and southern Norrland in the early 1990s indicate a population of about 700.

When wolves were declared protected animals in 1966, after centuries of intense persecution, there were probably fewer than 10 individuals left in Sweden. A tiny remnant survived until 1977, when a dozen or so wolves must have crossed over from Finland, and in 1978 the species bred in Norrbotten for the first time since it had been protected. But these wolves soon disappeared from Norrbotten, at the same time as a few individuals appeared much further south, in the borderland between Värmland and Hedmark in Norway. With the exception of 1986 wolves have bred in

Värmland every year since 1983. Migrating wolves spread; some of them died in road accidents, others were shot, but isolated individuals recolonised old districts and after 1991 pairs were established in Dalarna and in the Härjedalen–Hälsingland area. In the winter of 1993/94 there were about 25 wolves in Sweden.

The bear population was in a serious state at the turn of the century and several decades onwards, but it was saved by improved protection. Since the 1940s it has had a more favourable development than any other of the large predators. In the early 1990s the population was estimated to be about 620. With an annual licence to kill 30–40 bears the population continues to grow slowly and spread.

0. Vanished
Black stork 1933
White stork 1954
Great bustard c. 1860
Puffin 1959
Barn owl 1984
Roller 1967
Middle spotted
 woodpecker 1980
Crested lark 1989

1. Endangered
Black-necked grebe
Lesser white-fronted
 goose
Kentish plover
White-backed wood-
 pecker
Corn bunting

2. Vulnerable
Garganey
White-tailed eagle
Montagu's harrier
Gyrfalcon
Peregrine
Quail
Spotted crake
Corncrake
Dunlin (ssp. *schinzii*)
Little gull*
Caspian tern
Sandwich tern
Black tern
Eagle owl*
Shore lark
Tawny pipit

3. Rare
Bar-tailed godwit
Kittiwake
Snowy owl
Hoopoe
Grey-headed wood-
 pecker
Great reed warbler
Greenish warbler
Arctic warbler
Penduline tit
Golden oriole
Serin
Redpoll (ssp. *cabaret*)
Little bunting

4. Care-demanding
Red-throated diver
Black-throated diver
Red-necked grebe*
Slavonian grebe*
Cormorant (ssp. *si-
 nensis*)
Bittern
Grey heron
Whooper swan
Bean goose
Barnacle goose
Pintail*
Scaup*
Long-tailed duck
Honey buzzard
Red kite
Marsh harrier
Hen harrier*
Goshawk*
Golden eagle
Osprey
Kestrel*
Capercaillie
Partridge
Crane
Avocet
Little ringed plover
Golden plover*
Ruff*
Jack snipe*
Great snipe*
Black-tailed godwit
Curlew*
Arctic skua

Lesser black-backed
 gull (ssp. *fuscus*)
Little tern*
Guillemot
Stock dove
Ural owl
Great grey owl
Kingfisher
Black woodpecker*
Lesser spotted
 woodpecker

Three-toed woodpecker*
Sand martin
Yellow wagtail
 (ssp. *flava*)
Red-breasted flycatcher
Bearded tit
Nutcracker
Hawfinch

* Species with regionally
 different threat status

PERCENTAGE REDLISTED BIRD SPECIES

1:10 000 000

☐ Total number of
 bird species
 in the region

■ Percentage redlisted
 bird species

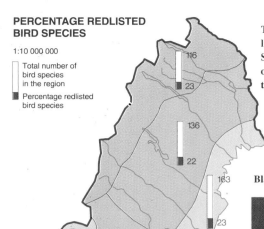

The percentage of red-listed species differs very little from region to region; southern and central Sweden have the highest percentage, the interior of Norrland and the southern mountain districts the lowest. (S176)

Black-necked grebe *Podiceps nigricollis*

The occurrence of red-listed birds generally reflects the total number of species in different parts of Sweden. The largest number of threatened species are to be found in a broad zone running from immediately south of the Norrland boundary from northern Uppland to Närke. Other areas with many threatened species are north-eastern Skåne, Öland and the coast of Kalmar. (S177)

A young gyrfalcon *Falco rusticolus* in its mountain environment. There are scarcely 100 pairs of gyrfalcons in Sweden. This bird is one of the vulnerable species.

Birds

For most birds it is large-scale forestry and agriculture that are the major threats. Forestry is a threat above all to the specialised species that require old forests and forests containing many dead trees. Species requiring deciduous forests also suffer badly in the modern forest landscape. These are the factors that have led to the recent extinction of the middle-spotted woodpecker in Sweden and the sharp decline of several other woodpecker species. The threat from agriculture is above all large fields and fewer remnant biotopes (forest edges, wooded islands in fields, natural meadows etc), lack of food due to pesticides and herbicides and more effective drainage. These factors have made fields the poorest of all Swedish biotopes for birds.

Agriculture has in the long term reduced the number of forest birds since it is largely forests that have been turned into fields; but agriculture has historically also helped many new species which we regard as natural today but which would not exist if there was forest everywhere. These "agricultural" species have, however, mainly been encouraged by various old types of cultivation. Each phase of exploitation has its winners and its losers.

NUMBER OF REDLISTED BIRD SPECIES

1:5 000 000

Number/square (25 X 25 KM)

39
35
30
25
20
15
10

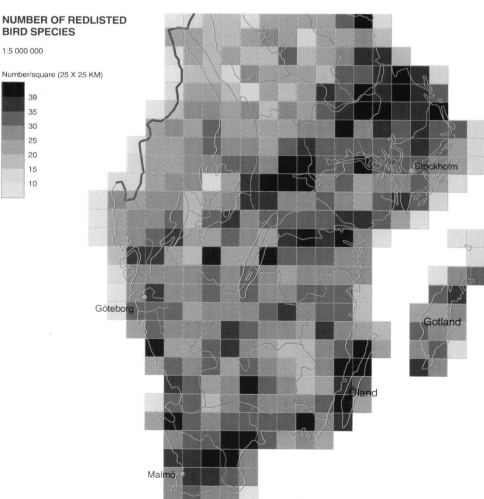

DISTRIBUTION OF LESSER WHITE-FRONTED GOOSE

Anser erythropus

- Before 1950
- 1960-1980
- • 1990-1994

Lesser white-fronted goose
resting on Öland

BREEDING COLONIES OF CASPIAN TERN

Sterna caspia

Caspian terns on their nest at one of
about 40 Swedish colonies.

Agriculture, and in more recent times silviculture, too, have affected wetland birds negatively because of all the great drainage schemes of the past few hundred years. Today's restoration of wetlands brings new hope for several species.

Fortunately enough toxic substances no longer seem to be a serious threat to birdlife in Sweden, thanks to the increasingly strict control of pesticides. Acidification has not yet, as far as we know, threatened any species of birds, but may become harmful since it affects such large areas.

LESSER WHITE-FRONTED GEESE

The lesser white-fronted goose *Anser erythropus* is one of the most endangered bird species in Sweden and northern Europe. At the turn of the century and later there were some 5,000 breeding pairs in Fennoscandia, perhaps 2,000 of which were in Sweden. In the early 1990s, in the same area, there were only about 50 breeding pairs, 5–10 of which were in Sweden.

The reason for this decline may be connected with the destruction of biotopes and hunting during migration and in the winter resorts, but also with the fact that breeding and moulting areas now are more frequently disturbed by recreational fishing in particular. The increase in the number of foxes may also have affected the species' possibilities to breed and moult. (S178)

CASPIAN TERNS

The only occurrence of the Caspian tern *Sterna caspia* in west and northwest Europe is in the Baltic area. There has been a considerable decline since 1970, when the population was estimated to be about 2,200 pairs and there were 44 known colonies. In 1992 the number of known colonies was 25, comprising about 1,500 pairs, 500 of which were in Sweden. An important factor in the decline of this tern is probably conditions in its winter areas, such as the severe drought in the Sahel zone. Other factors are the expansion of mink in certain archipelagos, pollution of the nutrient rich inland waters where the terns fish, disturbance of nesting sites, and so-called protective shooting at fish ponds and salines in Central and Southern Europe and in winter resorts along the Niger's flood area in Mali. (S179)

Amphibians and Reptiles

Three species and one subspecies of Sweden's six reptiles are red-listed as requiring protection. Amphibians are one of the most severely affected groups of animals in the Swedish fauna; of the 13 species no fewer than nine are red-listed. There are several reasons: draining of wetlands in agricultural land, afforestation of natural pastures, draining of forestland and conversion of deciduous forest to spruce plantations are among the most important factors. The planting of fish and crayfish, filling-in of ponds, road-building and other impairment of biotopes has also destroyed many amphibian populations.

One species, the fire-bellied toad, became extinct in Sweden in 1960, but has now been re-introduced. The current situation for three species, the spade foot toad, the green toad and the natterjack, is very critical. The green tree frog has declined greatly in the 20th century and lost half of its distribution area. Thanks to habitat protection and the restoration of ponds this species now has better prospects of surviving.

SOME RARE AND THREATENED AMPHIBIANS

1:2 500 000

- (hatched) *Pelobates fuscus*, previous distribution
- (dot) *Pelobates fuscus*, present distribution
- (dot) *Rana dalmatina*
- (dot) *Bufo viridis*
- (+) *Bufo calamita*

(S180)

Agile frog *Rana dalmatina*

Green toad *Bufo viridis*

Natterjack *Bufo calamita*

Spade foot toad *Pelobates fuscus*

Rana dalmatina has a scattered distribution area in south-east Sweden. The population is the remains of a previously more continuous habitat. This species spawns in shallow fens and other ponds without fish in large forest areas dominated by deciduous trees and has suffered from spruce planting and the end of grazing as well as by draining and the infilling or removal of small wetlands.

Pelobates fuscus is found in sandy agricultural areas in the southern half of Skåne. For some inexplicable reason this species has declined disastrously in recent years. After having occurred at several hundred sites it now lives in only a few areas, usually with but a few

individuals at each site. Unless this trend can be broken the species will vanish from Sweden.

Bufo viridis is rare on shore meadows and rocky areas in Skåne, Blekinge and on Öland. This species has declined rapidly and now lives at fewer than ten sites. It has, however, increased again in a few areas along the Sound, so the situation does not seem totally hopeless.

Bufo calamita occurs today in the archipelagos of the west coast and on shore meadows in Skåne and Blekinge. This species has declined greatly in Skåne and Blekinge over the past few decades.

Vänersborg
Linköping
Göteborg
Jönköping
Växjö
Halmstad
Kalmar
Öland
Kristianstad
Karlskrona
Malmö

TRIGLOPSIS QUADRICORNIS

1:10 000 000

Number of finds

● 8–15
● 3–7
● 1–2

Luleå

Sundsvall

Gävle

Stockholm

Göteborg

Malmö

**RED-LISTED
FISHES***
**(PISCES AND
CYCLOSTOMATA)**

0. Vanished
Sturgeon (c. 1900)

1. Endangered
Spring-spawning cisco
Sheatfish

2. Vulnerable
Moderlieschen
Stone loach
Gudgeon
Atlantic salmon
Fries' goby

3. Rare
Blue bream
Asp
Spined loach
Cottus koshewnikowi
Yarrel's blenny
Rock cock

4. Care-demanding
Sea lamprey
Brown trout
Arctic char
Grayling
Fourhorn sculpin

* in fresh *and* sea water

The sculpin *Triglopsis quadricornis* is an Arctic coastal fish also found in isolated populations in deep lakes. The lake and Baltic forms are Ice Age relics and grow to be not more than 35 cm long. The lake populations are threatened by acidification and other environmental pollution. (S181)

The sheatfish *Silurus glanis* is the largest freshwater fish in the world; the largest known Swedish record was 3.6 m long. It is a relict of the warm period which spawns only in warm summers. It lives in both lakes and rivers and used to be found in many more places than today. It is protected. (S184)

SILURUS GLANIS

Freshwater Fish

There are some 50 fish species in Swedish freshwater. Seven of these migrate between the sea and rivers, while the others live only in fresh or brackish water. Most of them belong to the carp (Cyprinidae) and salmon (Salmonidae) families.

The small number of species in Scandinavia is due to the fact that all life in freshwater died out during the Quarternary ice ages. Several species subsequently immigrated from various directions as the Baltic Sea developed. Today human influence on lakes and watercourses is the greatest threat to freshwater fauna. Some waters are severely polluted by nutrients and effluents, but fishing, shipping, draining and the like also affect freshwater life. The Museum of Natural History has investigated the occurrence of several of the endangered fish species. Their distribution prior to 1988 has been surveyed, using the collections in Sweden's natural history museums as a starting point. Thereafter field work established the current distribution of, in the first place, the small and often overlooked species.

BARBATULA BARBATULA

The stone loach *Barbatula barbatula* is about 15 cm long and lives on the beds of rivers with oxygen-rich water. A recent discovery in the Torne älv is considered to belong to a Finnish-Russian population. (S182)

The gudgeon *Gobio gobio* is an up to 12 cm long carp fish. It is threatened because of its limited distribution and its strict requirement of a sand or gravel bottom for spawning. (S185)

GOBIO GOBIO

COBITIS TAENIA

The spined loach *Cobitis taenia* is a little fish, at most 8 cm long. It is active at night and difficult to catch, so its distribution is not clearly known. (S183)

The moderlieschen *Leucaspius delineatus*, one of the carp family, grows to be not more than 58 mm long and lives in both running and stagnant water rich in weeds but with patches of clear water. It has disappeared from many of its previously known locations. (S186)

LEUCASPIUS DELINEATUS

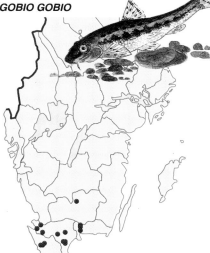

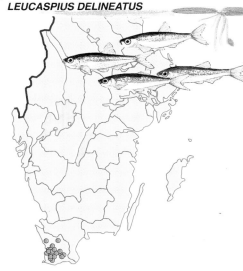

The giant oaks at Halltorps hage in central Öland are the hosts of several of Northern Europe's rarest beetles, including the longhorn beetle *Cerambyx cerdo*, which is protected at this site.

A cowpat is full of life—mostly flies and beetles. Many of these species have decreased greatly in the last hundred years. Some have even vanished from Sweden.

Invertebrates

The total number of invertebrates in Sweden is estimated to be about 30,000, almost 1,900 of which are on the red list. Approximately half of the red-listed species live in forests and the lack of dead trees—preferably large ones—is one of the most threatening factors for these animals.

Some 900 of the red-listed insects are threatened by various agricultural methods and here it is changes in or the discontinuation of grazing that is the single most significant factor. Many butterflies live on plant species that are found only on old meadow and pastureland have decreased. As cattle grazing has gradually decreased, the number of insects living in animal droppings has also decreased. Insects that flourish in sunshine and warmth such as many aculeate wasps and orthoptera decline in numbers when meadows and pastures become overgrown or are turned into plantations. For aquatic species it is mainly acidification, water regulation and changes in vegetation caused by over-fertilising that create a threat.

CHLAENIUS SPECIES

Chlaenius spp. are a kind of carabid beetle, about 15 mm long, represented by seven species in Sweden, all of which are red-listed. Most of them have a southerly distribution in Scandinavia and also occur in Central Europe.

Several species live on sunny lake shores with rich vegetation and in swampy areas. During the past few decades several of our carabid beetles have declined in number since many swampy areas have been drained and shore grazing is no longer practised in most districts, with overgrown meadows as a result.

AGRILUS MENDAX

Agrilus mendax, a wood-borer, is a beautiful but endangered species of beetle, 10–15 mm long, which mainly occurs in Russia but has also been found in southern Finland, the Baltic states and eastern Europe. Its larvae live under the bark of living rowan trees in sunny, warm sites, especially where the trunk has been damaged. Although the rowan is a common tree in Sweden, this beetle is found only at a few places. The species seems to require a large number of rowans, preferably on a south-facing slope, to survive.

SOME CHLAENIUS SPECIES

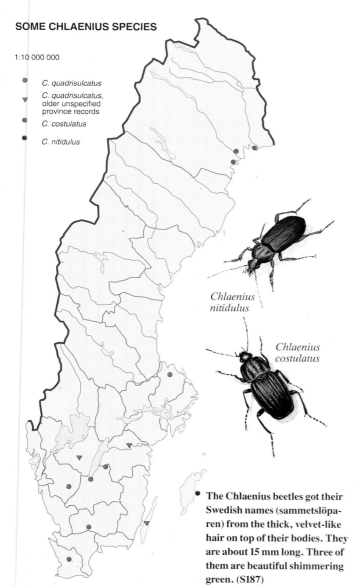

1:10 000 000

- C. quadrisulcatus
- C. quadrisulcatus, older unspecified province records
- C. costulatus
- C. nitidulus

Chlaenius nitidulus

Chlaenius costulatus

The Chlaenius beetles got their Swedish names (sammetslöparen) from the thick, velvet-like hair on top of their bodies. They are about 15 mm long. Three of them are beautiful shimmering green. (S187)

AGRILUS MENDAX

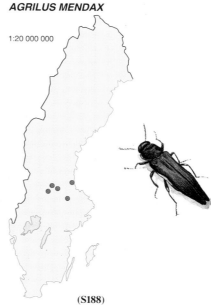

1:20 000 000

(S188)

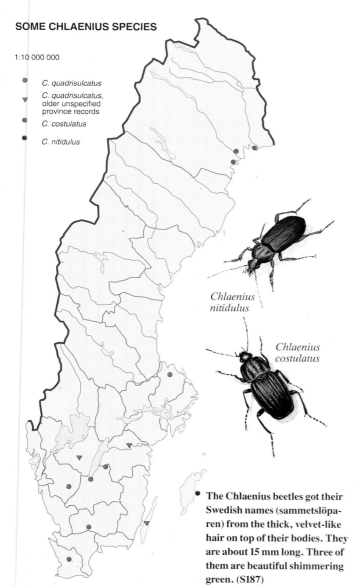

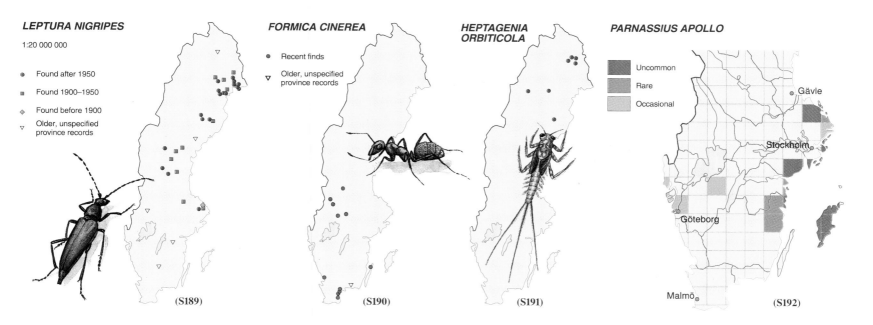

LEPTURA NIGRIPES

1:20 000 000

- Found after 1950
- Found 1900–1950
- Found before 1900
- Older, unspecified province records

(S189)

FORMICA CINEREA

- Recent finds
- Older, unspecified province records

(S190)

HEPTAGENIA ORBITICOLA

(S191)

PARNASSIUS APOLLO

- Uncommon
- Rare
- Occasional

Gävle

Stockholm

Göteborg

Malmö

(S192)

When moose gnaw the bark of living rowan trees, they damage the trunk, which has temporarily helped the beetle at a few of the Swedish sites. But when the moose population grows too large, the young trees have been so seriously damaged that the beetle has difficulty in finding suitable trees.

LEPTURA NIGRIPES

Leptura nigripes is a vulnerable, 16 mm long insect, one of the longhorn beetles. Its larvae live in birch and aspen tree stumps with white rot, especially those left after forest fires.

During the 19th century this longhorn beetle was found in several southern Swedish provinces, but has not been found south of Uppland in the 20th century. In Norrland, too, this species seems to have declined. The main reason seems to be fewer forest fires.

FORMICA CINEREA

Formica cinerea is an 8 mm-long, vulnerable, black relative of the ordinary wood ant. It loves warmth, occurring on warm, sandy deposits in the coastal districts of southern Sweden and on sandy fields in parts of central Sweden. It is also found at certain sites in neighbouring countries and in Central and Southern Europe to the Urals. This ant builds its nest on warm, sandy soil with little vegetation. Since it often occurs on open patches of sand, its inland sites are mainly threatened by spontaneous scrub and pine plantations.

HEPTAGENIA ORBITICOLA

Heptagenia orbiticola, a mayfly, is very rare and is listed as being in need of protection. It is about 10 mm long

and lives in running water in Norrland, where as a larva it crawls among stones. Like other mayflies it lives for only a few days as a winged insect. This species is harmed, like most other mayflies, by acidification, pollution and physical changes in water environments.

PARNASSIUS APOLLO

The Apollo butterfly *Parnassius apollo* was quite common until the 1950s, but since then has disappeared from many districts. The reasons for this sharp decline on the mainland are a matter of speculation. The most probable explanation is acidification. This species is now found only sporadically on the west coast, which is severely affected by acid deposition. Along the east coast it occurs only on calcareous soils, where the limestone may have a buffer effect on acidifying substances. On more acid soils the larvae probably do not manage to absorb the nutrients in the host plant. This plant, *Sedum telephium*, the orpine, has not, however, decreased on the mainland.

BULIN

Bulin *Ena montana*, a snail species, has its main distribution area in Central Europe. In Scandinavia this species occurs today only at a few sites on the deciduous tree-clad slopes along the east shore of Lake Vättern. It probably has difficulty in spreading, which is in the long term another threat to its survival in Sweden. It is possible that it can be spread passively, for example by birds or on windblown leaves, but the importance of this is unknown. When the motorway along Lake Vättern was built, several of its habitats were destroyed.

The Apollo butterfly *Parnassius apollo* has become less common in recent years and is nowadays seen mostly in districts with limestone bedrock.

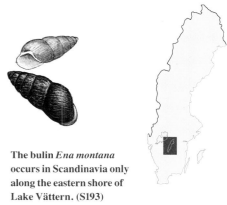

The bulin *Ena montana* occurs in Scandinavia only along the eastern shore of Lake Vättern. (S193)

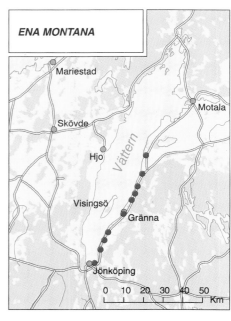

ENA MONTANA

Mariestad

Motala

Skövde

Hjo

Vättern

Visingsö

Gränna

Jönköping

0 10 20 30 40 50 Km

FOMITOPSIS ROSEA

1:10 000 000

Records/25 x 25 km square

■	53
	20
	10
	5

Luleå

Umeå

Sundsvall

Gävle

Stockholm

Göteborg

Malmö

Fomitopsis rosea grows almost exclusively on large spruce logs in old coniferous forests. Young specimens are unmistakeable by their beautiful pink pores, whereas older mis-coloured specimens can be mistaken for the common *Fomitopsis pinicola*. (S194)

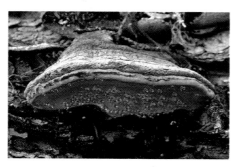

AURANTIOPORUS CROCEUS

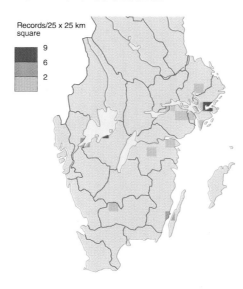

Records/25 x 25 km square

	9
	6
	2

Aurantioporus croceus grows only on old oak trees and is one of Sweden's rarest bracket fungi. It usually appears on the same trees for a number of years, but it quite often grows high up and hidden in holes, so it remains undiscovered. (S195)

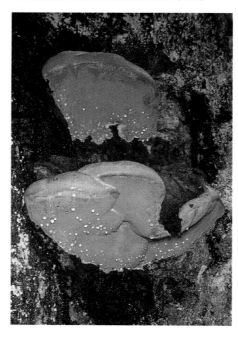

A few examples of threatened fungi that grow only in natural pastures and meadows.

Fungi

There are some 3,000 macrofungi in Sweden, 20% of which are red-listed. Fungi are most seriously threatened by changes in agricultural and forestry methods and by the effects of air pollution on the chemistry of the soil.

The large-scale use of artificial fertilisers has meant that fungi no longer flourish in meadow and pastureland–at the same time as natural grazing land, rich in species, has to a large extent been replaced by fields poor in species.

In modern, cultivated forests the lack of old trees and fallen trees is the greatest threat, since the conditions for many species that live on wood have deteriorated.

Air pollution leads to acidification of the ground, which is harmful for most organisms, and to an unnaturally high level of nitrogen. Mycorrhiza-forming fungi suffer particularly when nitrogen levels rise.

BRACKET FUNGI AND CRUST FUNGI

There are about 800 species of bracket fungi, Polyporaceae, and crust fungi in Sweden. Most of them live only on dead wood. The present method of managing and exploiting forests has changed the environments of these fungi dramatically, making it more difficult for them to spread. The species that can grow only on large, old trees, such as *Aurantioporus croceus* on oak trees and *Fomitopsis rosea* on spruce, suffer badly. The latter is one of several bracket fungi which are used as indicators, since their presence suggests that other endangered species may also be present.

AGARICS, BOLETES, TOOTHED FUNGI, CLUB FUNGI

There are over 2,000 species of these groups in Sweden, most of which are terrestrial and many of which form mycorrhiza. A large number are uncommon, but it is not clear whether their existence is threatened. Particularly vulnerable groups are those that prefer old forest with long continuity and those that require a high pH in the soil. Among them are many Clavaria fungi such as *Gomphus clavatus*. Another group grow in unfertilised meadowland, including *Hygrocybe punicea*. Many of the species that form mycorrhiza with nemoral trees are also endangered, among them many boleti and agarics.

Clavaria inaequalis	Entoloma mougeotii	Hygrocybe punicea	Geoglossum difforme	Geastrum schmidelii	Boletus impolitus

HYGROCYBE PUNICEA

1:10 000 000

Records/25 x 25 km square

■	28
■	20
▨	10
▨	5

Luleå

Umeå

Sundsvall

Gävle

Stockholm

Göteborg

Malmö

Hygrocybe punicea

Hygrocybe punicea used to be common and a popular edible fungus. It prefers to grow in natural pastures rich in herbs, but also in deciduous forests with deep soil. Since it cannot tolerate artificial fertilisers it has decreased greatly in the 20th century and is now only locally common in districts where old types of cultivation are still in use. (S196)

GOMPHUS CLAVATUS

1:20 000 000

■	Two or more records
▨	One record

Gomphus clavatus grows in calcareous and clayey soil and prefers old, mossy spruce forests, but can also grow in beech forests. It appears in dense clusters, often as fairy rings, and makes excellent eating. Since it is both beautiful and rare, however, it should not be picked. (S197)

Gomphus clavatus

Lichens

About 250 of Sweden's 2,000 or so lichens are red listed, the majority of them in southern Sweden. More than 60% are found in forest environments, while about 30% grow on cliffs and bare rock. Approximately 35% live in the agricultural landscape. Only 2% of the red-listed lichens are found in the mountains.

Modern forestry methods have led to a lack of large, old trees and dead wood (logs and snags)—substrates that are essential for many species. Draining swampy forests has also led to a decline in the distribution of many lichens, since constant high humidity is vital for many of them. Air pollution is also an obvious threat, above all in south-west Sweden. Several species have declined sharply in this part of the country. Changes in agriculture have resulted in species tied to trees in meadows and pastures being disfavoured.

Menegazzia terebrata

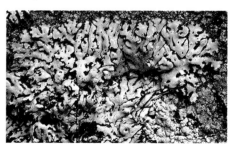

Flavoparmelia caperata

MENEGAZZIA TEREBRATA, RECORDS AFTER 1990

(S198)

FLAVOPARMELIA CAPERATA, RECORDS AFTER 1990

(S199)

MENEGAZZIA TEREBRATA AND HYPOGYMNIA PHYSODES

An example of a species that has been affected negatively by forestry is *Menegazzia terebrata*. This is similar to *Hypogymnia physodes* but it has many small holes on the upper surface of its thallus. *Menegazzia terebrata* occurs mainly on alders in swampy forest. It has also been found on mossy, shaded rocks. This species has a westerly distribution, but also occurs in eastern Sweden. Since it is dependent on high humidity and shade, it is sensitive to clear-cutting.

Flavoparmelia caperata grows mainly on deciduous trees, both in dense deciduous forests and in open or half-open terrain, such as the edge of a forest. A dozen or so sites have been reported over the years, but the species has disappeared from most of them, so that today it is known in only six places. The reason for its disappearance is mainly that its habitats have been destroyed by road building, new housing estates and the felling of deciduous trees.

PTEROGONIUM GRACILE AND HOOKERIA LUCENS

1:2 500 000

- ● Pterogonium gracile, present locality
- ○ Pterogonium gracile, earlier locality
- ◉ Hookeria lucens

(S200)

Hookeria lucens

Pterogonium gracile

Bryophytes

Some 240 of Sweden's 1,000 or so mosses are red listed. Changes in agricultural and forestry methods are the greatest threats, but air pollution affects many negatively.

Hookeria lucens occurs in shaded, moist places close to running or dripping water, usually on soil but sometimes on tree roots or stones. Its characteristic light-green, shining carpets make it easy to identify, so most of its sites have probably been discovered. Since the first record was made in the early 19th century this species has been found in some 30 places. However, it has disappeared from over ten of them and is now known to exist in about 20 places, all in the south-west of Sweden. Draining and other changes in water flow are the greatest threats. The dependence of this species on constant high humidity means that it runs a great risk of dying out in clear-cuttings. It also seems to be sensitive to pollution in watercourses.

Pterogonium gracile is an example of a species that has lost ground because of air pollution. It grows at the base of cliffs shaded by deciduous trees and is found only in the south-west of Sweden, where it has been found at 45 sites since the 19th century. It has disappeared from 30 of these and is weaker at 10 of the remaining 15. The size of the populations varies greatly from site to site. At the most densely populated one it covers about one square metre, while at the weakest one it covers only about 20 square centimetres. Sensitivity to air pollution is indicated by the fact that this moss has mostly disappeared from sites near to towns like Göteborg, where it has disappeared from 20 or so sites within a radius of some 20 km.

Neckera pennata is found in most of Sweden, but mainly concentrated in Uppland and Gästrikland. This species grows only in old forests, on deciduous trees with nutritious bark, mainly maple, aspen and lime. It is a good indicator of long forest continuity, that is, there has been forest at that place for a very long time. Over the years this species has been found at a total of some 150 sites. A survey early in the 1990s showed that it had disappeared from 30 sites, mainly because of tree felling. The great interest in red-listed bryophytes during recent years has, however, led to the discovery of a number of new, previously unknown sites, about 70 since 1990. This tendency, that previously unknown sites of red-listed species are located, is also very evident for other groups of plants and animals.

Neckera pennata grows in old forests on deciduous trees like aspen, maple and lime. It is rare but has been discovered at a fairly large number of previously unknown sites during the 1990s.

NECKERA PENNATA

1:10 000 000

- ● Locality found after 1990
- ◉ Locality found before 1990
- ○ Vanished

(S201)

Stoneworts often form underwater vegetation in shallow pools and ponds in calcareous areas. *Chara aspera* photographed on Gotland.

Stoneworts

Stoneworts are a group of plants that are found in both fresh and salt water. They look more like vascular plants than algae and all in all 33 species have been found in Sweden. No fewer than 27 of them are red-listed—an unusually large proportion in comparison with other plant groups.

Eutrophication is the most serious threat. These algae are among the first to die out as a result of eutrophication, being affected indirectly by the increased growth of epiphytic algae and plant plankton resulting from larger supplies of nutritious salts, which shades the plants growing under the surface.

These algae can spread rapidly to new pools but they are then outcompeted by other underwater plants. The decreasing number of new pools and temporary ponds, for example flooded areas along rivers, is therefore another reason why many such algae are endangered in our cultural landscape. However, newly-built fish and crayfish ponds, gravel pits and quarries function to some extent as substitute habitats.

These algae have also disappeared from many acidified lakes; the mechanism underlying this decline is, however, not known.

In moderately eutrophied, shallow lakes certain large algae such as *Chara tomentosa* and *Nitellopsis obtusa* can cover vast areas, forming dense populations with a biomass of more than 3 kg per m². Fluctuations in the size of algae populations have occurred in several Swedish bird lakes, which has affected the number of breeding and resting water birds. The best documented examples of this are at Tåkern in Östergötland and Krankesjön in Skåne, two of Sweden's most frequented bird lakes.

Tolypella nidifica occurs exclusively in salt and brackish water. It has decreased both in the south Baltic and along the west coast, probably owing to eutrophication. (S202)

Nitella gracilis grows mainly in shallow water both in ponds and along the shores of lakes. It is threatened because its habitats are eutrophied or have disappeared. (S203)

Chara rudis occurs only in large, calcareous lakes. It has disappeared from many eutrophied lakes—probably because of a lack of light. (S204)

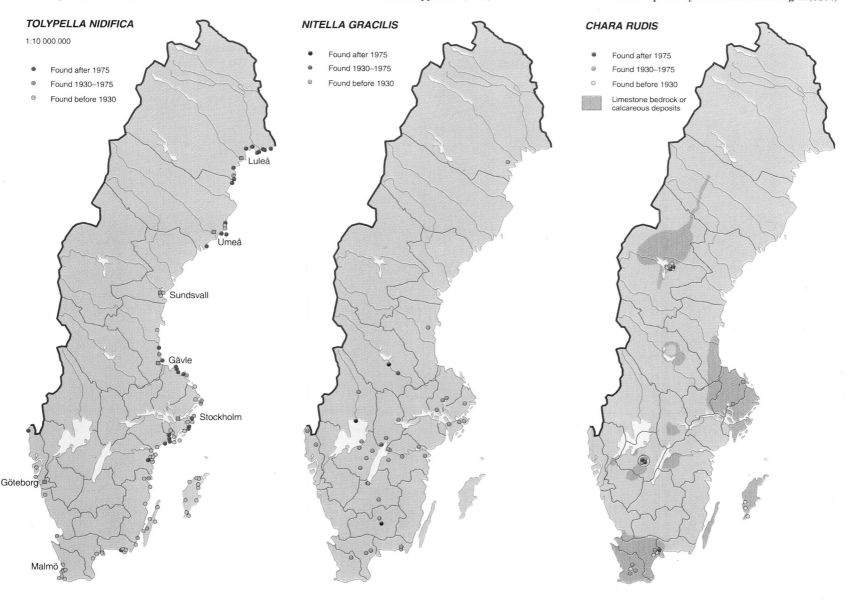

TOLYPELLA NIDIFICA

1:10 000 000

- Found after 1975
- Found 1930–1975
- Found before 1930

NITELLA GRACILIS

- Found after 1975
- Found 1930–1975
- Found before 1930

CHARA RUDIS

- Found after 1975
- Found 1930–1975
- Found before 1930
- Limestone bedrock or calcareous deposits

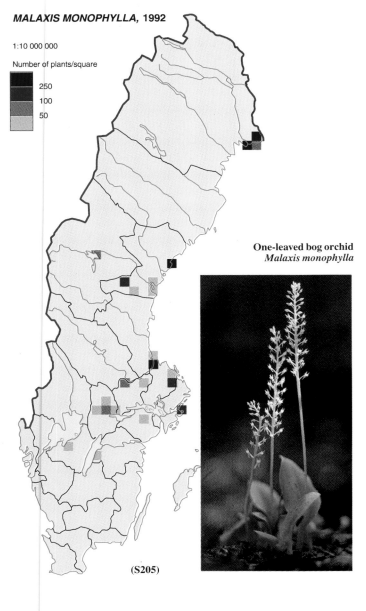

1:10 000 000

Number of plants/square

250
100
50

One-leaved bog orchid
Malaxis monophylla

(S205)

VASCULAR PLANTS

Approximately 450 of Sweden's 2,000 or so vascular plants are red listed, that is, just over 20%. These species occur mainly on agricultural land (69%) and to a lesser extent in other environments, such as forests (15%) and wetlands (14%).

The old cultivated landscape of meadows, little manuring, poorly weed-cleaned sowings and no pesticides favoured many species. As agriculture was modernised, the distribution of many of these species was dramatically reduced. One example is the weed lamb's succory *Arnoseris minima*, which used to be common but is now red listed. This annual species is found on poor, sandy soil. The reasons for its decline are probably both tree planting and no longer letting land lie fallow. The use of fertilisers and herbicides may also have a negative effect.

Forest vascular plants are mainly threatened by increasingly dense and dark forests as a result of planting spruce and fewer deciduous trees, but also when forests previously used for grazing spontaneously become denser.

The vetch *Vicia pisiformis* does best on warm, south-facing slopes on dry, nutritious soil. It prefers light, half-open habitats with bushes and deciduous trees. This vetch is known to exist at some 20 sites in southern central Sweden and is here at the northern limit of its distribution area. Low night temperatures in summer strongly inhibit the production of flowers and thus seeds, which may explain this limit. The expansion of scrub and coniferous tree plantating are the direct causes of its disappearance from many of its Swedish sites. Studies have shown that this vetch has little genetic variation within and among populations.

Draining swampy forests and other wetlands has had a negative effect on several species, such as the one-leaved bog orchid *Malaxis monophylla*. This species grows in fens and swampy forests containing lime and is dependent on the soil being "stirred" to prevent competition from other species. This "stirring" may be caused by the hooves of cattle or wild animals, ice movement in areas close to shores or natural water movement in the soil. Less grazing in outfields is therefore another explanation for the dramatic decline of this orchid in the 20th century. It is known from historical records in about 190 sites, but a survey in 1992 found it in only just over 50 of them. Only 25 of the sites had more than 10 individual plants. All in all 3,259 individual plants were found, 2,069 of them in bloom. The one-leaved bog orchid is red listed in Sweden, Finland and Norway and in many other European countries. It is not found in Denmark.

● 3 sites
◉ 2 sites
○ 1 sites

Lambs' succory *Arnoseris minima* is a weed that has almost completely disappeared from our fields as a result of modern agricultural methods. (S206)

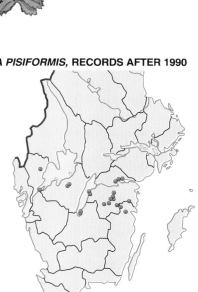

Vicia pisiformis occurs rarely on warm south-facing slopes in a belt across southern Sweden. (S207)

Vicia pisiformis is one of Sweden's largest pea plants. The shoots, which can be several metres long, climb in bushes in half-open, deciduous forests. It has decreased in recent years, mainly because the forests where it flourishes are becoming overgrown.

Migration, Movements and Dispersal

Mammals' Movements

Animals move from one place to another for several possible reasons. An example of large-scale movements involving many individuals and long distances is the seasonal migration of reindeer between forest and mountain districts, which may be compared to birds migrating to more southerly lands. In a narrower perspective individual animals will move to find food or a mate, to escape from predators and so on.

In order to be able to describe how animals move about in the terrain individuals have to be identified and located. Usually it is necessary first to capture and mark the animal. In open countryside it is often helpful to fit the animal with some easily visible identification in the form of a numbered collar, ear marks or patches of colour on their coats, for example.

In recent years it has become more and more common to fit a radio transmitter, which makes it possible to determine the animal's position at every moment, in the dark and in dense vegetation, at great distances. The latest technology even utilises various satellite systems. In this way scientists can study a wide range of movement, from the long migrations of wild reindeer in remote tundra areas and the movement of polar bears round the Arctic Sea to the journeys of a shrew along the edge of a field.

The movements of animals may be categorised as: *movement within a home range, dispersal, migration* and *nomadism.*

MOVEMENTS WITHIN THE HOME RANGE

An animal's home range is the area in which it moves during its normal, daily activities. Since movements are not uniform every day, our picture of the size of the home range will depend on the length of time each animal is followed.

Most species spend most of their active time searching for food. This creates a pattern which is closely governed by the amount and location of food in the area. If the food is spread out over too large areas, more energy will be spent on finding it than the food provides. In this situation an animal will probably choose to migrate or nomadise.

A special type of home range is what is called a *territory*. Such areas are usually defended by males that drive other animals of the same species and sex off their territory. Territorial boundaries are usually defined in the terrain, for example by scent marking. In some cases, however, the territories may be flexible, that is, an individual defends a limited area around it or round another individual.

The area changes as the animal moves about.

The size and appearance of home ranges can vary a great deal from species to species. Large animals need larger areas than small ones to meet their energy needs. This is true of both herbivores and predators. Predators often have considerably larger home ranges than herbivores of the same size since, unlike the herbivores, they cannot so easily predict where to find their food.

To be able to get information about the movements of brown bears in their home ranges and in different seasons they are fitted with transmitters.

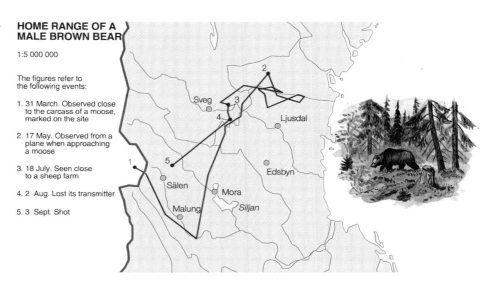

HOME RANGE OF A MALE BROWN BEAR

1:5 000 000

The figures refer to the following events:

1. 31 March. Observed close to the carcass of a moose, marked on the site
2. 17 May. Observed from a plane when approaching a moose
3. 18 July. Seen close to a sheep farm
4. 2 Aug. Lost its transmitter
5. 3 Sept. Shot

Predators in particular may sometimes have extremely large home ranges. The example on the map shows how a three-year-old male bear *Ursus arctos* has moved. This investigation was carried out in 1989 by means of radio location. The home range was about 23,600 km² in area. (S208)

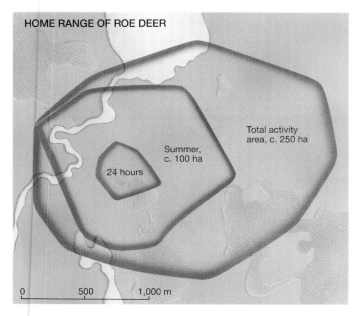

HOME RANGE OF ROE DEER

Total activity area, c. 250 ha

Summer, c. 100 ha

24 hours

0   500   1,000 m

The size of the home range of a roe doe *Capreolus capreolus* during a summer day, during the whole of a summer (June–August) and during a whole year. The example is from a forest environment. In richer districts, often with many farms, the home ranges are smaller.

HOME RANGE OF BADGER, TRACK MAY 24–25

Badger sett
21.03   01.05

Area of concentrated movements

0.00

Badger sett
02.35   03.45

23.40

22.00

Badger sett

22.45

23.05   23.25

23.10

0   500   1,000 m

The way an animal moves is to a high degree affected by the local food resources. The activities of the badger *Meles meles* are to a high degree governed by the availability of cultivated land where it can find food such as worms. For this reason it spends less time in forests and other places where the soil is poor and offers less food. The picture shows how a badger fitted with a transmitter moved one night in May.

SOME EXAMPLES OF MIGRATION

1:5 000 000

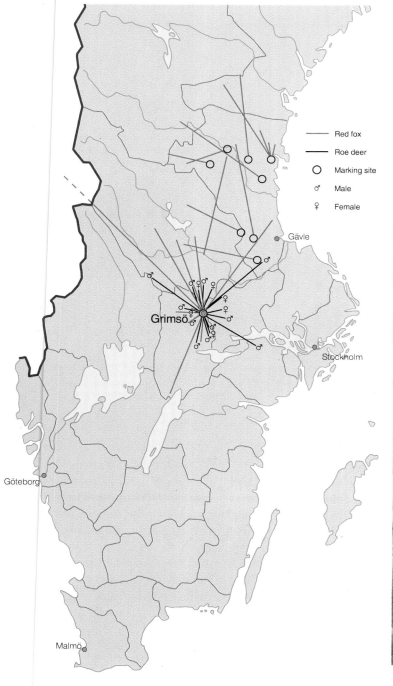

— Red fox
— Roe deer
○ Marking site
♂ Male
♀ Female

Gävle

Grimsö

Stockholm

Göteborg

Malmö

Radio marking makes it possible to follow an animal's movements in detail.

Map left. Examples of emigration by roe deer *Capreolus capreolus* and fox *Vulpes vulpes*. Usually it is young animals that emigrate, often long distances from their birth place. (S209)

DISPERSAL

When an animal is said to disperse, it means that it emigrates from its birth place to an area where it chooses to breed. This type of movement is in a one-way direction; the animal does not return to its original home.

With most species it is young animals not yet sexually mature that emigrate. The tendency to emigrate is often stronger among males than among females. Competition for females may result in many males leaving an area.

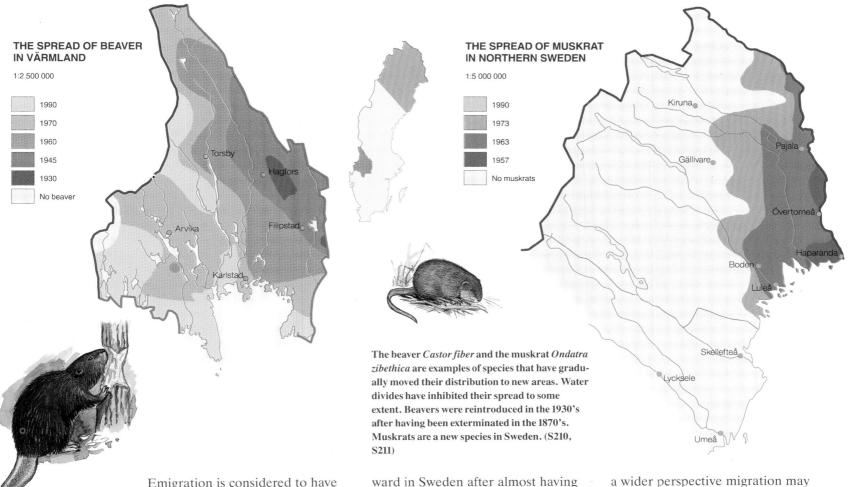

**THE SPREAD OF BEAVER
IN VÄRMLAND**

1:2 500 000

- 1990
- 1970
- 1960
- 1945
- 1930
- No beaver

**THE SPREAD OF MUSKRAT
IN NORTHERN SWEDEN**

1:5 000 000

- 1990
- 1973
- 1963
- 1957
- No muskrats

Torsby

Hagfors

Arvika

Filipstad

Karlstad

Kiruna

Pajala

Gällivare

Övertorneå

Haparanda

Boden

Luleå

Skellefteå

Lycksele

Umeå

The beaver *Castor fiber* and the muskrat *Ondatra
zibethica* are examples of species that have gradually moved their distribution to new areas. Water
divides have inhibited their spread to some
extent. Beavers were reintroduced in the 1930's
after having been exterminated in the 1870's.
Muskrats are a new species in Sweden. (S210,
S211)

Emigration is considered to have
several causes according to the species involved. One theory is that emigration—and hence immigration as
well—has to take place to maintain
a large genetic variation. Alternative
theories claim that the real reason
may well be competition for partners
or for food.

Dispersal may result in a species
colonizing areas where it previously
did not live. One of the classic examples is the way roe deer spread northward in Sweden after almost having
been exterminated in the early 19th
century. This species not only re-
gained its previous distribution area
in southern Sweden but continued to
spread northward. Today roe deer are
found even in the most northerly
parts of Sweden.

MIGRATION

An animal is said to migrate if it per-
forms regular and seasonal movements between two or more areas. In
a wider perspective migration may
also include movements within
a home range.

Originally scientists considered that
animals migrated to avoid periods of
poor food supply or quality. Nowadays, however, this idea has been re-
versed; migrations are undertaken to
find places which offer optimal conditions for giving birth and rearing
offspring. In Scandinavia there are
large, regular seasonal changes in climate and food supply, which create
migration patterns among, for example, the northern big herbivores (reindeer, moose and roe deer).

NOMADISM

A nomadising animal moves in an un-
predictable way and is often found
further and further away from the
place where it was first observed.
Thus these animals do not establish
fixed home ranges but often move
across much larger areas than stationary animals.

This behaviour might be expected
in poor areas (particularly those with
food shortages), in areas with extreme
weather situations and/or where resources are unevenly distributed over
large areas and difficult to predict in
time and space. Examples are the
herds of gnu in Africa, wild reindeer
in the tundra areas of northern Canada and some kangaroo species which
live in desert-like landscapes in Australia.

It is common in Norrland for moose *Alces alces* to move from their summer resorts on high land to special winter districts where
they gather in large numbers. This migration is repeated every year and often by tradition follows the same routes.

Interior of the closed-down Kleva mine in Småland, which is now protected for its hibernating bats.

BAT MIGRATIONS

Bats which live on insects find that food is in short supply in the autumn. Insect-eating birds have only one option—to migrate. Bats can solve the problem by:

- ☛ hibernating on the spot,
- moving to areas with better conditions for hibernating (= shorter hibernation period), or
- like birds, moving to areas where there are insects.

The majority of Swedish bats choose the first alternative, hibernating. There is evidence that *Nyctalus noctula* and *Pipistrelli nathusii* can choose to move to areas with better hibernating conditions. Experience up to now indicates that the central Swedish population of *Nyctalus noctula* regularly migrates to Skåne, but not often further south. Two recoveries, however, suggest that the Swedish population of *Pipistrellus nathusii* hibernates on the continent, as do those from the Baltic states.

There are a few other species which migrate at least short distances or between summer colonies and hibernating places. The extremely rare bat *Myotis dasycneme* probably does the same, and *Vespertilio murinus*, which lives mainly in farming districts in the summer, moves into towns in the autumn to mate and later to hibernate in large, high buildings.

No European species of bat makes use of the possibility of moving to areas where there is food, as insect-eating birds do.

Hibernating bats *Myotis daubentoni* on the wall of a mine gallery.

A long-eared bat *Plecotus auritus* on its way into its hibernating place in an old mine. Småland's Taberg.

BAT RECOVERIES
Pipistrellus nathusii

Between 1985 and 1992 14,529 bats of 15 different species were marked at the Pape bird station in the south-west of Latvia. The dominant species was *Pipistrellus nathusii* (almost 90%). The map shows how recoveries of these bats were made in the Netherlands, Belgium, France, Germany, Italy, Slovenia, Estonia, Lithuania and Belarus. This bat has been found in Sweden as far north as northern Uppland as well as on Gotland and Öland. There are a few observations from southern Finland. At Ottenby on Öland and at Falsterbo these bats have been observed migrating across the sea to the south and south-west, so it is likely that this species regularly flies across the sea between its summer and winter ranges. (S212)

Vomb

Pape

● Recovery
ringed in Skåne

● ringed in Pape

Starlings *Sturnus vulgaris* gather in flocks before migrating to the south-west.

Bird migration

Many of Sweden's breeding bird species migrate annually between their breeding sites and more or less distant winter areas. But there are other types of migration as well. Geese, for example, can fly long distances to special moulting places, which are not where they winter, and some species may move between different breeding places from year to year.

There are birds in the Swedish fauna that have the most varied migration patterns. Species with extremely long migration routes are the common tern and the arctic tern. Arctic terns journey as far south as to the waters of the Antarctic. Many Swedish migrating species, including several insect-eating warblers, spend the winter in Africa south of the Sahara. Some species fly to presumed winter quarters in Asia—the bluethroat, the scarlet rosefinch and the rustic bunting, for example. Many ducks, buzzards, thrushes and finches migrate to more or less remote parts of Europe and North Africa. Yet others, like the waxwing and the redpoll, stay where there is a good supply of berries or seeds in the winter, so they can be found in various areas from one winter to the next.

HOW DO BIRDS FIND THEIR WAY?

The shortest distance between two places on the earth's surface is along a great circle route, but navigating along this line requires continual changes of direction. Flying along a fixed compass course is longer, unless the two places happen to be on the same meridian. Some birds' migration routes, from northern Siberia to West Africa, for example, more or less follow great circle routes.

How is it possible for birds to orientate themselves in time and space? The results of a classic experiment using ringed starlings are interesting. While migrating from north-east Europe to west Europe 11,000 starlings were netted in Holland and taken to Switzerland, where they were released. The young starlings continued to fly south-west and landed up in Spain, while the old birds flew north-west to their normal winter quarters in northern France and southern England. This result has been interpreted to show that young starlings have a strong preference in the autumn to fly in a certain direction which was innately determined and which took them to Spain. The older, more experienced birds, however, choose to fly towards a previ-

The blackbird *Turdus merula* breeds generally in both forests and towns. In a poll a few years ago this well-known species, loved not least for its song, was elected the national bird of Sweden.

INTERNATIONAL
RECOVERIES OF
BLACKBIRD

Area where the recovered birds were ringed as nestlings

Area of many recoveries

Site of occasional recoveries

The blackbird is a partial migrant. It stays all the year round in built-up areas, but forests are mostly "emptied" of blackbirds in the winter. The map shows recoveries abroad of blackbirds ringed as nestlings in Sweden. (S213)

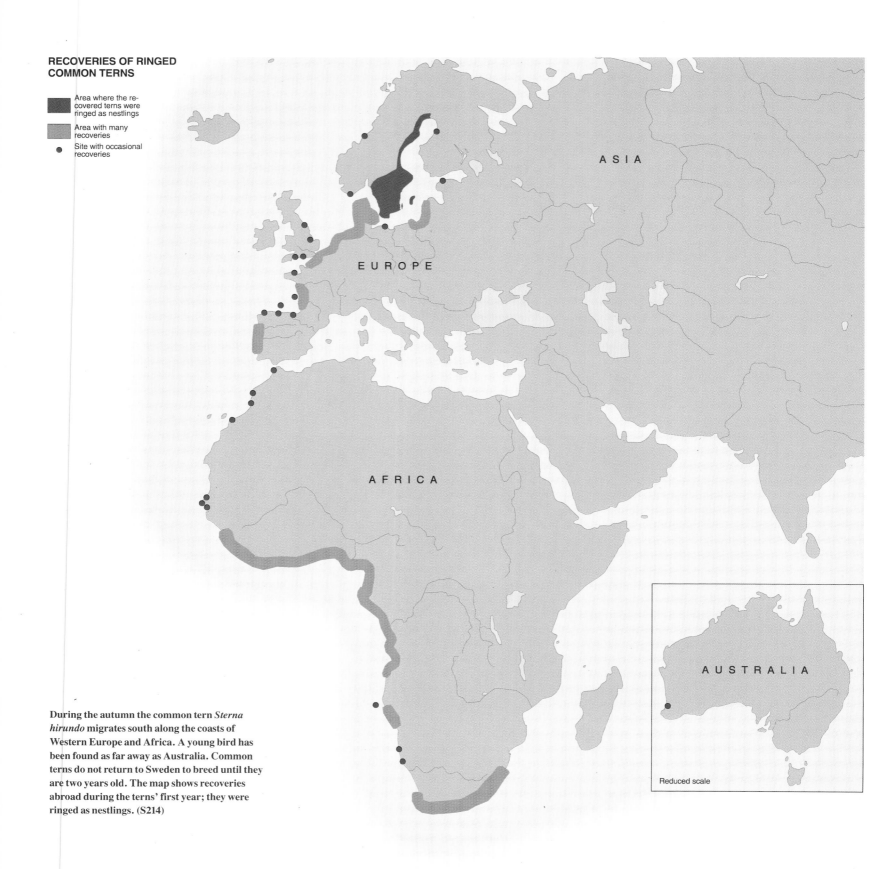

RECOVERIES OF RINGED COMMON TERNS

■ Area where the recovered terns were ringed as nestlings

▨ Area with many recoveries

● Site with occasional recoveries

ASIA

EUROPE

AFRICA

AUSTRALIA

Reduced scale

During the autumn the common tern *Sterna hirundo* migrates south along the coasts of Western Europe and Africa. A young bird has been found as far away as Australia. Common terns do not return to Sweden to breed until they are two years old. The map shows recoveries abroad during the terns' first year; they were ringed as nestlings. (S214)

Common terns are seen from May to August on most lakes and rivers in southern and central Sweden as well as along the whole of the Swedish coast. Most of the year, however, they live along the coasts of West and South Africa.

ously known goal rather than continuing in the inborn direction when this would take them away from their goal.

A distinction is made between the compass orientation and the goal orientation of birds. The young starlings in the experiment fly by compass orientation, while the older birds' flight towards their previously known winter quarters is an example of goal orientation or navigation. The fact that birds are able to navigate to a previously known place has also been proved by moving nesting birds from their nest to an unknown place, from which they have found their way back. This ability is not limited to migratory birds but includes species like homing pigeons which are related to the non-migratory rock dove.

Cage experiments using hand-bred migratory birds have proved that birds have an innate time schedule for their migration and that they can use the sun, the stars and the magnetic compass to navigate in a certain direction.

RECOVERIES OF WARBLERS RINGED IN SWEDEN

- ● Reed Warbler
- ● Sedge Warbler
- ● Marsh Warbler

Reed warblers are common in the reed beds round lakes in southern and central Sweden.

The reed warbler *Acrocephalus scirpaceus*, the sedge warbler *A. schoeno-baenus* and the marsh warbler *A. palustris* are three closely related species. They migrate from Sweden in quite different directions to reach their winter quarters. (S215)

Sedge warblers prefer wet meadows and shrubland, especially near lakes with reed, but outside southern and central Sweden they are also found in scrubland in the northern mountain districts.

Marsh warblers (far right) nest in tall-herb vegetation in southern Sweden.

SWEDEN — THE GULF OF GUINEA, THERE AND BACK

The first migration of a songbird, a reed warbler, for example, to tropical West Africa, may go something like this:

A few weeks after the fledgling has left its nest it parts from its parents and siblings. As soon as it has finished moulting, a number of preparations for migration may be observed. The daily rhythm is altered before the night journeys and fat is stored round the intestines and under the skin as fuel supplies. The bird now has to manage to migrate by itself, by means of its innate programme and continuous learning.

*

To help it orientate the bird has a built-in compass which uses the angle of the lines of force of the earth's magnetic field, but after learning the bird may make use of other compasses. On clear nights the bird has observed the apparent movement of the stars in relation to the stationary pole star and the constellations closest to that star. The bird now has these stars as guiding marks for navigation. It probably also gets information from the setting sun as well as perhaps from the polarisation patterns of sunlight.

*

One night towards the end of August the first stage of the flight begins. After only a few hours the bird lands again and when dawn breaks it looks for a suitable resting place, stays there a few days and then sets off on another lap. To begin with the journeys are not more than perhaps 100 km a night. After a month or so the bird has come to the Iberian peninsula and thanks to an innate programme, and perhaps influenced by the coastline, it changes its course from south-west to south or south-south-east. The fat reserves have been topped up before flying across the Sahara. The stages are longer now and the rest periods shorter. When the bird approaches its winter quarters just north of the Gulf of Guinea, the migratory pressure decreases under the influence of the innate time schedule.

*

When flying back to the breeding place in the spring the journey is faster and, as recoveries have shown, often along a more direct route. Probably the bird can in some way, by relating its last resting place to the goal, fly straight there. How this orientation takes place is, however, still a mystery.

Distribution of
European eel

Ocean currents of importance
for the European eel

Iceland

Scandinavia

Yellow eel

Atlantic Ocean

Glass eel

Europe

North America

Fully-grown larva,
almost one year,
c. 75 mm

Larva, some
months old,
c. 25 mm

Resently hatched
larva c. 6 mm

Silver eel

Sargasso Sea

Africa

The European eel *Anguilla anguilla* spawns in the Sargasso Sea and the larvae are then carried by ocean currents across the Atlantic to the coasts of Europe—a distance of more than 7,500 km! After a period of growth, which for females can be up to 20 years, eels return to the Sargasso Sea, where they spawn before they die. (S216)

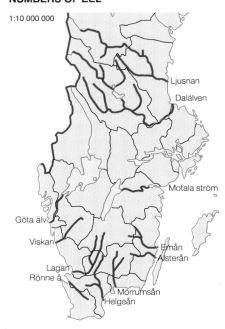

WATERCOURSES WITH LARGE NUMBERS OF EEL

1:10 000 000

Ljusnan

Dalälven

Motala ström

Göta älv

Viskan

Emån
Alsterån

Lagan
Rönne å

Mörrumsån
Helgeån

The map shows watercourses in southern and central Sweden where eels are particularly frequent. (S217)

Eel Migration

It is presumed that the reason why the European eel *Anguilla anguilla* has its spawning area in a sub-tropical part of the Atlantic is that the North American and the Euro-asiatic continental plates were closer together more than a hundred million years ago. At that time the Atlantic eel species' prehistoric forefathers spawned in a considerably smaller ocean. The land masses subsequently moved apart while the ideal spawning place remained on the American side of the present Atlantic Ocean.

The journey of the willow-leaf-shaped eel larvae from the Sargasso Sea to Europe takes seven to ten months. In August–September they are found off the coasts of Europe and North Africa, where they are transformed into elvers or glass eel, that is, practically transparent young eels but with a normally-shaped body. When the water temperature approaches +10°C, some of them start to swim up a river along the west coast. Others travel farther into the Baltic and after five to eight years are perhaps found in Lake Mälaren or the river Dalälven.

Eels seem to be more or less continually travelling during their growth phase, that is, the yellow eel stage. After growing for a number of years in the sea or in fresh water they become silver eels, with a black back and a silver belly. They are then ready for their long swim across the Atlantic back to the Sargasso Sea. The females are older and larger (10–20 years, 0.5–1 kg) than the males (5–10 years, 0.1 kg) on their return journey. It is strategically more favourable for the females to grow a little larger so that they can provide more spawn. After spawning all eels die, so completing the cycle.

Brown trout migration

The brown trout *Salmo trutta* lives in various environments ranging from small streams to large oceans, but it can spawn only in fresh water, since its eggs and the newly-hatched fry cannot maintain their water balance in salt water. Brown trout spawn practically exclusively in running water with a suitable gravel bed where the female can bury her spawn.

Brown trout may be classified as stationary or migratory. Stationary brown trout move between various feeding and wintering places in a river. In contrast, migratory brown trout stay only a few years in a river before the smolt migrate out to sea. After

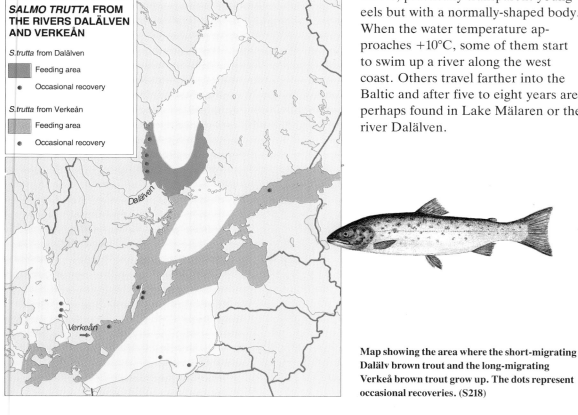

SALMO TRUTTA FROM THE RIVERS DALÄLVEN AND VERKEÅN

S. trutta from Dalälven

Feeding area

Occasional recovery

S. trutta from Verkeån

Feeding area

Occasional recovery

Dalälven

Verkeån

Map showing the area where the short-migrating Dalälv brown trout and the long-migrating Verkeå brown trout grow up. The dots represent occasional recoveries. (S218)

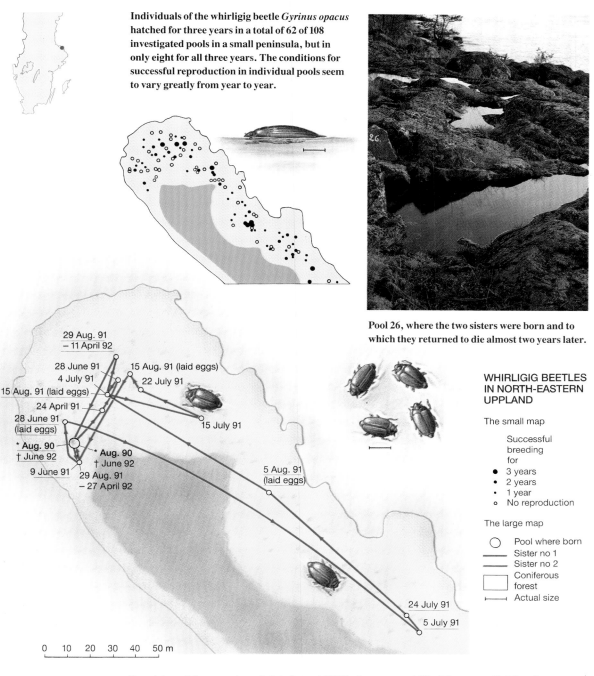

Individuals of the whirligig beetle *Gyrinus opacus* hatched for three years in a total of 62 of 108 investigated pools in a small peninsula, but in only eight for all three years. The conditions for successful reproduction in individual pools seem to vary greatly from year to year.

Pool 26, where the two sisters were born and to which they returned to die almost two years later.

WHIRLIGIG BEETLES IN NORTH-EASTERN UPPLAND

The small map

Successful breeding for
- 3 years
- 2 years
- 1 year
- No reproduction

The large map

○ Pool where born
—— Sister no 1
—— Sister no 2
▢ Coniferous forest
⊢——⊣ Actual size

Two sisters of *G. opacus* born in late August 1990 in the same pool (No.26) were studied for a long period. After having visited and laid eggs in several pools in the area in 1991, something almost unbelievable happened: they returned to their home pool in May 1992 after having survived a second winter. One of them which was in a bad state then laid a last clutch of eggs before she and her sister died at the place where they had been born almost two years earlier. (S219)

High Life in a Whirligig Beetle Community

Most people have seen the small, shining black beetles that, like dodgem cars, chase insects across the surface of a pond. Whirligig beetles are often seen in flocks of as many as a thousand individuals.

Sweden's largest whirligig beetle genus, *Gyrinus*, with eleven species, is found in all sorts of waters throughout the country below the tree line—from large lakes and rivers to small, temporary pools. *Gyrinus opacus* can colonise and develop in pools less than 0.5 m² in area. This species has been closely studied on a small pine-covered peninsula in north-east Uppland.

Whirligig beetles remain active until ice forms on the water. Only adults survive the winter. They mate in April–August and the eggs are laid on stationary objects in the water. Most of the females hatched in the summer reproduce in the same year they are born, so *G. opacus* has two generations a year in this area.

A fundamental dilemma for a whirligig beetle is whether it should spend all its life at the pool where it was born, or move to another pool. In the first case it runs the risk of mating with its siblings, which in small populations without immigrants can lead to genetic defects in the long run. In the Uppland study a small number of females reproduced during their first year at the pool where they were born. But most of the summer generation migrated to other pools, where they laid their eggs. More males than females remained loyal to their home pool. This type of behaviour is typical of animals, where the males defend a limited resource, like the behaviour of, for example, sparrows defending their territory.

Females stay a shorter time than males when they come to a new pool, which might suggest that they are more demanding. Females also seem to visit and stay more often at pools which have no other *G. opacus* or only one individual. This can be interpreted as showing that the females increase their reproductive success best by choosing pools that provide the best possible opportunities for their eggs and larvae, while the males do best by mating with as many females as possible.

In the area studied in Uppland the males lived longer than the females. Only a few percent of all those born survived two winters, that is, lived about two years as adults.

some time they return to spawn in the same river they were born in.

Smolting means that brown trout adapt physiologically, morphologically and in behaviour to life in the sea. When this takes place depends on the size of the smolt, which in turn depends on the climate and type of river. Smolt from rivers in southern Sweden can migrate when they are one year old, while those in northern Sweden are perhaps five years old.

How brown trout, like salmon, find their way back to the same river they were born in is still a mystery. It used to be believed that it was only the smell of the water that led salmon and trout home. Today it is presumed that it is a complex learning process in-

volving the water's chemistry and appearance. Ocean currents and the earth's magnetic field may also be significant factors.

In the sea, brown trout stay close to the river in which they grew up. An example of this is the Dalälven brown trout, which grows up along the coast of Uppland and Gästrikland, in the Åland archipelago and along the west coast of Finland. There are, however, brown trout that migrate long distances. An example is the Verkeå brown trout in Skåne, which migrates round the whole of the Baltic and parts of the Bothnian Bay before returning to the Verkeå to spawn.

Hunting and Fishing

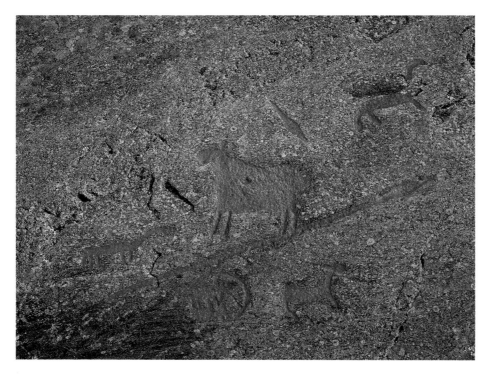

The people that first settled in Sweden hunted in order to get food and skins for clothing, but also later to protect domestic animals from predators. The great importance of hunting is shown in many rock carvings.

Several provincial law books from the 13th and 14th centuries contain regulations concerning hunting. Magnus Eriksson's legal code dated 1351 gave the king the sole right to hunt all royal game, that is, moose and deer. In some periods roe deer and even swans were counted as royal game!

During the 16th and 17th centuries the royal hunting privileges grew, but the nobility, too, were given more and more rights. It was not until 1789 that the land-owning peasantry were allowed rights to hunt on their own land.

Hunting went on all through the year, with no respect for young animals, deep snow or snow crust. Attempts to limit hunting were made. The first protective measures were taken with the formation of the Swedish Hunters' Association in 1830. Several species were protected and closed seasons began to be introduced.

Nevertheless, the 19th century saw many wild animals threatened. It was above all the large species like moose and roe deer and the large predators —wolf, bear, lynx and wolverine—that were still being hunted too intensively. In fact the authorities encouraged the hunting of the large predators. Birds of prey also suffered from this blind hatred of predators.

Our knowledge of the biology and environmental requirements of different species improved greatly as the 19th century came to a close, which resulted in better hunting laws and shorter open seasons. In an international perspective as well, Sweden has well-organised hunting seasons today. In fact, there has probably never been so much wild game available for hunting in modern times as there is today.

DYNAMIC DEVELOPMENT OF MOOSE

In the early 19th century moose were found only in a few districts in central Sweden. After a period of no hunting between 1825 and 1835, they were hunted even more intensively, especially in the winter, but this was forbidden as early as 1836. Thereafter hunting was allowed only in the late summer and autumn. By the end of the century moose were distributed almost as widely as today, but the populations were much smaller.

The number of moose decreased, especially during the First World War when poaching was rife. The hunting season was further reduced around 1920 and slowly the population began to recover. In the 1930s it became possible to hunt moose under licence, which, together with other measures, meant that the number of moose shot in the 1960s was almost 30,000 a year.

A properly managed moose population has a great growth potential. In the late 1970s the reproduction rate was at times more than 60%. In just

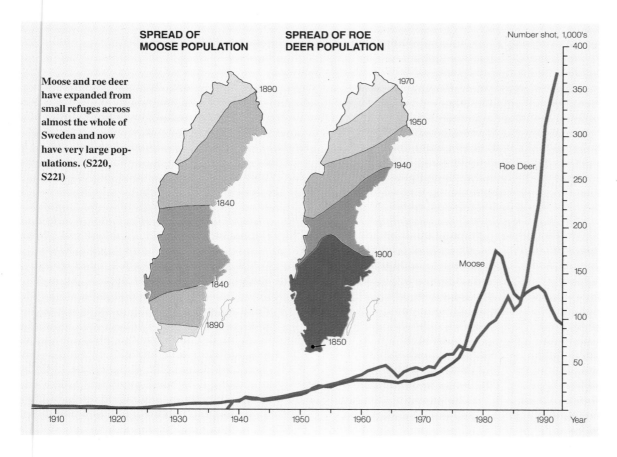

SPREAD OF MOOSE POPULATION

SPREAD OF ROE DEER POPULATION

Number shot, 1,000's

Roe Deer

Moose

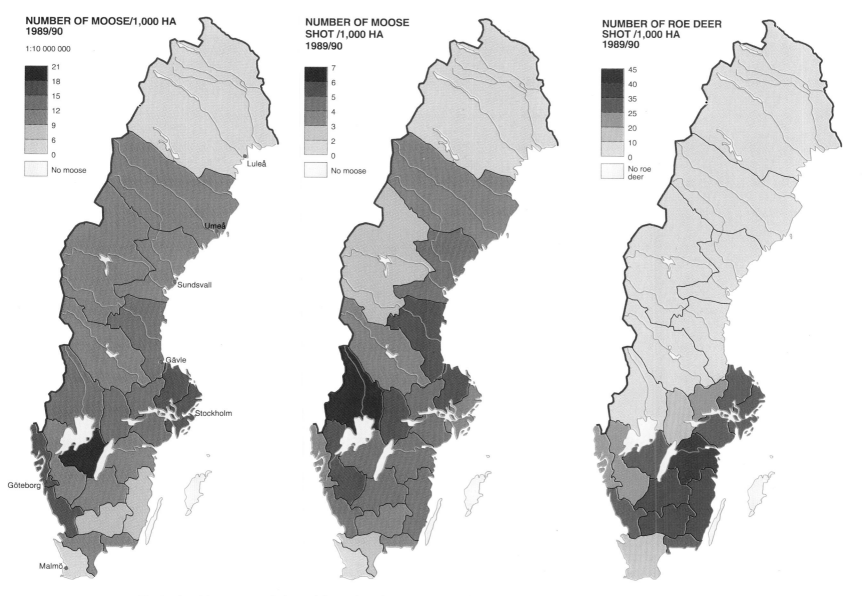

NUMBER OF MOOSE/1,000 HA 1989/90

1:10 000 000

21
18
15
12
9
6
0

No moose

Luleå
Umeå
Sundsvall
Gävle
Stockholm
Göteborg
Malmö

NUMBER OF MOOSE SHOT /1,000 HA 1989/90

7
6
5
4
3
2
0

No moose

NUMBER OF ROE DEER SHOT /1,000 HA 1989/90

45
40
35
25
20
10
0

No roe deer

The density of the moose population and the numbers shot reach a peak quite far south in Sweden, in the provinces round Lake Vänern, for example. (S222, S223)

Roe deer, now spread over almost the whole country, have very dense populations south of limes norrlandicus. The map shows estimated figures for the numbers shot in various counties. (S224)

From the age of three to four years old, moose cows normally have two calves a year, which allows relatively large numbers to be shot and/or a rapid growth in the population.

a few years the number shot doubled and in the record year of 1982 it reached nearly 175,000. The large moose population caused great damage to both forests and crops.

A continuing high level of culling has brought the population down to a more reasonable level. However, the demand for a rapid reduction resulted in varied numbers—in some areas the population is just about right, in others it is too small. In order to achieve a well-balanced moose population in the most effective way hunters, landowners and land-users are now cooperating. Research continues, methods for counting moose populations are being developed and computer models are playing an important part in population management. One of the latest developments is that the supply and utilisation of grazing grounds are being recorded.

ROE DEER — HARDIER THAN EXPECTED

In the mid—19th century there were no more than a couple of hundred roe deer left in Sweden. They found a sanctuary on a few estates in central Skåne. Improved hunting regulations and a better understanding of gamekeeping resulted in the species spreading again into southern Värmland and along the coast of Uppland in the early 20th century. By the 1970s roe deer had reached as far north as north-west Västerbotten and Tornedalen. Changes in forestry, smaller numbers of predators and the end of domestic grazing probably helped roe deer to spread north so rapidly.

Thanks to recent mild winters and the dramatic decline of the fox population the number of roe deer has now reached a level that was scarcely conceivable before.

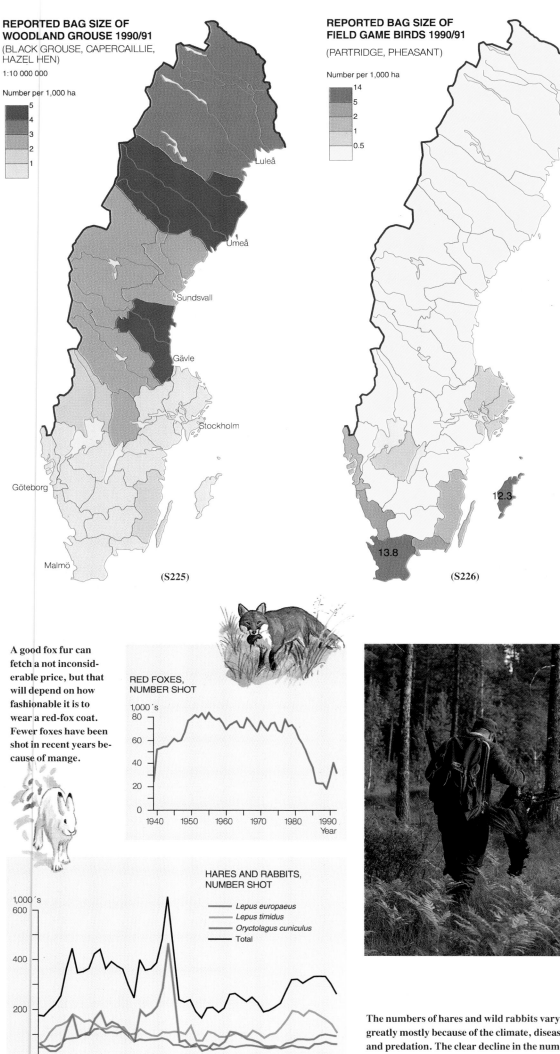

REPORTED BAG SIZE OF WOODLAND GROUSE 1990/91

(BLACK GROUSE, CAPERCAILLIE, HAZEL HEN)

1:10 000 000

Number per 1,000 ha

5
4
3
2
1

Luleå

Umeå

Sundsvall

Gävle

Stockholm

Göteborg

Malmö

(S225)

REPORTED BAG SIZE OF FIELD GAME BIRDS 1990/91

(PARTRIDGE, PHEASANT)

Number per 1,000 ha

14
5
2
1
0.5

12.3

13.8

(S226)

A good fox fur can fetch a not inconsiderable price, but that will depend on how fashionable it is to wear a red-fox coat. Fewer foxes have been shot in recent years because of mange.

RED FOXES, NUMBER SHOT

1,000´s

80
60
40
20
0

1940   1950   1960   1970   1980   1990
Year

HARES AND RABBITS, NUMBER SHOT

1,000´s

600
400
200
0

— Lepus europaeus
— Lepus timidus
— Oryctolagus cuniculus
— Total

1940   1950   1960   1970   1980   1990
Year

The numbers of hares and wild rabbits vary greatly mostly because of the climate, diseases and predation. The clear decline in the number of wild rabbits shot is the result of myxomatosis, which killed off most of the population in the early 1960s.

HUNTING GAME BIRDS AND OTHER SMALL GAME

Even if the major financial value of hunting lies mainly in moose and roe deer, game birds and other small game are not unimportant. Bearing in mind the large variations in climate and habitats in Sweden, and the relatively good supply of game, the conditions for successful hunting are good.

In southern Sweden the bags are mostly of pheasant, partridge, hare and rabbit, while in the northern provinces mountain hare, capercaillie, black grouse and grouse are more common. Duck, fox, marten and mink are hunted throughout Sweden.

THE VALUE OF HUNTING

One of the results of hunting is about 20 million kg of high-quality meat. At 50 kronor a kilo that makes about one billion kronor. A theoretical calculation of the value of hunting rights—35 billion hectares of hunting grounds at 40 kronor—gives a value of about a billion and a half kronor.

There are some 320,000 hunters in Sweden. Each year they spend almost ten million days hunting or managing game, which makes hunting one of the major recreational activities in Sweden. In urban areas only every twentieth adult man goes out hunting, whereas in rural areas the figure is one in four. There are few women hunters, about five per cent.

The capercaillie *Tetrao urogallus* is Sweden's largest fowl. A cock can weigh more than four kg. Capercaillies are often found in swampy forest during the autumn shooting season.

Retrieving dogs are commonly used when hunting birds. This is in part a legal requirement.

The Swedish fishing industry employed in 1995 about 10,000 people; some 3,500 are fishermen and about 6,500 work in the canning industry, fish delivery, shipyards and equipment production.

COMMERCIAL LAKE–FISHING

1:5 000 000

Salmon *Salmo salar*
Brown trout *S. trutta*

Char *Salvelinus salvelinus*

Whitefish *Coregonus* sp.

Vendace *C. albula*

Pike *Esox lucius*

Pike–perch
Stizostedion lucioperca

Perch *Perca fluviatilis*

Eel *Anguilla anguilla*

Other

Lake Vänern 1,158 tonnes

Lake Mälaren 278 tonnes

Lake Hjälmaren 196 tonnes

Lake Vättern 145 tonnes

Other lakes 483 tonnes

About 75 per cent of the total freshwater catch of fish, which in 1992 amounted to 2,307 tonnes with a value of 35 million kronor, comes from Lakes Vänern, Vättern, Mälaren and Hjälmaren. (S227)

CATCHES OF SALT–WATER FISH IN SWEDEN

1,000 tonnes

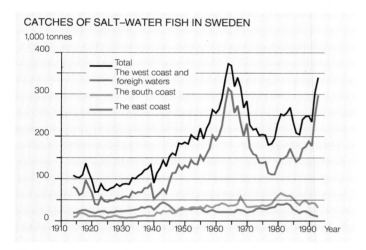

Total
The west coast and
foreign waters
The south coast
The east coast

The increase up to the mid–1960s was mainly the result of extensive Swedish fishing in the North Sea. The catches decreased in the 1970s mainly because the herring population declined in the North Sea. In 1977 Norway and the EU extended the fishing zones in the North Sea, which seriously affected Swedish fishing potential. The increase in the total catch over the past few years is mainly due to fishing for animal feed in the Baltic.

SWEDISH FISHING 1993, LANDED WEIGHT AND VALUE

	Tonnes	1,000 SEK
Freshwater fish	508	6 252
Eel	1 016	42 860
Salmon	883	18 779
Vendace	280	2 347
Whitefish	351	4 117
Plaice	456	8 711
Witch flounder	385	10 638
Cod	15 524	152 196
Haddock	1 169	11 197
Coalfish	4 200	23 418
Herring/Baltic herring	64 483	112 646
Sprat	3 433	12 272
Mackerel	3 270	9 424
Fish for animal feed*	233 301	153 598
Prawns	864	43 570
Shrimps	2 171	64 268
Other	3 447	63 335
Total	**335 741**	**739 628**

*Mainly herring, sprat and blue whiting used to manufacture fish meal and oil.

COMMERCIAL FISHING

Cod is the most important deep-sea fish for Sweden; in the late 1980s cod alone accounted for more than 50% of the total income from deep-sea fishing. Since then, however, catches have decreased dramatically, especially in the Baltic. Other deep-sea fish of importance are herring, prawns, shrimps and fish for animal feed. The latter, which is mostly used to produce fishmeal and oil, has become more and more important during the past few years. The most important fish for coastal fishing are eel and salmon. Pike-perch, eel, vendace, whitefish, pike, char, salmon, brown trout and perch are the most common fish caught in lakes.

Since several species run the risk today of being over-fished, there is increasing interest in more selective fishing methods, that is, methods which as far as possible sort certain

COMMERCIAL SEA–FISHING 1993

1:30 000 000

Tonnes

1,000
500
100
10
1

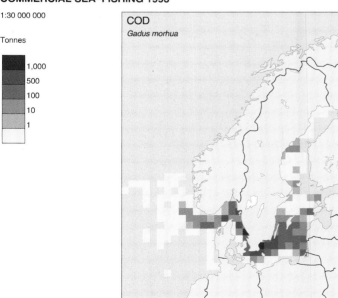

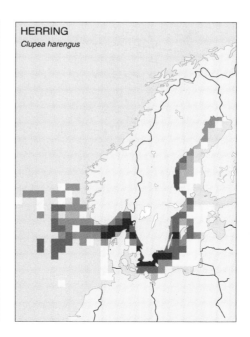

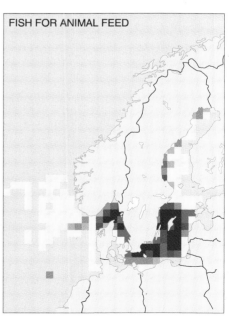

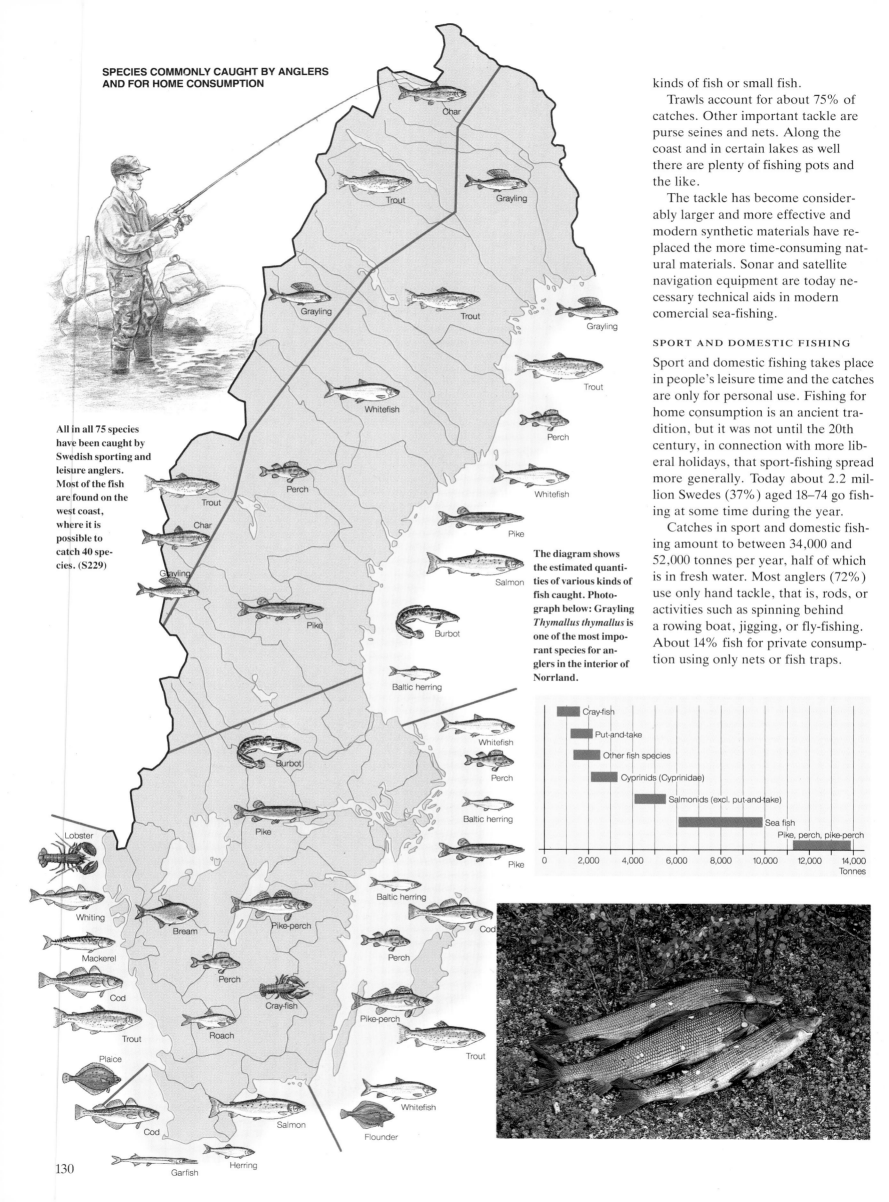

SPECIES COMMONLY CAUGHT BY ANGLERS AND FOR HOME CONSUMPTION

All in all 75 species have been caught by Swedish sporting and leisure anglers. Most of the fish are found on the west coast, where it is possible to catch 40 species. (S229)

The diagram shows the estimated quantities of various kinds of fish caught. Photograph below: Grayling *Thymallus thymallus* is one of the most important species for anglers in the interior of Norrland.

kinds of fish or small fish.

Trawls account for about 75% of catches. Other important tackle are purse seines and nets. Along the coast and in certain lakes as well there are plenty of fishing pots and the like.

The tackle has become considerably larger and more effective and modern synthetic materials have replaced the more time-consuming natural materials. Sonar and satellite navigation equipment are today necessary technical aids in modern comercial sea-fishing.

SPORT AND DOMESTIC FISHING

Sport and domestic fishing takes place in people's leisure time and the catches are only for personal use. Fishing for home consumption is an ancient tradition, but it was not until the 20th century, in connection with more liberal holidays, that sport-fishing spread more generally. Today about 2.2 million Swedes (37%) aged 18–74 go fishing at some time during the year.

Catches in sport and domestic fishing amount to between 34,000 and 52,000 tonnes per year, half of which is in fresh water. Most anglers (72%) use only hand tackle, that is, rods, or activities such as spinning behind a rowing boat, jigging, or fly-fishing. About 14% fish for private consumption using only nets or fish traps.

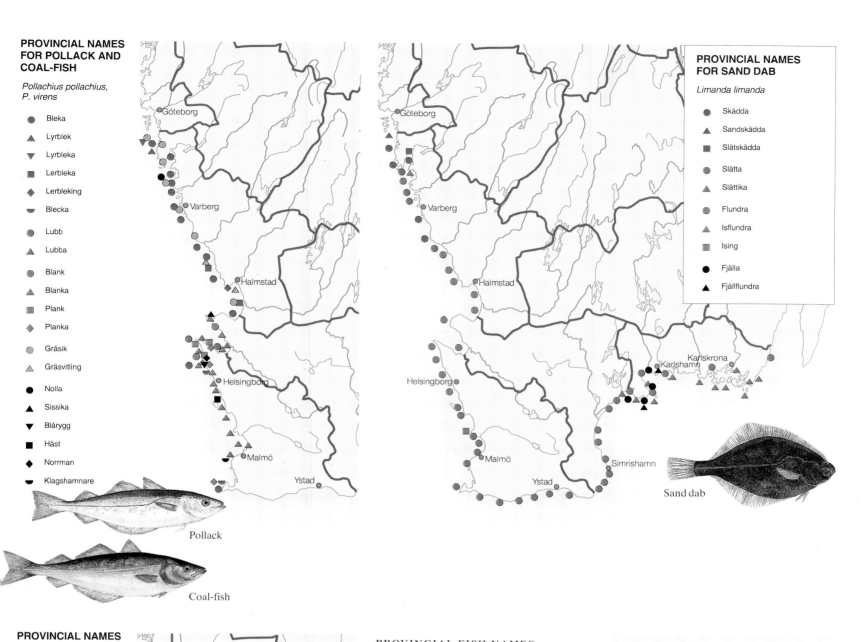

PROVINCIAL NAMES FOR POLLACK AND COAL-FISH

Pollachius pollachius,
P. virens

- Bleka
- Lyrblek
- Lyrbleka
- Lerbleka
- Lerbleking
- Blecka
- Lubb
- Lubba
- Blank
- Blanka
- Plank
- Planka
- Gråsik
- Gräsvitling
- Nolla
- Sissika
- Blårygg
- Häst
- Norrman
- Klagshamnare

Pollack

Coal-fish

PROVINCIAL NAMES FOR SAND DAB

Limanda limanda

- Skädda
- Sandskädda
- Slätskädda
- Slätta
- Slättika
- Flundra
- Isflundra
- Ising
- Fjälla
- Fjällflundra

Sand dab

PROVINCIAL NAMES FOR GREY GURNARD

Eutrigla gurnardus

- Knot
- Knote
- Knoting
- Gnate
- Gnot
- Gnoding
- Knorr
- Knorrhane
- Väderhane
- Skomakare
- Skräddare
- Smed
- Sillkung

Grey gurnard

PROVINCIAL FISH NAMES

Nowadays we expect every species of fish to have a fixed name which is used all over Sweden. But in the old days such linguistic norms did not apply. Anyone who needed to talk about fish used names and terms that varied from district to district or from village to village and which did not at all need to follow what we consider to be the correct zoological terminology.

The maps show how commercial fishermen's traditional Swedish names for sand dab, coalfish and gurnard vary from place to place in Blekinge, Skåne and along the west coast. Certain marks indicate several sources in the area. The fish that have or have had great economic importance have fairly uniform names. The name *slätta* for sand dab, for example, occurs along the whole coast. Eel, salmon and pike are other examples of fish that are important for the economy and whose names have been widespread for many years.

Pollack and coalfish are quite similar in appearance and are of no real economic importance, so they had to share names and there were many of them, often derogatory: *bleka* (pallid), *planka* (plank) and so on. Gurnard was of very little value, too; it is difficult to handle because of its spikes and it also makes a funny buzzing noise. This encourages fantastic names which lived on in the culturally rather isolated fishing villages.

Domestic Animals and Cultivated Plants

The process of domestication is continuous, so that our domestic animals are changing all the time. Ödhumbla cattle and Skåne geese are two old breeds that have been preserved.

Use of domestic animals and cultivated plants at various periods since the Ice Age. The time scale is given in ¹⁴C-years.

When the edge of the ice sheet still lay across central Sweden some 10,000 years ago, the first crops were being cultivated in the Near East. Perhaps the reason was that the climate became drier and warmer and the amount of game decreased when the forests were partly destroyed by drought. In fact, agricultural cultures arose quite independently of each other at several other places in the world such as the Andes in South America and in the Far East.

From the Near East the farming culture spread slowly, reaching Sweden about 6,000 years ago. It then spread rapidly across southern and central Sweden—perhaps because of a harsher climate with colder winters that demanded planning and food storage.

FROM WILD SPECIES TO DOMESTIC ANIMAL

An animal species becomes domestic after a change over many generations. *Domestication* means that mankind controls the development of the species to fit his needs. Thus domestication is quite different from taming, which is a fairly short and simple procedure for most animals. Animals that live in herds are easier to domesticate than species with a strong territorial sense, since man is then able to take over the role of flock leader.

Man domesticated certain species in order to get a regular supply of meat and hides and to be less dependent on hunting. Secondary products like blood, milk, wool and manure were utilised later, perhaps in the order given above.

As far as we can see today, all our domestic animals came to Sweden as already domesticated species. Several of them, sheep and goats, for example, came from the mountain regions of the Near East. Cattle and pigs probably also came from there, even though they were very much later given "fresh blood" from aurochs and wild boar. The horse was domesticated on the steppes of Ukraina.

This development has continued and populations have adapted to varying needs and environments such as fertile meadowland and poor pine heaths. And our national breeds have evolved: mountain cattle, Småland cattle, the Öland horse, the Skåne goose and many others.

Most of our cultivated plants were brought to Sweden and, like the domesticated animals, many of them come from the Near East. As mankind's living conditions have changed, the species have changed. Emmer and einkorn have been replaced by other cereals giving better yields; the cultivation of common millet *Panicum miliaceum* and buckwheat *Fagopyrum esculentum* has in principle ceased. Species that we look upon today as weeds, like rye-brome *Bromus secalinus* and gold-of-pleasure *Camelina sativa*, were once cultivated; they gave a poor yield but provided an important complement if the rest of the harvest failed.

1,000 years B.P.	9		6	5	4	3	2	1
	Mesolithic			Neolithic	Bronze Age	Iron Age		Modern Age

Dog

Sheep
Goat
Pig
Cattle

Horse
Cat
Rabbit
Goose
Hen
Duck

Emmer
Einkorn
Naked barley
Hulled barley
Wheat
Small spelt
Bromus secalinus
Camelina sativa
Millet
Oat
Rye
Flax
Pea
Bean
Buckwheat
Oil plants
Sugar -beet

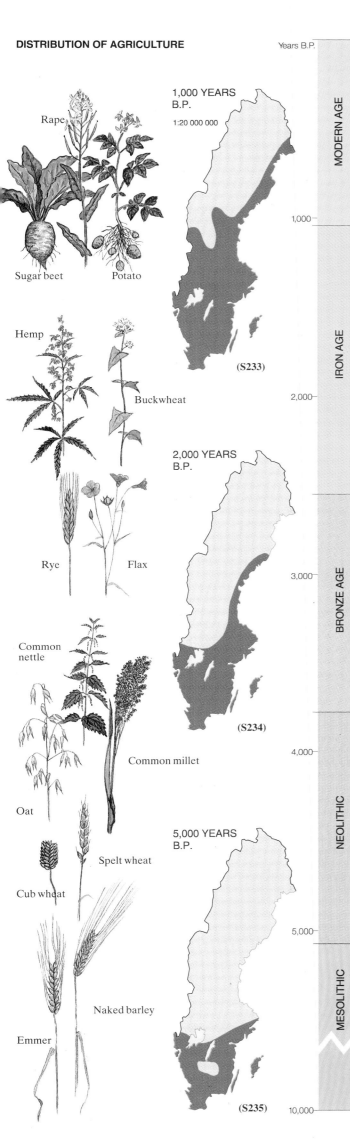

Rape

Sugar beet   Potato

Hemp

Buckwheat

Rye   Flax

Common
nettle

Common millet

Oat

Spelt wheat

Cub wheat

Naked barley

Emmer

Years B.P.

**1,000 YEARS
B.P.**

1:20 000 000

(S233)

**2,000 YEARS
B.P.**

(S234)

**5,000 YEARS
B.P.**

(S235)

1,000

2,000

3,000

4,000

5,000

10,000

MODERN AGE

The most common cereals during the Middle Ages were rye, wheat and barley, and later oat was cultivated widely. During the past century Sweden has gained a large number of new crops, including sugar-beet and oil plants. The horse was still the primary riding and pack animal and oxen and cows were used as draught animals. New domestic animals which came in more recent times were turkeys, domestic rabbits and doves.

IRON AGE

During the Iron Age cultivated crops like wheat, barley and oat began to be more and more important alongside cattle-farming. Rye was introduced. When these crops failed, corn spurrey *Spergula arvensis* and other present-day weeds were also probably used. Buckwheat was introduced at the end of the Iron Age. Flax became common as a textile plant but also for its oilseed along with gold-of-pleasure *Camelina sativa*. Towards the end of the Iron Age hemp was commonly cultivated, perhaps because of the need for thick ropes and hawsers for the larger ships. Woad *Isatis*

tinctoria was probably introduced as a dye.

New domestic animals were hens and cats, but the latter were not common. Sheep became more important as producers of wool.

BRONZE AGE

Domestic animals were still more important than cultivated crops. Oat was introduced but not much cultivated. It is possible that wild oat was also cultivated; it was in any event a common weed in the oat fields. Beans were introduced and for a time millet was also cultivated. Yarn was spun from the fibres of the stalks of common nettles.

Domestic cattle, pigs, sheep and goats were common, as were dogs. Up to then sheep had primarily been kept for their meat, fleece and milk, but as their wool

improved they also provided raw material for textiles. Local breeds of hornless ewes began to appear.

Horses came to Sweden early in the Bronze Age and were used mostly as riding and pack animals. Geese were also kept as domestic animals, but whether they were domestic geese or tamed greylag geese is uncertain.

NEOLITHIC

Man began to cultivate the land and keep domestic animals. Apart from dogs the first domestic animals were pigs, goats, sheep and cattle. Dogs were larger and sturdier. During the farming era of the Stone Age domestic animals were considerable more important than cultivated crops. The first cereals were emmer and spelt wheat and several kinds of barley: einkorn, naked barley and hulled barley. Probably rye-brome *Bromus secalinus* and fat hen *Chenopodium album* were also cultivated, as well as peas towards the end of the period.

MESOLITHIC

Dogs were the only domestic animals. They were probably spitz types about 50 cm high at the shoulder. Sweden's oldest canine finds date back about 9,000 years. The first cereals came to Sweden towards the end of this period, perhaps as ritual offerings from people south of the Baltic where agriculture had already commenced. But grain was cultivated on

a very small scale. It is possible that more domestic animals were introduced at the end of the hunting era of the Stone Age.

Wild Plants as Food and Medicine

Reed *Phragmites australis* is a useful plant that has been neglected. There are estimated to be at least 100,000 ha of reed in Sweden, with a total annual energy content of at least 1.3×10^{12} kcal!

Acorns are less well-known as food than hazel nuts, probably because of their bitter taste. The bitterness can be removed, however, by soaking them in water or more simply by roasting them.

In Sweden's wild flora there are two species that are used more than any other: Scots pine and Norway spruce. They have been cultivated for centuries all over the country and are the foundation of our most important export industry. There is rather little use made of our other wild plants today compared with the past, when they were essential for survival. These plants gave not only food and medicine but also building materials and material for tools, clothes, dyes and much more.

Some 250 wild plants were probably used in Sweden as food, and at least the same number for medicinal purposes. But it is long since wild plants were widely used for such purposes; we have to go several thousand years back to the late Stone Age before we can find any widespread use. The Bronze and Iron Ages saw the introduction of cultivated crops, which reduced the importance of wild plants as food. But medicinal plants were still in use in the present century.

Common knowledge of useful wild plants has now mostly been lost, but during the 18th and 19th centuries as well as during the two world wars the authorities and scientists tried to persuade poor people to make greater use of wild plants.

Sweden may seem to lack edible wild plants, but thanks to its varied countryside there are in fact a surprising number of useful species. Wild berries and fungi do not provide much energy and have little importance as "real" food; roots, nuts, seeds and some lichens are considerably more important. Calculations have shown that wild-growing food in Sweden would be enough for about 30,000–50,000 people per year. Fishing in lakes and along the coast, seasonal hunting and a "realistic" utilisation of wild plants are included in these calculations.

WILD BERRIES AND FUNGI

In spite of their low energy value and although we use more energy picking them than we get from eating them, more than 80% of the Swedish population spend some time every year

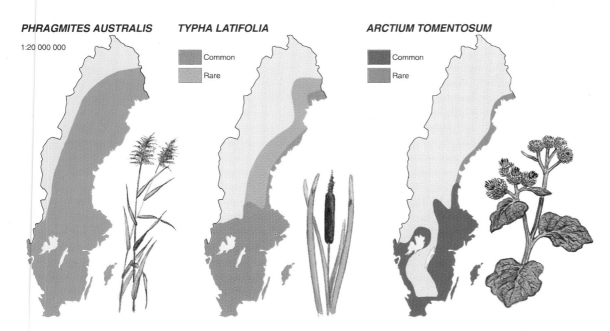

PHRAGMITES AUSTRALIS

1:20 000 000

TYPHA LATIFOLIA

- Common
- Rare

ARCTIUM TOMENTOSUM

- Common
- Rare

Every part of the reed *Phragmites australis* can be used for various purposes. The root stores sucrose and has a sweet taste, whether it grows in salt or fresh water. (S236)

Bulrush *Typha latifolia* contains a great deal of starch and is used as fodder. The marrow and shoots of the root and the basis of the stalks are edible, yet this species has seldom been used for food in Sweden. The down, that is, the seed hair, can be useed as insulating material. (S237)

The woolly burdock *Arctium tomentosum* is a biennal with a root that can grow to a large size, up to 30 cm long and 5–10 cm thick. It has a mild taste and a high energy content; carbohydrates makes up 15% of its weight when fresh. (S238)

Percentage of Sweden's
production of cowberries
blueberries and
cloudberries

350 l/person and year

75%

40 l/person and year

25%

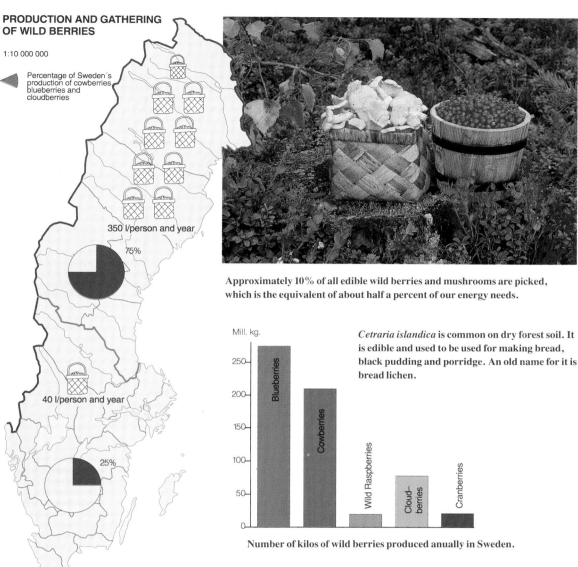

Approximately 10% of all edible wild berries and mushrooms are picked,
which is the equivalent of about half a percent of our energy needs.

New shoots of pine are sweet and contain about 50
mg of vitamin C per 100 g.

Mill. kg.

250

200

150

100

50

Blueberries

Cowberries

Wild Raspberries

Cloud—berries

Cranberries

Cetraria islandica is common on dry forest soil. It
is edible and used to be used for making bread,
black pudding and porridge. An old name for it is
bread lichen.

Number of kilos of wild berries produced anually in Sweden.

**Picking wild berries
and mushrooms plays
an invaluable role for
recreation—to get ber-
ries and mushrooms
free and at the same
time get exercise and
fresh air is a benefit
worth nurturing.
There are plenty of
berries and mush-
rooms! (S239)**

picking wild berries. The significance
of wild berries in the national diet has
varied over the years. Up until the end
of the 19th century forest berries were
used now and then as food. But at the
end of the 19th century up to about 1915
there was a large market for cowberries
Vaccinium vitis-idaea. Exports to Germany were particularly large, as much
as 10 million kilos in 1903. Blueberries
Vaccinium myrtillus also enjoyed pop-
ularity in the wake of "the cowberry
rush".

The results of an investigation carried out by the Swedish University of
Agricultural Sciences show that nature
produces more than one billion litres of
blueberries, cowberries and wild raspberries *Rubus idaeus.* To these cloudberries *Rubus chamaemorus*, cranberries *Vaccinium oxycoccos* and
a few other wild berries should be
added. We pick at most 7% of all
available berries, that is, a maximum
of about 80 million litres.

Picking mushrooms is a more recent activity in Sweden. An investigation at the Swedish University of
Agricultural Sciences shows that not
more than 50% of the population
pick mushrooms at any time during
the year, but interest seems to be

growing. About 800 million kilos of
edible fungi are produced annually, of
which 3% at most, about 22 million
kilos, are picked.

FOOD AND MEDICINE FROM THE
CONIFEROUS FORESTS

Pine needles are very rich in vitamin
C, closely followed by spruce and
juniper. The contents increase the further north one goes and the colder it
is. About 400 mg of Vitamin C per
100 grams of fresh pine needles has
been found in January at Pajala, for
example! The shoots of coniferous
trees, especially pine, are very tasty in
the spring.

Bark from young trees has the
same energy content as berries, and it
can be ground or boiled. The "bark-
bread" of the famine years used the
inner bark of old pines, however—
somewhat surprisingly, as that kind of
bark has a lower food value than bark
from young trees.

The fresh, clear resin from pine
and spruce kills bacteria and can be
applied directly to a wound. Certain
lichens, *Usnea* spp. and *Cladonia ar-
buscula*, contain usnic acid which is
also a bactericide that can be applied
to wounds. Lichen has usually been

thought of as famine food, but it is better than that; *Bryoria* spp and *Cetraria
islandica* contain lichenin and can be
used as food not only for reindeer.

MANY USEFUL PLANTS GROW
IN MIRES

Many people think of mires as "use-
less" land. Some peat is harvested—
mainly for fuel—on a fairly small
scale, but in fact mires contain many
useful plants.

Willow *Salix* spp. and goat willow
Salix caprea contain salicylic acid
which is used for fevers, headaches
and even for washing wounds. Labrador tea *Ledum palustre* and bog
myrtle *Myrica gale* can be used as in-
secticides. Bog bilberry *Vaccinium
uliginosum* is often neglected but is in
fact better than the blueberry, since it
has a higher energy content and its
vitamin C content is ten times higher.

Dried *Sphagnum* spp can absorb
and retain liquid 20 times its dry
weight and it is also slightly antisep-
tic. Cleaned and dried it would make
a good bandage. Humified Sphagna,
that is, peat, could in principle act as
an ion exchanger, and tests have
shown that it can be used to purify
water.

Butterwort *Pinguicula* **spp. (above) and sundew** *Drosera* **spp. (right)**

Names and Uses

We can work out how plants were used in the old days by studying their names. These dialect names reflect popular ideas about the world of plants, which often differ from the usual classification in our floras. Many species of plants have the same name; thus Sw *tåtel* (hairgrass) in popular botany applies to all grasses that have a stalk crowned by a panicle. Dialect plant names are collected in Sweden's dialect and folklore archives in Lund, Göteborg, Uppsala and Umeå.

BUTTERWORT AND SUNDEW

Butterwort *Pinguicula* spp. and sundew *Drosera* spp. are known by some 40 different names which mostly indicate how they were used in the household. In northern and central Sweden they were of great importance for dairy produce. To preserve

fresh milk and ensure a good supply all through the year it was turned into curdled milk, but this required a starter either consisting of curdled milk or prepared with butterwort or sundew. Whether in fact it is possible to make curdled milk with butterwort has been questioned—the method has sometimes been attributed to folklore. But controlled tests have proved that it is quite possible, even though it is not always successful.

The Swedish prefix *tät*, for example in *tätmjölk* (curdled milk) and *tätört* (butterwort) is one of several Germanic and Indo-European words that mean thicken or curdle. *Tät* in names like *tätgräs* and *tätte* refer to the curdling process. Various Swedish names like *skyrgräs*, *långmjölksgräs*, *filgräs*, *filbunksgräs*, *segmjölksgräs* and *tjockmjölksgräs* refer to the names of milk products. Butterwort and sundew were called *myrtätte* or *myrsyra* after both the product and the place

The most common Swedish names for *Pinguicula* spp. and *Drosera* spp. north of the boundary on the map are *tätgräs* and *sileshår*. Elsewhere these names are limited in use or have only been found sporadically. (S240)

In some areas both *tätört* and *sileshår* are used to make curdled milk, and there they have the same name since they were used for the same purpose. (S241)

In areas where curdled milk was not common, the making of it was connected with fantastic popular tales. People often knew the name of the plant but could not identify it. (S242)

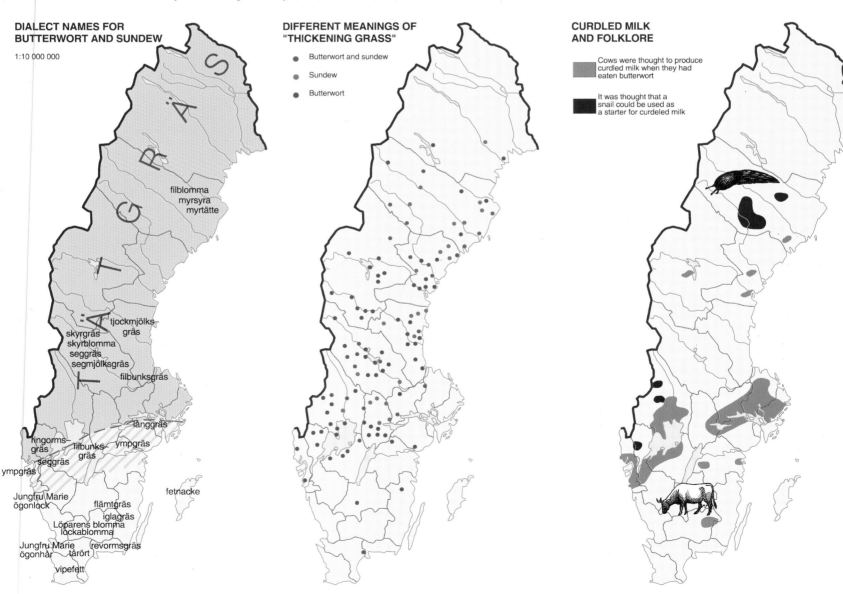

DIALECT NAMES FOR BUTTERWORT AND SUNDEW

1:10 000 000

TÄTGRÄS

filblomma
myrsyra
myrtätte

tjockmjölks-
gräs
skyrgräs
skyrblomma
seggräs
segmjölksgräs
filbunksgräs

långgräs

ringorms-
gräs filbunks-
gräs
seggräs
ympgräs

ympgräs

Jungfru Marie
ögonlock
flämtgräs
iglagräs
Löparens blomma
lockablomma
Jungfru Marie
ögonhår revormsgräs
tårört
vipefett

fetnacke

DIFFERENT MEANINGS OF "THICKENING GRASS"

● Butterwort and sundew
● Sundew
● Butterwort

CURDLED MILK AND FOLKLORE

Cows were thought to produce curdled milk when they had eaten butterwort

It was thought that a snail could be used as a starter for curdeled milk

DIALECT NAMES OF MEADOW SWEET

1:5 000 000

JOHANNES-GRÄS

PERSMÄSSGRÄS

Korsgräs

Skråv

BYTTLOCKGRÄS

Skråv

Byttlockgräs

Skråve

KORSGRÄS

ÖLGRÄS

Ölgräs

BÖRTNE

HÄR-KRÅKS-GRÄS

Härkolv

ÄLG-GRÄS

BYTTGRÄS

Luktgräs

Älgsbrodd

Algräs

Mjölkandesgräs

Mjölkan-desgräs

ÄLGGRÄS

Rönngräs

Alagräs

Mjölkandes-gräs

Kalygräs

Ölgräs

ARM-GRÄS

Majgräs

ÄRM-GRÄS

Mörtan-gräs

ÖL-GRÄS

Kallgräs

MAJ-GRÄS

Bigräs

KARSÖTA

MÖ-GRÄS

Majgräs

Älggräs

Bigräs

Bigräs

Älggräs

MÖRTGRÄS

Bigräs

KARÖRT

Ölblomma

BRAKE

MJÖDÖRT

KALLGRÄS

BRÄSKE

Meadowsweet *Filipendula ulmaria* has 30 or more dialect names; some of them are given on the map. Half of them are so well substantiated that it has been possible to indicate their distribution areas. Besides these established names, there are many more sporadically used ones, some of which are on the map. (S243)

under the name *igelgräs* (leech grass) because it was thought that they caused "liver leeches" (liver flukes) in sheep. Sundew is also called *Jungfru Marie ögonhår* (the Virgin Mary's eyelashes), *Jungfru Marie ögonlock* (eyelids), *ögongräs* (eye grass) and *tårört* (tear grass). These names may be explained by the similarity of the leaves to eyelids, but the plant has also been used as an eye ointment. It is called *locka blomma* (spider-flower) because it traps spiders and insects and *Löparens blomma* because it was one of the seven plants which a man called "Löparen" used to cause abortion. The names *revormsgräs* and *ringormsgräs* (ringworm grass) refer to its use in veterinary medicine.

MEADOWSWEET

There are various explanations for the different names for meadowsweet *Filipendula ulmaria*. A third of them are connected with its uses. Three of them refer to beer and mead, which were flavoured with its leaves. The name *mjödört* (meadwort) is found in Skåne. *Mörtgräs*, used in Västergötland and eastern Värmland, is a combination of *mjödört* and *mjödgräs*. An early 14th-century source from southern Västergötland names a *Miodyrtaedal*, and in Medelpad it was called *ölgräs* (beer grass).

Meadowsweet has a strong scent which can be used to get rid of the dank smell in wooden bowls—the name *luktgräs* (scented grass) is found here and there. The names *karsöta*, *kassöta* in Östergötland, *karört*, *kargräs* in Småland, *byttgräs* in Dalarna, Gästrikland and Hälsingland and *byttlockgräs* in Jämtland and Ångermanland show that the plant was used to clean bowls and tubs.

Many sources tell that beehives were rubbed with meadowsweet to attract bees, as the names *bigräs* and *biros* in Småland and Västergötland suggest. An explanation of the name *majgräs* (May grass) in Bohuslän and Dalsland is that it was in May that beehives were prepared for use—so it was in May that meadowsweet had to be gathered.

The two most northerly names, *persmässgräs* and *johannisgräs*, refer to its flowering period in late June. The name *älggräs* was probably originally *äl-gräs* = *algräs* (alder grass), indicating where it grew. *Älggräs* probably has nothing to do with *älg* (moose), but it likes to grow among alder trees (Sw *al*).

where they grew (*myr* = mire).

Löpe (rennet) is a term known throughout Scandinavia apart from Denmark and southern Sweden, but also in other areas where Norsemen used to live, such as Shetland, Orkney, Scotland, northern England, Ireland and a few places in the south of France. In Scandinavia plant names can clearly be connected with various milk products, but elsewhere we can only identify the names.

In southern Sweden, where curdled milk was unknown, the plants had quite different names. Butterwort was the less known of the two, so only a few sporadic occurrences are known. *Fetnacke* ("Fatneck") is connected with thick leaves and *vipefett* ("lapwing grease") comes from the belief that lapwings rubbed themselves against the leaves. *Flämtgräs* ("Panting grass") was used to cure oxen that had trouble with their breathing.

Butterwort, sundew and a few other plants were lumped together

New Knowledge

Abisko scientific research station, dating back to 1903, functions as a base for research in the mountains. The emphasis is on plant ecology and meteorology, the dynamics of plant populations, latitude and altitude limits, local variations in climate and so on.

Tjärnö Marine Biological Laboratory in northern Bohuslän is a centre of research and teaching for marine biology. Its work includes in particular environmental monitoring, analyses of coastal environments and information to the public on marine environments.

Stensoffa Field Station near Krankesjön at Revingefältet in Skåne. The picture shows various current research activities: from the left, pheasant aviaries, frog ponds, bird-orientation experiments using magnets, aviaries for small birds, ponds and bird boxes for starlings.

Our knowledge of plants and animals has developed over thousands of years. For early man it was essential to know where animals lived and how they behaved if there was to be a successful hunt. Knowledge of plants and their distribution was also vital for survival.

Much later research developed a more academic character and individual scientists began to describe the flora and fauna they saw in their home districts and later on journeys within and outside Sweden. These more systematic investigations, which were already evident in the 17th century, have continued to the present day, resulting in extensive collections and printed works.

In the 1970s the authorities launched an important survey of nature in connection with the national physical survey, at both the local and the national level. The National Environmental Protection Agency, for example, has promoted national surveys of various landscape types such as primeval forests, wetlands, meadows and pastures. Since 1991 The National Board of Forestry has been surveying swamp forests which are of special conservation interest and since 1993 also key woodland biotopes (biotopes containing valuable flora and fauna).

Much of the new knowledge of the distribution of plants and animals which is emerging today is based on team work, however, in which amateur and non-profit organisations are making major contributions; examples of these are province floristic surveys, the Swedish Bird Atlas and Project "One Step Ahead", but also a multitude of projects for individual species or groups.

THE ROLE OF RESEARCH

Ecological research has grown stronger in the past few decades and become more and more specialised in such areas as behavioural ecology, population ecology and ecosystem ecology. Our universities and university colleges have increased in number and there are also today more than 50 field stations where teaching and research are carried on.

More recently we have acquired a great deal of new information about individual species or groups of organisms thanks to research projects. Accurate surveys of the occurrence and distribution of populations have helped us to understand the factors that are vital for diversity and how this diversity changes from place to place.

Biogeographical research has for a time focussed on the distribution pattern of plant and animal populations, above all in investigations that are based on questions concerning island biogeography, biotope fragmentation, metapopulations, landscape ecology and dispersal biology. To make a comparison with the now classic works of zoologist Sven Ekman and botanist Eric Hultén, what we lack today are mainly scientific methods for explaining the large-scale distribution of species more clearly; in other words, we need to know the factors that determine the externalz geographical boundaries of our plant and animal populations.

New techniques are developing, using automated data recording, position determination via satellite and surveying by means of geographical information systems. It is to be hoped that these aids will awaken fresh interest in large-scale geographical research.

Station	Governing body	Research	Teaching	Employees	Beds
Abisko	KVA	x	x	10	80
Aneboda	University of Lund	x	x	–	18
Ar	University of Stockholm	x	x	9	–
Asa	SLU	x	x	7	49
Askö	University of Stockholm	x	x	6	40
Balsgård	SLU	x	x	37	8
Bjertorp	SLU	x	–	3	–
Bogesund	SLU/KTH	x	x	–	–
Brunsberg	Forestry Research Inst.	x	–	8	3
Ekebo	Forestry Research Inst.	x	–	17	2
Ekenäs	Oscar and Lili Lamm's Foundation	x	–	2	25
Enaforsholm	Royal Academy of Agriculture and Forestry	x	–	–	60
Forsmark	N. Board of Fisheries	x	–	–	2
Grimsö	SLU	x	x	30	40
Gårdsjön	IVL	x	x	–	–
Götala	SLU	x	–	2	–
Hemavan	Lars Färgares gård Foundation	–	x	–	40
Jädraås	SLU	x	x	14	50
Karlskrona	N. Board of Fisheries	x	x	6	–
Kivik	SLU	x	x	3	2
Klubban	University of Uppsala	x	x	3	40
Kristineberg	KVA & University of Göteborg	x	x	50	60
Kronlund	University of Umeå	x	x	5	73
Kuolpavare	SLU	x	–	–	–
Kälarne	N. Board of Fisheries	x	–	9	–
Lanna	SLU	x	–	3	1
Lysekil	N. Board of Fisheries	x	–	30	–
Lönnstorp	SLU	x	–	2	–
Norrbyn	University of Umeå	x	x	20	22
Norrmalma/ Erken	University of Uppsala	x	x	4	30
Offer	SLU	x	–	2	2
Ringhals	N. Board of Fisheries	x	–	2	–
Rånna	SLU	x	–	5	1
Röbäcksdalen	SLU	x	x	65	2
Siljansfors	SLU	x	x	4	8
Simpevarp	N. Board of Fisheries	x	–	2	2
Stensoffa	University of Lund	x	x	2	20
Stenstugu	SLU	x	–	4	–
Studsvik	University of Stockholm	x	–	18	–
Sunnäs	Swedish Hunters' Ass.	x	–	3	6
Svartberget	SLU	x	–	9	10
Sävar	Forestry Research Inst.	x	–	26	2
Tjärnö	Universities of Göteborg and Stockholm	x	x	30	60
Torslunda	SLU	x	–	3	2
Tovetorp	University of Stockholm	x	x	3	56
Tullbotorp- Tullgarn	University of Stockholm	x	x	–	24
Tönnersjö- heden	SLU	x	x	4	10
Ultuna	SLU	x	x	8	–
Vindelfjällen	County Adm. Board	x	x	–	36
Vojakkala	SLU	x	–	3	–
Ås	SLU	x	–	1	–
Älvkarleby	N. Board of Fisheries	x	x	2	–
Ätnarova	SLU	x	x	1	–
Öjebyn	SLU	x	–	13	2
Ölands Skogsby	University of Uppsala	x	–	4	12
Öregrund	N. Board of Fisheries	x	–	12	–
Östads Säteri	IVL/University of Göteborg	x	x	–	–

IVL = Institute for Water and Air Pollution Research
KTH = Royal Institute of Technology, Stockholm
KVA = Royal Academy of Sciences
SLU = Swedish University of Agricultural Sciences

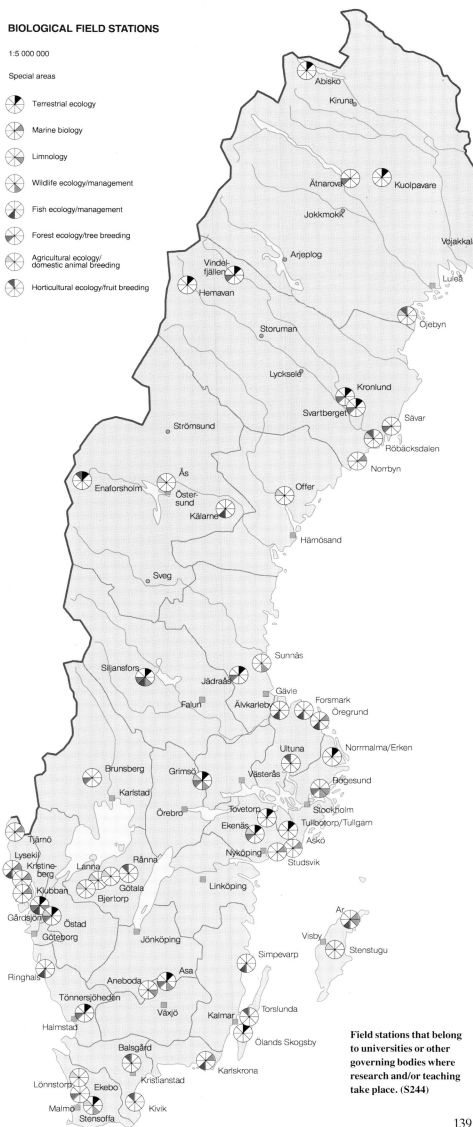

BIOLOGICAL FIELD STATIONS

1:5 000 000

Special areas

Terrestrial ecology

Marine biology

Limnology

Wildlife ecology/management

Fish ecology/management

Forest ecology/tree breeding

Agricultural ecology/ domestic animal breeding

Horticultural ecology/fruit breeding

Field stations that belong to universities or other governing bodies where research and/or teaching take place. (S244)

139

A survey team collecting data at one of the National Forest Survey sample areas.

The National Forest Survey

Ever since 1923 the state of Sweden's forests has been followed in a sample survey system called the *National Forest Survey*. Ever since it was started this survey has been the state's instrument for measuring changes in Sweden's forest resources. The first survey, which was carried out in 1923–29, was the result of general concern that the country's forest resources were running out; timber supplies for the growing forest industry were thought to be threatened. The second survey was carried out in 1938–53. These first two surveys were carried out county by county over a long period of years. It was not until all the counties had been surveyed that the results for the whole country could be compiled. But since 1953 the whole country is surveyed every year. The Department of Forest Survey at the University of Agricultural Sciences in Umeå is now responsible for these national surveys.

The survey's methods have been improved over the years and the contents adapted to meet new needs. Since 1953 all data has been collected from sample areas placed along the sides of survey blocks. These are squares or rectangles whose sides are between 200 and 1,800 m long. Since 1983 permanent sample plots have also been surveyed at fixed intervals, usually of five years. Information from these plots is particularly valuable for studying changes from year to year. The relatively sparse samples taken in the National Forest Survey usually allow reports only at the county level, but methods are now being developed to utilize information from satellites. This will make it possible to report on much smaller areas such as municipalities.

The National Forest Survey has traditionally provided information which has met the needs of forestry, that is,

Damage to young plantations caused by grazing moose is a serious problem for forestry in many places. (S246)

The map shows how the percentage of deciduous trees of the total volume of timber has changed since 1923 in different parts of the country. (S247)

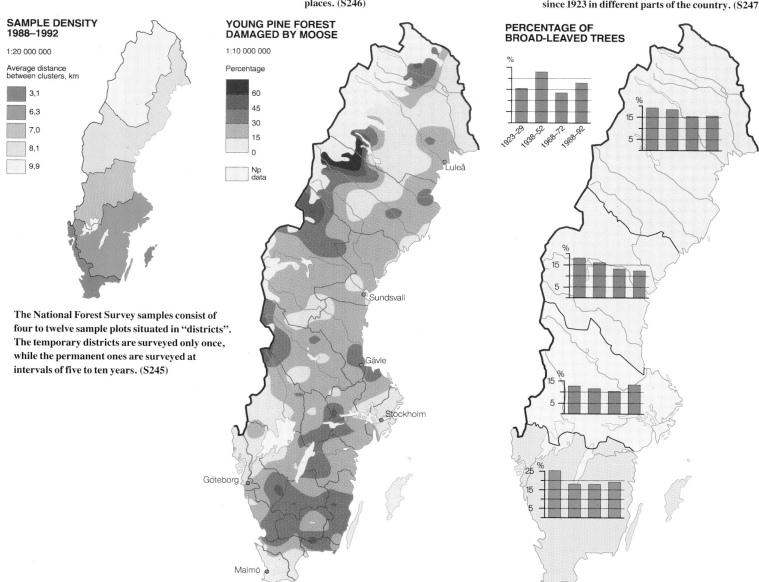

SAMPLE DENSITY
1988–1992

1:20 000 000

Average distance
between clusters, km

- 3,1
- 6,3
- 7,0
- 8,1
- 9,9

The National Forest Survey samples consist of four to twelve sample plots situated in "districts". The temporary districts are surveyed only once, while the permanent ones are surveyed at intervals of five to ten years. (S245)

YOUNG PINE FOREST
DAMAGED BY MOOSE

1:10 000 000

Percentage

- 60
- 45
- 30
- 15
- 0
- No data

PERCENTAGE OF
BROAD-LEAVED TREES

Luleå

Sundsvall

Gävle

Stockholm

Göteborg

Malmö

FOREST TYPES AROUND TÄFTEÅ

0   500   1000 m

Dominating tree

- Pine *Pinus sylvestris*
- Spruce *Picea abies*
- Birch *Betula pubescens, Betula pendula*
- Other broad-leaved trees
- Bare forest land

- Village
- Agricultural land

Täfteå

The map shows the distribution of various types of plantations in an area east of Umeå. This map has been produced by combining information from satellite images and the National Forest Survey sample plots. (S248)

data on the volume of timber available and its composition, forest growth and the amount of felling. In recent years, however, increasing interest has been given to data which describes the forests in a wider, environmental perspective. Ever since its start in 1923 the results of the survey have been used to formulate and follow up forestry policies. The material has also been used widely in forestry research.

As early as 1961 the National Forest Survey was complemented by soil mapping. This investigation, which continued up to 1975, resulted in Sweden's only complete soil map and maps of the pH value of soil and its sensitivity to acidification. Between 1983 and 1987 an extensive soil and vegetation inventory of the permanent plots was made by the National Forest Survey. This includes a detailed survey of ground vegetation, and since 1983 of lichens and algae on trees, as well as soil sampling and description. A reinventory of these sample plots was started in 1993 and is due to be completed in 2002. The Department of Forest Soils, SLU Uppsala, is responsible for this mapping work.

The National Forest Survey, in combination with The National Survey of Forest Soils and Vegetation, provides excellent opportunities for studying the changing state of the environment. This investigation can relatively easily be complemented with new areas of interest and—apart from maintaining its traditional role in forming forestry policies and aiding forestry research—is expected to play a vital role in the more intensive environmental monitoring which is developing.

Rosebay willow herb *Epilobium angustifolium* is a pioneer plant species which is favoured by human activities. It is, for example, common in newly clear-felled areas. (S249)

ROSE BAY
Epilobium angustifolium

1:10 000 000

Percentage of the forest area

- 2.0
- 1.0
- 0.5

- No data

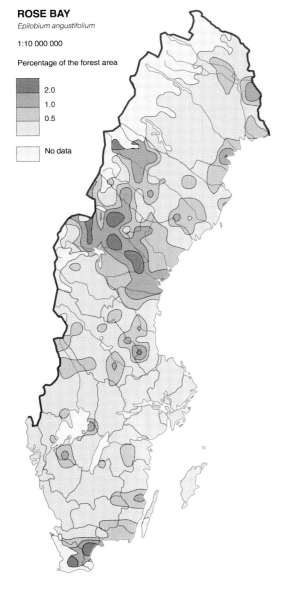

CALCIUMOXIDE IN THE GROUND

Percentage of weight

- 3.5
- 3.0
- 2.5
- 2.0
- 1.5
- 1.0
- 0.5

- No data

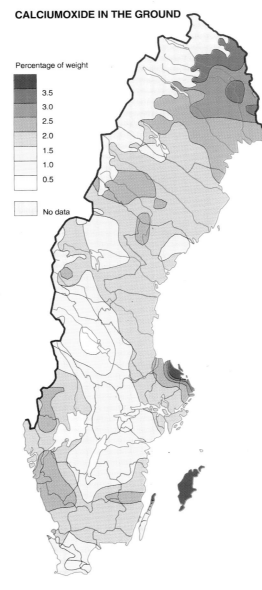

The map shows the presence of calcium in the form of calcium oxide (CaO) in soil samples taken at a depth of 50 cm. Calcium occurs in several minerals. Its most important function in plants is to stabilise the cell membranes. National Survey of Forest Soils and Vegetation, 1983–1987 (S250)

Province Floras

A province flora provides information on what plants grow in a province and where they grow. But the geographical units that botanists and zoologists use do not entirely correspond to the provinces—Lappland, for example, has been divided into five districts. There are, of course, also lists of plants in smaller areas such as municipalities or parishes, some of which are included below, especially when the latest province flora is quite old.

Province floras usually deal only with vascular plants, that is, flowering plants, grasses and the like, trees and bushes and ferns. There are also geographical lists of bryophytes, lichens and fungi.

The first province flora was in fact Linnaeus' *Flora dalekarlica*, which deals with Dalarna. It was written in 1734 but was not printed until 1873, so it did not influence the form of subsequent province floras. The first one to be published was Pehr Osbeck's *Utkast til Flora Hallandica*, dated 1788.

During the two hundred or more years that have passed since then there has been a steady stream of province floras and other such works—since 1830 about six every ten years. The early province floras often contained descriptions of plants and keys to help interested people determine which plant they had before them. More specific information about their occurrence in the province was often brief, however. Sites were given only for the rarest species, and even then rather vaguely.

Around 1900 province floras became more scientific; instead of describing a plant's appearance, lists were made of the distribution of each plant in the province. The exact location of less common species was given, but for common flowers only the names of the parishes where they were found. Initially maps were expensive to print, so they were not widely used in floras until the 1920s.

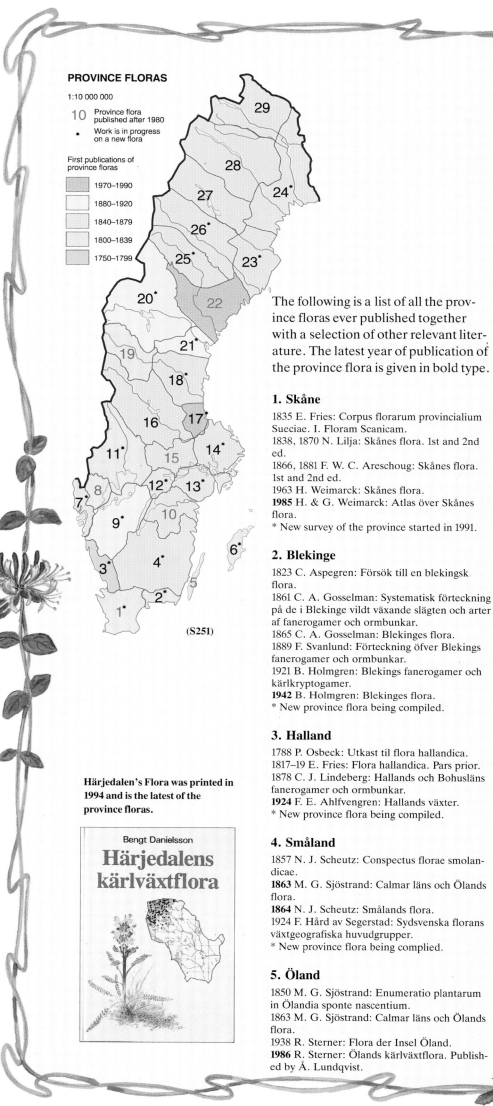

PROVINCE FLORAS

1:10 000 000

10 Province flora published after 1980

• Work is in progress on a new flora

First publications of province floras

- 1970–1990
- 1880–1920
- 1840–1879
- 1800–1839
- 1750–1799

(S251)

Härjedalen's Flora was printed in 1994 and is the latest of the province floras.

Bengt Danielsson
Härjedalens kärlväxtflora

The following is a list of all the province floras ever published together with a selection of other relevant literature. The latest year of publication of the province flora is given in bold type.

1. Skåne

1835 E. Fries: Corpus florarum provincialium Sueciae. I. Floram Scanicam.
1838, 1870 N. Lilja: Skånes flora. 1st and 2nd ed.
1866, 1881 F. W. C. Areschoug: Skånes flora. 1st and 2nd ed.
1963 H. Weimarck: Skånes flora.
1985 H. & G. Weimarck: Atlas över Skånes flora.
* New survey of the province started in 1991.

2. Blekinge

1823 C. Aspegren: Försök till en blekingsk flora.
1861 C. A. Gosselman: Systematisk förteckning på de i Blekinge vildt växande slägten och arter af fanerogamer och ormbunkar.
1865 C. A. Gosselman: Blekinges flora.
1889 F. Svanlund: Förteckning öfver Blekings fanerogamer och ormbunkar.
1921 B. Holmgren: Blekings fanerogamer och kärlkryptogamer.
1942 B. Holmgren: Blekinges flora.
* New province flora being compiled.

3. Halland

1788 P. Osbeck: Utkast til flora hallandica.
1817–19 E. Fries: Flora hallandica. Pars prior.
1878 C. J. Lindeberg: Hallands och Bohusläns fanerogamer och ormbunkar.
1924 F. E. Ahlfvengren: Hallands växter.
* New province flora being compiled.

4. Småland

1857 N. J. Scheutz: Conspectus florae smolandicae.
1863 M. G. Sjöstrand: Calmar läns och Ölands flora.
1864 N. J. Scheutz: Smålands flora.
1924 F. Hård av Segerstad: Sydsvenska florans växtgeografiska huvudgrupper.
* New province flora being complied.

5. Öland

1850 M. G. Sjöstrand: Enumeratio plantarum in Ölandia sponte nascentium.
1863 M. G. Sjöstrand: Calmar läns och Ölands flora.
1938 R. Sterner: Flora der Insel Öland.
1986 R. Sterner: Ölands kärlväxtflora. Published by Å. Lundqvist.

6. Gotland

1805—1806 G. Wahlenberg: Utkast till Gotlands flora.
1837 C. Säve: Synopsis florae Gothlandicae.
1869 G. Eisen & A. Stuxberg: Gotlands fanerogamer och thallogamer.
1897 K. Johansson: Hufvuddragen av Gotlands växttopografi och växtgeografi.
* Work in progress on new flora since 1983.

7. Bohuslän

1878 C. J. Lindeberg: Hallands och Bohusläns fanerogamer och ormbunkar.
1927 J. E. Palmér: Förteckning över Göteborgs och Bohus läns fanerogamer och kärlkryptogamer.
1945 H. Fries: Göteborgs och Bohus läns fanerogamer och ormbunkar.
1971 H. Fries: Göteborgs och Bohus läns fanerogamer och ormbunkar. 2nd ed.
* New survey of the province started in 1994.

8. Dalsland

1832 C. G. Myrin: Anmärkningar om Wermlands och Dalslands vegetation.
1859, 1868 L. M. Larsson: Flora öfver Wermland och Dal. 1st and 2nd ed.
1981 P.-A. Andersson: Flora över Dal.

9. Västergötland

1902 A. Rudberg: Förteckning öfver Västergötlands fanerogamer och kärlkryptogamer.
1967 K. Hasselrot: Västergötlands flora.
* New survey of the province started in 1984.

10. Östergötland

1861, 1874, 1880, 1901 N. C. Kindberg: Östgöta flora. 1–4 ed.
1977 E. Genberg: Östergötlands flora.
1992 E. Genberg: Östergötlands flora. 2. ed, published by F. Lind.

11. Värmland

1832 C. G. Myrin: Anmärkningar om Wermlands och Dalslands vegetation.
1859, 1868 L. M. Larsson: Flora öfver Wermland och Dal. 1st and 2nd ed.
1952 F. Hård av Segerstad: Den värmländska kärlväxtflorans geografi.
* Work in progress on new flora since 1982.

12. Närke

1758 A. Samzelius: Flora nericiensis. Published by S. Junell 1971.
1831, 1852 J. D. Gellerstedt: Nerikes flora. 1st and 2nd ed.
1866 C. Hartman: Landskapet Nerikes flora.
* Work in progress on new flora since 1989.

13. Södermanland

1852 H. Hofberg: Södermanlands phanerogamer och filices.
1871 K. F. Thedenius: Flora öfver Uplands och Södermanlands fanerogamer och bräkenartade växter.
1914 G. Andersson et al: Stockholmstraktens växter.
1937 E. Almquist & E. Asplund: Stockholmstraktens växter. 2nd ed.
* New province flora being compiled.

14. Uppland

1845 J. A. Schagerström: Conspectus vegetationis uplandiae.
1871 K. F. Thedenius: Flora öfver Uplands och Södermanlands fanerogamer och bräkenartade växter.
1914 G. Andersson et al: Stockholmstraktens växter.
1929 E Almquist: Upplands vegetation och flora.
1937 E. Almquist & E. Asplund: Stockholmstraktens växter. 2nd ed.
1965 E. Almquist: Flora upsaliensis.
* New survey of the province started in 1991.

15. Västmanland

1852 W. A. Wall: Westmanlands flora.
1877 J. E. Iverus: Beskrifning öfver Västmanlands fanerogamer och thallogamer.
1982 U. Malmgren: Västmanlands flora.

16. Dalarna

1734 C. von Linné: Flora dalekarlica. Published 1873 by E. Ährling.
1843 C. G. Kröningssvärd: Flora dalekarlica.
1879 C. Indebetou: Flora dalekarlica.
1949 E. Almquist: Dalarnes flora.
1993 L. Bratt et al: Hotade och sällsynta växter i Dalarna. Kärlväxter.

17. Gästrikland

1979 E. Lindberg: Gästriklands kärlväxter.
* New survey of the province started in 1990.

18. Hälsingland

1854 R. Hartman: Helsinglands cotyledoneae och heteronemeae.
1867 J. A. Wiström: Provinsen Helsinglands fanerogama vexter och ormbunkar.
1898 P. W. Wiström: Förteckning öfver Helsinglands fanerogamer och pteridofyter.
* New province flora being compiled.

19. Härjedalen

1834 M. G. Sjöstrand: Om Herjedalens naturbeskaffenhet och vegetation.
1839 K. F. Thedenius: Anmärkningar om Herjedalens vegetation.
1880 K. F. Dusén: Bidrag till Härjedalens och Helsinglands flora.
1908 S. Birger: Härjedalens kärlväxter.
1994 B. Danielsson: Härjedalens kärlväxtflora.

20. Jämtland

1884 P. Olsson: Jemtlands fanerogamer och ormbunkar.
1938 T. Lange: Jämtlands kärlväxtflora.
* New survey of the province started in 1987.

21. Medelpad

Collinder: Medelpads flora.
* New province flora being compiled.

22. Ångermanland

1990 J. W. Mascher: Ångermanlands flora.

23. Västerbotten

1878 C. J. Backman & V. F. Holm: Elementarflora öfver Vesterbottens och Lapplands fanerogamer och bräkenartade växter.
1926 S. Grapengiesser: Bygdeåtraktens flora. Svensk Botanisk Tidskrift 20: 366–405.
1982 S. Ericsson: Umeåtraktens kärlväxter. Natur i Norr 1: 2–71.
* New survey of Västerbotten started in 1977.

24. Norrbotten

1878 C. J. Backman & V. F. Holm: Elementarflora öfver Vesterbottens och Lapplands fanerogamer och bräkenartade växter.
1904 S. Birger: Vegetationen och floran i Pajala socken med Muonio kapellag. Arkiv för Botanik 3(4).
1909 A. Heintze: Växtgeografiska undersökningar i Råne socken. Arkiv för Botanik 9(8).
1925 H. Svenonius: Luleåtraktens flora. Svensk Botanisk Tidskrift 19: 431–484.
* New survey of Norrbotten started in 1988.

25. Åsele lappmark

1878 C. J. Backman & V. F. Holm: Elementarflora öfver Vesterbottens och Lapplands fanerogamer och bräkenartade växter.
1984 S. Ericsson: Åsele lappmarks kärlväxter. Natur i Norr 3: 82–170.
* New survey of Västerbotten started in 1977.

26. Lycksele lappmark

1878 C. J. Backman & V. F. Holm: Elementarflora öfver Vesterbottens och Lapplands fanerogamer och bräkenartade växter.
1924 D. & C. B. Gaunitz: Bidrag till kännedom om kärlväxtfloran i Sorsele socken av Lycksele lappmark. Svensk Botanisk Tidskrift 18: 128–140.
1930 E. Vretlind: Från östra Lappland. Om kärlväxtfloran i Malå socken i lidernas region. Svensk Botanisk Tidskrift 24: 58–110.
* New survey of Västerbotten started in 1977.

27. Pite lappmark

1878 C. J. Backman & V. F. Holm: Elementarflora öfver Vesterbottens och Lapplands fanerogamer och bräkenartade växter.
1943 T. Arwidsson: Studien über die Gefässpflanzen in den Hochgebirgen der Pite Lappmark.
1962 G. Wistrand: Studier i Pite lappmarks kärlväxtflora med särskild hänsyn till skogslandet och de isolerade fjällen.
1981 G. Wistrand: Bidrag till Pite lappmarks växtgeografi.

28. Lule lappmark

1878 C. J. Backman & V. F. Holm: Elementarflora öfver Vesterbottens och Lapplands fanerogamer och bräkenartade växter.
1925 T. Å. Tengwall: Die Gefässpflanzen des Sarekgebietes.
1939 G. Björkman: Kärlväxtfloran inom Stora Sjöfallets nationalpark.
1950 S. Selander: Kärlväxtfloran i sydvästra Lule Lappmark.

29. Torne lappmark

1860 C. P. Laestadius: Bidrag till kännedom om växtligheten i Torneå Lappmark.
1878 C. J. Backman & V. F. Holm: Elementarflora öfver Vesterbottens och Lapplands fanerogamer och bräkenartade växter.
1910 H. G. Simmons: Floran och vegetationen i Kiruna.
1911 E. Sterner: Jukkasjärviområdets flora. Arkiv för Botanik 10(9).
1919 T. C. E. Fries: Floran inom Abisko nationalpark. Arkiv för Botanik 16(4).
1952 O. Hedberg et al: Botanical investigations in the Pältsa region of northernmost Sweden.

CAREX GLOBULATA IN HÄRJEDALEN

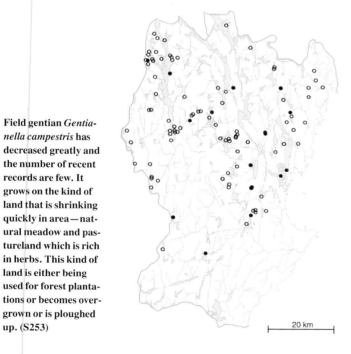

Carex globularis is a sedge with a northern and eastern distribution in Sweden. It is common in swampy spruce forests in Norrland but does not grow at all in the mountains or nearby. (S252)

50 km

GENTIANELLA CAMPESTRIS IN DALSLAND

Field gentian *Gentianella campestris* has decreased greatly and the number of recent records are few. It grows on the kind of land that is shrinking quickly in area — natural meadow and pastureland which is rich in herbs. This kind of land is either being used for forest plantations or becomes overgrown or is ploughed up. (S253)

20 km

PROVINCE FLORAS TODAY

Increasing interest in the environment has also led to increasing interest in studying plants; in the late 1970s a new generation of province floras saw the light of day. There is in almost every province now a new survey in progress for a new flora; they have already been published for Skåne, Öland, Dalsland, Östergötland, Västmanland, Härjedalen and Ångermanland.

These modern floras have a wider aim than the earlier local lists. The central purpose is still to provide an exhaustive description of where the various plants have been found, and maps are an obvious medium for such information. Sites of unusual plants are often specified to the nearest 100 metres or so. In addition herbaria and previous literature are studied in the search for earlier records. When old and new data are compared it often appears that the distribution of plants has changed. A plant may have become less common, like the field gentian *Gentianella campestris* in Dalsland, because the species' habitat is disappearing. But it may also have become more common, like the blackthorn *Prunus spinosa* in Småland, which has been encouraged by the spread of scrubland.

Modern province floras also attempt to analyse why a particular plant is found in one area but not in another. It is often easy to understand what limits the spread of a species in general but the finer details of the pattern may be more difficult to explain. Canadian waterweed *Elodea canadensis* flourishes in water containing plenty of nutrients, but why is it found in only some of Skåne's many such watercourses?

Province floras also describe what type of habitat each plant occurs in. Similarly, these floras state whether the plant is *permanent* or *occasional*; some plants such as sunflowers or tomatoes cannot seed or spread in our climate, so although they often appear on sea shores, waste dumps and road verges they always disappear.

Information is also usually given about where and when a plant was first seen in the province. Of Sweden's vascular plants more than half, 58% in fact, have immigrated since about 1700.

HOW IS A PROVINCE FLORA MADE?

Let us take the present Småland flora as an example. Like most of the modern province floras the preliminary research was done by team work for which the joy of discovery was the only wages. The value of the voluntary efforts is very great: in terms of money, almost 17 million kronor.

The 31,426 km² of the province were explored for a period of twelve years, 1978–89, with altogether 380 people taking part. So that areas where the flora was less rich should

Examining collected plants is an important stage in the preparation of a province flora.

ELODEA CANADENSIS IN SKÅNE

20 km

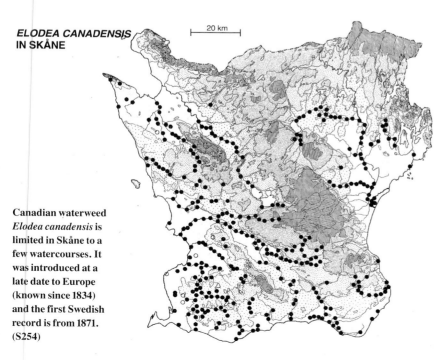

Canadian waterweed *Elodea canadensis* is limited in Skåne to a few watercourses. It was introduced at a late date to Europe (known since 1834) and the first Swedish record is from 1871. (S254)

Blackthorn *Prunus spinosa* has spread as a result of the way agricultural areas have been abandoned and overgrown in southern Sweden. Although it cannot survive the cold climate in the high, inner parts of Småland, it grows along Vättern with its mild climate. (S255)

BLACKTHORN IN SMÅLAND

50 km

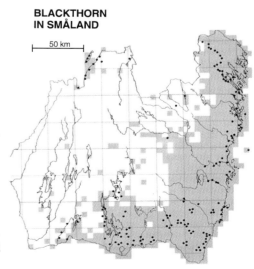

Province flora surveys are in progress in Skåne...

... and in the mountain districts

Below. The presence of the fungus *Haploporus odorus* and the lichen *Lobaria pulmonaria* indicates a forest type that hosts many threatened animals and plants.

Above. An excursion to Luottåive, 20 km² of mire and forestland which thanks to One Step Ahead's records was set aside as a Crown reserve in 1989. The first find in Sweden of the beautiful bracket fungus *Antrodiella citrinella* was made in the spruce forest on the north side of the mountain.

also be well investigated, the province was divided into 1,432 5×5 km squares. The goal was to find as many plant species as possible in each square.

But not all of them are ever discovered; many plants grow only at a few places in each square. In order to find every single one it would be necessary to search each square metre. It is estimated that about 85% of all the plants were found, which required 4–5 days' work for each square. The data was fed into a computer, and for each plant at least one site per square and biotope was noted. This makes it possible to some extent to follow up the records, to see, for example, whether certain species are disappearing more rapidly than others.

Some plants are difficult to identify, so the material has to be collected and pressed to prove that the information is correct. An occurrence may also be very unexpected, and then further proof is needed to confirm it.

Experts usually check that the plants have been correctly identified.

One Step Ahead

Modern forestry methods have seriously reduced the space available for biotopes as well as species. That is why the Swedish Society for the Conservation of Nature at Jokkmokk started the forest group called One Step Ahead in the late winter of 1987 to survey, conserve and protect forest environments. At that time we knew little about the state of biodiversity in the Norrbotten forests. One Step Ahead developed a survey method whose purpose was to identify biotopes containing valuable flora and fauna. This method can be used all the year round and is so simple that amateurs can manage it, at the same time as it is so exact that forest companies, authorities and researchers can make use of it.

INDICATOR SPECIES — SIMPLE AND FUN

Instead of trying to make complete lists of species, One Step Ahead concentrates on a sample group of species which have very special needs in their environment; these are called indicator species.

The occurrence of old forest indicators, most of which are threatened, makes it possible to distinguish particularly valuable forests worth preserving which contain many other demanding plants and animals. Indicator species also provide information about forest history and what type of protection or consideration when felling timber is needed to maintain biological diversity. The method is easily taught and a surveyor can start with just a dozen species. Today about 150 indicator species are used in the project, mainly lichens and fungi.

One Step Ahead's surveys have revealed a large number of hitherto unknown sites of rare species in the interior of Norrbotten. The uncommon fungus *Sarcosoma globosum* and the beautiful Norrland orchid *Calypso bulbosa*, for example, grow in spruce forests close to watercourses at Messaure.

DIVERSITY REDUCED

The impoverishment of biodiversity has proceeded rapidly in the past few decades. During the boom of the 1980s one forest stand containing endangered and vulnerable species was felled per day in Jokkmokk. Although large areas of forests, particularly those close to the high mountains, are protected, several of the biologically most valuable forest types containing the most threatened species are not nature reserves.

One Step Ahead's hierarchical system for estimating the continuity of logs (dead fallen trees) in spruce forests consists of bracket fungi that grow on the logs. The system applies in the first place to upper Norrland and is used to find and evaluate forests which have a high conservation value. Similar hierarchical systems are now being worked out for other parts of Sweden.

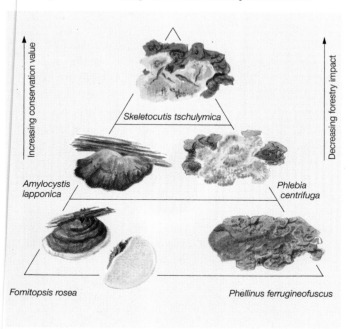

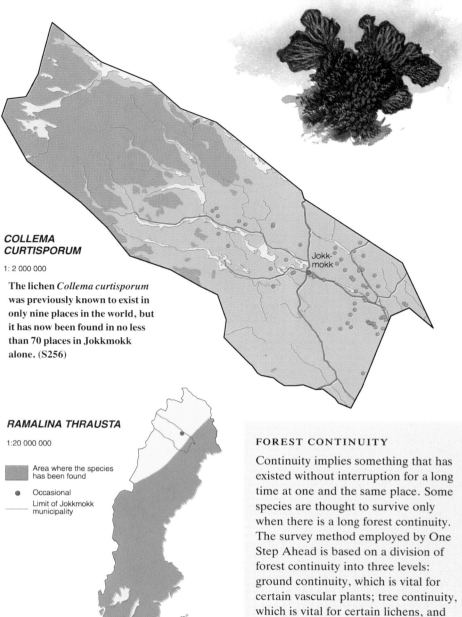

COLLEMA CURTISPORUM

1: 2 000 000

The lichen *Collema curtisporum* was previously known to exist in only nine places in the world, but it has now been found in no less than 70 places in Jokkmokk alone. (S256)

RAMALINA THRAUSTA

1:20 000 000

- ▨ Area where the species has been found
- ● Occasional
- ▢ Limit of Jokkmokk municipality

The map shows the previously known distribution of *Ramalina thrausta*. This lichen has now vanished from virtually the whole of that area, mainly due to new forestry activities. One Step Ahead has, however, discovered more than 60 new sites in Jokkmokk. (S257)

A LAST HAVEN

The inner parts of the Norrbotten forests—"the forgotten land"—have proved to be a last haven for many animals and plants. Calypso *Calypso bulbosa*, the bracket fungus *Haploporus odorus*, and the lichens *Evernia divaricata*, *Calicium adaequatum* and *Ramalina thrausta* are examples of threatened species which have their richest occurrences in this part of Sweden. The lichen *Collema curtisporum* has been found, in Jokkmokk alone, in about 70 places, growing on aspen in mixed forests containing many threatened species. This species has its main distribution in the world here.

FOREST CONTINUITY

Continuity implies something that has existed without interruption for a long time at one and the same place. Some species are thought to survive only when there is a long forest continuity. The survey method employed by One Step Ahead is based on a division of forest continuity into three levels: ground continuity, which is vital for certain vascular plants; tree continuity, which is vital for certain lichens, and log continuity (dead and fallen trees), which is vital for certain wood-inhabiting fungi.

The National Wetland Survey

During the 1970s wetlands became increasingly threatened by draining and peat extraction, so in 1983 the National Environmental Protection Agency, in cooperation with the county administrative boards, launched a survey to find wetlands of great conservation value. By the year 2000 the whole of Sweden will be covered.

Great efforts have been made to develop a basic, uniform method which can be used to survey wetlands throughout Sweden. Where necessary this method has also been adapted to suit regional conditions. The basic idea of the survey is to investigate all wetlands of a certain minimum size in

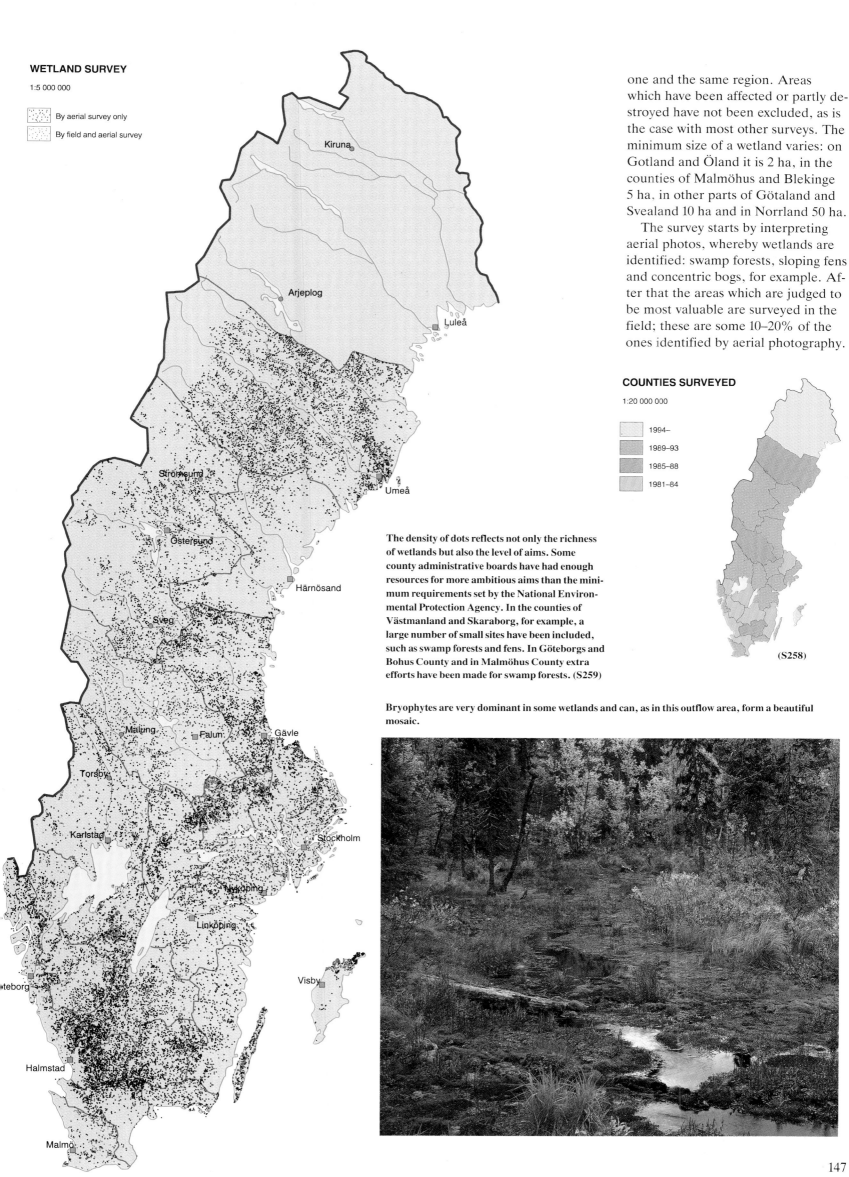

WETLAND SURVEY

1:5 000 000

By aerial survey only

By field and aerial survey

Kiruna

Arjeplog

Luleå

Strömsund

Umeå

Östersund

Härnösand

Sveg

Malung

Falun

Gävle

Torsby

Karlstad

Stockholm

Nyköping

Linköping

Visby

Göteborg

Halmstad

Malmö

one and the same region. Areas which have been affected or partly destroyed have not been excluded, as is the case with most other surveys. The minimum size of a wetland varies: on Gotland and Öland it is 2 ha, in the counties of Malmöhus and Blekinge 5 ha, in other parts of Götaland and Svealand 10 ha and in Norrland 50 ha.

The survey starts by interpreting aerial photos, whereby wetlands are identified: swamp forests, sloping fens and concentric bogs, for example. After that the areas which are judged to be most valuable are surveyed in the field; these are some 10–20% of the ones identified by aerial photography.

COUNTIES SURVEYED

1:20 000 000

1994–

1989–93

1985–88

1981–84

(S258)

The density of dots reflects not only the richness of wetlands but also the level of aims. Some county administrative boards have had enough resources for more ambitious aims than the minimum requirements set by the National Environmental Protection Agency. In the counties of Västmanland and Skaraborg, for example, a large number of small sites have been included, such as swamp forests and fens. In Göteborgs and Bohus County and in Malmöhus County extra efforts have been made for swamp forests. (S259)

Bryophytes are very dominant in some wetlands and can, as in this outflow area, form a beautiful mosaic.

SURVEYED WETLANDS

County	No	Total area, ha
Stockholm	640	12 000
Uppsala	794	40 000
Södermanland	579	19 000
Östergötland	693	20 000
Jönköping	1 336	91 000
Kronoberg	1 801	89 000
Kalmar	982	26 000
Gotland*	323	8.000
Blekinge	357	12 000
Kristianstad	844	30 000
Malmöhus	360	9 000
Halland	1 308	52 000
Göteborgs- och Bohus	613	15 000
Älvsborg	1 254	84 000
Skaraborg	1 279	40 000
Värmland	854	76 000
Örebro	976	41 000
Västmanland	1 389	44 000
Kopparberg	1 163	273 000
Gävleborg	2 110	127 000
Västernorrland	652	59 000
Jämtland	2 124	413 000
Västerbotten	4 326	814 000
Norrbotten**	29	
Total	**26 786**	**2 394 000**

*not completed **pilot survey

Predominant or "interesting" vegetation is then described and usually a list is made of the species found, with their frequency noted on a three-grade scale. All in all 338 bryophyte species, 876 vascular plant species and 177 bird species have been found. All the data is stored in the Environmental Protection Agency's wetland data base.

Vegetation Maps

As natural resource and environmental questions become increasingly important in our lives, the demand for "ecological data" grows. Since vegetation reflects climate, hydrology, geology, soil, topography and land use, for example, information about vegetation provides a useful basis for physical planning, environmental monitoring, environmental impact analysis, flora and fauna conservation, site-adapted forestry and landscape ecological planning. A vegetation map can also provide valuable information for outdoor leisure activities, hunting, and picking wild berries.

VEGETATION TYPES SURVEYED FROM THE AIR

Data on vegetation is obtained by interpreting aerial photos taken with IR film which is sensitive to reflection from vegetation in the infra-red area, that is, just above visible light.

A vegetation map records 50 or so vegetation types as well as the age of forests and their development phases. In addition there is special information about vegetation areas which are smaller than the smallest mapping unit (0.25–1 ha). Vegetation data is built up according to a standard classification system in the National Land Survey's data base.

NATIONAL LAND SURVEY VEGETATION DATA BASES

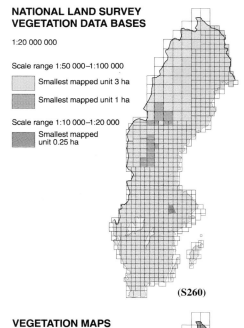

1:20 000 000

Scale range 1:50 000–1:100 000

Smallest mapped unit 3 ha

Smallest mapped unit 1 ha

Scale range 1:10 000–1:20 000

Smallest mapped unit 0.25 ha

(S260)

VEGETATION MAPS

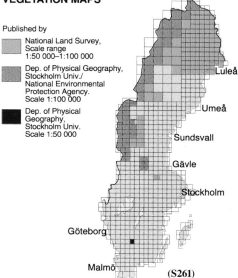

Published by

National Land Survey, Scale range 1:50 000–1:100 000

Dep. of Physical Geography, Stockholm Univ./ National Environmental Protection Agency. Scale 1:100 000

Dep. of Physical Geography, Stockholm Univ. Scale 1:50 000

Luleå
Umeå
Sundsvall
Gävle
Stockholm
Göteborg
Malmö

(S261)

VEGETATION MAPS — SIGNPOSTS TO NATURE

Vegetation maps are important in the identification of habitats. There is a close connection, different for different species, between vegetation type and occurrence. Common species will probably be found in several vegetation types, while rare species will often have very special environmental demands. Certain species occur in more than one vegetation type or in border zones between vegetation types. Sometimes special demands concerning size or spacing have to be fulfilled for a species to occur.

A natural forest, which is characterised by long continuity, has a richer variety of trees and structures than a cultivated forest. Rare species are often connected with natural forests. Information on a vegetation map may be combined with other information regarding topography, soil type, the nutrient status of land and from historical maps in a geographical information system (GIS) in order to locate such forests.

Map of bird habitats based on the vegetation map, right. Rustic buntings are closely connected with wet forests and forest mires. Jack snipes are rare birds connected with large, open, wet mires. Common sandpipers are a common species that flourishes on stony beaches. (S262)

BIRD HABITATS

1:50 000

Habitat congenial for

Rustic Bunting *Emberiza rustica*

Jack Snipe *Lymnocryptes minimus*

Common Sandpiper *Actitis hypoleucos*

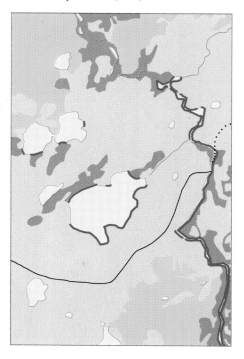

Part of the vegetation map of Norrbotten (29L NV). Layers of vegetation types known to favour certain species of bird have been extracted with the aid of GIS.

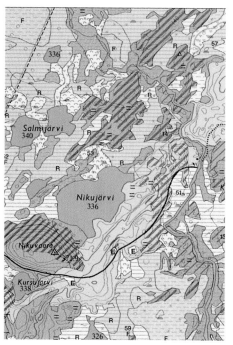

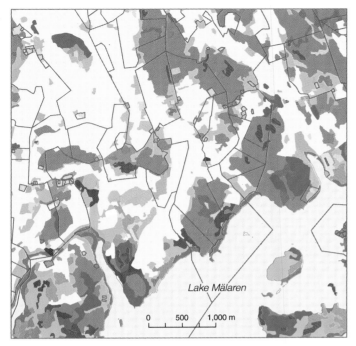

Lake Mälaren

0   500   1,000 m

This section shows the vegetation data base in its basic version for an economic map sheet (5×5 km) near Västerås (10G9g Rytterne). (S263)

VÄSTERÅS — AN EXAMPLE

Vegetation data bases are used in Västerås as a part of the planning material when, for example, working on sustainable development (Agenda 21). These data bases can help to build up a picture of the landscape which will make it possible to find areas of rich biodiversity. Core areas, together with neighbouring areas of similar types, can form a network of possible habitats for threatened plants and animals. A selection has been made of important natural values in the Mälar region such as nemoral forests, moist-wet fertile areas and old uneven-aged and multilayered forests.

The ecological functions of vegetation types can be illuminated by analysing them in geographical information systems (GIS) in which various conditions can be simulated.

DECIDUOUS FOREST

- Mixed nemoral forest
- Ash dominated forest
- Oak dominated forest
- Wet decidouos forest
- Decidouos forest
- Not decidouos forest
- • Nemoral tree
- —— Estate boundary

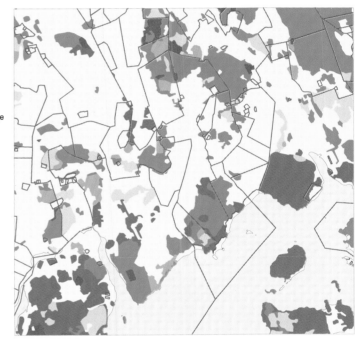

Information has been retrieved from the vegetation data base to make a map showing different types of deciduous forests and individual large nemoral trees.

AGE OF FOREST STANDS

- Clear-felled area
- Young forest
- Thinning phase
- Grown-up forest
- Old forest of varying age
- Not forestland
- —— Estate boundary

Similarly information about forest age classes has been highlighted in a special map.

BIO-DIVERSITY

- Nemoral forest
- Moist areas
- Wet areas
- Rich soils
- Old forest of varying age
- • Nemoral tree
- —— Limit of forest area
- —— Estate boundary

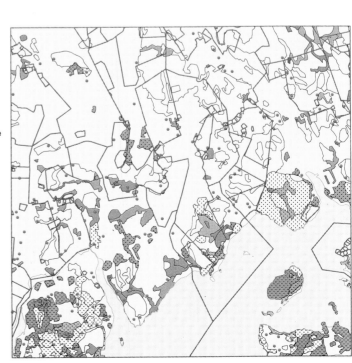

Where nemoral forests and old forests of varying age coincide, a specially rich fauna and flora may be expected. (S279)

Sampling by sieving—an initial volume of 20 litres of litter is passed though a fine-meshed sieve. Animals are then picked out manually at the laboratory from the 2–3 litres that pass through the sieve.

Survey of Terrestrial Fauna

Between 1921 and 1981 the Museum of Natural History in Göteborg carried out an intensive project to collect certain terrestrial invertebrate groups. This project was launched and supervised by the then curator, Hans Lohmander, between 1921 and 1960. After his death the survey was continued by Henrik W. Waldén, and the large area which Waldén had already investigated in Svealand was combined with the areas investigated by Lohmander. The survey covers southern Sweden up to northern Dalarna, with an extension along the east coast up to northern Ångermanland; it comprises an area of 191,600 km².

The main groups of the survey are woodlice, millipedes, centipedes, pseudoscorpions and terrestrial molluscs (slugs and snails). At times freshwater molluscs, spiders and some insect orders have also formed part of the material collected. The main methods of collection were sieving ground litter, bagging and direct collection.

The aim of the survey was initially to study the species' ecological and geographical behaviour, make comparisons between regions and reconstruct historical processes. But gradually the material's usefulness for nature conservation has become more important. For the study of how human activities—above all forestry and acidification—have affected terrestrial fauna, re-surveying old sites has proved to be valuable.

All in all some 22,000 sites were investigated. In addition some 2,000 sites in the area north of the northern limit were investigated to give some

TERRESTRIAL INVERTEBRATE SURVEYS

1:10 000 000

Intensively surveyed areas:

within the terrestrial invertebrate survey 1921–1981
outside the terrestrial invertebrate survey proper 1956–1994

Extensively surveyed areas 1956–1994

Areas not surveyed

Limes norrlandicus

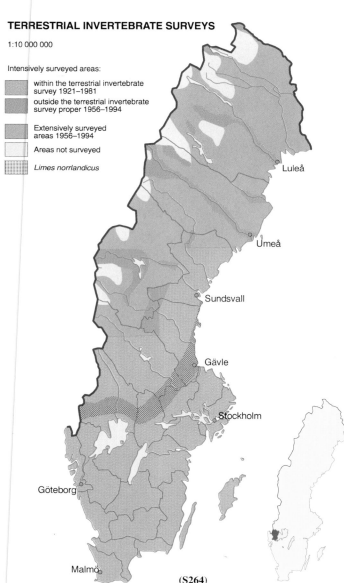

Luleå
Umeå
Sundsvall
Gävle
Stockholm
Göteborg
Malmö

(S264)

DISTRIBUTION PATTERNS OF TERRESTRIAL MOLLUSCS – EXAMPLES FROM DALSLAND

Nesovitrea hammonis is a very common snail that lives in many different kinds of environments. Divided dots show the presence of colour variety: greenish-white parallel with the usual brown variant. (S265)

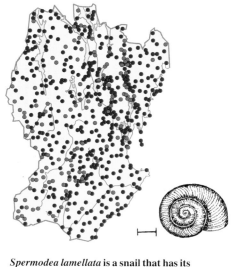

Oxyloma pfeifferi is a moisture-loving species of snail that is not found in poor soils in the west. (S266)

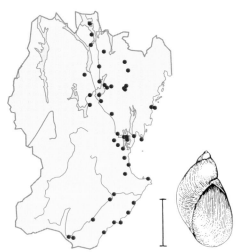

Spermodea lamellata is a snail that has its northernmost Swedish occurrences in Dalsland. These are offshoots of the species' main clearly western–sub-oceanic distribution. (S267)

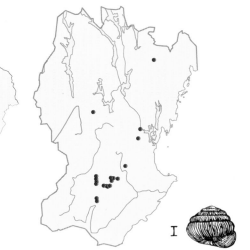

Macrogastra ventricosa is a snail limited to nemoral forest biotopes on the limestone bedrock of Dalsland group. The occurrences in Dalsland are the most northern in Sweden. (S268)

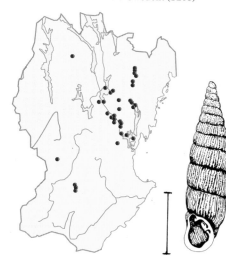

coverage of this part of Sweden. There is also material (mainly molluscs) collected by other people using similar methods. The total number of sites approaches 28,000, and the number of specimens collected is between 5 and 10 million. For molluscs alone the total number of recorded finds is probably about 300,000. Each site was carefully recorded, giving the date and its location and description. To allow the material to be processed quickly and smoothly and to create easily-managed search routines, however, it has first to be computerised and provided with co-ordinates. This work is now in progress.

With the aid of different coloured rings it is possible to identify individual birds. This method is used to study, for example, the survival, reproduction and movement patterns of white-tailed eagles.

When ringing birds nowadays information about the birds' size, weight, fat reserves and moulting is noted, as well as traditional data such as species, sex, age, time and place. When nestlings are ringed, the size of the brood and the number of addled eggs or dead young in the nest are noted as a matter of routine.

SWEDISH ORNITHOLOGICAL SOCIETY, REGIONAL REPORTING COMMITTEES

SOF's 32 regional reporting committees play a key role in monitoring the bird fauna. Each committee collects information, passing it on for analysis and compilation to the rarity committee or the central reporting committee. (S269)

Monitoring of Bird Fauna

Studies of bird fauna and its changes are probably better than for any other group of organisms. These studies are to a large extent carried out by amateurs, members of the Swedish Ornithological Society (SOF).

Every observation of very rare birds is documented in detail on a special form. As for the 100 or so less rare species all information is sent to the central reporting committee which also compiles and publishes an annual report. These reports cover more than half the bird species found in Sweden.

Certain uncommon and threatened species are also studied in special projects which, apart from investigating the population, also include active measures to support the species in question by providing food, guarding nesting sites and releasing birds bred in captivity.

Surveys of breeding birds and of winter birds have been carried out since 1975 on a large scale to follow up changes. This is done on a voluntary basis by SOF, but at a few places also within the framework of the Environmental Protection Agency's program for environmental control (PMK). Another project which has been in progress since 1959 is to count on a regular basis waterfowl during the winter season. These counts are made simultaneously all over Europe and are co-ordinated by the International Waterfowl and Wetlands Research Bureau.

RINGING

Ringing, which was introduced almost 100 years ago, was a milestone on the road to our knowledge of the dispersal of birds from their hatching places, their long migrations, local territory, length of life and so on. Perhaps the most important factor is that it has been possible to follow the fate of individual birds thanks to their number and reporting address. Birds can also be marked individually in other ways, by dyeing their feathers, and using wing marks, collars or coloured rings, for example.

The first person to ring bird successfully was a Dane, H. Chr. C. Mortensen. After a number of experiments he ringed 162 starlings in 1899 with rings of aluminium. A taxidermist, Gustaf Kihlén, was Sweden's first bird ringer. In 1911 he ringed 76 rough-legged buzzards and one pintail duck and the following year 78 rough-legged buzzards near Kiruna. The first two buzzards were found on 8 October 1911, strangely enough on the same day, one in Småland and one 35 km south of Moscow. In 1913 the Museum of Natural History in Stockholm began to ring birds and later the Swedish Hunters' Association and SOF. Since 1960 all ringing has been administered from a centre at the Museum of Natural History in Stockholm.

1:10 000 000

Number of ringed birds

30,000
20,000
10,000
5,000
1,000

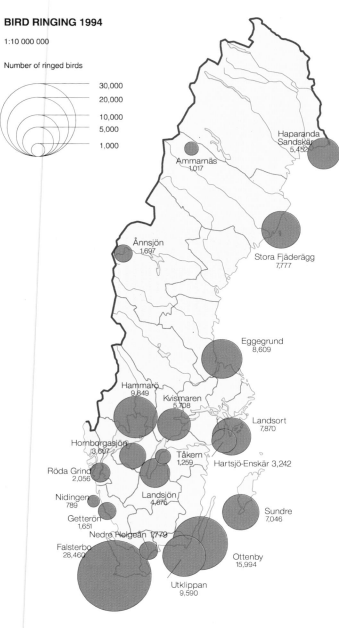

Ammarnäs
1,017

Haparanda
Sandskär
5,452

Ånnsjön
1,697

Stora Fjäderägg
7,777

Eggegrund
8,609

Hammarö
9,849

Kvismaren
5,708

Landsort
7,870

Hornborgasjön
3,697

Tåkern
1,259

Hartsjö-Enskär 3,242

Röda Grind
2,056

Nidingen
789

Landsjön
4,676

Getterön
1,651

Sundre
7,046

Nedre Holgeån 1,779

Falsterbo
28,460

Ottenby
15,994

Utklippan
9,590

The number of birds ringed at permanent ringing points and bird stations in Sweden during 1994. More than half of all ringing in the country is now done at permanent ringing points and as a rule with completely standardised routines which make it possible to compare years and ringing points. (S270)

Species	Ringed	Recovered	% Recovered
Mute swan *Cygnus olor*	11,559	5,444	47
Canada goose *Branta canadensis*	7,594	1,645	22
Eider *Somateria mollissima*	10,750	1,175	11
Goshawk *Accipiter gentilis*	11,177	1,777	16
Osprey *Pandion haliaetus*	10,017	1,090	11
Snipe *Gallinago gallinago*	10,035	712	7
Common sandpiper *Actitis hypoleucos*	16,613	222	1,3
Common tern *Sterna hirundo*	21,498	287	1,3
Blackbird *Turdus merula*	53,902	1,120	2,1
Reed warbler *Acrocephalus scirpaceus*	199,677	1,018	0,5
Willow warbler *Phylloscopus trochilus*	526,882	688	0,1
Great tit *Parus major*	232,949	1,425	0,6
Lapland bunting *Calcarius lapponicus*	1,141	1	0,1
Rusting bunting *Emberiza rustica*	1,508	0	0
Ortolan bunting *Emberiza hortulana*	1,218	8	0,7
Totals, 331 species	5,250,324	69,539	1,3

The table shows the extent of ringing and the frequency of recoveries for a number of bird species between 1960 and 1990, and the total figures for all the 331 species ringed during this period.

It is important that the address on the rings is well known and comprehensible in many languages. That is one reason why ringing in many countries is organised by museums of natural history. Another reason is the need for continuity, since discoveries can be expected many years after birds are ringed. All birds which are reported by some other person than the ringer himself and birds checked by their ringer if they are found more than 10 km from the ringing place are counted as rediscoveries. Of course most birds die young, but their potential age is often remarkably high, as ringed discoveries have proved. The following international reports of ringing may be mentioned as examples: oyster-catcher 36 years, arctic tern 33 years, guillemot, black-headed gull and herring gull 32 years, curlew 31 years, honey buzzard 28 years, starling 20 years, swallow 16 years and reed warbler 11 years.

Survey of Bats

The most effective method for surveying bats is to use an ultra-sound detector which transforms their orientation calls into audible sound. The various species can be identified by differences in frequency, rhythm and sound quality. This technique was first used in Sweden in 1978, resulting in surveys of several provinces in southern and central Sweden. The distribution of most bat species in Sweden is now well known.

These surveys are carried out both broadly and in detail. The broad survey aims in the first place to find species-rich habitats for bats with the help of maps and to survey these places. Examples of such places are castles, country houses and old mill towns, old deciduous and coniferous forests, and lakes and watercourses close to such places.

If a more complete survey is required, a systematic investigation can be carried out using 5×5 km squares. If the work is to be effective, suitable places have to be selected for this purpose, too, but they can also include old stone bridges, wind and watermills, sawmills, churches and large farms. The selected places are visited at least twice, and in those cases where a threatened or rare species is recorded, an attempt is made to locate nursery colonies.

A bat investigator with ultra-sound detector, headphones and headlamp.

NOCTULE IN SKÅNE
Nyctalus noctula

1: 2 500 000

Kristianstad

Lund

Malmö

(S271)

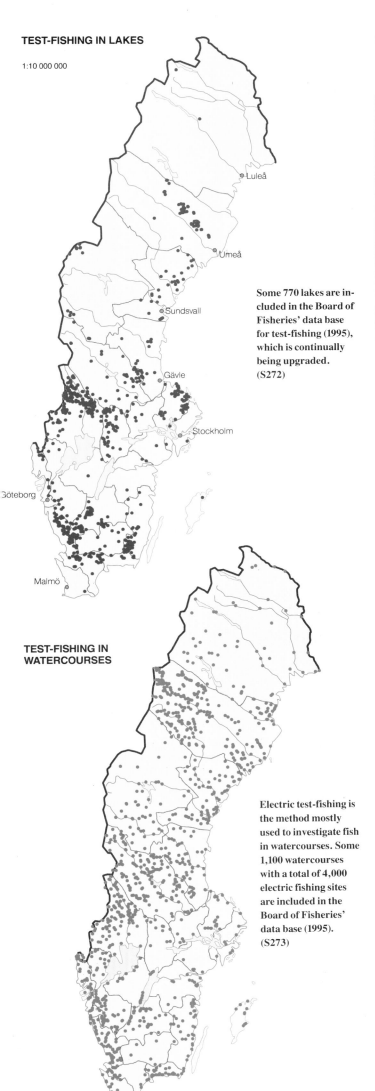

Luleå

Umeå

Sundsvall

Gävle

Stockholm

Göteborg

Malmö

Some 770 lakes are in-
cluded in the Board of
Fisheries' data base
for test-fishing (1995),
which is continually
being upgraded.
(S272)

**TEST-FISHING IN
WATERCOURSES**

Electric test-fishing is
the method mostly
used to investigate fish
in watercourses. Some
1,100 watercourses
with a total of 4,000
electric fishing sites
are included in the
Board of Fisheries'
data base (1995).
(S273)

Test-fishing nets are put out in the evening and
emptied in the morning.

A catch from net test-fishing is analysed. The
composition of the mesh in the net ensures that
fish of all species and sizes can be caught.

Test-fishing

Test-fishing is carried out in order to
investigate how many fish there are
and of what species in a lake or wa-
tercourse. Two methods are mainly
used for test-fishing today: *electric
test-fishing* in running water and *net
test-fishing* in lakes.

Electric test-fishing involves passing an electric current through the
water by means of a generator and
two electrodes. When fish enter the
electric field their muscles are affected so that they swim towards the
source of the current. When they are
close to this source, they are stunned
and can be caught with a bag net. The
fish are identified, counted and measured, and then released unharmed
into the water.

When net fishing is used, a fixed
number of nets are put out depending
on the size and depth of the lake to
be investigated. In order to get as
representative a catch as possible, the
lake is divided up into vertical depth
zones. The net has several different
sizes of mesh so that the catch will
represent as closely as possible the
type of fish and their various sizes in
the lake. These nets catch fish rang-

ing from three centimetres long up-
wards. The fish are identified, measured and weighed. Usually other
tests are made as well, for age, for
example.

Simply performed test-fishing can
provide answers to questions such as
whether the brown trout in a stream
or the roach in a lake managed to
spawn successfully the previous year,
while more detailed testing can provide information about the distribution of salmon and brown trout in
a river or the interaction between
roach and perch in a lake. Test-fishing
clearly reflects the pollution water has
been exposed to. Thus the results of
test-fishing can tell us much about water quality, which makes it a vital part
of environmental monitoring.

Test-fishing is mainly carried out
by the Swedish Institute of Freshwater
Research, the National Board of
Fisheries and the county administrative boards. There are also data bases
at the Institute of Freshwater Research in which all test-fishing results
are stored. This data can be used to
analyse changes in Swedish watercourses and lakes.

Authors

Ahlén, Ingemar, 1936, Professor, Swedish University of Agricultural Sciences

Andersson, Henrik, 1967, fishery biologist, Swedish Institute of Freshwater Research

Andersson, Lars, 1959, National Land Survey, Luleå

Andersson, Åke, F.L., 1938, wildlife ecologist, Swedish Hunter's Association

Angelstam, Per, 1953, Reader, Swedish University of Agricultural Sciences

Berglund, Björn E., 1935, Professor, University of Lund

Bjärvall, Anders, Ph. D., 1938, National Environmental Protection Agency

Björse, Gisela, 1968, District Forest Officer, Swedish University of Agricultural Sciences

Blindow, Irmgard, Ph. D., 1957, University of Lund

Bogelius, Anders, 1956, Senior Administrative Officer, National Board of Fishery

Brusewitz, Gunnar, Dr. h.c., 1924, author and artist, Rimbo

Cederlund, Göran, 1948, Reader, Swedish University of Agricultural Sciences

Ehnström, Bengt, 1937, Research Officer, Swedish University of Agricultural Sciences

Eliasson, Claes U., 1953, Research Technician, Lindesberg

Fries, Sigurd, 1924, Professor Emeritus, University of Umeå

Fritz, Örjan, 1962, biologist, County Administrative Board of Halland

Fürst, Magnus, Ph. D., 1931, Associate Professor, Swedish Institute of Freshwater Research

Gerell, Rune, 1933, Reader, University of Lund

Gustafsson, Lena, 1950, Reader, Swedish University of Agricultural Sciences, from 1/1 1994 Forestry Research Institute, Uppsala

Gärdenfors, Ulf, Ph. D., 1953, Swedish Threatened Species Unit, Swedish University of Agricultural Sciences

Hallingbäck, Tomas, 1949, biologist, Swedish Threatened Species Unit, Swedish University of Agricultural Sciences

Hamrin, Stellan F., Ph.D., 1944, Director, Swedish Institute of Freshwater Research

Ihse, Margareta, 1943, Reader, University of Stockholm

Ingelög, Torleif, F.L., 1946, Director, Swedish Threatened Species Unit, Swedish University of Agricultural Sciences

Janzon, Lars-Åke, Ph. D., 1945, National Museum of Natural History

Johansson, Annie, 1966, Ph. D. Student, University of Linköping

Johansson, Olof, 1958, ecologist, AssiDomän

Jonsell, Bengt, 1936, Professor, The Bergius Foundation, The Royal Swedish Academy of Sciences

Järvi, Torbjörn, 1944, Professor, National Board of Fishery

Karlsson, Thomas, Ph. D., 1945, National Museum of Natural History

Karström, Mats, 1957, biologist, Vuollerim

Kempe, Göran, 1951, Research Officer, Swedish University of Agricultural Sciences

Kornhall, David, 1928, Reader, University of Lund

Kåmark, Bengt, 1950, Principal Administrative Officer, National Board of Fishery

Källman, Stefan, Ph. D., 1954, Head of Education and Training, Civil Defence League

Larje, Rita, B. A., 1936, National Museum of Natural History

Larsson, Inger, 1945, Reader, University of Stockholm

Larsson, Karl-Henrik, Ph. D., 1948, University of Göteborg

Liljegren, Ronnie, Ph. D., 1945, University of Lund

Lindberg, Per Sigurd, 1950, biologist, Enskede

Linder, Per, 1957, District Forest Officer, Swedish University of Agricultural Sciences

Lingdell, Pär-Erik, 1948, engineer, Skinnskatteberg

Löfroth, Michael, 1957, Principal Administrative Officer, National Environmental Protection Agency

Mattsson, Jan-Eric, Ph. D., 1949, University of Uppsala

Moberg, Roland, 1939, Reader, University of Uppsala

Nilsson, Anders N., 1953, Reader, University of Umeå

Näslund-Landenmark, Barbro, 1955, Principal Administrative Officer, National Land Survey

Pettersson, Jan-Olof, 1933, District Forest Officer, Chairman of The Swedish Hunter's Association

von Proschwitz, Ted, Ph. D., 1957, Museum of Natural History, Göteborg

Påhlsson, Lars, 1934, Reader, The County Administrative Board, Malmö

Rafstedt, Thomas, 1944, biologist, Älvsjö

Renberg, Ingemar, 1945, Professor, University of Umeå

Rosén, Ejvind, 1942, Reader, University of Uppsala

Ryman, Svengunnar, 1946, Curator, Botanical Museum, University of Uppsala

Stolt, Bengt-Olov, Ph. D., 1936, National Museum of Natural History

Svensson, Bo W., 1941, Reader, University of Uppsala

Svensson, Mikael, 1962, biologist, University of Lund

Svensson, Sören, 1937, Reader, University of Lund

Tyrberg, Tommy, B. A., 1948, engineer, FFV Aerotech AB

Waldén, Henrik W., F. L., 1925, former Curator at the Museum of Natural History, Göteborg

Wickström, Håkan, 1951, fishery biologist, Swedish Institute of Freshwater Research

Wiederholm, Torgny, 1944, Reader, Swedish University of Agricultural Sciences

Williamsson, Mats, 1960, biologist, National Land Survey, Luleå

Apart from these authors a large number of people have assisted in the collection of data and other information for the production of maps and text. Special mention should be made of: Gunnar Broberg, University of Lund; Bo Fernholm, Lars Imby, Sven O. Kullander och Per Lindskog, National Museum of Natural History; Christina Lindahl, National Environmental Protection Agency; Johan Nitare, National Board of Forestry; Richard Bradshaw, Roger Svensson and Martin Tjernberg, Swedish University of Agricultural Sciences; Birgitta Bremer, Gunnar Eriksson and Håkan Tegelström, University of Uppsala; Gun Wallenberg, Västerås municipality, Olle Persson, Nacka; Dan Olofsson, Norrköping; Leif Andersson, Töreboda.

Literature and references

Ahlén, I. 1977. *Faunavård. Om bevarande av hotade djurarter i Sverige.* Skogshögskolan – Naturvårdsverket. Uppsala. Solna.

Ahlén, I., Andrén, C. & Nilson, G. 1995. *Sveriges grodor, ödlor och ormar.* ArtDatabanken och Naturskyddsföreningen. Uppsala and Stockholm. 2. ed.

Ahlén, I., Boström, U., Ehnström, B. & Pettersson, B. 1986. *Faunavård i skogsbruket. Allmän del.* Skogsstyrelsen.

Ahlén, I. & Tjernberg, M. 1996. *Rödlistade ryggradsdjur i Sverige – Artfakta.* ArtDatabanken. Uppsala.

Alexandersson, H., Ekstam, U. & Forshed, N. 1986. *Stränder vid fågelsjöar. Om fuktängar, mader och vassar i odlingslandskapet.* LTs förlag. Stockholm.

Almgren, G. 1984. *Ädellövskog – ekologi och skötsel.* Skogsstyrelsen. Jönköping.

Andersson, S. (ed.) 1988. *Fåglar i jordbrukslandskapet.* Vår Fågelvärld, suppl. nr 12.

Anthon, H. 1982. *Myggor och flugor i färg.* AWE/Gebers. Stockholm.

Anthon, H. 1982. *Getingar, bin och andra steklar i färg.* AWE/Gebers. Stockholm.

Aronsson, M., Hallingbäck, T. & Mattsson, J.-E. (ed.). 1995. *Rödlistade växter i Sverige 1995.* ArtDatabanken. Uppsala.

Bellman, H. 1985. *Heuschrecken, beobachten, bestimmen.* J. Neumann-Neudamm Gmbh & Co. Melsungen.

Bernes, C. (ed.). 1994. *Biologisk mångfald i Sverige.* En landstudie. Monitor 14. Naturvårdsverket, Solna.

Bjärvall, A. & Ullström,S. 1995. *Däggdjur. Alla Europas arter*. Wahlström & Widstrand. Stockholm.

Björck, S. 1995. *Review of the History of the Baltic Sea, 13.0 – 8.0 ka BP*. Quaternary International 27: 19–40.

Chinery, M. 1993. *Insekter i Europa*. Bonniers. Stockholm.

Coulianos, C.-C. & Holmåsen, I. 1991. *Galler. En fälthandbok om gallbildningar på vilda och odlade växter*. Interpublishing. Stockholm.

Curry-Lindahl, K. 1991. *Våra fiskar*. Norstedts. Stockholm.

Dal, B. 1978. *Fjärilar i naturen. Europas dagfjärilar. Nordeuropa*. Wahlström & Widstrand. Stockholm.

Danmarks Dyreliv. Band 1 (1984)-. Köpenhamn. Several volumes that cover the whole of Scandinavia: 2. *Nordens målere*; 3. *Nordeuropas pyralider*; 4. *Nordeuropas prydvinger*; 5. *Nordens ugler*.

Danmarks Fauna. Vol 1-, 1907-

Ehnström, B., Gärdenfors, U. & Lindelöw, Å. 1993. *Rödlistade evertebrater i Sverige 1993*. Databanken för hotade arter. Uppsala.

Ehnström, B. & Waldén, H. 1986. *Faunavård i skogsbruket. Den lägre faunan*. Skogsstyrelsen. Jönköping.

Ekman, S. 1922. *Djurvärldens utbredningshistoria på Skandinaviska halvön*. Bonniers. Stockholm.

Ekstam, U., Aronsson, M. & Forshed, N. 1988. *Ängar*. LTs förlag. Stockholm.

Ekstam, U. & Forshed, N. 1992. *Om hävden upphör*. Naturvårdsverket förlag. Solna

Entomologisk Tidskrift, 1-, 1880-

Eriksson, J. et al 1973–1988. *The Corticiaceae of North Europe*. 1–8. Fungiflora. Oslo.

Fauna Entomologica Scandinavica. Vol 1-, 1973-. Leiden & Köpenhamn.

Fauna och Flora, 1-, 1906-

Foucard, T. 1990. *Svensk skorplavsflora*. Interpublishing. Stockholm.

Groombridge, B. (ed.) 1992. *Global Biodiversity. Status of the Earth's Living Resources*. Chapman and Hall. London.

Gullander, B. 1963. *Nordens svärmare och spinnare*. Norstedts. Stockholm.

Gullander, B. 1971. *Nordens nattflyn*. Norstedts. Stockholm.

Gustavsson, R. & Ingelög, T. 1994. *Det nya landskapet*. Skogsstyrelsen. Jönköping.

Gärdenfors, U., Hall, R., Hansson, C. & Wilander, P. 1988. *Svenska småkryp. En bestämningsbok till ryggradslösa djur utom insekter*. Studentlitteratur. Lund.

Hallander, H. 1989. *Svenska lantraser*. Blå Veberöd.

Hallingbäck, T. & Holmåsen, I. 1995. *Mossor. En fälthandbok*. Interpublishing. Stockholm.

Hansen, L. & Knudsen, H. 1992. *Nordic macromycetes. Vol 2. Polyporales, Boletales, Agaricales, Russulales*. Nordsvamp. Köpenhamn.

Hultén, E. 1971. *Atlas över växternas utbredning i Norden*. Generalstaben. Stockholm

Ingelög, T. 1981. *Floravård i skogsbruket. Allmän del*. Skogsstyrelsen. Jönköping.

Ingelög, T., Thor, G. & Gustafsson, L. (ed.). 1984. *Floravård i skogsbruket. Artdel*. Skogsstyrelsen. Jönköping.

Ingelög, T., Thor, G., Hallingbäck, T., Andersson, R. & Aronsson, M. (ed.). 1992. *Floravård i jordbrukslandskapet. Skyddsvärda växter*. Databanken för hotade arter. Uppsala.

Jensen, B. 1993. *Nordens däggdjur*. Stockholm.

Johansson, O., Ekstam, U. & Forshed, N. 1986. *Havsstrandängar*. LTs förlag. Stockholm.

Jonsson, L. 1992. *Fåglar i Europa med Nordafrika och Mellanöstern*. Wahlström & Widstrand. Stockholm.

Kerney, M. P. & Cameron, R. A. D. 1979. *A Field Guide to the Land Snails of Britain and North-west Europe*. Collins. London.

Kindvall, O. & Denuel, A. 1987. *Sveriges vårtbitare och gräshoppor (Orthoptera)*. Fältbiologerna. Stockholm. 3. ed.

Krok, Th. O. B. N. & Almquist, S. 1994. *Svensk flora. Fanerogamer och ormbunksväxter*. Liber Utbildning. Stockholm.

Liljegren, R. & Lagerås, P. 1993. *Från mammutstäpp till kohage. Djurens historia i Sverige*. Lund.

Lindroth, C. H. 1993. *Våra skalbaggar och hur man känner igen dem*. Fältbiologerna. Stockholm.

Löfroth, M. 1991. *Våtmarkerna och deras betydelse*. SNV Rapport 3824. Naturvårdsverket. Solna.

Moberg, R. & Holmåsen, I. 1990. *Lavar. En fälthandbok*. Interpublishing. Stockholm.

Mossberg, B., Nilsson, S. & Persson, O. 1994. *Svampar i naturen*. Wahlström & Widstrand. Stockholm.

Mossberg, C., Stenberg, L, & Ericsson, S. 1992. *Den nordiska floran*. Wahlström & Widstrand. Stockholm.

Nordström, F., Wahlgren, E. & Tullgren, A. 1941. *Svenska fjärilar*. Nordisk Familjeboks förlag. Stockholm.

Påhlsson, L. (ed.). 1994. *Vegetationstyper i Norden*. TemaNord 1994:665. Nordiska Ministerrådet. Köpenhamn.

Risberg, L. 1990. *Sveriges fåglar*. Vår Fågelvärld, suppl. nr 14.

Rosenberg, E. 1995. *Fåglar i Sverige*. Norstedts. Stockholm.

Ryman, S. & Holmåsen, I. 1992. *Svampar. En fälthandbok*. Interpublishing. Stockholm.

Ryvarden, L. 1976–78. *The Polyporaceae of North Europe*. Fungiflora. Oslo.

Sandhall, Å. 1987. *Trollsländor i Europa*. Interpublishing. Stockholm.

Selander, S. 1987. *Det levande landskapet i Sverige*. Bokskogen, Göteborg. 3. ed.

Sjörs, H. 1956. *Nordisk växtgeografi*. Scandinavian University Books. Stockholm.

Sjörs, H. 1971. *Ekologisk botanik*. Biologi 10. Almqvist & Wiksell. Stocholm.

Skogsvårdsstyrelsen i Gävleborgs län. 1995. *Art- och biotopbevarande i skogen*. Skogsvårdsstyrelsen. Gävle.

Svensk Botanisk Tidskrift, 1- , 1907-

Svensk Insektfauna. Vol 1-, 1903-

Svensson, I. 1993. *Fjärilkalender*. Kristianstad.

Svensson, R., Wigren-Svensson, M. & Ingelög, T. 1993. *Hotade åkerogräs. Biologi och bevarande i allmogeåkrar*. Databanken för hotade arter, Nilson & Co. Uppsala och Borås.

Sveriges Natur, Årsbok, 1-, 1910-

Vår Fågelvärld, 1- , 1942-

Wilson, E.O. 1995. *Livets mångfald*. Brombergs. Stockholm.

Nomenclature

The names of plants, fungi and animals are mostly taken from the following publications. There may be a few deviations for various reasons, such as later agreement about minor changes.

Bryophytes. Söderström, L., Hedenäs, L., & Hallingbäck, T. 1992. *Checklista över Sveriges mossor*. Myrinia 2: 13–56.

Lichens. Santesson, R. 1993. *The lichens and lichenicolous fungi of Sweden and Norway*. SBT-förlaget. Lund.

Fungi. Since fungi are dealt with in a very large number of books, we list only the species mentioned in the Atlas together with the names of the botanists who first described them.
Amanita citrina (Schaeff.) Pers.
Amylocystis lapponica (Romell) Sing.
Antrodiella citrinella Niemelä & Ryv.
Aurantioporus croceus (Pers.: Fr.) Murrill
Boletus impolitus Fr.
Clavaria inaequalis Müller: Fr. ss. Petersen
Cortinarius praestans (Cordier) Gill.
Daedaleopsis septentrionalis (P. Karst.)
Entoloma mougeotii (F.) Hesler
Fomitopsis pinicola (Sw.: Fr.) P. Karst.
Fomitopsis rosea (Alb. & Schw.: Fr.) Murrill
Geastrum schmidelii Vitt
Geoglossum difforme Fr.
Gomphus clavatus (Pers.: Fr.) S.F. Gray
Haploporus odorus (Sommerf.: Fr.) Bond. & Sing.
Hygrocybe punicea (Fr.) Kumm.
Laurilia sulcata (Peck) Pouzar
Mycena crocata (Schrad.: Fr.) Kumm.
Phellinus ferrugineofuscus (P. Karst.) Bourd. & Galz.
Phlebia centrifuga P. Karst.

Piptoporus betulinus (Bull.: Fr.) P. Karst.
Puccinia persistens Plowr.
Sarcosoma globosum (Schmidel: Fr.) Casp.
Skeletocutis tschulymica (Pil t) Keller

Vascular plants. Krok, Th. O. B. N. & Almquist, S. 1994. *Svensk flora. Fanerogamer och ormbunksväxter.* 27:e ed. Esselte. Stockholm.

Molluscs. Nordiska Kodcentralen 1993. *Code list M3 Mollusca.* Naturhistoriska Riksmuseet. Stockholm.

Crustaceans. Enckell, P. H. 1980. *Kräftdjur. Fältfauna.* Lund.

Butterflies and Moths. Gustafsson, B. (ed.). 1995. *Catalogus Lepidopterorum Sueciae.* Naturhistoriska Riksmuseet. Stockholm.

Beetles. Lundberg, S. 1995. *Catalogus Coleopterorum Sueciae.* Naturhistoriska Riksmuseet. Stockholm.

Hemiptera. Coulianos, C.-C. & Ossiannilsson, F. 1976. *Catalogus Insectorum Sueciae. VII. Hemiptera-Heteroptera.* 2 ed. Entomologisk Tidskrift 97:10–173.

Ants. Douwes, P. 1975. *Sveriges myror.* Entomologisk Tidskrift 116:83–99.

Bees. Janzon, L.-Å., Svensson, B. G. & Erlandsson, S. 1991. *Catalogus Insectorum Sueciae. Hymenoptera, Apoidea. 3. Megachilidae, Anthophoridae and Apidae.* Entomologisk Tidskrift 112:93–99.

Orthoptera. Holst, K. T. 1986. *The Saltatoria (Bush-crickets, crickets and grasshoppers) of Northern Europe.* Fauna Entomologica Scandinavica, Vol. 16.

Fish and Cyclostomata. There is no one work at present which uses a nomenclature consistently followed by Scandinavian marine zoologists. A standard work is: Eschmeyer, W.N. 1990. *Catalog of the genera of recent fishes.* California Academy of Sciences.

Amphibians and Reptiles. Ahlén, I., Andrén, C. & Nilson, G. 1995. *Sveriges grodor, ödlor och ormar.* ArtDatabanken och Naturskyddsföreningen. Uppsala and Stockholm.

Birds. Risberg, L. 1990. *Sveriges Fåglar.* Vår Fågelvärld, supplement nr 14. Stockholm.

Mammals. Wilson, D. E. & Reeder, D.M. 1993. *Mammal Species of the World—A Taxonomic and Geographic Reference.* Smithsonian Inst. Press. Washington & London. 2 ed.

Acknowledgements for illustrations

AdB = ArtDatabanken, SLU (Swedish Threatened Species Unit, Swedish University of Agricultural Sciences)
G = Greatshots
N = Naturfotograferna (Agency for Nature Photographers, Sweden)
NRM = Naturhistoriska Riksmuseet (National Museum of Natural History)
SLU = Sveriges lantbruksuniversitet (Swedish University of Agricultural Sciences)
SNA = Sveriges Nationalatlas (National Atlas of Sweden)
VMI = Våtmarksinventeringen, Naturvårdsverket (Wetland Survey, National Environmental Protection Agency)

Page
2 Map Gunnar Brusewitz
6 Photo top part of Olaus Magnus' *Carta Marina* 1539, coloured edition
Photo bottom from Olaus Magnus' History of the Nordic People
7 Portrait top Marten Mijtens the Elder
Portrait bottom Joakim Streng
8 Map SNA, data Gunnar Brusewitz
Portrait J. H. Scheffel 1739
9 Map and drawings top Hans Sjögren, data Robert E. Fries 1950 and B. Danielsson & G. Burenhult 1991
Portrait top J. Haagen after P. Krafft the Younger
Portrait bottom J. G. Sandberg, postumous 1930
Drawing bottom right Gunnar Brusewitz
10 Portrait top Gunnar Brusewitz
Drawings top J. W. Palmstruch
Portrait bottom M. Mollard
Drawing bottom Gunnar Brusewitz
11 Portrait top Gunnar Brusewitz
Portrait middle R. Widing
Drawing right Wilhelm von Wright
Drawing bottom Llewellyn Lloyd
12 Painting top Bruno Liljefors, Art Museum of Göteborg
Drawing middle left Gunnar Brusewitz
Photo middle unknown photographer
13 Portrait Gunnar Brusewitz
Photo right Hans Pettersson
Drawing bottom C. A. M. Lindman
14 Drawings Nils Forshed,
Diagram Hans Sjögren after Björn E. Berglund
15 Maps SNA, data

S. Björck 1995 and for 14 000 Erik Lagerlund
Drawings Nils Forshed
Diagram Hans Sjögren after B. E. Berglund 1968
16 Maps SNA, data S. Björck 1995
Drawings Nils Forshed, bottom after Leif Kullman
17 Maps SNA, data S. Björck 1995
Drawings Nils Forshed
18–21 Maps SNA, data Björn E. Berglund
Drawings Nils Forshed, data B. E. Berglund and Ronnie Liljegren and R. Liljegren & P. Lagerås 1993
22 Drawings Nils Forshed
Photo middle Tommie Jacobsson/N
Photo bottom Lennart Mathiasson/N
23 Maps SNA, data Gisela Björse, Richard Bradshaw, Daniel Michelson and The National Forest Survey, SLU
24 Maps SNA, data Gisela Björse, Richard Bradshaw, Daniel Michelson and The National Forest Survey, SLU
Photo Tommy Lennartsson
25 Map top Hans Sjögren after H. Walter 1979 and Nationalencyklopedin
Map bottom SNA after Nationalencyklopedin
26 Map SNA, data O. Gjærevoll 1992
Photo middle Claes Grundsten/N
Photo bottom left Peter Ugander/N
Photo bottom right Jan Töve/N
27 Map SNA, data Nordic Council of Ministers
Photo Klas Rune/N
28 Maps SNA, data B. Pedersen 1990
29 Maps top SNA, data Tomas Hallingbäck, AdB
Maps middle SNA,

data Michael Löfroth
Photo top Peter Gerdehag/G
Photo middle Tommie Jacobsson/N
Photo bottom Kennet Bengtsson/N
30 Maps SNA, data R. Moberg & I. Holmåsen 1992
Photo top left Bengt Ekman/N
Photo top right and middle left Ingmar Holmåsen/N
Photo middle right Tomas Hallingbäck
Photo bottom Jan-Peter Lahall/G
31 Map top left SNA, data J. Eriksson & Å. Strid 1969
Map top middle SNA, data Svengunnar Ryman
Map top right SNA, data T. Niemelä 1971
Maps two bottom left SNA, data Svengunnar Ryman
Maps two bottom right SNA, data L. Lange 1974
Photos Ingmar Holmåsen/N
32 Maps SNA, data H. W. Waldén
Drawings Barbara Landelius
33 Map SNA, data E. Hultén 1971, O. Gjærevoll 1990, T. Nilsson 1995
Drawings Nils Forshed
34 Map top SNA, data G. Svärdson 1979, A. Waterstraat 1990
Map bottom SNA, data Lars Imby
Diagram SNA, data Ulf Gärdenfors, AdB
Drawings Nils Forshed
35 Map top SNA, data E. Hultén & M. Fries 1986
Map middle left SNA, data E. Heiss 1983, N. N. Vinokurov 1982, C.-C. Coulianos & E. Sylvén 1979
Map bottom left SNA, data P. Lindskog 1991
Maps middle right and bottom right SNA, data E. Hultén 1971
Drawings Nils Forshed
36 Map NOAA–11 GAC Image, © SSC Satellitbild 1993
37 Map top SNA after E. Hultén 1971 and SNA/Geology
Map middle SNA after L. Risberg 1990
Map bottom SNA after E. Hultén 1971
Diagram SNA, data Per Angelstam
Drawing Nils Forshed
Photo top Bengt S. Eriksson/N
Photo middle Bengt Lundberg/N
Photo bottom Bengt Hedberg/Naturbild
38 Maps SNA, data B. W.

Svensson 1992
Photo upper Bertil
K. Johansson/N
Photo lower Ingmar
Holmåsen/N
39 Map SNA
Diagram Hans Sjö-
gren, data Skogsstatis-
tisk Årsbok,
Skogsstyrelsen
41 Diagram Hans Sjö-
gren, data Nordic
Council of Ministers
Photo Hans Pettersson
42 Map top Dep. of Phys-
ical Geography, Stock-
holm Univ.
Map bottom SNA, da-
ta Stefan Ericsson
Diagram SNA, data
Martin Tjernberg,
AdB
Drawing top Hans Sjö-
gren, data E. Zachris-
son, Geological Survey
of Sweden
Drawings bottom Nils
Forshed
43 Map top Dep. of Phys-
ical Geography, Stock-
holm University
Drawing top Hans Sjö-
gren, data E. Zachris-
son, Geological Survey
of Sweden
Drawing bottom Hans
Sjögren
44 Drawings Nils
Forshed, data Åke
Berg, Bengt Ehn-
ström, Lena Gustafs-
son, Tomas
Hallingbäck
Diagram left SNA,
data The National
Forest Survey, SLU
Diagram right SNA,
data Martin Tjernberg,
AdB
45 Maps top SNA, data
The National Forest
Survey, SLU
Map bottom SNA, da-
ta Project Production-
Environment, SLU
46 Map top right SNA,
data National Forest
Survey, SLU
Maps bottom left SNA,
data The National Sur-
vey of Forests, Soils
and Vegetation, SLU
Drawings Nils Forshed
Photo Hans Strand/G
47 Maps SNA, data The
National Forest Sur-
vey, SLU
Drawings Nils Forshed
Photo left Axel Ljung-
quist/N
Photo middle Kenneth
Bengtsson/N
Photo right Jan
Schützer/N
48 Map SNA, data
L. Kardell & A. Ek-
strand 1990, Skogssty-
relsen: Fjällnära
skogar 1989
Diagram Hans Sjö-
gren, data Per Linder
Photo Björn Uhr/N
49 Maps SNA, data
B. Mossberg, L. Sten-
berg & S. Ericsson
1992

Photo Jan Grahn/N
50 Maps SNA, data The
National Forest Sur-
vey, SLU
Photo Bengt Lund-
berg/N
51 Map SNA, data VMI
Diagram middle SNA,
data M. Löfroth 1994
Diagram bottom SNA,
data Martin Tjernberg,
AdB
52 Maps SNA, data VMI
Photo Alf Linder-
heim/N
53 Maps SNA, data VMI
Photo left Tore Hag-
man/N
Photo middle Klas
Rune/N
Photo right Lennart
Mathiasson/N
54 Maps SNA, data VMI
55 Maps top SNA, data
M. Löfroth
Maps middle and bot-
tom SNA, data VMI
Drawings Nils Forshed
Photo Michael Löfroth
56 Map and diagram
SNA, data Meadow
and Pasture Survey,
National Environmen-
tal Protection Agency
Drawing Nils Forshed
57 Map and diagram
SNA, data Meadow
and Pasture Survey,
National Environmen-
tal Protection Agency
Drawings Nils Forshed
Photo Tore Hagman/N
58 Diagram bottom SNA,
data C. Bernes 1994
Diagram bottom right
SNA, data Martin
Tjernberg, AdB
Drawings Nils Forshed
Photo top left and bot-
tom Peter Gerdehag/G
Photo top right Jan
Töve/N
59 Map SNA, data Mead-
ow and Pasture Survey,
National Environmen-
tal Protection Agency
Maps right SNA, data
Leif Andersson
Drawing Nils Forshed
60 Photo top Claes
Grundsten/N
Photo middle Tero
Niemi/Naturbild
Photo bottom Bengt
Ekman/N
61 Map top left SNA, da-
ta Ejvind Rosén and
Martin Zobel
Maps top right SNA
after U. Ekstam,
R. Jacobson, M. Matt-
son & T. Porsne 1984
Map middle SNA, da-
ta Nils Ryrholm
Map bottom SNA,
data R. Moberg &
I. Holmåsen 1992.
Drawing Nils Forshed
Photo Jan-Peter La-
hall/G
62 Drawing Hans Sjögren
after Ejvind Rosén
Photo top Axel Ljung-
quist/N
Photo middle right
Claes Grundsten/N

Photo bottom right Jan
Töve/N
Other photos Ejvind
Rosén
63 Map left SNA, data
Olof Johansson
Map right SNA, data
L. Ericson & H.-G.
Wallentinus 1979
Drawings Nils Forshed
Photo Tore Hagman/N
64 Map SNA, data Per Si-
gurd Lindberg
Drawings Nils Forshed
Photo Beng Hedberg/
Naturbild
65 Map SNA, data Rune
Gerell and Lunds
stadsingenjörkontor
Drawings Nils Forshed
Photo Rolf Nyström/
Naturbild
66 Lithograph Agneta
Gussander
67 Table Ulf Gärdenfors,
AdB
68 Map SNA, data Åke
Berg and Martin
Tjernberg, AdB
Drawing Hans Sjögren
69 Maps SNA, data
Svensk Fågelatlas,
University of Lund
70 Map SNA, data Swed-
ish Institute of Fresh-
water Research
Photo top Ulf Ris-
berg/N
Photo middle Bengt
Lundberg/N
71 Map left SNA, data
Ulf Gärdenfors, AdB
Maps right SNA, data
Anders N. Nilsson
Drawings Nils Forshed
72 Map left SNA, data
E. Hultén 1971
Map right SNA, data
Project Production-
Environment, SLU
Photo Peter Gerde-
hag/G
73 Maps and diagram
SNA, data Tomas Hal-
lingbäck
Photo Jan-Peter La-
hall/G
74 Maps SNA, data
Tomas Hallingbäck
Drawings Nils Forshed
Photo Jørn Bøhmer
Olsen/G
75 Drawings Nils Forshed
after Tomas Halling-
bäck
76 Map Hans Sjögren, da-
ta H. Tegelström 1989
Photo upper Torbjörn
Skogedal/Myra
Photo lower U. Skarén
77 Map top left Hans Sjö-
gren, data P. Taberlet
& J. Bouvet 1994,
P. Taberlet, J. E.
Swenson, F. Sandegren
& A. Bjärvall 1995
Map top right Hans
Sjögren, data U. La-
gercrantz & N. Ryman
1990
Map bottom left Hans
Sjögren, data
M. Lönn, H. C. Pren-
tice & H. Tegelström
1995
Photo middle left Bo

Kristiansson/N
Photo middle right
Lennart Mathiasson/N
Photo bottom Ingmar
Holmåsen/N
78–85 Map SNA, data Claes
Grundsten, the county
administrative boards,
and local clubs of
Swedish Ornithological
Society
86 Photo top left Pär Do-
meij/G
Photo top right Peter
Gerdehag/G
Photo middle Lars Jar-
nemo/N
Photo bottom Lars
Dahlström/Tio
87 Diagram Hans Sjö-
gren, data Martin
Tjernberg, AdB
Map SNA, data S. Ek-
man 1922, Sören
Svensson
Drawing Nils Forshed
Photo Heikkiillamo/
Naturbild
88 Maps SNA, data
S. Ekman 1922,
L. Risberg 1990,
G. Aulén 1988 and
Tommy Tyrberg
Drawings Nils Forshed
Photo Bengt Lundb-
erg/N
89 Map left SNA, data
A. Enemar 1957,
H. Källander 1970 and
Sören Svensson
Map middle SNA, da-
ta Tommy Tyrberg
Map right SNA, data
S. Durango 1946 and
Tommy Tyrberg
Photo top Tero Niemi/
Naturbild
Photo middle Bengt
Lundberg/N
Drawing Nils Forshed
90 Map left SNA, data
K. Engström 1952 and
Sören Svensson
Map middle SNA, da-
ta E. Fabricius 1983
and Tommy Tyrberg
Map right SNA, data
P.-E. Jönsson 1988,
Tommy Tyrberg
Maps bottom left and
middle SNA, data
Tommy Tyrberg
Map bottom right
NRM
Drawings Nils Forshed
Photo Klas Rune/N
91 Maps top SNA, data
S. Ekman 1922, Sören
Svensson, Tommy Tyr-
berg
Maps bottom SNA,
data S. Ekman 1922,
S. G. Nilsson 1982 and
Tommy Tyrberg
Drawing Nils Forshed
Photo top Jan-Peter
Lahall/G
Photo middle Peter
Gerdehag/G
92 Maps SNA, data Lars
Lindell and Tommy
Tyrberg
Photo Bengt Ekman/N
93 Drawings and diagram
Hans Sjögren, data
Åke Andersson and

Tommy Tyrberg
94 Maps SNA, data Mar-
gareta Ihse
Drawing top middle
Nils Forshed
Drawings right Eivor
Granbom
95 Maps National Land
Survey
Drawing Nils Forshed
96 Four upper maps
SNA, data Ted von
Proschwitz, Museum
of Natural History,
Göteborg
Four lower maps SNA,
data Lars-Åke Janzon,
NRM
Drawing Nils Forshed
Photo Torkel Hag-
ström
97 Maps SNA, data C. U.
Eliasson 1991
Drawing Nils Forshed
Photo left Kenneth
Bengtsson/Naturbild
Photo right Klas
Rune/N
98 Map top left SNA, da-
ta C. Bernes 1994
Map top right SNA,
data National Survey
of Forests, Soils and
Vegetation, SLU
Map (bottom) and dia-
gram SNA, data Pro-
ject threatened lichens
in southern Sweden,
University of Lund
Photo Tomas Halling-
bäck
99 Maps SNA, data Pro-
ject threatened lichens
in southern Sweden,
University of Lund
Drawings Nils Forshed
100 Maps SNA, data
Swedish Institute of
Freshwater Research
Photos Ulf Risberg/N
101 Diagram SNA, data
John Andersson, Dan-
marks Geologiske
Undersøgelser
Drawings Gunnel
Eriksson
Photo Fredrik Ehren-
ström/N
102 Maps SNA, data Torg-
ny Wiederholm, SLU
and National Environ-
mental Protection
Agency
Photo upper Ingemar
Ahlén
Photo lower Inge
Lennmark
103 Maps SNA, data AdB
Photo Bengt Lund-
berg/N
104 Drawing Nils Forshed
Photo middle Åke W.
Engman/N
Photo bottom Folke
Hårrskog/N
105 Maps SNA, data
Anders Bjärvall
Photo top Rolf Ny-
ström/Naturbild
Photo middle Bo Kris-
tiansson/N
106 Maps SNA, data
Svensk Fågelatlas,
University of Lund
Photos Bengt Lund-
berg/N

Index

159

National Atlas of Sweden

A geographical description of the landscape, society
and culture of Sweden in 17 volumes

MAPS AND MAPPING

From historic maps of great cultural significance
to modern mapping methods using the latest advanced technology. What you didn't already
know about maps you can learn here. A unique
place-name map (1:700,000) gives a bird's-eye
view of Sweden. Editors: Professor Ulf Sporrong,
geographer, Stockholm University, and Hans-
Fredrik Wennström, economist, National Land
Survey, Gävle.

THE FORESTS

Sweden has more forestland than almost any
other country in Europe. This volume describes
how the forests have developed and how forestry
works: ecological cycles, climatic influences, its
importance for the economy etc. One of many
maps shows, on the scale of 1:1.25 million, the distribution of the forests today. Editor: Professor
Nils-Erik Nilsson, forester, National Board of
Forestry, Jönköping.

THE POPULATION

Will migration to the towns continue, or shall we
see a new "green wave"? This volume highlights
most sides of Swedish life: how Swedes live, edu-
cation, health, family life, private economy etc.
Political life, the population pyramid and im-
migration are given special attention. Editor:
Professor Sture Öberg, geographer, Uppsala
University, and Senior Administrative Officer
Peter Springfeldt, geographer, Statistics Sweden,
Stockholm.

THE ENVIRONMENT

More and more people are concerning themselves
with environmental issues and nature conser-
vancy. This book shows how Sweden is being
affected by pollution, and what remedies are
being applied. Maps of protected areas, future
perspectives and international comparisons.
Editors: Dr Claes Bernes and Claes Grundsten,
geographer, National Environmental Protection
Agency, Stockholm.

AGRICULTURE

From horse-drawn plough to the highly-mechan-
ized production of foodstuffs. A volume devoted
to the development of Swedish agriculture and its
position today. Facts about the parameters of
farming, what is cultivated where, the workforce,
financial aspects etc. Editor: Birger Granström,
state agronomist, and Åke Clason, managing director of Research Information Centre, Swedish
University of Agricultural Sciences, Uppsala.

THE INFRASTRUCTURE

Sweden's welfare is dependent on an efficient infrastructure, everything from roads and railways
to energy production and public administration.
If you are professionally involved, this book will
provide you with a coherent survey of Sweden's
infrastructure. Other readers will find a broad
explanation of how Swedish society is built up and
how it functions. Editor: Dr Reinhold Castens-
son, geographer, Linköping University.

SEA AND COAST

The Swedes have a deep-rooted love for the sea
and the coast. This volume describes the waters
which surround Sweden and how they have
changed with the evolution of the Baltic. Facts
about types of coastline, oceanography, marine
geology and ecology, including comparisons with
the oceans of the world. Editor: Björn Sjöberg,
oceanographer, Swedish Meteorological and
Hydrological Institute, Göteborg.

CULTURAL LIFE, RECREATION
AND TOURISM

An amateur drama production in Hässleholm or
a new play at the Royal Dramatic Theatre in
Stockholm? Both fill an important function. This
volume describes the wide variety of culture activities available in Sweden (museums, cinemas,
libraries etc), sports and the various tourist areas
in Sweden. Editor: Dr Hans Aldskogius, geographer, Uppsala University.

SWEDEN IN THE WORLD

Sweden is the home of many successful export
companies. But Sweden has many other relations
with the rest of the world. Cultural and scientific
interchange, foreign investment, aid to the Third
World, tourism etc. are described in a historical
perspective. Editor: Professor Gunnar Törn-
qvist, geographer, Lund University.

WORK AND LEISURE

Describes how Swedes divide their time between
work and play, with regional, social and age-
group variations. The authors show who does
what, the role of income, etc, and make some pre-
dictions about the future. Editor: Dr Kurt V.
Abrahamsson, geographer, Umeå University.

CULTURAL HERITAGE AND
PRESERVATION

Sweden is rich in prehistoric monuments and historical buildings, which are presented here on
maps. What is being done to preserve our cultural heritage? This volume reviews modern cultural
heritage policies. Editor: Dr Klas-Göran Selinge,
archeologist, Central Board of National Antiqui-
ties, Stockholm. Ass. Editor: Dr Marit Åhlén,
runologist, Central Board of National Antiqui-
ties, Stockholm.

GEOLOGY

Maps are used to present Sweden's geology – the
bedrock, soils, land forms, ground water. How
and where are Sweden's natural geological resources utilised? Editor: Curt Fredén, state geologist, Geological Survey of Sweden, Uppsala.

LANDSCAPE AND SETTLEMENTS

How has the Swedish landscape evolved over the
centuries? What traces of old landscapes can still
be seen? What regional differences are there?
This volume also treats the present landscape,
settlements, towns and cities, as well as urban and
regional planning. Editor: Professor Staffan
Helmfrid, geographer, Stockholm University.

CLIMATE, LAKES AND RIVERS

What causes the climate to change? Why does
Sweden have fewer natural disasters than other
countries? This volume deals with the natural
cycle of water and with Sweden's many lakes and
rivers. Climatic variations are also presented in
map form. Editors: Birgitta Raab, state hydro-
logist, and Haldo Vedin, state meteorologist,
Swedish Meteorological and Hydrological Institute, Norrköping.

MANUFACTURING AND SERVICES

Heavy industry is traditionally located in certain
parts of Sweden, while other types of industry are
spread all over the country. This volume contains
a geographical description of Swedish manufac-
turing and service industries and foreign trade.
Editor: Dr Claes Göran Alvstam, geographer,
Göteborg University.

GEOGRAPHY OF PLANTS
AND ANIMALS

Climatic and geographical variations in Sweden
create great geographical differences in plant and
animal life. This volume presents the geographical distribution of Sweden's flora and fauna and
explains how and why they have changed over the
years. There is a special section on game hunting.
Editors: Professor Ingemar Ahlén and Dr Lena
Gustafsson, Swedish University of Agricultural
Sciences, Uppsala.

THE GEOGRAPHY OF SWEDEN

A comprehensive picture of the geography of
Sweden, containing excerpts from other volumes
but also completely new, summarizing articles.
The most important maps in the whole series are
included. Indispensable for educational purposes. Editors: Professor Emeritus Staffan Helmfrid, National Atlas of Sweden, Stockholm.

- Special editor
- Production
- Sales

Kiruna

Luleå

Umeå

Gävle

Uppsala

Örebro   Stockholm

Linköping   Norrköping

Jönköping

Göteborg

Höganäs
Lund

1:20 000 000

The work of producing the National Atlas
of Sweden is spread throughout the country.